Terrorism, Organised Crime and Corruption

Terrorism, Organised Crime and Corruption

Networks and Linkages

Edited by

Leslie Holmes

Professor of Political Science, the University of Melbourne, Australia
Recurrent Visiting Professor, Graduate School for Social Research, Warsaw, Poland and University of Bologna, Italy

Edward Elgar
Cheltenham, UK • Northampton, MA, USA

Published by
Edward Elgar Publishing Limited
The Lypiatts
15 Lansdown Road
Cheltenham
Glos GL50 2JA
UK

Edward Elgar Publishing, Inc.
William Pratt House
9 Dewey Court
Massachusetts 01060
USA

Paperback edition 2010

A catalogue record for this book
is available from the British Library

Library of Congress Cataloguing in Publication Data
Terrorism, organised crime and corruption : networks and linkages / edited
by Leslie Holmes.
     p. cm.
  Includes bibliographical references and index.
  1. Terrorism. 2. Organized crime. 3. Corruption. I. Holmes, Leslie.
  HV6431.T486 2007
  363.325—dc22
                                    2006028689

ISBN 978 1 84542 537 1 (cased)
ISBN 978 1 84980 048 8 (paperback)

Printed and bound by MPG Books Group, UK

Contents

Tables

Abbreviations and Acronyms

ACC	Anti–Corruption Commission
AFP	Australian Federal Police
AML	Anti–Money Laundering
ASEM	Asia–Europe Meeting
ASIC	Australian Securities and Investments Commission
ASIO	Australian Security Intelligence Organisation
ATM	Automatic Teller Machine
AWB	Australian Wheat Board
BBC	British Broadcasting Corporation
BCCI	Bank of Credit and Commerce International
B2B	business to business
CCC	Corruption and Crime Commission
CDPC	(Committee on Crime Problems)
CEE	Central and Eastern Europe
CEEC	Central and East European country
CESAA	Contemporary European Studies Association of Australia
CJC	Criminal Justice Commission
CLERP	Corporations Law Economic Reform Program
CMC	Crime and Misconduct Commission
CMEA	Council for Mutual Economic Assistance
CoE	Council of Europe
CPI	Corruption Perceptions Index
CTCU	Counter-Terrorism Coordination Unit
CTED	Counter-Terrorism Executive Directorate
EBBOY	Encyclopaedia Britannica Book of the Year
EBRD	European Bank for Reconstruction and Development
EC	European Community
EEA	European Economic Area
EFTA	European Free Trade Area
ELN	(National Liberation Army)
EMU	Economic and Monetary Union
ESRs	Eight Special Recommendations
ETA	(Basque Fatherland and Liberty)
EU	European Union

FARC	(Revolutionary Armed Forces of Colombia)
FATF	Financial Action Task Force
FBI	Federal Bureau of Investigation
FCPA	Foreign Corrupt Practices Act
FDI	Foreign Direct Investment
FIG	Financial and Industrial Group
FIU	financial intelligence unit
FOZZ	(Foreign Debt Servicing Fund)
FRs	Forty Recommendations
FSA	Financial Services Authority
FSB	(Federal Security Service)
GDP	Gross Domestic Product
GRECO	(Group of States against Corruption)
HREOC	Human Rights and Equal Opportunity Commission
ICAC	Independent Commission Against Corruption
ICV	Islamic Council of Victoria
IFC	International Financial Corporation
IGO	Intergovernmental Organisation
IL	International Law
IMF	International Monetary Fund
IMU	Islamic Movement of Uzbekistan
IOU	I owe you
IRA	Irish Republican Army
ISPAC	International Scientific and Professional Advisory Council
ITU	International Telecommunication Union
JHA	Justice and Home Affairs
JI	Jemaah Islamiyah
KADEK	(Freedom and Democracy Congress of Kurdistan)
KGB	(Committee of State Security)
KOR	(Committee for the Defence of Workers)
KYC	Know Your Customer
MGC	Multidisciplinary Group on Corruption
MLRs	Money Laundering Regulations
MONEYVAL	(Select Committee of Experts on the Evaluation of Anti-Money Laundering Measures)
NATO	North Atlantic Treaty Organisation
NCCT	Non-Cooperative Countries or Territories
NCTC	National Counterterrorism Center
NFL	National Football League
NGO	Non-Governmental Organisation

NSCOC	National Service for Combating Organised Crime
NSW	New South Wales
NT	Northern Territory
OAS	Organization of American States
OCC	Official Corruption Commission
OECD	Organisation for Economic Co-operation and Development
OLAF	(European Anti-Fraud Office)
OMRI	Open Media Research Institute
OPI	Office of Police Integrity
PCAI	Parliamentary Commissioner for Administrative Investigations
PHARE	(originally) Poland and Hungary: Assistance for Restructuring their Economies
PIC	Police Integrity Commission
PKK	(Kurdistan Workers' Party)
PRC	People's Republic of China
PZU	(Polish Office of Insurance)
QLD	Queensland
RFE/RL OCTW	Radio Free Europe/Radio Liberty Organized Crime and Terrorism Watch
RICO	Racketeer Influenced and Corrupt Organizations
ROSC	Report on the Observance of Standards and Codes
SA	South Australia
SLD	(Democratic Left Alliance)
STR	Suspicious Transaction Reporting
SWB/EE	Summary of World Broadcasts/Eastern Europe
TI	Transparency International
TNC	Transnational Corporation
UK	United Kingdom
UN	United Nations
UNODC	United Nations Office on Drugs and Crime
UNSC	United Nations Security Council
USA	United States of America
VAT	Value Added Tax
VCAT	Victorian Civil and Administrative Tribunal
WA	Western Australia
WMD	Weapons of Mass Destruction
WTO	World Trade Organisation

Contributors

Mark DaCosta Alleyne is Associate Professor in the Department of Communication at Georgia State University, having moved there in 2005 from the University of California at Los Angeles. His publications include *Global Lies? Propaganda, the UN and World Order* (2003).

Frank Bovenkerk is Professor of Criminology at the Willem Pompe Institute for Criminal Law and Criminology at the University of Utrecht. Together with Michael Levi, he edited *The Organized Crime Community: Essays in Honor of Alan A. Block* (2006).

Diana Bowman is a Research Fellow in the Monash Centre for Regulatory Studies, Faculty of Law at Monash University. She has published in the areas of governing nanotechnology, public accountability, public–private partnerships, and utility regulation.

Bashir Abou Chakra is a practising lawyer in the Lebanese Lawyers' Bar Association in Lebanon. He has specialised in the internationalisation of crime and criminal justice. He is now also a Legal Consultant/Investigator for the Intellectual Property firm Saba & Co., whose mission is to combat organised piracy, fraudulent activities and counterfeiting (including smuggling of these), and infringements of trademarks and patents.

Adam Czarnota is Associate Professor in the School of Law and Co-Director of the European Law Centre, University of New South Wales, Sydney, and Senior Fellow at the Contemporary Europe Research Centre, University of Melbourne. Together with Wojciech Sadurski and Martin Krygier, he co-edited *Spreading Democracy and the Rule of Law? The Impact of EU Enlargement for the Rule of Law, Democracy and Constitutionalism in Postcommunist Legal Orders* (2006).

Rémy Davison is Lecturer in International Relations in the School of Political and Social Inquiry and a member of the Global Terrorism Research Unit at Monash University. He is also a Fellow of the Contemporary Europe Research Centre at the University of Melbourne. His recent publications include *The*

New Global Politics of the Asia-Pacific, co-authored with Michael Connors and Jörn Dosch (RoutledgeCurzon, 2004).

Maarten van Dijck is a Senior Researcher at the Tilburg University, the Netherlands and affiliated with the research project 'Assessing Organised Crime and Human Security in the Balkan Region'. He co-edited (with Petrus C. van Duyne, A. Maljevic, K. von Lampe and J. Newell) *The Organisation of Crime for Profit: Conduct, Law and Measurement* (2006).

Petrus C. van Duyne is Professor of Empirical Penal Science at the Tilburg University, the Netherlands. He initiated the annual Cross–border Crime Colloquia in Europe. Together with Michael Levi, he co-authored *Drugs and Money: Managing the Drug Trade and Crime Money in Europe* (2005).

George Gilligan is Senior Research Fellow in the Department of Business Law and Taxation at Monash University. He has taught at the University of Cambridge, Exeter University and Middlesex University in the UK, and La Trobe University, the University of Melbourne and Monash University in Australia. His most recent book is *Crime, Truth and Justice: Official Inquiry, Discourse, Knowledge* (2004, co-edited with John Pratt).

Leslie Holmes is Professor of Political Science, and Deputy Director of the Contemporary Europe Research Centre, at the University of Melbourne. His most recent book is *Rotten States?: Corruption, Post-Communism and Neoliberalism* (2006).

Pete Lentini is Co-Convenor of the Global Terrorism Research Unit, School of Political and Social Inquiry, Monash University. He has previously served Monash University as a Deputy Head and Head of the School of Political and Social Inquiry, and Associate Dean (Research), Faculty of Arts. Together with Marika Vicziany and David Wright-Neville, he co-edited *Regional Security in the Asia Pacific: 9/11 and After* (2004).

Peter Shearman was until recently Associate Professor of Political Science at the University of Melbourne and is now a Principal Fellow of the Contemporary Europe Research Centre. His most recent books are *European Security after 9/11* (2004), which he co-edited with Matthew Sussex, and *Australian Security after 9/11* (2006), co-edited with Derek McDougall.

Yuri Tsyganov moved to Australia in 1998 from Russia, where he had been a researcher at IMEMO, Russia's leading international relations institute attached to the Academy of Sciences. For several years after arriving in Australia, he conducted research into corruption in Russia and Central Europe at the University of Melbourne. He has recently taken up a public service position in Canberra, while retaining his Fellowship at the Contemporary Europe Research Centre. He is the author of *Russian Policy Toward Northeast Asia: In Search of a New Approach* (2003).

Preface and Acknowledgements

Together with the Contemporary European Studies Association of Australia (CESAA), the Contemporary Europe Research Centre (CERC) at the University of Melbourne has been organising an annual international conference for many years. In the early 2000s, we decided to conduct an experiment; rather than focus on a given problem purely in the European context, we would compare the situations in Europe and Australia, with a view to identifying resonances and, in turn, being able to suggest areas in which either side could usefully learn from the other. This comparative approach proved to be a success; attendances at the conferences increased, and we were able to demonstrate to Australianists and Europeanists that they could often learn much of relevance from each other.

The present volume is based on the November 2003 annual CERC conference (though all papers were updated in 2005), at which we again adopted this comparative approach. The first versions of most of the chapters in this book were presented there. However, when we came to consider publishing a book based on the conference, it was soon agreed that there was an obvious hiatus; how could we publish a collection on terrorism, corruption and organised crime that did not include a chapter on US perspectives? At least since 11 September 2001 ('9/11'), terrorism had moved to the top of the international security agenda, and everyone was anxious to have as deep an understanding of it – including of its financing – as possible. I am very grateful to Mark Alleyne (at the time he was approached, of the University of California at Los Angeles, now of Georgia State University) for agreeing to produce a chapter at short notice on an American perspective on terrorism and an aspect of its links to corruption.

This volume considers the three types of crime both individually and in terms of bilateral and trilateral connections. As the editor, I consciously avoided insisting on a standardised format in each chapter, or on standardised definitions; while such homogeneity is sometimes appropriate, particularly in collections intended for use as textbooks, it can also stifle the creative approach. Moreover, diversity – allowing authors to seek their own paths – is often more enlightening than uniformity and tidiness. Given that so many of the terms used in this study remain contested, insistence on agreed definitions would have been both artificial and misleading, since they could create a false impression of a higher level of consensus among analysts – even among the small number included in this volume – than really exists. While I tend to prefer deliberative to agonistic approaches to democracy, I accept that there are times when compromise – here referring to the use of agreed terms – can result in outcomes that not only suit none of the discursive participants, but also none of the observers.

Another point about terminology is that 'networks' is used here in the everyday sense of an interconnected group or system, not in the more technical sense used in network theory (diktyology) or its specifically social version, social network analysis. Unfortunately, many of the methods used by anthropologists, sociologists and other social scientists for analysing networks are not available for research into the types of phenomena studied in this collection, largely because of the secrecy surrounding them and the related difficulties involved in interviewing and observing members of criminal groups.

There are many individuals and organisations to thank for their assistance in bringing about the conference, and hence this book. First, I would like to thank all the contributors, some of whom came literally half way around the world to participate in our conference. Many of them would have been unable to participate had it not been for the generous funding provided by CESAA, the Global Terrorism Research Unit at Monash University, the National Europe Centre (Australian National University, Canberra) and the Royal Netherlands Embassy – to each of which I express my sincere gratitude. For invaluable administrative assistance, I wish to thank Dora Horvath, Zoe Knox, Suzy Mueller, Iva Pauker and Tony Phillips.

Leslie Holmes
Melbourne

1. Introduction

Leslie Holmes

GROWING AWARENESS

On 27 July 2003, there was an attempted military coup in the Philippines. It was soon put down. But it is worth noting the principal reason given by the rebels for the uprising: they were protesting against corruption, and the close collaboration between corrupt officials (especially in the military) and terrorists (*Philippine Star* online, 31 July 2003, visited May 2005; *South China Morning Post*, 1 August 2003: 11). This identification of connections between corruption and terrorism in a specific context was relatively new. But even the recognition by governments and official agencies of the full significance – economically, socially, politically and in security terms – of organised crime and corruption, and of the connections between these, is relatively new. A few pieces of evidence will support this contention; the choice here is highly selective, since further examples are provided in subsequent chapters.

In April and May 1996, the then heads of the CIA (John Deutch) and the FBI (Louis Freeh) both warned the US Congress that Russian organised crime and corruption were already undermining the Russian system, and could pose a threat to the USA. Towards the end of that year, former CIA head James Woolsey claimed that officials in the Russian Ministries of Defence and the Interior were, ' ... very much in bed with Russian organized crime groups' (all from Webster 1997: esp. 3, 51). Shortly after this, in 1997, President Clinton became the first US president to recognise officially, publicly and explicitly the *interconnectedness* of corruption and organised crime. This was followed in May 1998 by the publication of the USA's first ever 'International Crime Control Strategy', which was the principal outcome of President Clinton's October 1995 Decision Directive 42, calling for a specific program to address the dangers of international crime to the USA. In this, it was argued that organised crime gangs and 'disreputable business interests sometimes aligned with them' use 'corrupt political connections' to avoid fair economic competition, and that 'Organized crime now uses bribery as one of its primary tools to establish front companies aimed at gaining control of legitimate businesses and penetrating the legitimate economy' (*International Crime Control Strategy* 1988: 18, 81). The US government had begun to recognise that official corruption (that is, committed by officers of the state) and organised crime feed off each other, and often work hand in glove.[1] A prime example of this is people smuggling (usually referred to in official US documents as alien smuggling), which, together with its close relative human trafficking, could not occur on the scale it does globally were it not for corrupt officers of the state – particularly in customs, the police, and sometimes the military – colluding with criminal gangs to circumvent various states' and international laws.[2]

But awareness has been developing rapidly in recent years, and an increasing number of cases, and the ramifications of these, are being reported. In February 2005, for example, Australian authorities publicly announced their concern that Chinese crime gangs (misguidedly described in the media as Mafia) had been corrupting senior police officials in Papua New Guinea. Among the many negative implications of this were that this was further delegitimising a regime already suffering from a low level of popular support; this could lead to mass unrest and hence instability, with possibly profound knock-on security effects in the whole region. Another serious aspect of this, which could directly impact upon Australia, was the limited evidence that this collusion was facilitating people-smuggling and drug-trafficking (*The Age* [Melbourne], 19 February 2005: 1–2).

Even more recent than the official awareness of bilateral connections between organised crime and corrupt officials is the acknowledgement of either bilateral links between corrupt officials or organised crime gangs and terrorists, or trilateral ones between these three groups. The *International Crime Control Strategy* (1998: 17) referred to above acknowledged that terrorists sometimes use 'drugs trafficking and other criminal activities to finance their operations', and in this sense implicitly recognised some overlap between organised crime and terrorism. However, the often close and direct ties were yet to be acknowledged. Moreover, the USA's growing awareness of networks was well ahead of that of most other countries and international organisations. The situation changed dramatically following 9/11. A few examples of official recognition since September 2001 will highlight the fact that a rapidly growing number of governments and international organisations now acknowledge that connections can and do exist, and that they pose significant dangers.

Some 330 people, many of them children, were killed as a result of a terrorist hostage-taking exercise in Beslan, Northern Ossetia (Southern Russia) in early September 2004. Shortly after the incident, Russian Prosecutor General Vladimir Ustinov acknowledged that controlling terrorism in the future would be much more difficult than it should be because of so many corrupt Russian officials – particularly in the security forces – colluding with terrorists and/or crime gangs.[3] A survey conducted by the Levada polling organisation in September 2004 revealed that more than 50 per cent of Russians believed that the Beslan incident had been possible largely because of corrupt officials. There were at least three significant ways in which corrupt officials were assisting terrorists.[4] First and perhaps most obviously, they were allowing suspicious people through security checks in return for bribes. Second, they were selling arms on the black market. The final way was more indirect. According to President Putin's advisor on Chechnya, up to 80 per cent of the aid being allocated by the central Russian authorities to southern Russian regions was not reaching its intended destination – the poor of the region – because of corrupt officials. This sense of being forgotten or treated indifferently by Moscow was cited as a reason why more citizens would be attracted to terrorism than would otherwise be the case (*Guardian*, 17 September 2004: 19).[5] Still in Russia, the Federal Security Service (FSB) reported in mid-2002 that the number of attempts by organised crime gangs to sell components for both chemical and nuclear weapons was increasing (cited from a Russian source in Curtis 2003b: 71). Clearly, a prime market for such components would be terrorist groups.

In February 2005, the Irish police announced that a number of arrests had been made in connection with a major bank robbery (£26 million or €38 million – at that time, the largest theft of cash in British history) committed in December 2004.[6] Whilst the direct involvement of the Irish Republican Army (IRA), a terrorist organisation, was still not proven conclusively at the time of writing, a member of Sinn Fein – the political wing of the IRA – was among those arrested. Indeed, the IRA has been described as 'Ireland's most proficient robber of banks' (*Washington Post* online, 18 February 2005, visited February 2005). The Irish police revealed that they considered this robbery to be part of a money-laundering operation. Moreover, a report released by the Independent Monitoring Commission in early February 2005 claimed that Sinn Fein had at least *sanctioned* a series of robberies in Ireland, including the major one in December (*BBC News* online, 10 February 2005, visited February 2005). Sinn Fein had just weeks earlier denied any involvement in the robbery, and had used its indignation as an excuse to withdraw its earlier offer of a complete decommissioning of arms. But the arrests resulted in serious embarrassment for the president of Sinn Fein, Gerry Adams, who returned to Ireland from Spain on hearing of Sinn Fein arrests. Although he denied any involvement on the part of either Sinn Fein or the IRA, many believed this was a cover-up. Following the arrests, the Irish Justice Minister called the IRA, ' ... a colossal criminal operation' (all from *New York Times*, 19 February 2005: A8), while the Conservative (UK) Spokesperson on Northern Ireland, David Lidington, had a few days earlier criticised Sinn Fein for its involvement with '... an armed and active criminal gang' (*BBC News* online, 10 February 2005, visited March 2005). A number of arrests relating to the robbery were made in November 2005, including of individuals alleged to be members of Sinn Fein.[7]

One other aspect of this Irish case deserves mention. A large sum of money was discovered in February 2005 at a Northern Irish country club known to be popular with police officers. On the day following the discovery, Northern Irish police investigators confirmed that the cash was part of the money stolen from the Northern Bank. It remains to be seen whether or not a connection between organised crime gangs, terrorists and corrupt police officers can be proven on the basis of this find and related developments. But there are certainly grounds for strong suspicion. Another European case, which involves at least bilateral linkages – between the Basque terrorist organisation ETA and the Italian organised crime group the Camorra – was identified by Italian authorities in the early 2000s; there were also allegations of connections between these two and corrupt elements of the Czech military (Curtis and Karacan 2002: 9–10; for further information on linkages between organised crime and terrorists in Europe see Sagramoso 2001).

Moving beyond Europe, Ecuadorian authorities announced in June 2005 that they had broken a drug-smuggling ring that had been using some of its profits to part finance a Lebanese Islamist group classified by the USA as a terrorist organisation (Hezbollah). The US State Department has long maintained that Islamist terrorist groups based in the Middle East were active in Latin America; and Hezbollah was accused by many of being responsible for a July 1994 terrorist attack on a Jewish centre in Buenos Aires that cost more than 80 lives (McDermott 2005).

While it might not be particularly surprising that governments have only recently begun to recognise the *connections* between organised crime and/or corruption and/or terrorism, it comes as a surprise to many to learn that it is also only recently that many Western governments, and in particular international organisations, have begun to take corruption itself seriously. Thus, it is only a little over a decade – May 1994 – since the issuance of what was described by Transparency International (TI) in 1996 as 'the first multilateral agreement among governments to combat the bribery of foreign officials' (Transparency International 1996: 15), namely the OECD's 'Recommendations on Bribery in International Business Transactions'. TI also claims that the European Union (EU) only began to take serious notice of corruption in 1995 (*TI Newsletter*, September 1996: 10) – while the UN Convention against Corruption was opened for signature as recently as December 2003.

But there has been an explosion of awareness, legislation, campaigning, and so on in recent years – to such an extent that some have questioned or openly criticised the growth of what might be seen as an anti-corruption industry (for example Krastev 2004). There is now even an 'International Day against Corruption' (9 December), on which, in 2005, the United Nations Office on Drugs and Crime (UNODC) launched its own anti-corruption campaign – 'You Can Stop Corruption' – oriented towards both civil society and individual citizens. Nevertheless, the fact remains that corruption is still a major problem around the world (for evidence, readers should consult the TI website), while crime-fighting authorities in many countries have in recent years become much more conscious of the potential dangers of organised crime, and of the linkages between its perpetrators and those responsible for combating them.[8] Citing Webster again (1997: 45), as of the mid-1990s, 'Corruption of the official Russian bureaucracy poses, in many ways, the most serious threat to the interests of the United States and other countries'. Although the threat from Al-Qaeda and related terrorist organisations has now supplanted this corruption as *the* primary perceived threat, the fact that there might be *indirect* linkages between corrupt Russian officials and Al-Qaeda demonstrates just how serious the terrorism–corruption–organised crime nexus is perceived to be in many quarters; both Western and Russian governments and media have claimed that there are links between Chechen terrorists and Al-Qaeda, for instance (particularly at the time of the Moscow theatre siege in October 2002 – http://www.newsmax.com/archives/articles/2002/10/24/ 162841.sht and http://cfrterrorism.org/groups/ chechens.html, both visited April 2005), so that the connections already noted between the former and corrupt Russian security officers represent such an indirect linkage.

As for the approach of international agencies to fighting the corruption– organised crime nexus, one early example is that of the Council of Europe (CoE). In June 1997, the Ministers of Justice of the then 40 member states of the CoE met in Prague to discuss 'Links between Corruption and Organised Crime' and devise ways to coordinate the international fight against them

(CoE website, visited August 2005). But the connections between the terrible twins (that is, corruption and organised crime) and terrorism were still to be widely acknowledged by governments and international agencies. President Clinton did refer to 'an unholy axis of new threats from terrorists, international criminals and drug traffickers' in January 1998 (*International Crime Control Strategy* 1988: 15), but this was still ultimately a vague and implicit recognition of the close ties that often exist between these phenomena, and did not explicitly identify corrupt officials as part of the security threat equation.

But as already noted, one of the numerous effects of 9/11 has been the belated and explicit recognition by many more Western governments (including the American and British) and international organisations that corruption, organised crime and terrorism *are* frequently bedfellows. To quote the Director of the Secretary General's Cabinet at Interpol, Stanley Morris (2002: 1), 'Corruption and terrorism are intrinsically linked. While corruption has money as its motive, terrorism requires money to further its ends'. Morris goes on to focus on the fight against money-laundering as one of the main tools for combating both corruption and the funding of terrorism, and in this context refers *inter alia* to the actions being taken by the Wolfsberg group of international banks and the OECD's Financial Action Task Force.

Another of many concrete outcomes of this rapidly rising awareness of linkages is the establishment in October 2001 of a 'Terrorist Finance Team', initially with just eight staff, within the *Economic Crime* (emphasis added) Unit of the UK's National Criminal Intelligence Service.[9] At about the same time that this new agency was established, the National Terrorist Financial Investigation Unit had its staff nearly quadrupled. If it were not for organised crime and corruption, terrorists would find it much more difficult to access weapons, for instance, and to finance their own operations; this has become more clearly the case in the 2000s, as governments have amended legislation to permit them to monitor potential money-laundering and suspicious bank accounts much more closely. Equally, one of the most common sources of the nuclear materials and conventional weapons organised crime gangs allegedly sell to terrorists is corrupt officials, particularly in the military, customs and police. And in an era when the distinctions between the state and the market have become increasingly blurred, even states can be involved in what could be called a 'triumvirate of evil'. North Korea, for example, has been accused on several occasions of participating in various forms of organised crime activity, including drug smuggling and illegal fishing.[10] Sometimes, the leaders of a regime that had struggled against organised crime can dramatically alter their stance once they lose power. Thus, the Taliban regime in Afghanistan strongly condemned the production of poppy-seed for heroin. But once the Taliban lost control of the state, they appear to have changed their attitude and encouraged the production and sale of opium, seeing possibilities in this for financing their efforts at fighting the new Afghan state and its Western supporters (*Economist*, 20 November 2004: 32).

So far, the focus has been primarily on the fact that it is only very recently that governments and international agencies have begun to appreciate the overlaps between corruption, organised crime and terrorism. But much of the academic community has also been relatively slow to appreciate the connections. Without exploring this in depth, three symbolically relevant pieces of information will suffice to endorse this point. First, a recent edition of as standard a work on organised crime as Howard Abadinsky's (2000) has a mere two pages on corruption in a book of almost 500 pages, and nothing directly on terrorism. Second, while there are numerous research centres that specialise in one or other of the three phenomena under consideration here, there are only a couple of major ones in the English-speaking world that focus on their interconnectedness. One is the Transnational Crime and Corruption Center (TraCCC) in Washington DC, which describes itself on its website as 'the first center in the United States devoted to teaching, research, training and formulating policy advice in transnational crime, corruption and terrorism' (visited July 2005). It was originally founded in 1995, but only included a focus on terrorism much more recently; it is headed by Dr Louise Shelley. The other is the Jack and Mae Nathanson Centre for the Study of Organized Crime and Corruption, based at York University in Toronto, and established in 1996. It does not mention terrorism in its mandate, although it has now begun to consider these linkages too. It is headed by Dr Margaret Beare.[11] Finally, the media and various research agencies have now also started to analyse the linkages between these three forms of crime. A good example is Radio Free Europe/Radio Liberty (RFE/RL), which has an (irregularly produced) 'Organized Crime and Terrorism Watch' online analysis that officially 'reports on crime, corruption and terrorism in the former USSR, Eastern Europe and the Middle East'. It too is new, dating from late 2001; prior to that, RFE/RL had only a report on crime and corruption. A second example is the Federal Research Division of the US Library of Congress, which began focusing on *linkages* only in the early 2000s (see for example Curtis and Karacan 2002; Miró 2003).

The reasons for this growing awareness are several. The most obvious recent one – the impact of 9/11 – has already been mentioned. But other factors were clearly at work before this. Three of the most significant are the impact of the end of the Cold War, the development of new measurement techniques, and globalisation, each of which is outlined here.

With the end of more than four decades of Cold War, the West did not have as readily identifiable an enemy as it had previously had. But in an era when many were claiming the terminal demise of the state in an era of globalisation, neo-liberalism and disintegrative identity politics, one of the areas in which states could still claim to have a role to perform was security. Yet the state's claim on funds to support its security role requires, or is at least strengthened by, the identification of an enemy or enemies. In general, other states appeared ever less likely to pose a serious threat to the leading Western states. But transnational organised crime and terrorism *could* be portrayed as a danger. Moreover, if these two phenomena could be linked to states that were likely to be seen as potential real threats to the West, so much the better. Thus was born the US government's concept of rogue states, which was subsequently replaced (in January 2002) by the notion of an axis of evil; states identified in this way were said *inter alia* to have close ties with terrorists and/or organised crime. The linking of these concepts to the need for an enemy is not necessarily to claim that there was a conspiracy and deliberate exaggeration on the part of Western states. Rather, agencies that had spent decades monitoring the communist threat now redirected their attention, and suddenly took far more notice of phenomena that had long been there, but that may have become more prominent.

The last point leads to another ramification of the end of the Cold War. This is that peoples who, until the end of the 1980s, had found it difficult to travel outside of the communist bloc, suddenly found this far easier. Since early post-communism also represented a time of high levels of social and economic insecurity, it is not surprising that corruption and transnational organised crime increased in and from the region. The situation was compounded by the violent disintegration of former Yugoslavia. One effect of this was that it intensified the desire of more and more people from the region to flee. But another ramification was that many of those who had been fighting were tempted and had the wherewithal to continue their violence and/or to engage in the illegal sale of decommissioned arms and munitions once the various wars were over. In short, this situation contributed to the rise of new criminal gangs in South-Eastern Europe. All this was unquestionably a major factor explaining the growing awareness in Western Europe – which was geographically adjacent to these unstable and troubled transition states – of the security threat posed by organised crime and corruption.

A third effect of the end of the Cold War was that Western states that had, until the end of the 1980s, often turned a blind eye to corruption and other unsavoury aspects of countries they wanted to retain in or attract to the Western camp now felt far less need to do so; this argument is made forcefully and persuasively by, among others, Moisés Naím (1995).

Finally, many Western states may have become more introspective or self-reflexive in the 1990s, and more willing to 'wash their dirty linen in public' than they had been during the Cold War, when communist states would have been able to use the West's self-reporting of corruption to their own propaganda advantage.[12] Of course, Western corruption *did* get reported in the West during the Cold War; in a democracy in which the media are performing their watchdog functions properly, this is to be expected. Nevertheless, the sheer increase in the reporting of corruption, which can be demonstrated empirically (McCoy and Heckel 2001), represented a marked change.

Perhaps because of the new focus on corruption and transnational organised crime – this is less clearly the case with terrorism – in the 1990s, there was a substantial increase in attention to measurement methodologies. With reference to the former, for instance, the first Corruption Perceptions Index produced by Transparency International appeared in 1995, just before the first Public Expenditure Tracking Survey (PETS) was conducted (in Uganda; see Reinikka *et al.* 2002) – while most of the World Bank experiential surveys of corruption were conducted in the late 1990s and early 2000s. It is quite possible that the impression that both corruption and transnational organised crime (see Woodiwiss 2003: esp. 13) have become more of a problem since the early 1990s is in part related to the fact that analysts have been attempting to measure them with greater sophistication and enthusiasm than in earlier decades.

Globalisation is a concept that became a household term in the 1990s. Like the Cold War factor, there are various dimensions of it that help to explain both the apparent rise of terrorism, organised crime and corruption, and growing official awareness of the security implications of these. Many of these aspects are analysed in subsequent chapters, so that only a few key elements will be referred to here. The rise of the internet has made the internationalisation of crime easier through greatly facilitated communication, at the same time as it has opened up possibilities for new types of crime (for example e-mail scams; theft and fraud relating to online banking). At the same time, the liberalisation of international trade encouraged by neo-liberal or Washington Consensus policies has contributed to what Ohmae (1990, 2005) has called the 'borderless' world.[13] The rise of this so-called borderless world

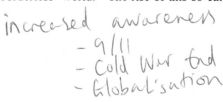

has in many cases made it easier for criminals of various kinds to move between countries. But many states have ambiguous attitudes towards the liberalisation of borders. While many welcome it if it increases the flow of licit goods and capital, they do not advocate free movement either of what they consider to be illicit capital and goods, or of *all* people. Thus, at the same time as Ohmae and others talk of a borderless world, there has been a strengthening of border control around the expanded EU (leading some to refer to Fortress Europe), Australia, and more recently the USA (for example with its 2006 declared intention substantially to extend its existing fence along the border with Mexico), as states and regions seek to limit illegal migration and the movement of criminal funds. Unfortunately, this increases the demand for, *inter alia*, people smuggling, which in turn creates additional opportunities for criminality.

DEFINITIONAL ASPECTS OF TERRORISM, ORGANISED CRIME AND CORRUPTION

Having established that official awareness of the linkages between terrorism, organised crime and corruption is a relatively recent – but now accelerating – development, it is appropriate to consider briefly what the three terms actually connote. One important reason is that this can help us better understand *why* organisations and academics find it so difficult to analyse these phenomena and to obtain reliable data on them. Of course, the latter problem is to no small extent because of the secrecy surrounding all three types of criminality, which in turn creates major difficulties in investigating them and securing convictions, and helps to explain why so much of our information about them is soft and/or inferential. But the problem is compounded by the fact that the definitions and boundaries of all three concepts are fuzzy and disputed. Rather than suggest concise and precise definitions, which are notoriously contentious – for instance, because of cultural differences – a better approach is to conceptualise and identify them through sets of criteria.

Like the concepts of organised crime and corruption, the term *terrorism* is contested. More than two decades ago, one analyst identified no fewer than 109 definitions (Schmid 1983: 119–52), while a much more recent Russian analysis identified 'between 100 and 200' conceptions of terrorism, but maintained that none of them was considered authoritative ('a classic' – Gavrilin and Smirnov 2003: 4). Our preference is to sidestep the minefield of dictionary-style definitions. Instead, for an action to be *identified* here as terrorism, it needs to meet the following set of criteria:

1. It involves violence, both actual and threatened, which often appears to be random and is designed to incite widespread fear (that is, intimidate).[14]
2. It disregards conventional rules of warfare, typically drawing no distinction between combatants and non-combatants in directing its violence.
3. It ultimately has a political objective, though this may be purely negative (revenge; anarchy), negative as a first stage (for example, destruction of a state or regime, but with a longer term aim of creating a new political unit or regime), or unclear to those not involved in the terrorist activity; the political objective may also be connected to religious objectives.
4. Its perpetrators consciously break the state laws of countries in which they operate.[15]
5. Its perpetrators usually seek publicity for their cause.[16]
6. It is not *per se* oriented towards material benefit.
7. It is carried out by non-state actors.[17]
8. It must be perceived by a significant proportion of the target population and/or the state as terrorism.

An important point to note is that this checklist includes in several places terms such as typically and normally. This is deliberate, and reflects the difficulties involved in producing a universally valid set of criteria. Conversely, it implicitly recognises the diversity of terrorist activity, which is an advantage of such an approach.

Letizia Paoli (2002) claims that the term organised crime is an ambiguous catchphrase. She emphasises the inconsistency in the literature concerning the very concept of organised crime, and proceeds to argue that most so-called organised crime is in fact very *disorganised* and small-scale, and will remain so.[18] She further maintains that such major large-scale criminal organisations as do exist are often involved in *legal* economic activity, so that the term organised *crime* can be misleading. Paoli and others (such as Bäckman 1998) who have questioned the meaning, significance, scale and nature of organised crime sometimes overstate their cases, but there is unquestionably some truth in many of their contentions. Certainly, there is no universal agreement in the literature, or between organisations dealing with this phenomenon, on how to define it. Given the preference here for identifying phenomena through checklists rather than short definitions, activities will be classified as examples of *organised crime* if they meet the following eleven criteria:

1. They are necessarily carried out by a group (at least three persons) that may, but need not and often does not, include officials.[19]
2. They are carried out by a group that normally has limited (exclusive) membership, for instance on the basis of ethnicity, family ties, place of origin or a common prison background.[20]
3. They are carried out by a group that is structured, and often hierarchically organised, albeit in very diverse ways.[21]
4. They are to a large degree coordinated, rather than spontaneous.
5. They are carried out by a group that is durable.
6. They are carried out by a group that exists primarily for the sake of material benefit.
7. They are usually targeted (that is concentrating on a particular type or types of criminal activity, such as drug-trafficking, prostitution, gambling, forgery or arms smuggling).
8. They are necessarily, and at least in part, consciously unlawful.
9. They typically involve violence, either actual or threatened.
10. Their perpetrators do not typically seek publicity.
11. They must be perceived by a significant proportion of the population and/or the state as constituting organised criminal activity.[22]

In addition to reminding the reader of the reasons for, and advantages of, the use of terms such as typically and often, it should be further noted that the above criteria make no reference to transnationalism. While organised crime can – and, it appears, increasingly does – operate across national boundaries, this is not *per se* a distinguishing feature, merely a characteristic of a sub-group of organised crime gangs.[23]

The criteria used here for identifying *corruption* are different again. Thus, for the purposes of this study, an action or non-action (the latter might include deliberately turning a blind eye in return for some reward) should in principle meet five criteria in order to qualify as an example of corruption:

1. It must involve an individual or a group of individuals occupying a public office, typically a state position; in short, it must involve officials, whether elected or appointed.
2. The public office must involve a degree of decision-making or law-enforcing or state-defensive authority. Hence, and controversially, while

military officers could be corrupt, ordinary soldiers – particularly conscripts – would be excluded under this definition. Similarly, even though they might be state employees, a postal delivery worker or a train driver could not be corrupt under this approach.

3. The officials must commit the act at least in part because of either personal (vested or private-regarding) interest and/or the interests of an organisation to which that official belongs (for example a political party), if these interests run counter to those of the state and society.

4. The officials act (or do not act) partly or wholly in a clandestine manner, and are aware that their actions (non-actions) either are or might be considered illegal or improper. In cases of uncertainty, the officials opt not to check this – not to subject their actions to the so-called sunlight test (that is they are not prepared to allow open scrutiny of their actions) – ultimately because of intended interest-maximisation.[24]

5. It must be perceived by a significant proportion of the population and/or the state as corrupt.[25]

This checklist for assessing whether an action or non-action constitutes corruption is less problematic than an actual definition, but is not watertight. For instance, it does not cover the situation in which a politician openly promotes favourites who are not the best qualified candidates for a position, since this does not meet the fourth criterion. Nevertheless, it does address most situations that would be widely perceived as corrupt.

All three terms identified here by means of sets of criteria are contested and, ultimately, socially constructed and labeled. Thus a terrorist campaign can be construed as a justified fight for freedom; particular examples of organised crime are seen by some as 'protective' in a basically positive sense; and some forms of corruption can be widely perceived as a useful 'greasing of the cogs'.[26] Ultimately, the way in which phenomena are to be interpreted will depend largely on either the majority viewpoint (a more objective perspective, in the sense that it can be measured), a normative judgment (more subjective, based on the particular ethical codes of individual observers), or a combination of these.[27] This is why the final criterion cited in each of our three checklists refers to perception.

Another caveat is that some of the variables are common across at least two checklists. For instance, both corrupt officials and organised crime gangs can operate primarily for material gain, while attempting to avoid detection (related to variables referring to conscious law-breaking) is a common – if obvious – feature of most examples of all three types of crime. Thus the lists have to be taken as packages, and it makes no sense to isolate individual variables and use them independently of the others in a given list.

A final point to note about the checklists is that they approximate to abstract, Weberian-style ideal types. The reason they can only approximate is because of the inclusion of escape valves – the use of terms such as normally and typically – in some of the criteria. Unfortunately, while the inclusion of such terms allows for variety and nuancing when aggregating diverse groups and activities, and in this sense is advantageous, it does compromise the capacity to produce pure forms of each type of crime. On the other hand, emphasising this point about ideal types, and pushing our checklists as far as possible in the direction of such pure forms, helps to highlight an important point about the approach adopted here. This is that actual, real world groups and actions sometimes straddle two or even three of the types of crime analysed in this volume. But this does not mean that the concepts themselves have to be blurred – any more than Max Weber's three ideal types of legitimation have to be blurred, even though, in the real world, systems and regimes do sometimes display features of more than one of his three modes (as Weber himself acknowledged). The relevance of this should become clear in the concluding chapter of this book, where calls for a fudging of terms are rejected; the point is more appropriately addressed there, since the chapter urges consideration of a fourth type of crime, and the argument can be better made when related to all four types.

OBJECTIVES AND FOCI

Europe – the primary focus of this book – has witnessed numerous major corruption scandals in recent years. While the problems of corruption in post-communist Central and Eastern Europe (CEE) are frequently rehearsed (see for example Miller *et al.* 2001; Karklins 2005; L. Holmes 2006), it must not be forgotten that leading EU countries (as well as other Western states, including the USA), such as Belgium, France, Germany and Italy have also experienced major scandals since the beginning of the 1990s (see Della Porta and Mény 1997; R. Williams *et al.* 2000; Bull and Newell 2003). Europe is also home to two of what many analysts see as the world's five major organised crime groupings (the Italian 'mafia' broadly understood; the Russian 'mafia'[28]). Other groupings apparently visited Europe before the 1990s, but had gone largely unnoticed before 1992–93 and/or had not previously been active there; the Japanese Yakuza is a prime example (Sterling 1994: 118, 127–8). Europe has also long been subject to terrorism. In addition to the recent bombings in Madrid and London, the most prominent examples in the past three decades have been the Red Brigades in Italy, the Baader-Meinhof gang (Red Army Faction) in Germany, the IRA in Ireland and the UK, Action Directe in France, PKK (renamed KADEK in 2001) in Turkey, and ETA in Spain and Southern France (for a listing and brief introduction to the major terrorist groups, both in Europe and globally in recent decades, see Wilkinson 2001: xi–xvi). Our second focus, Australia, was once seen as largely isolated from some of the less desirable criminal and violent developments elsewhere. But it has now been forced closer to centre stage. The Bali bombings in 2002 were one of the more widely-publicised manifestations of this, while often deadly gangland warfare in Melbourne in the first few years of the new millennium drew comparisons with 1920s Chicago. One of the objectives of this book is to analyse recent changes and evidence relating to the three types of crime in Europe, Australia and elsewhere, both individually and in terms of their interconnectedness.

It would be all too easy to focus on the sensational aspects of this topic. But we shall largely leave the more colourful aspects to the mass media and journalistic accounts.[29] Having considered evidence of corruption, organised crime, terrorism, and the bi- and trilateral relations between these, a second objective is to consider the deeper implications of the interconnectedness of these three phenomena. The impact can be classified under three headings – governance, domestic legitimacy and international legitimacy – each of which is outlined here.

One of the most unfortunate implications of both 9/11 and the increasing technological sophistication of organised crime, corruption and terrorism is that more and more states are now placing collective security and crime fighting concerns above respect for individual human rights and civil liberties. Thus, the 'triumvirate of evil' is impacting upon the bedrock of most Western conceptions of democracy, which in turn affects our conceptions of optimal structures and operational modes of governance. Several authors in this volume touch on various aspects of this theme.

It has traditionally been maintained that a major drawback of corruption is that, if it is perceived by publics to be systemic, it can undermine particular types of regime and even system legitimacy (a problem that is compounded if there is evidence of widespread collusion between corrupt officials and organised crime gangs), notably legal-rationality. Yet many citizens are inconsistent on this issue. If voters who are otherwise critical of corruption have to choose in an election between a candidate who is seen to be corrupt but effective (for example in reducing unemployment and increasing GDP growth rates), and another with a cleaner but less dynamic and effective reputation, they will often choose the former.[30] Perhaps it is time fundamentally to reconsider the traditional (especially Weberian) notions of legitimation modes. Particularly in the period since 9/11 – when, as noted, the salience of the rule of law has declined in many Western states[31] – it appears that eudaemonism (here meaning good economic performance, broadly conceived), sometimes linked with official nationalism, has become more important than legal rationality as the principal domestic legitimator of the modern state. But if this is the case, it is also time to analyse the normative and practical problems associated with this change.

Legitimacy operates also at the international level. One dimension of this relates to a state's approval by the international community. As elaborated in Chapter 5, when the EU released its country-specific assessments of ten CEE applicants for membership in 1997, only one factor was common to *all* summaries of the political issues to be addressed urgently in each country: corruption. Applicant states were informed that they would be considered ineligible for admission to the EU unless they could demonstrate a serious commitment to reducing this. This is one aspect of international legitimation or delegitimation (depending on a government's response). Another is exemplified by the World Bank and the OECD, which are two among many international organisations that sometimes financially penalise countries that require economic assistance, but which are seen to be too tolerant of corruption, organised crime and/or terrorism. If the argument about the connections between economic performance and domestic legitimacy is valid, it becomes clear how this lack of international legitimacy and financial support can directly impact on regime and system legitimacy *within* a given country. Often, the World Bank and other agencies argue that what is needed is governance reform – so that the linkages between governance, legitimacy, and the 'triumvirate of evil' come sharply into focus.

In light of all this, a book that analyses the three phenomena, problematises them, provides evidence on them both individually and in terms of their interconnectedness, and considers the governance and other reforms most likely to reduce their impact, is both timely and necessary. By comparing European experiences with Australian and American, academic depth can be combined with practicality. Despite our full awareness of the potential problems of comparative analysis, such as insufficient sensitivity to cultural and structural differences, it is maintained that the potential advantages of better understanding through vicarious experience – the benefits of not having

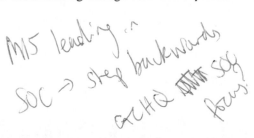

to 'reinvent the wheel' – outweigh the disadvantages, as long as the limitations and dangers of transposition are constantly borne in mind.

The reference to networks and linkages in the title of this book is primarily to connections *between* the three types of crime on which we focus, rather than between different entities – crime gangs, terrorist organisations, and so on – *within* each of these three categories, such as those known to have existed between the IRA and the Colombian terrorist organisation FARC (Revolutionary Armed Forces of Colombia), or between Italian and Albanian traffickers. But there is also a need for much more detailed research into two other types of network and linkage. The first is that forged between communities, states and international organisations seeking to combat them. The second is perhaps less obvious, but is in many ways just as important. This is the linkages that form between communities and criminals. Some research has already been conducted on this (for example in the cases of organised crime in Italy, drug cartels in Colombia, and the Taliban in Southern Afghanistan, while Pete Lentini's chapter in this volume also considers an aspect of this), but there is a need for far more. Unless an attempt is made to understand how and why various kinds of criminal are sometimes embedded in communities whose members are aware of their neighbours' illegal activities but do not report them to the authorities, there will be less progress in combating these three types of behaviour than there could and should be. While much more research needs to be conducted into this aspect of networks and linkages, greater awareness of the significance of such connections will advance us. In the concluding chapter, a plea is also made to expand analyses from three to four types of sometimes-related crime.

Reference was made above to some of the numerous problems involved in defining the three phenomena under examination here. Given these problems and disagreements, it is not surprising that measuring each of them is also fraught with difficulties. One indication of this is the recent publication of a book of some 300 pages devoted largely to the various problems relating to the methods used by Transparency International and other organisations for measuring corruption (Sampford *et al.* 2006). Another is the fact that when, in April 2005, the USA's newly-established (August 2004) National Counterterrorism Center (NCTC) published statistics on the number of terrorist attacks and victims there had been worldwide in 2004, it immediately came under criticism for using an overly-narrow definition and approach, and soon (July 2005) published a revised set of figures. Thus, whereas the earlier set had indicated that there had been 651 'significant' attacks, in which 1907 people had lost their lives, the updated set identified 3192 attacks, in which

28,433 people had been killed, injured or kidnapped (*EBBOY 2006*: 208; NCTC website, visited March 2006). The 2005 figures rose substantially, with 11,111 terrorist attacks noted worldwide (of which approximately 30 per cent were in Iraq), resulting in the deaths of almost 15,000 non-combatants. When these 2005 data were released, the Deputy Director of the NCTC acknowledged that even the *revised* figures for 2004 were too low (all from *Washington Post*, 29 April 2006: AO1). Data on organised crime, particularly across several jurisdictions, are also highly problematical. Often, this is for similar reasons to those that explain the difficulties in obtaining comprehensive and reliable data on corruption, such as cultural differences, definitional disagreements, and so on (see Burnham 2003). As just one symbol of the difficulties involved, the UNODC (United Nations Office on Drugs and Crime) only began to publish estimates of the volume of the illegal narcotics market as recently as 2005. According to the first such report, based on 2003 data, the volume of the illicit narcotics market was calculated at US$13 billion at the production level, and US$322 billion at the retail level (allowing for seizures and other losses) (*EBBOY 2006*: 208). Such figures, even if rubbery, not only provide some idea of the sheer scale of the drugs market – in which corrupt officials, organised crime gangs, and some terrorist organisations (sometimes called narco-terrorists) are all involved – but also a clear indication of the *reasons* for such involvement; the profit margins can be, quite simply, huge.[32]

The last point leads to another that research suggests should be reconsidered. Those who maintain that corruption, organised crime and/or terrorism are primarily a function of poverty need to counter Vincenzo Ruggiero's argument that it is the potential rewards of crime, not necessity, that attract most of its perpetrators. Thus he concluded in a recent study that '… the excess of resources and opportunities, rather than the lack of both, is the major cause of criminal activity' (Ruggiero 2000: 178).[33] In the nineteenth century, Alexis de Tocqueville argued convincingly – in his theory of rising expectations – that poverty alone is hardly ever the stimulus for revolution. Along similar lines, it is maintained here that poverty *per se* is rarely the trigger for the kinds of growth in anti-social and anti-statist behaviour analysed in this volume.[34] There must be leadership, opportunities, and – often closely related to the opportunity context – either a perception of potential major change or *actual* major change to stimulate such growth. Poverty can and frequently does provide fertile soil for all three broad phenomena under consideration here, but does not in itself adequately explain the growth in any of them.

STRUCTURE

The structure and logic of this book can now be elaborated. The collection basically divides into two sections. The first comprises chapters that are primarily comparative in their thematic coverage. In the next chapter, Frank Bovenkerk and Bashir Abou Chakra point out that terrorism and organised crime were for a long time analysed by different research communities. It was not until the 1980s that the two groups of scholars began to collaborate more closely, as it emerged that illicit drug production and trafficking sometimes funded terrorist campaigns. An interesting point revealed by comparative analysis is that, whereas the social origins of organised crime gang members and terrorists tend to be different, there exist similarities between the types of personality attracted to both organised crime and terrorism; in this context, the authors argue that the attraction to power is an element that has been inadequately emphasised and researched. Having identified areas of agreement and common interest between the two groups of researchers, Bovenkerk and Abou Chakra argue that there remain fundamental disagreements on the extent of collusion between the two types of criminality. While some analysts maintain that the two are closely linked and even converging, others point out that the same limited number of cases of collusion is cited repeatedly, and that there is a shortage of detailed empirical evidence. In the final part of their analysis, the authors make a plea for much more empirical research on collusion, to determine which of the two schools is closer to the truth. In this context, they propose an agenda of eleven questions that should guide future research.

Pete Lentini's focus in Chapter 3 is specifically terrorism. But his is a comparative approach, in that he looks at the lot of Moslems in both Europe and Australia (though with greater emphasis on the latter), and from more theoretical perspectives. Having drawn a distinction between anti-terrorism and counter-terrorism, his particular focus is on the ways in which a 'them-us' divide (marginalisation, alienation) might be avoided, and the growth of terrorism pre-empted, through the pursuit of more inclusionary policies of multi-culturalism, which appears to have been a largely effective approach in Australia, albeit not entirely problem-free. A major plank of such an approach is cultural citizenship, which he sees as a necessary third strand of citizenship. Lentini addresses the thorny problem of the legitimacy of the modern state, and how this might be enhanced as a way of attracting people who might otherwise be tempted to identify with other social constructions. He also identifies some of the problems associated with the concept of cultural citizenship, and points out that, ultimately, anti-terrorist and counter-terrorist policies and practices need to be tailor-made for specific societies and circumstances.

In Chapter 4, Rémy Davison considers the efficacy of 'soft' law regimes (that is using non-binding norms and precepts, as distinct from legal treaties) in combating financial crime, especially money-laundering; there is a particular focus in his chapter on the OECD's Financial Action Task Force (FATF) and, to a lesser extent, measures adopted by the EU and CoE. Although he addresses this issue primarily in the context of terrorism, much of the argument applies also to the other two forms of crime analysed in this volume. Davison argues that the FATF has been relatively successful, despite the actions of the NCCTs (Non-Cooperative Countries or Territories), and that this is an encouraging sign for those combating terrorism, corruption and organised crime. Nevertheless, there remain various problem areas, which he highlights.

Chapter 5 analyses the linkages between corruption and organised crime in CEE. Following a brief overview of the evidence on examples of such linkages, and of public perceptions of the nexus and its ramifications, the reasons for collusion are explored. There is a particular emphasis on the impact of the communist legacy, the effects of the multiple and simultaneous transition, and the ramifications of neo-liberalism. The fourth part of the chapter considers and evaluates some of the governance measures that can be and are being taken to combat both types of crime in CEE; it also highlights some of the dilemmas faced by authorities that seek to combat corruption and organised crime within a post-communist context that, at least putatively, seeks to promote democracy and civil rights. The conclusions explore the dynamism of the corruption and organised crime situation in recent years, and warn against unquestioning acceptance of deterministic views of the future that tend to be deeply pessimistic.

Chapters 6 through 11 constitute the second part of the collection, and are primarily concerned with terrorism and/or corruption and/or organised crime in particular parts of the world, both macro-regions and individual countries. This said, many of these chapters make more widely applicable theoretical points on the basis of their case studies. The chapter by Petrus van Duyne and Maarten van Dijck on cartels in the Dutch construction sector demonstrates that even countries with relatively clean images can and do experience cosy relationships that, in many cases, are improper. For instance, such relationships often undermine competition, to the disadvantage of the consumer. In practice, they also frequently involve the payment of bribes to civil servants, and thus corruption.[35] The authors show that the Dutch authorities have not only often turned a blind eye to the operation of cartels in the cement industry, but actually sought to *reduce* public perceptions of impropriety in the 1990s by decriminalising violations of the anti-cartel legislation, redefining them as mere administrative transgressions. Actions that in many ways closely resembled those associated with overt organised crime were not treated as such by the authorities, in part because the Criminal Code did not cover them. Yet the authorities' approach, van Duyne and van Dijck argue, has sometimes been ambiguous, and there *have* been investigations of allegations of organised criminal activity and corruption relating to the construction industry. The authors explore and explain the reasons for such ambiguity, which include historical tradition, the need to react to popular outrage, and a widespread lack of enthusiasm for new rules imposed on the Netherlands by the EU.

In Chapter 7, Yuri Tsyganov explores what he sees as the re-emergence in Russia of pre-communist (traditional) linkages and cooperation between economic, social and political groupings, some of which can be described as clans. He explores the ways in which clans seek to enhance their interests through what is sometimes called state capture, and through control of the mass media. Tsyganov analyses the popular expectations that Putin's accession to power would result in a clampdown on these groups and activities, but argues that these hopes have been dashed. While there has been some change under the present Russian president, it is more a matter of new clans (the so-called *chekisty*) seeking to oust and replace the old ones (oligarchs), and a return to power of the *nomenklatura*, rather than the removal of such types of grouping altogether from the economic and political scene. Tsyganov also shows how corruption has become a bargaining chip in the struggle between the new, old, and resurgent groupings.

The focus of Adam Czarnota's chapter is corruption in the post-communist states of CEE, with particular reference to Poland. He maintains that post-communist states are obsessed with corruption, and seeks to explain this. A major plank of his argument is that CEE citizens have been profoundly disappointed by the hypocrisy of their post-communist authorities; while proclaiming the importance of, and their adherence to, the rule of law (part of what he sees as the visible part of transformation), these authorities are in fact often corrupt (which is a component of the hidden part). But the populace can see through these machinations; since corruption and the rule of law are mutually exclusive, this hypocrisy undermines faith and trust in the new systems. In light of this, Czarnota argues that a commitment to the rule of law was introduced prematurely and too inflexibly in the CEE states; since it could not have been introduced properly in the early stages of transformation, it would have been better to delay it, so as not to tarnish its image, with the resultant popular cynicism towards the concept that is now so evident. Czarnota argues that corruption is a functional response to the post-1989 need to modernise post-communist socio-economic systems, but that it then becomes entrenched and self-reproductive (structural), petrifying and delegitimising the modernisation process and the new systems as its relationship with them deepens and becomes interdependent.

Chapter 9 is a collaborative effort between two academics from Monash University, George Gilligan and Diana Bowman. Their analysis begins with a general discussion of the phenomenon of corruption, in particular the problems involved in attempting to find a universal definition of it, its costs, and various responses that have been adopted by governments and other agencies around the world. They then focus specifically on corruption in Australia, providing a detailed analysis of the various agencies at both federal and state level that have a remit to counter corruption. They examine these agencies' various powers, functions, resources and outputs. The chapter concludes with a discussion of some of the thorny problems involved in evaluating governance initiatives that seek to counter corruption.

The question of why a popular Labour prime minister in the UK would so strongly support key aspects of the foreign and defence policy of a conservative (parts of it neo-conservative) group of Republicans in the USA – most notably the notion of a 'global war on terror' and the invasion of a sovereign state (Iraq) on the pretext of pre-emption – is addressed by Peter Shearman in Chapter 10. Is this just another example of Britain's putatively closer affinity with the USA than with continental Europe? Shearman challenges the notion that Blair's support for the 'war on terror' related primarily to traditional Anglo-American ties, seeing it more in terms of a genuine – if misguided – *moral* commitment to a particular type of warfare. Far from being mere emulation of Washington's policy, London reached the decision to participate in the invasion of Iraq because of Blair's own strongly held ethical and religious beliefs. Moreover, Blair had reached many of his general positions on international relations and security *before* George W. Bush had even become president, and had already made an original contribution to the re-conceptualisation of international politics. He had formulated his innovative ideas very much in response to what had been happening in former Yugoslavia during the 1990s; if anybody was emulating anyone else, it was Bush of Blair, not vice versa. This said, and as part of his overall argument concerning Blair's originality, Shearman highlights important differences between Blair's thinking and that of the Bush administration. However, he also demonstrates that there are both contradictions and dangers in Blair's approach, even if it is the prime minister's own. Among these are that Blair's policies will further stimulate terrorism and organised crime.

Having considered motivations for the British approach to the so-called war on terror in the previous chapter, Chapter 11 analyses the motivations of the Bush administration. In a thought-provoking chapter, Mark Alleyne begins by considering recent challenges to the neo-realist state-centric school of international relations from globalisation and constructivist theories, both of which he outlines. Following this is a section on the ramifications of liberalisation in the global economy in recent decades, which Alleyne sees as having contributed both to the rise of corporate power and irresponsibility, and to a weakening of the state; it also played into the hands of terrorists. The third section considers the shock of 9/11, and the ways in which the US administration produced a discourse designed to persuade its own population and other states to accept the notion of a war on terror and the need to fight this. In order to construct a recognisable enemy, given that it was not a state or states as such, the US government identified individuals (Osama bin Laden; Saddam Hussein) and regimes (the Taliban in Afghanistan, Baathism in Iraq) that would symbolise the new enemy and be seen as hostile to basic values considered part of Western identities, including democracy and freedom. The Bush administration used official nationalist legitimation techniques to boost patriotism in the US, increase citizen surveillance and reduce civil liberties. But these developments were not the most important ones, according to Alleyne, for whom changes in the neo-liberal financial system have been even more significant. There was a new emphasis on the need for corporate surveillance, particularly in the financial sphere, which increased the power of the state in its role as protector. The powers of the FATF were increased, to identify a specific role for the organisation in combating terrorist financing. By 2005, the UN had at last come close to full recognition of the potential links between terrorism, organised crime and corruption; in his proposals for restructuring the UN, Kofi Annan listed anti-terrorism measures *immediately* before those designed to counter organised crime and corruption – which were treated together. In his fourth section, Alleyne considers the diverse reasons for states joining the US-led 'war on terror', and why some states would not join. He also explains why some states might not even want to join the US lead in suppressing terrorist financing, before concluding his analysis.

It is argued in the concluding chapter that, while this collection has sought to contribute to a better understanding of the triumvirate of terrorism, organised crime and corruption, a fourth player needs to be factored into the networks equation. That player is corporate and white-collar economic crime, which both researchers and those on the front line fighting crime need to analyse *in part* in the context of interconnectedness with one or more – depending on the precise circumstances – of the three types of crime considered in this volume.

CONCLUSIONS

Overall, this volume will lend weight to those criminologists and political scientists (for example Godson and Olson 1993; P. Williams 1994; Buzan *et al.* 1998; Buzan and Little 2000) who have argued in favour of a reconceptualisation of our notions of security. In realist paradigms, security threats are primarily between states. While states still have an all-important role to play in security, this volume demonstrates that one of the most serious threats to them can emanate from their own officers, collaborating with groups that have little or no regard for either states or their citizens. Until the state can trust its own officers, the 'war on terror' and the struggle against organised crime will enjoy at best only limited success. In extreme cases, where official corruption is endemic in a country, the state itself can be under threat. It is not only the neo-liberal international financial system that has undermined the modern state; neo-liberalism in the domestic context has also contributed to this weakening. Inasmuch as neo-liberalism displays little regard for bureaucratic social capital or trust, it can atomise state officials and undermine their loyalty, rendering them more susceptible to illicit temptation – corruption, links with organised crime, and the possibility of engaging with other improper networks. Western states may now be seeking to reassert themselves vis-à-vis the neo-liberal international financial system. But unless they also modify or reverse their neo-liberal stance domestically, they are likely to continue to have corruption and related criminality as major problems for the foreseeable future. There are linkages of which they still appear to be largely unaware.

NOTES

1. There is empirical evidence of a 'very strong level of association between the index for levels of organized crime and the index for public sector corruption' (Buscaglia and van Dijk 2003: 22). This does not prove a direct connection, but, coupled with our limited knowledge of actual examples of collusion, strongly suggests close links between the two types of crime.

2. Interpol draws a useful definitional distinction between people smuggling and human trafficking: 'Trafficking is distinct from smuggling insofar as the traffic of human beings involves the exploitation of the migrant, often for purposes of forced labour and prostitution. People smuggling simply implies the procurement, for financial or material gain, of the illegal entry into a state of which the individual is neither a citizen nor a permanent resident' (Interpol website, visited March 2006).

3. Mark Kramer (2005: 221) maintains that, 'Russian units in Chechnya have been plagued by rampant corruption and have been linked with narcotics trafficking, prostitution rings, illegal arms dealing and kidnappings for ransom'. He concludes (p.267) that 'Russia would undoubtedly have fared better in Chechnya were it not for the corruption, cronyism, indifference and administrative incompetence that pervade the Russian army, security forces and political system'.

4. For earlier strong circumstantial evidence of links between Chechen terrorists and Russian state officials (including security forces) see *East European Constitutional Review*, 12 (2–3), 2003: 43.

5. In late January 2005, the Russian parliamentary commission investigating the Beslan events announced that Russian and Beslan government officials had been involved in the attack, and there was optimism in some quarters that the commission's final report would be revealing and highly critical. However, these hopes were dashed. When the report was finally and belatedly submitted at the end of 2005, it was criticised for basically exonerating the authorities, since it made only weak references to government 'miscalculations', rather than serious criticisms (*Pravda.RU* online, 28 December 2005, visited March 2006; see too *BBC News* online, 26 December 2005, visited March 2006).

6. Interestingly, in terms of resonances and connections between Europe and Australia, the bank (Northern Bank in Belfast) was a subsidiary of the National Australia Bank. However, the National Australia Bank sold this to a Danish bank in 2005.

7. It should not be assumed that it is only Catholic terrorist and paramilitary organisations that have connections with organised crime in Ireland. In 2001, the Royal Ulster Constabulary (that is the Northern Irish police) claimed that 43 out of 78 identified crime gangs had current or past links with either Catholic or Protestant paramilitary organisations (*Guardian*, 23 March 2001: 3)

8. A useful source for details on organised crime is the International Association for the Study of Organized Crime (IASOC), founded in 1984. Its website was established in December 2001, and includes an Organized Crime News section. One recent example of collusion is provided by the conviction in April 2006 of two retired police officers, who were found guilty of acting as 'hit-men' for a US cosa nostra family at the same time as they were working for the New York Police Department as detectives (*New York Times*, 7 April 2006: 1). There have also been several cases of Australian police officers being involved with organised crime syndicates in drug-trafficking – see for example *Australian*, 27 December 2005: 4.

9. There had been a Terrorist Finance Unit attached to the Northern Ireland Office since 1993; this developed from the Anti-Racketeering Unit that was established in 1988. An important difference between the 1993 unit and the similarly named newer organisation is that the 2001 version explicitly recognised terrorism as a truly international and global phenomenon.

10. North Korea was considered to be the second largest foreign supplier of illicit drugs to the Russian Far East until the late 1990s (Nomokonov 2000). During the 1990s, several North Korean state officials were detected attempting to smuggle drugs into Vladivostok (*Izvestiya* 17 December 1996; *Vladivostok News*, 2 March 2001), and it was alleged that some were acting on behalf of their government. A more recent claim is by the head of the Australian Federal Police, Mick Keelty, who has stated his belief that the North Korean government was involved in a drug smuggling operation that was intercepted by Australian authorities in April 2003. This related to the so-called Pong Su affair (named after the ship that was found to be transporting 150 kg of heroin) that resulted in prison sentences of more than 20 years each to three North Koreans (*Echo* [Australia], 18 May 2006: 4). More generally on the involvement of North Korea in money-laundering, counterfeiting and illicit drugs see *Washington Post*, 25 April 1999: A21.

11. For an example of her work comparing organised crime and corruption see Beare (2003).

12. An insightful analysis of factors explaining the rise of corruption awareness and reporting in Western Europe other than those considered here can be found in Blankenburg (2002).

13. The term Washington Consensus was coined in 1989 by John Williamson, who has recently and succinctly elaborated its ten key features (Williamson 2003).

14. The phrase 'appears to be random' refers to the perception of those affected by the terrorists' actions. The terrorists may well have a rationale for attacking particular individuals or groups, but have not revealed this, so as to increase fear among target populations.

15. The inclusion of the word state here is to acknowledge that some groups may believe they are following religious laws, which they see as taking precedence over a state's laws.

16. Even though Al-Qaeda's ultimate objectives remain disputed and often opaque, its leaders and members make frequent use of the internet to publicise their activities and speeches.

17. State actors can conduct acts of terror against sections of the population; Stalin, Hitler, Pol Pot, Mao and Saddam Hussein are prime examples. However, this should be called state terror, to distinguish it from the phenomenon focused on here, namely terrorism. State officials can be involved in terrorism; but they do so for personal reasons, not as part of state policy.

18. The term 'disorganised' crime has long been in circulation, and is associated with, inter alia, Peter Reuter (1983) and Richard Hall (1986). There was also a 1989 film with this title.

19. The assumption here is that officials participate for personal reasons, not on behalf of the state or actually using their state office; the latter case would constitute collusion between corrupt officials and organised crime. It should also be noted here that our own view is that three is too small a number of persons to constitute an organised crime gang, so that we sympathise with Paoli's point about so many examples being 'small-scale'. However, a large number of organisations have adopted three as the cut-off point, which explains the practice adopted here.

20. In a sense ironically, members of gangs often have to develop their own version of social capital, or at least trust; without this, it would be easier for authorities to penetrate their organisations, and for some individuals to take more than their 'fair share' of profits.

21. The phrase 'in various ways' is included here as a way of acknowledging that some groupings are decentralised; but even in such arrangements, there is usually a micro-hierarchy. Similarly, although some commentators argue that hierarchies are being replaced by networks, the latter still imply structure – and often even new forms of hierarchy.

22. This list has been influenced by Naylor (1997).
23. Some challenge the notion that organised crime is becoming more transnational, however, see for example Hobbs (1998). There is certainly evidence of a rise in local organised crime activity in some countries, such as China (Chu Yiu Kong 2002: 193). But the two trends – an increase in both transnational and local activity – are not incompatible.
24. Some corrupt officials openly flaunt the fruits of their improper activities, which raises questions about the concept of secrecy. But there is an important difference between flaunting the results of corruption and bragging about the actions or non-actions that sourced such results. More problematic are the cases of 'corruption' in which officials did or did not do something that is subsequently deemed improper, but which was not considered corrupt at the time the acts were committed. There have been numerous cases of alleged corruption in which officials appear to have been genuinely surprised that their actions or inactions might ever have been construed as corruption. Some have argued that the sunlight test is the ultimate determinant of whether or not an action or non-action constitutes corruption; while it usually is a good test, the type of case just cited reveals its limitations. This is a highly pertinent issue in transition states, since both legislation and values in the early stages following the collapse of the former systems are often ambiguous or essentially non-existent.
25. This list is almost identical to that in L. Holmes (2006): 30.
26. For a classic analysis of the protective role organised crime can play see Gambetta 1993. In one of the USA's best selling (and best titled!) books of 2005 and 2006, Levitt and Dubner (2005: 101-2) provide evidence of the 'caring' side of a Chicago-based crack-dealing gang. More generally on the 'protective' role of organised crime see Skaperdas 2001.
27. Another point to highlight here is that the notion of a 'majority viewpoint' can be problematical. Sometimes, the perspectives of the state and of a majority of the citizenry do not coincide. In such cases, it is up to analysts to state explicitly what they mean by 'a majority viewpoint'.
28. The term mafia is in inverted commas here because it is often used loosely nowadays, to refer to a wide range of organised crime gangs in many countries. Originally – and, strictly speaking, still – it refers only to organised crime syndicates originating in Sicily. But many use it generically to cover similar gangs elsewhere in Italy – notably the 'Ndrangheta in Calabria (on this see Paoli 2000), Sacra Corona Unita in Puglia (see Massari 1998), and the Camorra in the Naples area (see Behan 1996; Di Fiore 2005) – as well as much further afield. The most commonly cited additional three groupings are the Chinese (though Hong Kong based) Triads, the Japanese Yakuza and the Colombian drug cartels. However, many analysts nowadays add other groups to this list, including Albanian, Jamaican (especially Yardies in the UK), Nigerian and Turkish.
29. For book-length sensationalist (if fascinating!) analyses see Sterling (1994); Freemantle (1995).
30. In a six-country survey on political party financing conducted by the author in late 2003 and early 2004, respondents in Bulgaria, France, Germany, Italy, Poland and Russia were asked whom they would choose in an election – a somewhat corrupt but effective candidate, or a 'squeaky clean' but less effective candidate. The results from four countries – Bulgaria, Italy, Poland and Russia – were remarkably similar, with approximately 25 per cent of respondents opting for the more corrupt candidate. The figure was much lower in Germany – some 14 per cent – and rather higher (35 per cent) in France. It is possible – indeed likely – that many more citizens would vote for the more corrupt candidate in a real election.
31. The best example of this is the treatment of prisoners in Guantanamo Bay.

32. However, as in licit industry, the profits from organised crime do not necessarily filter through to the rank-and-file workers. Thus Levitt and Dubner (2005: 103) claim that many drug dealers at the street level actually make very modest incomes.

33. A similar position regarding organised crime is adopted by Finckenauer and Voronin (2001: 4), who argue that 'The fundamental causes of organized crime are actually quite simple – greed and demand'. They point out (p. 3) that the latter increases where goods are illegal (as with some kinds of drugs), highly regulated (as with guns), or simply in short supply.

34. Many of the best-known terrorists of the past three decades have been from relatively affluent backgrounds and have been well-educated; examples include Ilich Ramirez Sanchez (better known as Carlos the Jackal), Ulrike Meinhof (of Germany's Red Army Faction), and Osama Bin Laden. For an early analysis of the social backgrounds of terrorists see for example Weinberg and Davis (1989): 83-96.

35. For a disturbing picture of collusion, and its effects, between the building sector and corrupt officials in China see Ding (2001).

2. Terrorism and Organised Crime

Frank Bovenkerk and Bashir Abou Chakra

Organised crime and terrorism are usually viewed as two different forms of crime.[1] Organised crime focuses on economic profit and acquires as much of a share as possible in the market, particularly the illegal market, while terrorism is motivated by ideological aims and a desire for political change. The word 'terrorism' is not once mentioned in Abadinsky's handbook (1990) on *Organized Crime*, while in an influential study on *Political Terrorism*, Wilkinson (1974: 33) wrote, 'We shall exclude from our typology criminal terrorism which can be defined as the systematic use of acts of terror for objectives of private material gain'. As a result of this distinction between organised crime and terrorism, two separate bodies of criminology literature have emerged, different programs fund research into each, and information about each is taught in different courses. Any information gathered by criminal investigators who scrutinise the two phenomena is usually kept confidential, as they tend not to share their knowledge and insights.

A HYPOTHESIS OF CONVERGENCE

In recent years, doubts have nonetheless arisen as to whether there might not be some links between the two phenomena. This began with the discovery of *narco-terrorism*, when it became clear in the 1980s that drug trafficking was used to support the political objectives of certain governments and terrorist organisations. 'Terrorists are happy to seize any opportunity to call what they are doing political', wrote Ehrenfeld (1990: xix), 'and drug traffickers were always seen as purely criminal. When the two combine, terrorist organisations derive benefits from the drug trade with no loss of status, and drug traffickers who have forged an alliance with terrorists become more formidable and gain in political clout'. Various authors have now adopted this notion. 'Although they are distinct phenomena that should not be confused,' wrote Schmid (1996: 40) in an influential first article on this new phenomenon, 'there are links' and 'there is some common ground'.

In new books on both these phenomena, references are also made to other kinds of crime. In *Organised Crime*, Lyman and Potter (1997: 307) devoted a special chapter to terrorism and note that 'political agendas and profit motivation may be concurrent variables in many acts of terrorism'. In *The New Terrorism*, Laqueur (1999: 211) wrote an entire chapter about the cooperation between the two because 'in some cases a symbiosis between terrorism and organised crime has occurred that did not exist before'.

On 28 September 2001, just after the dramatic events of 9/11 in New York and Washington, the Security Council of the United Nations adopted a wide-ranging anti-terrorism resolution, and in article 9 (4) noted 'with concern the close connection between international terrorism and traditional organised crime'. It is still unclear what the close connection consists of, and this is to be the topic of further research. In an unpublished contribution presented at a conference of the International Scientific and Professional Advisory Council (ISPAC) of the United Nations Crime Prevention and Criminal Justice Programme in Courmayeur in 2002, Schmid suggested that there may be connections that take the form of associations, alliances, cooperation, confluence, convergence or symbiosis. Other analysts (Williams and Savona 1995; Schweitzer 1998; Williams and Godson 2002) went further and suggested the theoretical possibility that, in concrete cases, terrorism can mutate into organised crime and vice versa. Some (Dishman 2001; Makarenko 2001) even consider the possibility that terrorism and organised crime might totally converge and become one and the same. Makarenko (2003) makes an interesting classification effort by placing various types of convergence on a continuum, with organised crime at one end and terrorism at the other. This leads to the question: how do specific underground organisations move from one type to the other?

Various authors keep referring to more or less the same examples, the FARC in Colombia, Sendero Luminoso in Peru, guerrilla fighters in Chechnya, the Abu Sayyaf Group in the Philippines, the IMU in Uzbekistan, and a few others. It is striking that none of them provides a thorough empirical analysis of any of these cases, and the evidence cited never goes much deeper than a good media account. This is not meant to belittle good journalism; but reporters may miss asking the appropriate analytical questions, such as those proposed at the end of this contribution.

Some specialists in organised crime or terrorism doubt the existence of any clear connections between the two. Schmid cited two authorities in his Courmayeur paper of 2002: Mark Galeotti, who noted that 'until now, fears of international alliances between terrorists and criminals have proven to be exaggerated', and Louise Shelley, who suggested that links occur less frequently than people believe, and that there are far more connections with politicians. Naylor (2002: 56–7) found some examples of opportunistic alliances between the two. Indeed, some guerrilla organisations or some of their militant members do resort to simple criminality. Yet upon closer inspection, some supposed alliances often prove to be merely fictional. 'At the end of their cooperation the two groups usually end up on opposite sides of the barricades.' It is striking that most authors generally fail to present empirically based analyses to prove their cases. According to Schmid in his 2002 paper: 'They are making little more than educated guesses'.

Who is right? In the following, we first survey the theoretical considerations presented by the supporters of the confluence hypothesis. It is not sufficient simply to demonstrate, as is generally done, that there exist structural similarities between the two types of crime. We also want to comprehend the mechanisms enabling them to work together. Subsequently, we would like to address the arguments of authors who deny the existence of any such connections or do not believe they are of any significance. This brings us to the question: in the event of any such links or merger, which of the two is likely to emerge in the long run as the dominant type? When it comes to combating this new phenomenon of collaboration and possible convergence, this is of essential importance. In a short final section, a number of central questions that should play a role in concrete empirical research are presented.

WHY LINKS OR EVEN METAMORPHOSIS?

A number of political and economic developments have brought terrorism and organised crime into each other's territory. There are also a number of clear structural similarities that would appear to make collaboration advantageous for both of them. In addition, both types of organisations can be expected to attract the kind of personalities that reconcile the two types of criminal activities. We shall briefly address these three complexes of factors.

Firstly, there is the matter of globalisation. In this era of accelerated globalisation, organised crime and terrorism are both internationally on the rise and both have witnessed enormous changes in recent decades, when major insights on them entered the field of criminological theory. There are thousands of criminal organisations and hundreds of terrorist groups in the world. Hess, who has conducted a great deal of research on terrorism in the past, noted: 'When I look back today at the time of the Red Brigades, the

Baader Meinhof Gang, the Weathermen, the whole range of phenomena we studied as terrorism 20 years ago, I tend to become nostalgic .... Most terrorism was rather provincial' (Hess 2003: 345). Williams and Godson (2002: 311), writing about organised crime today and comparing it with the situation in the past, concluded that it 'has reached levels in the post-Cold War world that have surprised even close observers'. The world has opened up, the borders have faded or are no longer as well guarded, the market has been globalised, financial and commercial mergers and the deregulation of state intervention have provided new opportunities. Moreover, communication technology is presenting unanticipated new technological possibilities. Large-scale migration across the globe has also created new emigrant and refugee communities that can serve as both recruitment bases and hiding places (Makarenko 2001).

The convergence authors note a similarity between people who commit crimes and those who throw bombs: they have a common enemy, the state in general, and its law enforcement agencies in particular. In recent years such hostility has turned to international organisations that have created political frameworks to combat both transnational organised crime and international terrorism.

Both types of criminals operate in secrecy in the underworld, and they use the same infrastructure for their activities and the same networks of corruption and white-collar crime. Both use the same kind of tactics: they engage in international smuggling, money laundering, counterfeiting, kidnapping, extortion and various kinds of violence. Napoleoni (2003: 128–32) describes 'the Mosque Network' that began with Saudi charities and now stretches into countries of Europe that have been shown to have links with Osama bin Laden's network. Recruited young terrorists raise their money through smuggling, ransom, automobile theft and extortion.

Organised crime and terrorism cross paths; they help or submit to one another, which makes them dependent on each other. International organised crime can use the power apparatus of political crime to create the social and economic context that makes their profitable activities feasible. Terrorists need funding from such activities to pursue their own agendas. When terrorist groups are still small, they do not need many resources, but when they grow into insurgent or guerrilla groups that aspire to control a larger region, they have greater needs (Naylor 2002).

The end of the Cold War, the existence of weak and even failed states, and the rise of new surrogate or shadow states are only a few of the political changes that facilitate cooperation in the underworld. The end of the Cold War meant in many cases an end to the sponsoring of terrorist organisations by states in the two power blocks. The organisations had no choice but to look for new sources of funding, and provide their own funding by organising crime themselves or extorting money from criminal organisations and legitimate business via '*revolutionary taxation*'.

Weak states characterised by limited state control easily fall prey to organised crime – Sicily and Colombia are the standard examples – but terrorists can also target them. Sometimes 'black holes' – pockets of political instability within such countries – have been filled in with irregular armed groups. Failed states in Africa (Sierra Leone, Somalia, Liberia) or Asia (Afghanistan) made it possible for organised crime to work with national plutocrats or local warlords who plundered the countries' diamonds, gold, tropical timber, exotic species of animals, and so on. The distinction between terrorism and organised crime – and even corruption – becomes obscured because the plutocrats and warlords utilise terrorist methods as well.

New economic formations are emerging that completely disregard national borders. They follow their own logic of territorial development in the form of shadow states. A cultural anthropologist from Notre Dame University (Indiana, USA) terms them 'surrogate sovereigns' (Nordstrom 2004). They are largely hidden from view, and they provide some of the world's unstable economies and marginal political regions with arms, mercenaries and luxury commodities. Figures of this kind collaborate with ambitious political entrepreneurs who aspire to both economic power and political control.

Of major concern is the fear of terrorists obtaining access through the aforementioned sovereigns to weapons of mass destruction (WMD), or else to the means, raw materials and technical know-how for producing such weapons. The threat of having a few individuals, rather than just rogue states, coming to possess such weapons is ever more real. A black market in nuclear, biological and chemical materials is emerging, and growing links between organised crime and terrorism further fuels this fear. There are no doubts as to Al-Qaeda's repeated attempts to acquire WMD, albeit with varying degrees of success. It is of no surprise that its leaders are still actively seeking to do so through the black market. Al-Qaeda is alleged to have tried on at least eight different occasions to acquire uranium and other radiological materials, possibly for use in a 'dirty bomb', and is reported to have succeeded in one case.[2] It can safely be assumed that Al-Qaeda is now able to complete small-scale, fairly rudimentary attacks using chemical and perhaps also biological agents. It is also highly likely that they are in possession of the necessary materials and technical ability to assemble 'dirty bombs'.

In retrospect, one possible and particularly disturbing scenario is the development of a strategic alliance between criminal groups involved in WMD theft and smuggling and a terrorist group. Another possible situation is the active support of certain rogue states, suffering from malignant corruption and a symbiosis with organised crime, of terrorist plans to obtain WMD. Such an alliance or support would probably result in nuclear and biochemical materials being used in a terrorist attack. It may not be beyond the means of some terrorist groups to develop such weapons themselves; the example of Al-Qaeda is a case in point.

The structural similarities between organised crime and terrorism are striking. Organised crime researchers never tire of noting how few classical large-scale pyramidal or bureaucratically organised groups there exist in today's underworld. Students of terrorism point out that cell structures and networks rather than big organisations are becoming the rule. To a certain degree, both are correct. Yet the terms organised crime and terrorism are each used to refer to a range of very different criminal and political violence activities.

There are groups that organise crime by using private violence or the threat thereof; their crime consists of organised extortion. Their role is to provide a safe environment for concluding 'business' contracts, to ensure that agreements are respected and that disputes between 'business' partners are settled. They perform this role in places where the state completely or partially fails to guarantee contracts, such as Sicily (Gambetta 1993) or post-1989 Russia (Varese 2001; Volkov 2002). They are also active in places where the state de facto withdraws its own influence by proclaiming certain widespread economic activities to be against the law (the sale of alcohol, drugs or pornography, providing premises for prostitution or gambling). This kind of organised crime dominates all the illegal and some of the legal activities in a certain territory, whether it is a country, a region or a neighbourhood, and tends to establish a monopoly position (Schelling 1984). It may indeed, as is the case with certain activities in Russia, take the form of a hierarchic organisation.

The second kind of organised crime is linked to the production, smuggling and sale of illegal goods and services: trafficking in drugs or arms, smuggling of people, trafficking in women, loan sharking, trading in exotic species of animals and tropical timber, dumping toxic waste and so forth. Organisations that engage in these activities have no territorial aspirations and have every reason to stay out of the way of the authorities and their law enforcement agencies. Commercial crime organisations like this are far more numerous than the branches of the Mafia, Triads or Yakuza (which are examples of the first category), but are not stable and bureaucratically organised enterprises. They consist instead of networks of small and flexible groups of criminals or cells. This loose form of illegal business is functional in the competitive and changeable world of illegality, which makes it less visible to the law enforcement agencies (Reuter 1983).

Since there are so many categories of terrorist organisation, it is difficult to make any general statements about them. Though it is certainly true that all terrorist groups tend to frighten people by using or threatening to use extreme violence in their efforts to influence political developments, studies of concrete terrorist groups and their activities create the impression that the differences among groups are greater than the similarities (Cronin 2002). Terrorists aspire to left-wing or right-wing political aims, defend the rights of oppressed minorities, are religiously motivated or pursue single issue goals (for example the Animal Liberation Front, campaigns to close abortion clinics).

It is highly probable that the type of terrorism determines in part how it is organised and whether or not there is any collaboration with organised crime. The chance of cooperation with organised crime would seem to be greater in the case of politically motivated terrorist organisations than for example with 'crazy' groups. There are terrorists who operate in complete independence, but there are also those who are (or were) supported or even totally organised by (foreign) governments. One hypothesis might be that organised crime and terrorists work together more easily if and when they are supported, encouraged or helped in some way by a government or parts of one, such as intelligence agencies.

Let us return to the simple structure. One feature terrorist organisations have in common with organised crime of the (smuggling) organisation variety is that they by no means always have stable and well organised units, and are far more likely to consist of agglomerates of autonomous units. Schmid (2002) mentions the self-reliant lone wolf terrorist and refers to Tishkov, who sees a paradigm for the future in this type of 'leaderless resistance' terrorist. At any rate, this might hold true of the early stage of terrorism – and the majority of terrorist organisations never get past this stage. The need to become better organised emerges when they grow into insurgent groups or guerrilla armies.

There are bound to be differences in the forms of collaboration between these variants of organised crime and terrorism. We can assume it is more profitable for terrorists to collaborate with production, smuggling and sales organisations than with organised crime of the type that organises the underworld as a whole. And conversely, it is more advantageous for organised crime to collaborate with substantial organisations that really exert political influence than with the lone fanatic who attacks unexpectedly and only generates temporary panic.

To a certain extent, there is also a similarity in the type of persons involved in the two types of crime. Both types of organisation tend to recruit their members from the same reservoir of marginal segments of the population, which are subject to social, cultural or political frustration (strain theory). They offer status and personal rewards. Both types of organisation consist of people who are prepared to take risks, enjoy excitement and thrills, and scorn the norms of regular society. There may be a division of labour here. Terrorist groups might bring forth leaders, and the criminal underworld may produce people with the necessary operational and survival skills.

In addition, they have a major driving force in common, the yearning for status and power. In the first instance, this does not seem to be such a serious motivation. We imagine terrorists as fanatics willing to sacrifice their lives for a political ideal. At most, they can become world famous by blowing themselves up, but in doing so they forfeit their chances of exercising power or enjoying fame (infamy?) in this world. The factor of power does not often enter the picture in the literature on the reasons behind terrorism. But Silke (2003) points out how even inauspicious teenage suicide bombers may increase their status within their community by joining the terrorists' ranks. However, many terrorists remain alive and do not risk their own lives needlessly, and the personality descriptions we have of them demonstrate how much they enjoy fame and power (Hoffman 1998: 169–80). It is not without reason that so many terrorist movements are named after their charismatic leader. Ignatieff (2002) asked himself how terrorists can reconcile the fact that, in the name of higher ideals, they violate fundamental human rights, including the right to life and freedom. He calls those whose true motivation is oriented towards profit and power 'opportunistic nihilists', a term originally coined by Rauschning (1940) in his interviews with Adolf Hitler. The life stories of prominent contemporary terrorists such as Osama bin Laden or Ramzi Yousef make it clear that many of them belong in this category, as do leaders of the Colombian FARC, the IRA and Abu Sayyaf (Reeve 1999). It is also striking that almost all the present-day political leaders of Lebanon who began their careers as militias have also profited from drug cultivation in strengthening their political positions (Ehrenfeld 1990).

The true value of the power theme has not yet been assessed in the field of organised crime either. In examining why people join the Mafia, the first factor that comes to mind is the desire to enrich oneself. Yet, after consulting the testimonies of Italian turncoats, Paoli (2003: 151–4) concluded that the desire for power, especially local power, appears to be almost always a more important driving force than just the desire for wealth. Organised crime leaders always claim to operate in secrecy and to obey their own rule about keeping silent, but autobiographical gangster memoirs reveal how much they too enjoy fame and power (Firestone 1993). In this sense, the personality of the gangster bears a number of similarities to that of the opportunistic nihilist (Bovenkerk 2000).

Do the similarities render it easier to comprehend the connections and possible symbiosis? How can the phenomenon of terrorism becoming organised crime and vice versa be explained? When do rebels turn into felons? Or felons into rebels? These are once again questions to be addressed in careful case studies. All that can be done at this point is to suggest a number of possibilities.

1. In both organised crime and terrorist movements, the leaders are frequently very prominent; in fact the groups are often named after their leader. What happens if the leader dies or is imprisoned? Is it conceivable that the terrorist organisation will degenerate into a gang of robbers? This appears to have been the case with the group headed by the Uzbek rebel leader Juma Namangani, who is assumed to have perished in 2001, after which his gang went on randomly kidnapping for ransom.
2. What happens after insurgent terrorists lose the justification for their existence because the authorities have settled the political issue on which they focused? They might have become so accustomed to a certain life-style that they cannot give it up. Perhaps they have taken too much of a liking to exerting the kind of violence that is typical of terrorism. This appears to be one of the greatest obstacles facing Colombian presidents seeking a peaceful solution to the problem of terrorism. Rebel armies like the FARC and the ELN have built a life for themselves based on protection taxes from drug lords in the vicinity and kidnapping for ransom. They may even have developed into drug cartels themselves.
3. What happens to a Mafia family in dire straits because of the authorities' success in combating organised crime? Drug king Pablo Escobar had no qualms about murdering politicians, judges, police officers and even journalists, or intimidating them with techniques from the terrorists' repertoire. The Italian mafia has also attempted to intimidate the authorities and keep anti-mafia legislation from being passed by exploding car bombs at public buildings like the Uffizi Gallery in Florence. Some crime theorists

suggest that creating a general state of fear of terrorism promotes the advancement of organised crime. Is this really true?

4. There is also the possibility of widespread degeneration in the event of a lengthy armed conflict. A civil war 'may create a generation whose only skills, at what should be their peak productive years, are military; they therefore turn easily to criminal activity for survival even after the conflict winds down' (Naylor 2002: 82). If this is true, the future looks bleak for countries such as Liberia and Sierra Leone, since so many children are accustomed to soldiering and looting. Tishkov (2004) provides an ethnographic description of Chechen soldiers who became active in hostage-taking after the war.

OPPOSITE VIEWS ON A POSSIBLE NEXUS

In his report before the US House of Representatives' Committee on the Judiciary, Subcommittee on Crime, Frank J. Cilluffo, senior policy analyst at the Washington-based Center for Strategic and International Studies (CSIS), stated on 13 December 2000: 'Organised crime and terrorism have two different goals. Organised crime's business is business. The less attention brought to their lucrative enterprises the better. The goal of terrorism is the opposite. A wide-ranging public profile is often the desired effect. Despite this, the links between organised crime and terrorism are becoming stronger in regard to the drug trade.'

The division between the two is not based on the crimes committed, since they are partly the same, but on the reasons motivating the offenders. In the previous section, it was noted that both types of organisation recruit their members from frustrated segments of the population. Yet there is an important difference; individuals who participate in organised crime often come from the lower socio-economic classes, while it is not unusual for terrorists to be from the middle classes. This difference is not insignificant. There are persons among terrorists, brainwashed or not, who are driven solely by ideological principles and a political conviction. For them, terrorism is a way to force the authorities around the world to concede to their political, economic and social demands. They are not enthusiastic about collaborating with criminals in the traditional sense of the word, since this would entail the real risk of losing political credibility. In public at least, they downplay any involvement with criminals. Terrorists strive for an increased political following and look to the courtroom as a place to convince the world of the justness of their causes (Schmid 1996: 66).

To real career criminals, the conduct of politically motivated terrorists is incomprehensible and even weird. Why would anyone take such extreme risks without any prospect of eventually enriching themselves? Who would want to openly confront the authorities, instead of evading or corrupting them? Is it not much more sensible to keep illegal activities as concealed as possible? It is foolish to draw attention to oneself by using disproportional violence. The opportunities for organised crime are largely based on the idea of exploiting the existing imperfections in the economic and moral system of the state (the prohibition of certain substances such as drugs, the shortage of cheap legal workers, the high costs of processing waste, and so forth). Viewed from this perspective, organised crime is conservative. Solving social and political problems would put it out of business.

On the other hand, it is often surprising how easily ideological differences can be settled in the underworld. Ultranationalist Turks united in the Grey Wolves, and Kurd activists who joined forces in the PKK, were publicly each other's fiercest enemies in Turkey, as well as in the European and American Diasporas. Yet when it comes to smuggling heroin or people, the underworld is only too happy to work together (Bovenkerk and Yesilgöz 2004). In Lebanon, all political rivals – Christian, Sunni, Shi'ite Muslim or Druze – profited from the drug trade during the Civil War. War between ideologies stops at the edge of cannabis and poppy fields. There are many more examples of this kind. This mainly holds true of the leaders in both realms. They might come from different social backgrounds, but the common desire for power, and the personal wealth that goes with it, can easily steer the collaboration in the direction of predominantly organised crime.

Precise empirical research should be the ultimate arbiter on the issues discussed here. However, after weighing the arguments for and against the hypothesis of convergence, we tend to find the first more convincing. As we are speculating anyway, we would like to venture a conjecture about which of the two types of criminal organisation is likely to dominate and last the longer. Intuition tells us it is less probable that mafia dons will convert to terrorism than that terrorists will opt for the good life of real criminals. To anyone exposed to temptation, in the long run greed is stronger than ideology. The newly emerging hybrid group of 'organised criminal terrorists' would be the group of individuals to sponsor, support, and actively engage in terrorist activity, and thus try to promote their own personal interests or strive to acquire more power and wealth from their organised crime-linked activities.

Organised crime, in this perspective, would be the outcome of any merger that might take place. Whether this will indeed prove to be the case is an interesting research topic.

A RESEARCH AGENDA

In this chapter, we have repeatedly referred to the need for empirical research into possible links between terrorists and criminals. As Andreopoulos (1991: 226) noted, 'individual cases rather than a series of abstract assumptions can credibly constitute the building blocks of theory formation'. In all the cases where there is known or plausible collaboration between terrorists and organised crime, the following eleven questions, based on our analysis here, might serve as a research guideline:

1. Under what political constellations do these forms of collaboration emerge?
2. Which types of organised crime can easily cooperate with which variants of terrorism? And which types are less compatible?
3. Is there evidence of intervention by national or foreign authorities regarding the promotion of a collaboration process?
4. Which structural features possessed by such organisations point towards convergence?
5. Which types of alliance and convergence occur most frequently?
6. What exactly is their collaboration based on? What do the two organisations exploit in each other?
7. Is it true that both organisations recruit new members from the same socially frustrated sections of society?
8. How are differences in value orientations and class backgrounds of conventional criminals and terrorists resolved?
9. Is there evidence of a clear resemblance in how they strive for power?
10. Is all organised crime strictly centred around profit making, or are there exceptions where certain activities serve to acquire political spoils or gains?
11. Which element is dominant in the long run, the politico-ideological motivation or the criminal material one?

NOTES

1. An earlier (and shorter) version of this contribution was published in *Forum on Crime and Society*, 4 (1–2) (2004): 3–16.
2. 'WMD Terrorism and Usama Bin Laden' – http://cns.miis.edu/pubs/reports/binladen.htm, Center for Nonproliferation Studies, visited 20 June 2004.

3. Countering Terrorism as if Muslims Matter: Cultural Citizenship and Civic Pre-Emption in Anti-Terrorism

Pete Lentini[1]

INTRODUCTION

An event from the life of former Gambino crime family under-boss Sammy 'The Bull' Gravano illustrates this chapter's central concern:

> On Sunday mornings, Sammy usually accompanied his father to mass at the Church of Our Lady of Guadalupe. Down the block, they would pass a corner saloon. There would always be a cluster of men in front of it. They were all smartly dressed in suits, or in sharply creased slacks and Italian knit shirts. Sammy could see the glitter from the diamond rings many of them wore. There was often a crap game in progress right on the sidewalk with wads of bills being passed back and forth. Sometimes a police car parked there, and two or three of the men would saunter over and banter with the cops. Sammy could hear the laughter. He noticed that his father always stayed on the opposite side of the street. Some of the men would wave to him and call out, 'How you doin', Gerry?', and his father would nod back in acknowledgement. Finally, when Sammy was about eight he asked, 'Who are these men, Dad? Do you know them?'. 'Yes, I know some of them. They are not hard working nice people. They're bad people, *but they're our bad people*'. (Maas 1997: 5–6; emphasis added)

The main questions addressed below are: how can states dissuade members of marginalised communities (as, for instance, the Italian-Americans arguably were at the time the anecdote occurred) from identifying terrorists as 'our bad people'?; and how is it possible for a state to strengthen bonds of inclusion that help it to legitimate itself when it comes into conflict with another 'survival unit'? According to Mennell (1995), a survival unit is considered the entity that people believe can or will provide them with security, welfare and dignity, such as the nation-state, clan, religious group, or even subculture. Evidence drawn from Australian (and some European and American) experiences suggests that policies and practices that increase marginalised groups' status and dignity provide means for them to retain their cultural identity, and participate in broader political and social activities, reduce existential angst and alienation, and increase the potential for political, social and cultural inclusion. Pakulski (1997: 80) refers to this as cultural citizenship, and defines it as:

> . . . a new set of citizenship claims that involve the right to unhindered and legitimate representation, and propagation of lifestyles through the information systems in public fora. One can detect within them three substreams: the right to symbolic presence and visibility (versus marginalization); the right to dignifying representation (versus stigmatization); and the right to propagation of identity and maintenance of lifestyles (versus assimilation).[2]

In this chapter I attempt to apply Pakulski's notion of cultural citizenship to anti-terrorism measures. Anti-terrorism includes legislative- and policy-oriented approaches to contain terrorism, while counter-terrorism generally refers to law-enforcement and military operations against terrorists (J. White 2004). In particular, I examine the extent to which multiculturalism and cultural citizenship help to constitute a form of civic pre-emption against various forms of alienation that contribute to the occurrence of terrorism. I therefore seek to generate new understandings on how states can increase their legitimacy amongst their marginalised groups, and enhance their abilities to manage and reduce potential causes of terrorism.

Terrorism is a contested term with many definitions (Schmid 1993). For the purposes of this chapter, however, terrorism is defined as '... using, or threatening to use, violence against innocent people or non-combatants in order to effect political change and achieve political goals' by establishing a state of fear (Lentini 2003: 368). It is important to acknowledge that cultural citizenship alone cannot eradicate terrorism. It must be employed as part of a multi-vectored approach to reduce and manage terrorism's causes (Pillar 2001). Through expanded multi-cultural policies and cultural citizenship, states enhance the mechanisms for including marginal groups. Multiculturalism refers to policies and practices that protect and celebrate difference amongst ethnic and religious communities, and which include rights for them within the political system (Ang and Stretton 1998).

Terrorism occurs as a result of a breakdown in the legitimacy of the state. It occurs when particular groups and individuals fail to see the state as the primary survival unit. This process is a fusion of models proposed by Wright-

Neville (2004) and the late Ehud Sprinzak (1991, 1995, 1998). Disaffected groups first use established mechanisms to voice their grievances (activist/participant, Wright-Neville; crisis of confidence, Sprinzak). During this stage, activists utilise established political institutions and civil society to press their claims. Violence is not part of their overall strategy; their main objective is political reform. In the second stage (militant, Wright-Neville; conflict of legitimacy, Sprinzak), aggrieved groups still generally maintain non-violent measures. Nevertheless, since they believe that legitimate mechanisms for political change such as the ballot box are ineffective, or, as for instance in the case of the global Islamist organisation the Hizb ut-Tahrir, they consider the existing political arrangements illegitimate, they seek other mechanisms (Hizb ut-Tahrir n.d.). For some groups, this includes small-scale violence, like sporadic rioting or forms of direct action protest (Lacey 2001). It should also be acknowledged that in certain circumstances, organisations may have adopted these tactics because they had been rebuffed, sometimes violently, and felt that their means of conflict resolution needed to be more robust. During the final stage (terrorist, Wright-Neville; crisis of legitimacy, Sprinzak), actors resort to violence, believing that they have exhausted the means of non-violent approaches to conflict resolution.

The assertions here are confined to the status of ethnic and civic relationships affecting some diaspora Muslim populations and Islamist terrorism, as well as incidences of Islamic and Islamist activism and militancy. Islam is the faith revealed to the Prophet Muhammad in the 7th century CE. Islamism refers to implementing '. . . Islam in a comprehensive manner with particular emphasis on actualizing its ideals in the socio-political sphere' (Esack 2002: xi). As Wright-Neville (2004) demonstrates, using examples from South East Asia, not all forms of Islamism are violent.

TOWARDS AN ISLAMICALLY GROUNDED CONCEPTUAL TOOLBOX

As this study is concerned with Muslim communities, it may be useful to employ culturally relevant means for analysis. In this respect, Ibn Khaldun's concept of *asabiyya* or 'group loyalty, social cohesion or solidarity' is a reasonably appropriate framework. Khaldun contends that *asabiyya* is dynamic. As one group assumes ascendancy within a particular territory, other groups gradually begin adopting some aspects of the dominant *asabiyya*. Additionally, the dominant group also adopts some of the subordinate group's(s') *asabiyya*. For the present discussion, multicultural policies, and members' of marginalised communities engagement with cultural citizenship help maintain the *asabiyya* of these groups while permitting them gradually to adopt some of the dominant group's *asabiyya* (A. Ahmed 2003: 74). Ahmed contends that much of contemporary Muslim discontent, including those expressions that result in terrorism, is often the result of breakdowns in *asabiyya*. He maintains that *asabiyya* has been eroding in the Muslim world as a result of urbanisation, colonisation and post-colonial trauma and dislocation through voluntary and forced migrations. Consequences include a diminishing sense of Islamic *asabiyya* as it is overtaken by the new host countries' or regions' or cities' *asabiyya*. This, he argues, has led to the creation of a 'hyper-*asabiyya*' which is exclusivist and, in some circumstances, violent (A. Ahmed 2003: 74–90).

While it is important to incorporate cultural touchstones in the present analysis, it is necessary to include some important qualifications. First, Islam generally, and especially in Australia, is culturally, ethnically and linguistically diverse (Bouma *et al.* 2001; Saeed 2003: 1–2; 2004: 5). It encompasses many ethnic and cultural groups. According to the 2001 Census, there are 281,578 Muslims in Australia. The largest share of Australian Muslims, approximately 103,000, is Australian born. Nearly 80 per cent of Australia's Muslims are Australian citizens (Australian Bureau of Statistics data cited in Saeed 2004: 5).

Although the Arabic language (such as some prayers and commonly used expressions exchanged among believers) and some aspects of past and contemporary culture play important roles in Islam, not all Muslims are Arabs. Indeed Arabs comprise only some 20 per cent of all Muslims, and the states with the largest Muslim populations are non-Arab (Lapidus 2002: 832–33; Esposito 2002: 2). Hence there is not universal fluency in Arabic. Moreover, some Muslims harbour grievances towards some Arabs or elements of Arabic culture. Conversely, some Arab Muslims are hostile towards their fellow believers who do not comprehensively embrace their language, culture or religious attitudes. That the Gulf Arab states, and Saudi Arabia in particular, initially responded so weakly, and perhaps miserly, in providing financial assistance to their fellow Muslims in Southeast Asia – particularly Indonesia, which generally follows a much more tolerant interpretation of Islam – after the 26 December 2004 earthquake and tsunami disaster, is a case in point (Barton 2005; Eltahaway 2005). Second, Khaldun wrote about circumstances affecting tribesmen in 14th century Tunisia, where Muslims constituted a majority. Hence, there will not be a precise fit between his approaches and 21st century industrialised countries in which Muslims are visible but comparatively small minorities. Third, there are Islamic grounds on which attempts to establish a cultural context may fall short. For instance, noted Italian scholar of Arabic studies and Islam Francesco Gabrieli has written that the Prophet Muhammad 'condemned *asabiyya* as contrary to the spirit of Islam' in a hadith (Gabrieli n.d.).

Nevertheless, there are three reasons that make *asabiyya* an appropriate analytical tool in the present circumstances. First, although it was established earlier that Arabs do not comprise the majority of Muslims, they constitute a large share of Australian believers, Muslims of Lebanese extraction being the largest constituency. Moreover, '[a]pproximately 95,000 Muslims in Australia use Arabic' (Australian Bureau of Statistics data cited in Saeed 2004: 5). Therefore, including an Arab touchstone in the study has some relevance. Second, although Gabrieli noted some discrepancies between *asabiyya* and 'the spirit of Islam', Dr Maher Hathout, Senior Advisor, Muslim Public Affairs Council, and Spokesperson of the Islamic Center of Southern California has noted:

> The Prophet peace be upon him considered it a divisive factor that will lead to discord and actually prevent the more encompassing broad cohesiveness of the believers. In other words, he was denouncing what Professor Ahmed calls 'hyper-*asabiyya*' which may be called in Arabic '*ta-assub*', or fanatic exclusive belonging to a group or even to an idea or faith. (Hathout 2003)

Third, Spickard (2001) contends that Islam helped foster positive *asabiyya* by emphasising commonality in what was then multi-ethnic society. Hence he argued *asabiyya* always had a pluralist element to it. Therefore, it is possible to incorporate *asabiyya* as a category that is culturally relevant and insightful into the analysis.

The 'Abyssinian paradigm' is another culturally relevant reference point useful for a discussion of Muslim communities' inclusion in societies where they are in the minority. South African Muslim theologian and political activist Farid Esack (cited in an interview with Editors of *US Catholic Magazine* 2002: 16) notes:

> ... it is a problem for us Muslims that we have only two theological paradigms and precedents on which to base our lives, and that that limitation is in part responsible for the mess that we are in. The one is the paradigm of oppressed people in Mecca, and the other is a Muslim community that is in control in Medina. What we don't have is a model for co-existing with other people in equality.

But there is a third way, that can be called the Abyssinian paradigm, which refers to the time when the Prophet sent a group of his followers from Mecca to go to live in Abyssinia. They lived there peacefully for many years, and some of them did not return, even when Muslims were in power in Mecca. They made no attempts to turn Abyssinia into an Islamic state. They sent back good reports about the King under whom they were living and about how happy they were living there. This is the third paradigm that Muslims today need to revive, since it is crucial for the sake of human survival and coexistence.

Hence, the multicultural policies and practices should serve to uphold *asabiyya*, reduce hyper-*asabiyya/ta-assub*, and help to contribute to the construction of the 'Abyssinian paradigm' in practice. Moreover, these policies and practices, especially through a sense of cultural citizenship, should therefore reduce the potential for the delegitimation and alienation that can lead to the creation of 'enclave cultures' (Kimball 2002; Almond *et al.* 2003). Recent history demonstrates that, in many circumstances, terrorism or violence emanated from religious and other separatists. For instance, Aum Shinrikyo established special residential and industrial compounds within Japan for the cult, and purchased a ranch in Australia where its members tested weapons of mass destruction on sheep (Lifton 2000; Murakami 2001). It is alleged that members of a white separatist enclave in Elohim City, Oklahoma assisted Timothy McVeigh in the 1995 Oklahoma City Bombing (Hamm 2002).

It is important to reiterate that cultural citizenship cannot eliminate terrorism. However, it provides mechanisms for social integration that contain within them the potential to reduce the existential angst that fuels terrorism or gives it support.[3] Therefore, cultural citizenship as part of an anti-terrorist framework should potentially enable states to be better able to contain dissent within the Wright-Neville/Sprinzak categories of activism/crisis of confidence, or, in more severe circumstances, militant/conflict of legitimacy stages.

TESTING THE PROPOSITION

As previously acknowledged, cultural citizenship affords greater mechanisms for individuals and groups to maintain their dignity. This is extremely important for constructing anti-terrorist measures. Recent scholarship on Palestinian suicide bombers overwhelmingly indicates that their primary motivations are revenge and the desire to restore dignity (Margalit 2003; Moghadam 2003). Respondents to Valery Tishkov's anthropological study of the first war in Chechnya (1994–96) indicated that either they or individuals with whom they were closely acquainted began participating in armed struggle only after they had felt that the Russians had aggrieved them personally by harming them or their loved ones (Tishkov 2004).

Evidence from research in Europe further supports this contention. In a study based on ethnographic work interviewing French Muslims incarcerated for terrorism-related offences, Khosrokhavar (2003) reports that while many Muslims in France have been victimised, these men attempted to overcome victimisation through radicalism and attempted terrorism. He also stresses that their exposure through media to Palestinians' humiliation, their sense of collective suffering, and their desire to try to do something to rectify these feelings of disempowerment all contributed to their transformation. Hence he suggests that '… radicalisation occurs when the feeling of victimisation is overcome by a logic of self affirmation [and] self assertion'.

Khosrokhavar and Jeroen Gunning also emphasise the importance of maintaining strong diaspora communities as a means to counteract terrorism. Both note that although some 9/11 attackers came from a cell in Hamburg, they were not drawn from Germany's largely Turkish Muslim community. Rather, they were outsiders (Khosrokhavar 2003; Gunning 2003: 3). Moreover, they were radicalised when they were abroad, due largely to their distance from their original communities, and their feelings of liminality. It could also be argued that Frenchman Zacharias Moussaoui, the alleged twentieth 9/11 hijacker, also encountered a similar experience when he went to the UK to study. While there, he fell in with radicals in British mosques. They provided him with some form of succour while he faced poverty, communication difficulties, and cultural marginalisation (T. Ahmed 2004).

There is evidence to suggest that Australian government policies have been further advanced in these respects, and have helped to enhance Australian Muslims' sense of political, economic, social and cultural inclusion, from migration through to settlement and then to citizenship. Humphrey (2005: 146) argues that: 'Muslim immigrants have always approached Australia as a society in which they wanted to live good Muslim lives, a space of *dar al-Islam*, unlike Muslim immigrants in Europe who have mainly come to that position in the second generation'. The main difference, he contends, is related to the fact that 'As legal and illegal foreign workers in Europe, many were treated as temporary residents, whereas they came to Australia under migration and settlement schemes' (Humphrey 2005: 137).

However, Humphrey (2005) and Mansouri (2005) suggest that, since the beginning of the war on terrorism, the discourse on Muslims and Islam in

Australia has shifted from one of multiculturalism to one of risk, threat and otherness, particularly in relation to non-Australian Muslims such as asylum seekers. There have been examples of the policing of otherness, such as verbal and physical abuse of Muslims and destruction of property (Human Rights and Equal Opportunity Commission 2004: 43–76), acts in themselves that are arguably manifestations of terrorism. This fact highlights the importance of full citizenship for guaranteeing minority protection. It also suggests that many Australians still consider Muslims to be outsiders despite the fact that, as mentioned earlier, the largest share of Australian Muslims are Australian born.

As the examples cited below demonstrate, aspects of inclusion also influence how Australian Muslims respond to potential terrorists within their midst. French convert to Islam, Willie Brigitte, was allegedly dispatched to Australia to conduct terrorist operations or to form a terrorist cell. Although Brigitte made some inroads into Sydney's Muslim community, he remained for the most part an outsider – albeit one who was still able to find a wife and get married. The city's Muslim leaders made several statements in the media to suggest that they did not know him. For instance, they claimed that Brigitte did not pray in the city's main mosques. Moreover, they claim that they would have reported him to authorities had they known or heard that he was planning to engage in violence (Chulov 2003, 2004a; Forbes and Fray 2003; Harris 2003). It is possible a similar situation pertained in late-2001 in the case of Ahmad al Joufi, who entered Australia under a false passport as Hamoud Abaid al Anezi.[4] It has been alleged that al Joufi came to Australia to raise money and recruit volunteers to fight in Chechnya. Several Melbourne-based Muslims reported to the Victorian police that he had assaulted a number of community members. In addition, three of them accused al Joufi of being an Al Qaeda operative. In the end, al Joufi received a suspended sentence for these beatings and was deported. However, it is important to acknowledge that two of the three Muslims who originally made accusations to the police eventually withdrew their claims. In these circumstances, Victorian police suspect that there may have been some 'persuasion' in the matter (Kerin et al. 2002; Skelton 2002a, 2002b).

The al Joufi incident raises several significant points. First, that Melbourne Muslims went to the Victorian Police and reported the crimes indicates that mainstream Muslims living in diasporas, who constitute the overwhelming majority of members of this faith, continue to utilise existing legal mechanisms and institutions. This challenges the misinformed notion that Muslims will only follow Shariah, not the laws of the land, or that they seek to maintain separate existences from their fellow citizens, even if the Muslims had been born in the country in question (for example Laqueur 2003). It is acknowledged that there are instances of militant Islamists (and Islamist terrorists) who claim that they will only follow divinely revealed laws, and that they do not recognise and will not adhere to civic legal institutions or 'man made' laws (for example Hizb ut-Tahrir 1999: 7). Yet John L. Esposito notes that in the US, 'Native born Americans' made similar accusations (of an unwillingness to fit in) against Italian-Americans and Catholics during the late nineteenth and early twentieth centuries, and yet these groups have rapidly and successfully negotiated their cultures with a broader American culture. He argues further that, based on their current experiences and achievements, US and European Muslims will probably follow a similar trajectory (Muslims in Europe Post 9/11 2003). Even a more conservative commentator such as Walter Laqueur, who posits that most contemporary European Muslims maintain separatist tendencies, anticipates that they will eventually become more fully integrated into their 'host countries' mainstream societies. However, he is far less optimistic than Esposito on the rate and impact of this acculturation process (Laqueur 2003: 211).

Secondly, the Melbourne Muslims' contact with the Victorian Police, and their efforts to report crimes, suggest that they maintain some degree of confidence in, and therefore consider legitimate, the law enforcement branch of – and by extension – the Australian state. Hence, the Australian state in this circumstance maintains at least some modicum of credibility as a primary 'survival unit' amongst mainstream Australian Muslims. To revert back to the Gravano anecdote at the beginning of this chapter, the Melbourne Muslims did not view al Joufi as *'our bad guy'*, as for instance Gravano's father viewed some Italian-American mobsters. Rather, to the Melbourne Muslims he was just *'a bad guy'*, and they felt that it was their civic duty to report him. Moreover, they felt that the state: (a) was the proper authority to dispense justice; and (b) had the Muslims' trust that it had the ability to dispense justice. That Muslims perceive that the legal system and law enforcement officials will look after them properly is a positive step in countering potential delegitimation.

Thirdly, that two of the Muslims recanted their allegations against al Joufi is also important. On the one hand, it suggests that in the end some Muslims felt that the threat of violence or some other form of retribution by al Joufi or on his behalf may have been more likely than his detention. Hence, while they may have seen the state and its agents as the legitimate means of protection, they may not have had faith in them to execute their duties adequately. On the other hand, this event occurred within a timeframe that coincided with a fairly tense period of relations between Australian Muslims and the wider Australian public. In August 2001, anti-Muslim sentiment was sparked with the Howard government's tough stance on illegal migrants landing in Australia, most of whom were Muslims. Additionally, 9/11 also sharpened anti-Muslim elements within Australia. It is important to acknowledge that only a minority of Australians openly expressed such views, and that there were many instances of inter-faith dialogues conducted post-September 11. However, the fact remains that:

> The Australian Arabic Council recorded a twenty-fold rise in reports of discrimination and vilification of Arab Australians in the month after 11 September 2001. The Muslim Women's Association of South Australia received a 'significant number of reported incidents, specifically of discrimination and harassment against Muslims', most involving offensive verbal abuse of women. The Al Zahra Muslim Women's Association in Sydney also reported a 'phenomenal' increase in both discrimination and vilification reports. Many individual community members concurred that September 11 was a turning point. (HREOC 2004: 43)

Hence, from this time on, some – but certainly not all – members of the Australian Muslim communities closed ranks, and did not wish to alienate members of their own faith by openly siding with the state at the expense of their fellow believers, even if they did so in private. Some Muslim commentators criticised these actions (Akbarzadeh 2004; Aly 2004a, 2004b). In these circumstances of perceived stigma, ostracism, and even actual experiences of harassment and assault, some Muslims felt genuinely threatened. It is therefore possible to argue that some Muslims experienced a conflict between 'survival units'. Hence, some perceived the Muslim communities, as opposed to the Australian state, as more capable of protecting them. This case is instructive, because it reinforces the fact that legitimacy is not a permanent feature that states or their various institutions can always take for granted. Rather, they must constantly reaffirm their commitment to the terms of the social contract with their citizens in order to maintain their trust.

The Australian Government's response to the October 2002 bombings in Bali, which killed over 200 people including 89 Australians, created tensions between Australian Muslims and the state. Shortly after the attack, the Australian Federal Police (AFP) and the Australian Security Intelligence Organisation (ASIO) conducted a series of raids on the homes of Muslims in Western Australia and New South Wales believed to be associated with the Indonesian Islamist terrorist organisation Jemaah Islamiyah (JI) that conducted the bombing, and its alleged spiritual leader, Abu Bakar Bashir. While the raids unearthed a handful of potential terrorists, they also had the result of deeply alienating Muslims. Representatives of Muslim communities from these states and elsewhere criticised what they considered to be heavy-handed tactics that were largely unnecessary, reflective of unjustifiable racial profiling and the infringement of the rights and privacy of largely innocent residents and citizens, including women and children (Chulov and Greenlees 2002; Forbes 2002; Karnelas and Chulov 2002; Moore 2002; Nason 2002; Powell and Chulov 2002; West Australian 2002).

In Victoria too, police and intelligence services sought to question Muslims whom they felt may have had some links to JI or could help to advance their knowledge in the case; however, they were generally more restrained. Nevertheless, some Muslims in Melbourne still felt particularly aggrieved, and became more defensive in their outlooks. Representatives of the Victorian Police felt that the raids had significantly disrupted their relationships with the local Muslim and ethnic communities. Over the years they had created and maintained very positive interactions with the state's various Muslim organisations and other ethnic bodies. In order to re-establish their links with these communities and organisations, the Victorian Police, and in particular its Counter-Terrorism Coordination Unit (CTCU) formed a partnership with academics from Monash University and representatives from Victoria's ethnic and religious communities, legal bodies and trade unions to develop a new model of community policing in culturally diverse communities. The Australian Federal Government is currently funding this initiative (Sanders 2004).

A March 2002 evangelical Christian seminar on Islam and the war on terrorism, presented by Catch the Fire Ministries, further complicated the relationship between Australia's Muslim communities and the state. Muslims who attended the talk felt that the speakers' comments about Islam, the Prophet Muhammad, and the Qur'an were derogatory. They were not presented in a manner that would have been considered to be a constructive inquiry into the topic. Rather, they contended that Catch the Fire's exposition of Islam constituted religious vilification as established in the Victorian legal code (Crawford 2003; Zwartz 2003). The case came before the Victorian Civil and Administrative Tribunal (VCAT) in 2003. VCAT initially scheduled for the case to be heard over three days. However, it stretched well into the following year. In December 2004, Justice Higgins, who presided over the case, handed down an opinion declaring that the Catch the Fire Ministry's actions did indeed constitute religious vilification (Higgins 2004a, 2004b).[5]

Commentators raised concerns throughout case and after it concluded about the ruling's impact on freedom of speech (*The Age* 2004; Aly 2004c; Wallace 2004; Butler 2005; Rayner 2005). For instance, Federal Treasurer Peter Costello asserted that the case itself constituted an abuse of the Australian legal system and a devaluation of Judeo-Christian contributions to Australian society (Costello 2004). Gary Bouma, UNESCO Chair in Intercultural and Interreligious Relations – Asia Pacific, an ordained Anglican Priest and acclaimed commentator on the sociology of religion and Islam in Australia, noted that the case was not simply an issue of free speech. Rather, he contends that the case is more pertinent to responsible speech and how that speech is used to maintain relationships in an ethnically and religiously diverse community. Australians, he contended, had the right to freedom of speech. However, they also have the responsibility to portray others within the Australian community accurately, and have no right to demean or misrepresent them (Bouma 2004). Ironically, Costello's fellow front bencher and Minister for Multicultural Affairs, Peter McGuaren, echoed Bouma's sentiments in Melbourne in December 2004, in his comments at the launch of a major report on the importance of religion and multiculturalism's role in maintaining civic harmony and Australia's security in the war on terrorism (Cahill *et al.* 2004).

The VCAT decision could therefore be considered to be a manifestation of the upholding of minority rights. Indeed, one of the arguments presented in this chapter is that states are better able to reduce the chances of terrorism from representatives of minority groups when they respect those groups' rights and dignity. Nevertheless, there have been instances in which members of states' ethnic or religious majorities have concluded that governments have gone too far in protecting minorities' rights, and this has led to the emergence of right-wing terrorisms, as well as the increased lethality of anti-abortion terrorists in the US (Hewitt 2002: 41, 121–8; Mason 2002). Similar perceptions amongst segments of the Australian population have resulted in the rise of neo-populism, with the electoral successes of Pauline Hanson and the One Nation Party beginning in 1996, and the governing Liberal-National Coalition's adoption and mainstreaming of many of Hanson and One Nation's anti-affirmative action, anti-migrant rhetoric and policies (Markus 2001). It is therefore crucially important to acknowledge that states take risks when they employ anti-terrorist or counter-terrorist measures that infringe upon the rights of their ethnic and religious minorities. However, they also must face the possibility that in their pursuit of upholding minority rights, they may also trigger potentially hostile reactions from members of their states' ethnic or religious majorities or other minorities.

The Jack Roche case constitutes a third challenge to the relationship between Australian Muslims and the state. Roche, a British-born Australian convert to Islam, confessed to links with Abu Bakar Bashir. He also admitted to conducting reconnaissance on the Israeli embassy in Canberra with a view to bombing it, and plotting to assassinate Joseph Gutnick, a prominent Melbourne-based Jewish businessman. However, Roche made several attempts to inform the AFP and ASIO of his plans, and of JI's operations within Australia, before the Bali bombings. Additionally, another Australian Muslim convert – Ibrahim Fraser – contacted Australian authorities in an effort to warn them about Roche and his intentions and actions. In both cases, these Muslims' advances were ignored (Chulov 2004b; Daly 2004; Egan *et al.* 2004; Stewart *et al.* 2004).

It has been argued above that both the Catch the Fire case and the Roche/Fraser incidents complicate the legitimacy of the Australian state in the eyes of its Muslim communities. In these instances, Australian Muslims attempted to utilise Australian legal institutions and perform their civic duties by informing Australian police and intelligence services about potential terrorist activities. In the first instance they received negative responses from members of the mainstream Australian community and key Australian statespersons. In the latter, representatives of institutions empowered and mandated to protect Australian citizens ignored them. Hence, it is possible that these situations may have shaken some Australian Muslims' faith in their state's institutions. Moreover, it has been discouraging for some Muslims, who feel that, even when they are acting within the realm of the law and behaving like proper citizens, their actions are not properly acknowledged (Lentini 2004).

DISCUSSION AND CONCLUSION

Examples from the Australian experiences indicate that within some sectors of the Australian Federal Government, as well as in some of its states and law enforcement agencies, there is strong support for the employment of measures that protect minority rights and respect the dignity of religious communities – in this case Muslims – to reduce the potential for political violence.

However, as with all anti-terrorist and counter-terrorist measures, religiously and culturally responsive policies and practices cannot in themselves eradicate terrorism. As argued earlier, the best these strategies and tactics can do is to manage terrorism and reduce the factors that may fuel it.

That several Australians are currently incarcerated on charges of suspected terrorism or links to terrorist organisations is a testament to this assertion.[6] Moreover, it is important to stress that it would be impossible simply to apply the practices analysed above to other countries. States must develop anti-terrorist and counter-terrorist policies and practices with specific groups in mind. One approach will not fit all terrorist organisations. There are varying forms of terrorism, largely linked to identity groups with disparate grievances (real, exaggerated or imagined), histories, constituencies and objectives. As indicated above, legislation, policies and practices that enhance the rights of one group may be perceived as impeding those of others. Cultural citizenship is a sharply contested political terrain that both enhances and complicates states' abilities to combat terrorism.

It will be recalled that Jan Pakulski contends that cultural citizenship contains three sub-streams (symbolic presence and visibility versus marginalisation; dignifying representation versus stigmatisation; and the right to propagation of lifestyle versus assimilation). Recent events in Australia indicate that Australia's multicultural policies, and other decisions and practices that in general exemplify the first of each of Pakulski's pairs, help to maintain a positive cultural citizenship amongst its Muslim communities. Nevertheless, there have been challenges and threats to this relationship between the Muslims and the Australian state as a 'survival unit'. It is necessary to re-emphasise that Australian Muslims still maintain grievances concerning the Howard Government's policies towards Muslims, particularly non-Australian Muslims (Mansouri 2005). This includes its policies of mandatory detention for asylum seekers, many of whom are Muslims from South Asia and the Middle East. In addition, many Australian Muslims are angry at the Federal Government's participation in the US-led war in Iraq. And the Australian security agencies' initial failures to respond to Jack Roche and Ibrahim Fraser's warnings perhaps constituted a form of marginalisation which contradicted Pakulski's first criterion of cultural citizenship.

Yet it is important to acknowledge that symbolic presence – as well as actual presence – is maintained in other arenas. For instance, Australian Muslims and their representatives participate in key community and policy-making bodies (Cahill and Leahy 2004). The Victorian Police–Monash University–Community liaison example also demonstrates that Australian Muslim voices are included in debates on counter-terrorism issues that directly impact upon their community. Australian multicultural policies afford support for all faiths, and they enable its Muslims to practise their religion. This certainly helps to reinforce Pakulski's cultural citizenship criteria.

However, some policies and practices should be interrogated in slightly more detail. For instance, the Australian mass media, especially 'quality' dailies such as *The Australian* (national focus) and *The Age* (Melbourne) have *generally* tended to portray Australian Muslims positively only on *some* issues (for example Henderson 2002). In his long-term study of Australian press coverage of Muslims, Howard Brasted certainly notes that there have been instances of negative images. However, he also argues that the situation is neither static nor uniform: Muslims from former Yugoslavia have in general been depicted more positively than, for instance, Palestinian terrorists. His contention is that the Australian press does not engage in an 'Orientalist' discourse on Muslims and Islam. Rather, their coverage has been conditioned and influenced by 'journalistic methods and the marketing requisites of newspapers' (Brasted 2001: 222–3).

Even in instances in which Australian Muslims have been accused of heinous crimes, such as Mamdouh Habib and David Hicks, both incarcerated at Guantanamo Bay for allegedly being members of Al Qaeda,[7] the Australian quality press maintained that they were Australian citizens who deserved due legal process. They have criticised the Howard Government for permitting two Australian citizens to be victims of a miscarriage of justice by having them linger for years without a trial.[8] On other matters, some of the quality newspapers have not been as favourable towards Australian Muslims.[9] It should not be surprising, however, that tabloids like Melbourne's *Herald Sun* have *generally* been less favourable towards Australian Muslims.

Although the greatest share of Australian Muslims are working class (HREOC 2004: 214–15), there is an expanding middle class, including intellectual contributors to civil society, both overseas and Australian-born. These commentators amply defend and articulate various positions within the Australian Muslim communities to broader publics. This better enables Australian Muslims to exercise Pakulski's second criterion of cultural citizenship, namely generating dignifying representation. Academics Abdullah Saeed and Shahram Akbarzadeh, and public commentators such as ICV Board Member and Melbourne solicitor Waleed Aly, former ICV President Yasser Soliman, and Susan Carland (a former Australian Muslim of the Year) have represented and defended Australia's Muslims by emphasising their communities' commitments to living and working within the mainstream channels of multicultural and multi-faith frameworks.

Australia's multicultural policies provide opportunities for Australian Muslims to exercise a positive cultural citizenship that enables the maintenance of *asabiyya* and helps to establish some elements of an

Abyssinian paradigm in which Muslims, as part of a religious minority, are able to live in harmony under non-Muslim governance. Moreover, incidents like the VCAT decision in the Catch the Fire case further strengthen Australia's image as a viable 'survival unit'. The Australian state's continued maintenance of its Muslims' rights – despite its pursuit of some policies and practices which many Australian Muslims may find undesirable – has meant that malevolent Muslims' calls to violence have largely fallen on deaf ears within the Australian Muslim communities. Indeed, evidence presented in this chapter demonstrates that, by reporting actual or perceived acts of violence by members of their community to authorities, Australian Muslims clearly do not identify with their local co-religionists intending to commit violent acts – supposedly in their name – as 'our bad people'. By promoting tolerance and upholding justice for its Muslim citizens and residents, the Australian state helps to enable Australian Muslims to continue to refute and condemn these individuals' actions. Moreover, it permits Australian Muslims to experience Pakulski's third criterion of cultural citizenship, the right to identity and maintenance of lifestyles. Hence, these actions can help to reaffirm the Australian Muslims' loyalty to the state, and reduce the possibilities for delegitimation. Some Australian policies indicate that the state – or at least some entities within it – attempts to counter terrorism as if Muslims matter. Cultural citizenship in Australia has helped establish and may maintain some form of civic pre-emption, which enhances the state's ability to counter terrorism with the assistance of its marginalised communities.

NOTES

1. The author acknowledges the support of Monash University Research Fund (Networks and Netwars in the Asia-Pacific) and the Australian Research Council Linkage Grant Scheme (Counter-Terrorism Policing in Culturally Diverse Communities) in writing this chapter.

2. Cultural citizenship can be considered to be a third wave of citizenship, following on from a first wave of political citizenship (suffrage) and a second wave of socio-economic rights (welfare state) (Barbalet 1988; Appadurai and Stengou 2000). Nevertheless, it is important to stress that in certain circumstances cultural citizenship may not in fact be an extension of citizenship rights, but a substitution or a form of replacement for rights lost as a result of the decline in the welfare state. In other words, cultural citizenship reifies some of the forms of life politics, or lifestyle politics, that Giddens contends have emerged since the end of World War II, but especially from the 1960s and onwards. Nevertheless, they are also closely linked to attempts to assist, but are ultimately derived from, successful engagements in emancipatory politics that are in turn closely tied into the efforts of liberation movements and civil rights movements, such as gay rights, women's rights, and, for instance, indigenous rights (Giddens

1991: 209–31). Moreover, instances raised in this chapter suggest that cultural citizenship may in fact be insufficient for adequately protecting the rights of marginalised communities in the face of measures taken in the name of national security. It is entirely true that the Australian state is consciously seeking to uphold the rights of its Muslim citizens in the current anti-terrorism campaign. On the other hand, the Australian Federal Government is less vigilant in upholding the rights of Muslims who are not citizens, such as asylum seekers from the Middle East, Indonesia or other Muslim-dominated regions.

3. Nevertheless, it is important to acknowledge that such propositions are under scrutiny in some European contexts. European Muslims are encountering a backlash against them, and multicultural policies are being sorely tried following a Muslim's murder of Dutch film-maker Theo van Gogh (AFP 2004; AP 2004; Bichon 2004; Bremner 2004; Michelson 2004; The Times, AFP 2004). However, while condemning the action, Khan and Esposito (2005) perceptively note that:

> When a Dutch animal rights activist Valkert van der Graaf murdered a Dutch politician, Pim Fortuyn in 2002, it did not raise questions about the compatibility of the philosophy of rights and the West. But when a Dutch Muslim murders a Dutch film producer, it raises profound questions not just about Islam's compatibility with modernity and democracy but also about the ability of Western Muslims to live in a democratic society.

This anti-multicultural backlash has also been manifested in increased surveillance in European Mosques and over Muslim clerics. For instance, in Germany there are suggestions that khutbas (sermons) in Arabic or other languages be prohibited and only the vernacular permitted. France has also deported imams who have breached public order and human rights violations with their sermons and activities, and is seeking to train 'home-grown' clerics (Boyes 2004; Henly 2004). French legislation banning the wearing of religious symbols and clothing in some public spaces also complicates issues of multiculturalism within Europe.

4. I stress here the term 'possible' because there are arguments that the events recounted here may have been due to personal grievances that some Melbourne Muslims had towards al Joufi, and were not related to politics.

5. It is significant to acknowledge that, following the decision, Islamic Council of Victoria (ICV) President Yasser Soliman embraced his former adversary in the case, Pastor Danny Nallah, and stated: '. . . it's time to move forward and I hope we can talk to each other directly and try to develop understanding' (cited in Zwartz 2004).

6. Adelaide's David Hicks has been imprisoned in Guantanamo Bay since 2002. Jack Roche was imprisoned in 2004 and is serving a 9-year term for his aforementioned plans and actions. Jack Thomas, a Melbourne cab driver, was arrested in late 2004 for allegedly training in Al Qaeda camps and being ordered to establish an Al Qaeda sleeper cell in Australia. Thomas was released on bail in February 2005. Additionally Bilal and Maher Khazal have been extradited to Lebanon for allegedly playing a role in Hezbollah activities there.

7. At the time of writing, Habib had just been released and returned to Australia, and Hicks is still in Guantanamo Bay awaiting trial by Military Tribunal.

8. The discourse towards Habib began to change, however, following his 13 February 2005 interview on the Nine (television) Network's *60 Minutes*, particularly because of his failure to address his alleged activities in Afghanistan before 9/11, and his attempts to file for a disability pension from the Australian Government.

9. Headline analysis of Melbourne newspapers from 2002–04 helps to substantiate this claim. For instance, during this period there were nearly twice as many negative headlines in *The Age* concerning Australian Muslims as positive ones (15 and 8 respectively), and almost three times

more negative headlines than positive ones in the *Herald Sun* (17 vs. 6). Information has been derived from the Counter-Terrorism Policing for Culturally Diverse Communities project database. I am indebted to Rod Ling for maintaining this data set and providing these results.

4. 'Soft Law' Regimes and European Organisations' Fight Against Terrorist Financing and Money Laundering

Rémy Davison

INTRODUCTION

In 1995, Bernard Connolly's *The Rotten Heart of Europe: The Dirty War for Europe's Money* (Connolly 1996) raised its polemical sights and took aim at the architects of the European Union's (EU) Economic and Monetary Union (EMU) project. However, in condemning the Franco-German 'conspiracy' to take over 'Europe's money', the best-seller did not mention the quiet revolution that had been underway in Europe since 1990: the war against Europe's dirty money (Davison 1998b).

Money laundering describes a process whereby illegitimately obtained funds are converted into 'clean' assets or cash via the formal economy. Money launderers may employ means as diverse as legal gambling, legitimate bond or share investments, asset purchases, or simply the retail banking system, in order to conceal the origins of dirty money. The extent of money laundering worldwide is vast: using 1996 data, an IMF study estimates that the amount of money laundered annually is between two and five per cent of global GDP ($US800 billion – $US2 trillion) (IMF 2001: 21).[1] The IMF also estimates that between 5 and 28 per cent of the GDP of OECD economies is underground. In the Middle East and Asia, the figures are in the range of 13–71 per cent, while in Africa, the underground economy can account for 20–76 per cent (IMF 2001: 25). The infiltration of laundered money into the formal economy can destabilize economies, corrupt political systems, and provide an inaccurate picture of national accounts, leading to misleading fiscal estimates, financial misreporting, and exchange-rate and monetary volatility. As Urrutia (2004) argues, crime, dirty money and violence can have a serious impact upon the ability of states to effect macroeconomic adjustments. Dirty money has also proven a powerful incentive for collapsing states to engage in dubious activities, as evidenced by Russian mafia money laundering in Nauru. Given the volumes of money involved, together with its potential use for purposes such as arms purchases, human and drug trafficking, and criminal and terrorist financing, money laundering is scarcely a victimless crime.

Long before the terrorist attacks of 9/11, the EU, the Council of Europe (CoE), and the Organisation for Economic Co-operation and Development (OECD) had implemented a range of legal instruments designed to combat money laundering. Since 9/11, all three organisations have become actively engaged in the fight against terrorist financing. Moreover, the scope of activities undertaken by the EU, CoE and OECD is not limited merely to their members; various initiatives undertaken under their auspices, such as the OECD's Financial Action Task Force (FATF), are global in scope. That the most forceful and wide-ranging anti-money laundering (AML) legislation has emerged from Europe and the US is not surprising, as their affluence and relatively porous borders have made them major markets for illicit narcotics and human trafficking, as well as prime targets of terrorist activity. Unsurprisingly, the major targets for money laundering surveillance are banks and non-bank financial institutions. Increasingly, however, professionals (especially accountants and lawyers) who deal not only with significant financial transactions, but also with realisable assets, will be important players in the prevention of international crime and terrorist financing. Identifying ownership of funds or assets is the first task of anti-money laundering authorities.

This chapter provides a critical evaluation of a range of programs undertaken by the CoE, EU and FATF, such as AML initiatives, and countermeasures directed at terrorist financing. Organised crime and corruption are enormously complex areas; consequently, this chapter focuses predominantly upon the regulation of criminal and informal financial transactions. The aim of the discussion is to establish how effectively 'soft law' regimes have managed to regulate, monitor and impose rules and norms upon both member and non-member countries of regional and international organisations, such as the EU and FATF. The following section provides a brief overview of regime theory. Section two examines CoE initiatives, while sections three and four review recent EU legislation and FATF programs respectively.

'SOFT LAW' AND INTERNATIONAL REGIMES

The proposition that international regimes develop norms, values and legitimacy is a strongly-contested one within the international relations discipline. As Strange (1982) complained, the very concept of a regime is 'loose' and 'woolly'. However, proponents of regime theory argue that international regimes are essentially normative, and that the complexity of international affairs demands not fewer, but more regimes to operate the machinery of global governance (Keohane 1982). According to Keohane and Nye (2001), intergovernmental organisations (IGOs) have produced a body of both 'soft' and 'hard' international law designed to restrain the activities of states and other actors. Despite the distinction between 'hard' law (law-making treaties) and 'soft' law (non-binding precepts), Szasz (1997) argues that much international law is generally *observed* without enforcement mechanisms, and is enforced by the increasing rate of development of treaty-based law.

Regimes may also affect levels of corruption. Sandholtz and Gray's (2003) study asserts that while international regimes and the depth of integration strongly influence national levels of corruption, factors such as economic incentives, agenda-setting and rule-making are more important than international jurisprudence in affecting corruption levels. Sandholtz and Gray (2003: 761) essentially argue that increased interdependence (defined as 'international networks of exchange, communication, and organization') produces lower levels of corruption. From their 150-country survey, they conclude that international integration affects domestic policy making profoundly. However, domestic actors are driven primarily by 'utility calculations', rather than norms or values in themselves. They argue (ibid. 762–65) that the process of socialisation initiated by regime integration produces norm- and rules-based societies. Thus, the deeper the level of integration within an anti-corruption regime, the less the likelihood that a state will be disposed towards tolerance of corruption.

Nevertheless, realists maintain considerable reservations concerning the effectiveness of international regimes as proponents of norms, values and international law. According to Keohane and Nye's (2001: 2) modified structural realist perspective, states possess a mix of both 'hard' (military) and 'soft' power. 'Soft' power, as Keohane and Nye see it, involves persuading states 'to want what you want', and may involve a combination of diplomacy, market power and legitimacy.

The development of rules-based international regimes is usually within the control of an exclusive few. The EU's *acquis communautaire*, a 55-year collection of rules, norms, laws, treaties and conventions, was constructed largely by an EU dominated by intergovernmentalism, and the EU itself is a strongly *dirigiste* organisation in which the major players have traditionally been France, Germany and the UK. Effectively, the Big Three member states have constructed the 'rules of the game', primarily because they account for the largest proportion of EU GDP, and are consequently the largest contributors to the General Budget. Given this context, it is interesting to note that the OECD's FATF is built along similar lines. The FATF demands compliance from its member countries – with certain exceptions – but goes further than the EU in virtually compelling non-member countries to introduce minimum standards into their financial systems. In this respect, the FATF demonstrates the power that regimes backed by strong states (members of the OECD) exercise over weak states (Pacific Island states; transition states in CEE; developing countries in Southeast Asia and Africa). Thus, 'soft law' regimes do not necessarily use 'hard' power to ensure compliance among non-members; but their market power and ability to levy sanctions and other forms of discrimination virtually ensure that their demands result in at least some compliance.

COUNCIL OF EUROPE INITIATIVES

The first significant European intergovernmental initiatives targeting transnational crime occurred under the auspices of the Council of Europe, which established the European Convention on Mutual Assistance in Criminal Matters (Council of Europe 1959). The first European convention directed explicitly against terrorism was enacted by the CoE in 1977 (Council of Europe 1977). During the 1990s, the Council of Europe broadened the scope of its conventions to include confiscation of profits from the proceeds of crime (Council of Europe 1990); traffic in illegal narcotics (Council of Europe 1995); the establishment of the Group of States Against Corruption (GRECO) to implement the Council of Europe's anti-corruption conventions (Council of Europe 1998); and money laundering, search and seizure (Council of Europe 1997). During 2003, a number of CoE states signed or ratified the Criminal and Civil Law Conventions on Corruption. Turkey ratified the Criminal Convention on Corruption and acceded to GRECO. In September 2003, the Czech Republic ratified the Criminal Convention, which entered into force on 1 January 2004. In addition, Ireland ratified the Criminal Law Convention on

Corruption, while Romania has signed the Additional Protocol to the Criminal and Law Conventions on Corruption.

The Group of States against Corruption (GRECO)

The GRECO program was established under the auspices of the CoE. Its membership comprises most West and East European countries, the US, and some former Soviet republics (Estonia, Moldova, Latvia, Lithuania), with the notable exceptions of Russia and Ukraine. The principal aim of GRECO has been to ensure compliance with the legal instruments established by the CoE, such as the suppression of terrorism and anti-corruption conventions. The CoE has urged all member states to ratify these conventions and resolutions. However, unlike the EU, where legislation has 'direct effect' (that is member states are obliged to implement and enforce EU law within domestic jurisdictions – Davison 2002: 86), CoE conventions require individual ratification by member states. However, particularly in states which have only recently acceded to CoE membership, such as Moldova and the Baltic states, significant 'implementation deficits' have emerged, even when a state has fully ratified a convention. As former US representative to the FATF Joseph Myers notes, 'Too many countries pass these laws and then do nothing to enforce them' (quoted in O'Hara 2004: 17). However, some important reports on compliance with the CoE's legal instruments have emerged, such as the report on Liechtenstein, which have identified serious implementation deficits.

In order to surmount these problems, GRECO has established a four-stage process, comprising:

1. a two-round evaluation procedure;
2. a questionnaire;
3. GRECO evaluation reports;
4. GRECO Compliance Reports.

GRECO has issued a number of compliance reports that are delivered to the Statutory Committee of GRECO. Reports are confidential until authorised for release by the member country. A number of states, such as the Republic of Macedonia, have engaged in active consultation and cooperation with GRECO in order to address rampant corruption.[2] However, despite its adoption of a number of CoE and international conventions against corruption, the Republic of Macedonia has not enacted any legislation dealing with the prevention of corruption. This exemplifies the gap between the ratification of international conventions and the implementation of the necessary legal instruments within domestic jurisdictions. Exacerbating the problem is the fact that Macedonian governments have exceedingly limited means available to them to address issues such as terrorist financing and activities in certain parts of the country. Towns such as Tetovo, and most of Macedonia's western frontier, appear to be virtual fiefdoms of Islamic terrorists. In this respect, only parts of the country are subject to the central Macedonian government, and both NATO and the EU have proven reluctant to address this problem militarily, due to fears that the Macedonian government might collapse, resulting in a return to the civil strife of the 1990s (Debkafile 2002).

Council of Europe Anti-Money Laundering Measures

The Select Committee of Experts on the Evaluation of Anti-Money Laundering Measures (PC-R-EV; since 2002, MONEYVAL) was formed in 1997 by the CoE's Committee of Ministers to conduct mutual and self-assessment exercises of AML measures in CoE member countries that are not members of the FATF. Part of its brief is to conduct regular reviews into methods and trends of money laundering. Since 9/11, MONEYVAL has widened the scope of its activities to include countering terrorist financing.

A number of CoE members are not members of the FATF. These include Armenia, Azerbaijan, Bosnia-Herzegovina, Estonia, Georgia, Latvia, Lithuania, Republic of Macedonia, Malta, San Marino, Serbia-Montenegro, Slovakia and Slovenia. However, these countries are permitted to appoint up to three expert representatives to MONEYVAL. Certain representatives from IGOs may attend MONEYVAL in a non-voting capacity, including the FATF, Interpol, the Commonwealth Secretariat, the IMF, the United Nations Office on Drugs and Crime (UNODC), the UN Crime Prevention and Criminal Justice Division, the World Customs Organisation, the World Bank, the European Bank for Reconstruction and Development (EBRD) and the Offshore Group of Banking Supervisors.

MONEYVAL coordinates its activities with procedures and practices adopted by the FATF. MONEYVAL evaluations were developed in 1998 and implemented in 1999, with some additional guidelines. MONEYVAL's mutual evaluations culminate in a report with recommendations prescribing action. In the event of non-compliance, MONEYVAL has adopted a six-stage graduated process. Stages I–IV involve notification procedures, where MONEYVAL, the CoE's Director of Legal Affairs and the member state's relevant minister(s) are notified of non-compliance. The Stage V process involves a high-level mission to the country concerned. In the event of unsatisfactory progress following the implementation of Stages I–V, Stage VI procedures permit MONEYVAL to issue a public statement of non-compliance, in accordance with Recommendation 21 of the FATF. The MONEYVAL Plenary must then authorise the Chairperson to take any Stages I–V actions, but the Chairperson has the authority to take Stage VI measures without Plenary consultation.

MONEYVAL takes into account the practices and procedures of the FATF in its work. MONEYVAL is a sub-committee of the European Committee on Crime Problems (CDPC) of the CoE. Each of its 25 member countries is entitled to appoint three experts to MONEYVAL. Experts are selected based upon their expertise in legal issues relating to national and international AML instruments, supervision of financial institutions, and law enforcement matters. There are twice-yearly Plenary meetings of the Select Committee, at which national experts consider and adopt draft mutual evaluation reports of member states. In addition, the MONEYVAL membership includes experts from the past and current Presidency of the FATF and scientific experts appointed by the MONEYVAL Secretariat.

The CoE has also made efforts to develop a comprehensive policy to combat corruption over the past decade. A Multidisciplinary Group on Corruption (MGC) was founded in 1995. Based on its work, the CoE launched its Criminal Law Convention on Corruption in 1999 (Strasbourg Convention), according GRECO the responsibility for monitoring its implementation throughout signatory member countries. The CoE also adopted a Civil Law Convention on Corruption later in 1999, which was open for signature by both members and non-members of the CoE, as well as by EU member states.

Despite these initiatives, the level of ratification has been poor; only Moldova has implemented the Strasbourg Convention, for example. Moreover, the State Program for Fighting Crime, Corruption and Protectionism has a number of serious deficiencies, such as the omission of nepotism as a form of corruption.

EUROPEAN UNION INITIATIVES

The establishment of the Single European Market after 1992 not only provided increased opportunities for white-collar crime, but the concomitant deregulation of financial services also opened up new opportunities for money laundering and terrorist financing by both legitimate and criminal means. The 1991 collapse of the Luxembourg-based Bank of Credit and Commerce

International (BCCI) demonstrated the ineffectiveness of prudential supervision in both Luxembourg and the UK (the Bank of England supervised BCCI's commercial banking in Britain). BCCI was largely a case of management fraud, but it was involved with money laundering, and its funds were associated with drugs and arms trafficking. The EU Council of Ministers belatedly adopted the Second ('post-BCCI') Banking Directive in 1995, which ensured minimum supervision standards, equal to the US Bank Bill Amendments of 1992–93; the latter stipulated that US-registered banks were obliged to comply with US banking regulations. This was to ensure that Luxembourg banks, which operated the most lax banking regulations in the EU, achieved minimum EU standards. Foreign banks that do not comply with the Second Banking Directive are not permitted to operate in the EU (Rapid 1995). In 1991, the EU Council of Ministers introduced the Money Laundering Guidelines, which obliged all financial sector firms to report suspected money-laundering activities (Council of the European Union 1991).

AML Initiatives

The EU Commission issued its draft Third Money Laundering Directive in July 2004, which was approved by the Council of Ministers in December. The new Directive takes into account recent AML policy changes articulated by the FATF, the World Bank and the IMF, and consolidates and extends the measures outlined in the First (1991) and Second (2001) Directives.[3] The First Directive affected only those conducting financial business and related primarily to drug trafficking offences, whereas the Second Directive's scope extends beyond those conducting financial business and relates to criminal activity generally.[4] It also requires identification of all accounts containing more than €12,500 (Deloitte and Touche 2005: 5). In addition, the EU can also freeze the assets of suspected terrorists or terrorist organisations under the Financial Sanctions (Embargo) Regulations.

The Third Money Laundering Directive includes a new definition of money laundering to cover terrorist financing. It views money laundering as concealing or disguising the proceeds of serious crimes, and requires member states to engage in judicial cooperation in these matters (BNA Banking Report 2004: 35). The Directive advocates a 'risk-based approach' to AML, in line with the FATF's Forty Recommendations (FRs). This involves 'know-your-customer' (KYC) approaches and monitoring of account opening, and does not dilute the emphasis upon Suspicious Transaction Reporting (STR). The Third Directive also covers lawyers and notaries dealing with cash sums in excess of

€15,000, a measure opposed by the European Bar Association, which argued that there was 'no empirical evidence' that money laundering transactions on property were a regular occurrence, and that a €50,000 limit should be set (Council of the Bars and Law Societies of the European Union 2004: 2–3).[5] Indeed, the Third Directive has attracted hostile criticism from a wide range of professional associations throughout the EU in issue areas as diverse as the requirements for opening bank accounts (The Law Societies 2005: 9) to competition for business among 'regulated', 'self-regulated' and 'unregulated' professions.[6]

In extending the Second Money Laundering Directive, the Third Directive also targets terrorist financing in the following ways:

1. prohibitions upon credit and financial institutions keeping anonymous accounts or accounts with fictitious names;
2. prohibitions upon relationships with shell banks;
3. establishment of enhanced 'know-your-customer' requirements;
4. provisions for simplified due diligence in low-risk situations;
5. under certain conditions, allowances for due diligence to be carried out by third parties in other member states;
6. obligations on member states to establish financial intelligence units (FIUs) to combat money laundering and terrorist financing; and
7. requirement that member states establish licensing or registration systems for currency exchange offices, as well as for trust and company service providers (European Central Bank 2005: 1–2).

In late 2004, the Commission also recommended that member countries' law-enforcement agencies have full access to the records of financial institutions, and their transactions, although the enactment of legislation in this area is expected to take some time (Commission of the European Union 2004: 2).

Once the EU Council of Ministers' 2000 Convention on mutual recognition of restraint of assets and other judicial orders is fully implemented, seizure of assets and recovery of proceeds from money laundering and other illicit financial transactions will have Europe-wide application. In 2000, EU member states agreed to impose penalties on third countries considered 'particularly uncooperative' in fighting money laundering. A total of 19 countries have already been identified as 'uncooperative'. Prior to their accession to the EU, the 13 countries seeking EU membership were obliged to adhere to the AML regulations, including Hungary, which appeared on the original FATF Non-Cooperative Countries or Territories (NCCT) blacklist. Russia was cited by the

FATF as one of the most problematic countries in terms of money laundering during the 1990s, as the 1997–98 FATF-IX report noted (Financial Action Task Force 1998). However, the Russian Federation has enacted a number of pieces of legislation designed to combat money laundering, such as the 2001 *Law on Action to Combat the Laundering of Proceeds from Crime*, which brought Russia closer to the legislative standards adopted by the FATF and in the EU's Second Money Laundering Directive.

Program Octopus

As the EU commenced accession negotiations with the Central and East European countries (CEECs) during the 1990s, issues such as corruption and money laundering came to the fore. This was particularly relevant given that CEE members would have virtually unrestricted access to the EU's Single European Market, which had removed a large number of technical, fiscal and physical barriers to freedom of movement, as well as intra-EU trade. Consequently, the EU established two joint Octopus programs with the Council of Europe (Octopus I, 1996–98; and Octopus II, 1999–2000). The objectives of the Octopus initiatives were to ensure stability of democratic institutions, the rule of law, market economies, and social and economic progress (*European Report* 1999). The EU's Accession and CEEC Partnership agreements provide for application of the Justice and Home Affairs (JHA) pillar of the Maastricht Treaty (Davison 1998a: 78).

Under Octopus I, the EU provided training for police forces, civil servants, prosecutors and members of the judiciary involved in fighting organised crime and corruption. Octopus I also sought to identify legislative loopholes and weaknesses in CEECs, in addition to inter-agency cooperation on criminal matters and economic crime. Octopus II extended the reach of its program to include Albania, Croatia, the Republic of Macedonia, Moldova, Russia and Ukraine. Although schemes such as FALCONE and OISIN have been established to assist exchanges, cooperation and training of police and national security officers involved in fighting organised crime, relatively little participation by the applicant states was expected (Brown 1998). The final Octopus I report emphasised the need for participating countries to implement the necessary legal measures and institutional frameworks that would permit the investigation and prosecution of corruption and organised crime. In response to the Octopus I report, Octopus II developed targeted recommendations for action in participating countries, and its reports have had some influence upon the development of recent anti-corruption legislation introduced by the EU and the Council of Europe.[7]

The Asia–Europe Meeting (ASEM)

The ASEM dialogue process has produced a number of initiatives, applicable to all European and Asian member countries of ASEM; these include:

- ASEM Anti-Money Laundering initiative
- ASEM initiative on Trafficking in Women and Children
- ASEM Symposium on Law Enforcement Organs' Cooperation in Combating Transnational Crime
- The ASEM Anti-corruption initiative
- ASEM Cooperation in Promoting Awareness in the Young Generation on the Drug Problem (Asia-Europe Meeting 2002).

The 2002 Copenhagen ASEM summit (ASEM 4) declared that, in the short term, there would be full implementation of UN Security Council Resolution 1373 (2001) on combating terrorism in part through the prevention and suppression of its financing. In the medium term, ASEM partners declared they would work to implement the UN Security Council resolutions on counter-terrorism, as well as the FATF's Recommendations on Money Laundering (Dosch 2004: 114–15).

OECD INITIATIVES: THE FATF

The FATF was founded in 1990 following the 1989 G7 Paris summit.[8] Under the French presidency, FATF-I (1990) established three working groups dealing with money laundering statistics; legal matters; and administrative and financial cooperation. With backing from the UK, France, Switzerland and the US, FATF-I also adopted the original FRs, which Pieth and Aiolfi (2003: 360) describe as 'one of the most rigorous enforcement mechanisms known thus far in international law'. FATF-I expanded its initial membership to include Denmark, Finland, Greece, Hong Kong, Ireland, New Zealand, Norway, Portugal, Turkey and the Gulf Co-operation Council.[9] It is noteworthy that no Middle Eastern state is a member.

The Forty Recommendations

By 1996, more than 130 countries had adopted the 1990 FRs. Major revisions occurred both in 1996 – which sought to identify new money laundering techniques – and in 2003. The 2003 FRs included an expansion of due diligence processes for financial institutions; an extension of AML measures to designated non-financial businesses and professionals (for example, casinos, real estate agents, precious metals dealers, accountants, and lawyers); expansion of anti-money laundering requirements to include terrorist financing; and enhanced measures for high-risk customers and transactions.

Although the FRs are not legally binding, it is assumed that member countries will implement and adhere to them. However, states that adopt some or all of the Recommendations, but do not join the FATF, are targets for suspicion; adoption alone is not considered a commitment to combating money laundering. One reason for this is that non-FATF members do not undergo periodic mutual review by other FATF members; nor do they necessarily comply with the FATF's stringent internal evaluation process (Johnson and Lim 2002: 9). The review process comprises a range of surveys, including mutual review, a questionnaire, self-assessment, and a review by the FATF of all laws and regulations relating to AML activities. A draft report is prepared on the basis of this data, and the jurisdictions under review are granted the opportunity to comment on and discuss the draft prior to its submission to the FATF Plenary (Financial Action Task Force 2003b).

Between 1990 and 1995, the FATF released a number of Interpretative Notes to provide increased guidance on the FRs. In 1999, it sought to close the loophole in Recommendation 15, which did not oblige participating states to report suspicious transactions relating to tax matters. The FATF's Interpretative Note on Recommendation 15 stated that suspicious activities, including tax-related ones, should be reported, as money launderers may attempt to disguise a transaction as a tax matter.

The FATF categorises money laundering as a three-stage process:

1. *Placement* (placing illicit profits into the formal financial sector, or illegally transferring funds out of the country);
2. *Layering* (dividing or separating funds from their original source by employing a number of transactions – for example, through corporate vehicles established in off-shore financial centres).
3. *Integration* (placing laundered funds back into the formal economy) (Organisation for Economic Co-operation and Development 2001: 34).

The most effective source of AML and method of countering terrorist financing activities has been STR. STRs have led to successful prosecutions for fraud, illegal bookmaking, armed robbery and people trafficking. According to FATF member country reports, STRs are responsible for the initiation of between 90 and 100 per cent of all AML cases. A number of FATF member states have also implemented stringent AML regimes. The UK's Money Laundering Regulations (MLRs) (2001) give the Financial Services Authority (FSA) express powers to monitor compliance. In 2003, the FSA meted out several million pounds in fines on financial institutions, including to the Bank of Scotland and Abbey National, for regulatory failures and incomplete book-keeping. Consequently, financial institutions in Britain risk significant penalties if they fail to take the MLRs seriously (Dewhirst 2004).

The Eight Special Recommendations (ESRs)

The USA and UK moved quickly following the World Trade Center attacks to convene an extraordinary FATF plenary, which was held in October 2001. Their objective was to ensure that the crackdown on terrorist financing was implemented worldwide, not merely amongst the FATF's relatively small membership. The ESRs, adopted at the October meeting (see below), comprise significant addenda to the FRs, and aim to deny terrorist organisations access to the international financial system. The French government had strongly supported more rapid and widespread implementation of on-shore and off-shore financial regulation prior to 9/11, but the US had resisted increased monitoring of off-shore financial activities. Following the attacks, the US government supported the FATF's initiatives, particularly as the group extended its activities beyond the monitoring of money laundering to combating terrorist financing (Davison 2004: 73). FATF members agreed to implement the ESRs by June 2002, and the FATF is monitoring non-member states that either do not adopt the ESRs or else implement them inadequately. The FATF has also set a minimum standards requirement, in recognition of differences among countries' legal and financial systems (Salierno 2003: 16). The ESRs of 31 October 2001 related to the following (Financial Action Task Force 2001):

1. Ratification and implementation of UN instruments

2. Criminalisation of the financing of terrorism and associated money laundering
3. Freezing and confiscating of terrorist assets
4. Reporting suspicious transactions related to terrorism
5. International cooperation
6. Alternative remittance
7. Wire transfers
8. Non-profit organisations.[10]

Non-Cooperative Countries or Territories

In February 2000, the FATF published a set of 25 criteria relating to NCCTs that specified rules, practices and derogations that undermined or obstructed international cooperation on AML activities. In order to avoid countermeasures, and to be removed from the NCCT list, states must introduce legislation that implements all 25 criteria. In order to review NCCT compliance, the 2000 Plenary meeting established four regional groups (the Americas; Asia-Pacific; Europe; and Africa/Middle East). The review process comprises a range of surveys, including mutual review, a questionnaire, self-assessment, and a review by the FATF of all laws and regulations relating to AML activities. A draft report is prepared on the basis of these data, and the jurisdictions under review are granted the opportunity to comment upon and discuss the draft prior to its submission to the FATF Plenary.

The FATF published its first NCCT report in 2000, blacklisting 15 countries, including Russia and Liechtenstein (Johnson 2003: 40). In June 2001, two more European countries were added: Hungary and Ukraine. Hungary was delisted in June 2002, while FATF monitoring in June and October 2002 deemed Ukraine's progress inadequate. Following an 'inadequate progress' report in June 2001, Russia was deemed to have improved twelve months later and was delisted in October 2002; its progress was rated sufficiently highly for it to be admitted as a full member of the FATF in June 2003. Liechtenstein implemented FATF recommendations satisfactorily within one year and was delisted in June 2001. Liechtenstein and Hungary had strong incentives to achieve a FATF compliance rating, albeit for different reasons. Liechtenstein is a member of both the European Free Trade Association (EFTA) and the European Economic Area (EEA); the latter agreement compels member states to introduce into national law all Directives dealing with the EU Internal Market, which includes the three Money Laundering Directives and both Banking Directives. In Hungary's case, membership of the EU was at least partly at stake, leading to its compliance within twelve months of the FATF's blacklisting notification.

The FATF publishes a regularly-updated blacklist of jurisdictions that do not comply with the minimum standards established under the FRs and ESRs. STRs are required of all financial organisations in all FATF member countries. Under the FATF requirements, member countries' firms are obliged to report all transactions with either individuals or entities domiciled in FATF-blacklisted jurisdictions (Wright 2003: 367). Some states that initially made slow or inadequate progress on the FRs were subsequently removed from the blacklist. These included Hungary, Israel, the Marshall Islands, Nigeria and Russia. Following reviews, the FATF removed the Cook Islands, Indonesia and the Philippines from the NCCT list in February 2005. As of February 2005, only Myanmar, Nauru and Nigeria remained on the list, and countermeasures had been removed against even these states, due to the level of AML progress made.

The FATF has been the subject of criticism for focusing more intently on illicit off-shore activities in NCCTs than upon activities within its own members' jurisdictions. Banks in FATF member countries, including the UK, USA, Switzerland and Luxembourg, had experienced embarrassing reporting failures, particularly among the private banking sector (Pieth and Aiolfi 2003: 360). The latter undertook action itself, via the Basel Committee of Banking Supervisors, under the auspices of the Bank for International Settlements (BIS) and the G-20. The Committee produced the 12-member Wolfsberg Group in 1999, which agreed to exchange information on their internal AML rules. Directly following the 9/11 attacks, Wolfsberg banks investigated suspicious transactions, although the majority of payments in terrorist-related activities fall within the purview of retail banks (Pieth and Aiolfi 2003: 364).

Informal Channels of Finance

More recently, the FATF has increased its focus on informal financial flows, which have grown exponentially, as least partly as a consequence of the closing of loopholes in the formal financial sector. Alternative remittance systems, such as the widely-used *hawala* process, as well as cash couriers and so-called non-profit organisations – which are often established in certain jurisdictions with the express purpose of cleaning dirty money – have been employed by Al Qaeda to move funds through the global financial system.[11] *Hawala* systems have proven difficult to penetrate in various Middle Eastern and South Asian countries, which make use of gold trading instead of currencies, often to launder money. FATF members, such as Australia and Italy, have implemented legislation specifically aimed at dealing with gold money laundering in order to combat this problem (Financial Action Task Force 1998). One of the FATF's objectives has been to subject the informal, largely unregulated financial sector to the same types of restrictions and regulations as the formal bank and non-bank financial sector (O'Hara 2004: 17). However, this has proven to be an exceptionally difficult task. For example, *hawala* and cash-courier businesses are frequently operated by non-financial enterprises, which rely heavily upon transnational networks of personal or familial contacts, many of which are not readily identifiable by financial regulators. Moreover, as Jean-Louis Bruguière (2003) notes, terrorist groups increasingly employ 'micro-financing', or small-scale criminal activities, particularly credit card fraud, in combination with *hawala*, rendering transactions exceptionally difficult to trace.

Hawala financing circumvents the formal banking system and accounts for billions of dollars annually in international transactions. No actual cash may cross borders, and migrant workers sending money home employ this system daily (Looney 2002). Estimates suggest the *hawala* system transfers $US5 billion to Pakistan annually (almost 10 per cent of GDP), while Interpol estimates for 1998 suggest that the Indian economy holds around $US680 billion in *hawala* money (Baldauf 2002). Although *hawala* money senders may break many states' foreign transaction laws, small cash transfers (less than US$10,000) are entirely legitimate in many countries. However, the size and relative ease-of-use of the system means that it is readily open to exploitation for the purposes of terrorist financing. The lowest level of *hawala* regulation is in the Middle East and South Asia. However, even there a number of initiatives have emerged, such as Pakistan's Special Investigation Group, to monitor *hawala* transfers and investigate individuals and groups suspected of illicit financial transfers (Looney 2002).

The FATF has also sought to deny terrorists access to informal channels of finance. The ESRs give particular emphasis to alternative remittance systems and wire transfers. Even prior to 9/11, the broad adoption of the FRs by the IMF and World Bank in their 12 Key International Standards and Codes in 2000 means international organisations use a single set of standards for national reviews. At the time of writing, the World Bank, IMF and FATF were collaborating on the worldwide implementation of the FRs and ESRs (Johnstone and Brown 2004). In addition, US bank regulators have since 2000 also integrated FATF guidelines into their operating manuals. The impact of the post-9/11 anti-terrorist financing regime has made its presence felt even in

China; bank regulators in the PRC are increasingly careful about complying with US Bank Secrecy Act disclosures (O'Hara 2004).

The Effectiveness of the FATF

The significance of FATF initiatives should not be overstated. First, self-assessment guidelines mean that there is excessive dependence upon reporting by national governments. Second, the FATF relies heavily on EU and CoE GRECO and MONEYVAL reports, as well as on the third-party resources of the IMF and World Bank (M2 Presswire 2004: 1). For example, implementation of FATF recommendations in the Philippines is monitored by the US State Department (Roncesvalles 2004: 1). Third, the FATF itself has a staff of only ten, and an annual budget of less than US$2 million. Fourth, the FATF has no power of enforcement. Critics such as Chavagneux (cited in Godoy 2004b: 1) argue that even the NCCT list is unrepresentative, and corrupted by political pressures applied to the FATF by EU states. With the exception of Russia, none of the FATF's 31 member-states has ever appeared on the NCCT list, despite allegations of dubious practices in Switzerland and Luxembourg. For instance, Luxembourg's lax financial sector supervision and tradition of bank confidentiality placed it at the centre of the 1991 BCCI scandal.

Critics also claim that the FATF is highly selective about its targets. On the issue of bearer shares that could be utilised for money laundering purposes, outlined in the 2003 revisions to the FRs, Transparency International (TI) argues that of the three options available to the FATF, Recommendation 33 adopts the weakest measure; TI asserts that this demonstrates the FATF's inconsistency (Transparency International 2004a: 28). Chavagneux (cited in Godoy 2004b: 1) charges that France and the UK pressured the FATF to omit Monaco, and the Isle of Man and Jersey, respectively from the NCCT list. Certainly, it is true that no EU tax havens, such as the British Virgin Islands, were included among the NCCTs. In addition, the exclusion of French and British tax havens from the NCCT list, and the inclusion of tax shelters such as Panama and Nauru, is strongly suggestive of a strategy not only to implement AML initiatives, but also to eliminate global tax competition.

Furthermore, the effectiveness of AML measures – defined in terms of seizures – is questionable. In 2001, the FATF declared that only $US125 million in dirty money had been seized, which was a tiny fraction of the estimated $US1 trillion in laundered money transacted annually (Godoy, 2004b: 1).[12] In addition, the EU has attempted to dilute some of the FATF's recommendations, such as the requirement to attach AML information to all electronic transactions. The EU argues it comprises a single jurisdiction and that AML information is therefore only included in transfers to non-EU countries (*Compliance Reporter* 2003). In view of the belated detection of the Hamburg Al Qaeda cell in 2001, this ranks as a remarkable piece of complacency.[13]

The FATF has investigated countries such as Pakistan and Palestine that are alleged to be heavily involved in the financing of Al Qaeda and other terrorist groups. In 2004, Israeli authorities raided Palestinian banks, seizing millions of dollars in alleged terrorist funds. Elsewhere in the Middle East, somewhat belatedly, the FATF undertook a survey of financial practices in Saudi Arabia during 2004 (Godoy 2004a: 1). Although Saudi Arabia was declared clean by the FATF (Info-Prod Research 2004: 1), the inability of the FATF to undertake wide-ranging investigations of states' financial systems suggests that countries can present Potemkin villages that may conceal serious implementation deficits, even if the requisite national legislation is in place. As noted, the FATF relies heavily upon national self-assessments, reported government statistics and other official sources of information.[14]

Nevertheless, when the FATF demands compliance from NCCTs, most states have sought to accommodate its requests relatively promptly, due partly to the diminution of states' reputations as international financial centres, which has a demonstrably negative impact upon FDI (*Antara* 2003: 1). In Europe, applicants for membership or association agreements with the EU confront considerable obstacles unless they have implemented the FRs and ESRs, particularly the regulations concerning STRs. Moreover, significant policy outcomes – such as the ESRs – have resulted in bans on dealings with shell banks, which have no physical presence within the states in which they are regulated (*Compliance Reporter* 2003).

International cooperation and transparency is also of critical importance in conducting AML operations. For example, Aleksandr Vasilev of Russia's Federal Service for Financial Monitoring (Rosfinmonitoring) claims that there are few off-shore financial centres Rosfinmonitoring cannot access for information, as a result of cooperation between FIUs throughout most of the world. However, in its first two years of operation, although Rosfinmonitoring opened 250 files on money laundering, only 20 resulted in criminal proceedings and a mere two reached the courts (*Rossiiskaya Gazeta* 2004).[15] Although President Putin argues that the FATF and regional cooperation are instrumental in coordinating regional and international AML activities, Rosfinmonitoring argues that the FATF should go further. In 2004, Putin launched a Russian initiative to further international cooperation between law-enforcement agencies to combat illegal trade in weapons, drugs and other crime. This initiative found expression in the 2005 Russo-German agreement on AML, under which the two states' intelligence services will cooperate to counter money laundering (Deloitte and Touche 2004). Putin has also argued that the FATF should broaden its membership to encompass East and South Asia, transforming the FATF into a Eurasian group, in order to establish uniform international standards to counter criminals' income sources and terrorist financing (RIA News Agency 2004).

The Impact of FATF Blacklisting

In assessing the impact of the NCCT blacklist, the NCCTs may be divided into three groups of countries: delisted; delisted after 2 to 2½ years; and those which remained on the blacklist for more than 2½ years. Five states were removed from the blacklist within twelve months; these were the Bahamas, the Cayman Islands, Hungary, Liechtenstein and Panama. All implemented minimum standards in accordance with the FRs by June 2001. Seven countries were removed from the blacklist within 24–30 months, including Israel, Lebanon and Russia. A number of states in the third group remained on the blacklist as a consequence of insufficient progress or non-compliance. By October 2003, these were the Cook Islands, Egypt, Guatemala, Indonesia, the Marshall Islands, Myanmar, Nauru, Nigeria, the Philippines and Ukraine; by February 2006, however, only Myanmar and Nigeria remained on the NCCT list.

States from all three groups reacted very differently to the blacklist, from acceptance and rapid implementation of the FATF's FRs to denial, or even to unwillingness to concede the FATF's legitimacy. Yet in virtually all cases, there have been efforts to reform or restructure the financial system. Again, in virtually all cases, blacklisted states experienced or anticipated downturns in banking activity due to blacklisting. Indonesia, for example, argues that blacklisting has decreased investor confidence. Greater regulation has also led to capital flight. In response to the latter, Indonesia began a shift back towards a more regulated financial system, albeit unwillingly.[16] It remained blacklisted for almost 3½ years, due to insufficient progress.

Conversely, Liechtenstein acknowledged it had problems and sought to implement the FRs fully. It accepted that banking business would decline by putting AML initiatives in place, but chose to trade this off against a clean banking image. Liechtenstein remains a member of MONEYVAL. Hungary also accepted the FATF report, although it argued that the FATF had not taken sufficient account of the fact that Budapest had already committed to, or had prepared to enact, legislation that would place it in accordance with the FRs. Hungary is also a member of MONEYVAL.

There is a limited amount of empirical evidence linking AML regime-compliance with reduced incidence of money laundering. Masciandaro's studies of Italy (1995, 1999; Masciandaro and Filotto 2001) found that there is a strong relationship between banks and money-laundering activities where there is a well-developed illegal market. Despite Italy's full compliance with the FATF's recommendations, including the introduction of an anti-money laundering law in 1994 and implementation of the EU's Money Laundering Directive, the use of the Italian banking system as a conduit for illicit funds is extensive, exemplified by the high level of bank deposits originating from the informal economy. Johnson and Lim's (2002: 9) findings provide preliminary confirmation of a number of Masciandaro's hypotheses. They find that although there is a weaker bank/money laundering relationship in FATF member countries than elsewhere, this is not a universal pattern; there are in fact stronger bank/money laundering relationships in certain states that have implemented FATF recommendations, including Germany, Italy and Singapore. Nevertheless, there is a much more consistent pattern of the strength of this relationship in non-FATF states, such as South Korea.

In summary, the 'name and shame' approach of the blacklist, together with FATF monitoring, has apparently produced at least minimum compliance among NCCTs. Fear of loss of business, OECD sanctions or – in certain cases – US-threatened sanctions, has forced NCCTs to initiate at least some regulatory reform, resulting in tighter global AML measures.

CONCLUSIONS

September 11 brought a new urgency and dynamism to countering terrorist finance and AML in Europe, exemplified by the ESRs and the Third Money Laundering Directive. European organisations have embarked upon an ambitious, essentially normative project designed to introduce minimum standards to combat money laundering, terrorist finance and a burgeoning informal economy. That they have achieved this without widespread resort to financial or economic sanctions suggests that, at the macro level, 'soft-law' regimes can achieve significant regulatory outcomes, even in non-member jurisdictions. The FATF has become increasingly effective as an international standards-setting organisation. By publishing the 2000 NCCT blacklist – a list that is constantly under review – the FATF publicly questioned the legitimacy of certain states to operate as financial centres (Johnson 2003: 40). Although some OECD members, including Australia with the Financial Transaction Report Act 1988,[17] had unilaterally implemented AML legislation prior to the FATF's establishment, there was little incentive for states to formulate or implement AML initiatives. Blacklisting has to some extent forced states to address systemic problems.

The inability – or unwillingness – of states to fight corruption and money laundering can also have a direct impact upon their relationship with and, in some cases, membership of, the EU. This was the case with the inclusion of Liechtenstein and Hungary among the NCCTs. Their accession to the EEA and EU, respectively, had a significant impact upon the rapidity with which they sought to address FATF criticisms. Equally, European anti-corruption initiatives also affect non-member countries. In 1998, the EU rejected Ukraine's application for Associate membership, based among other things on its poor anti-corruption record (Andersen and Feuell 1999: 31). As an NCCT, Ukraine was forced to take AML measures seriously, which resulted in its delisting in February 2004 (Speer 2004: 390).

However, at the micro level, AML measures in themselves provide an unsatisfactory method of combating terrorist financing. The fact that the 9/11 hijackers utilised the formal US banking system, using a system of wire transfers, or merely bringing cash into the country, demonstrates that 'clean' money itself can be, and is, employed for the purposes of terrorism. As Cassella (2003) notes, this introduces the problem of 'reverse money laundering'. Moreover, the costs of implementing AML are spiralling. According to a 2004 KPMG report, bank AML costs rose 61 per cent 2002 through 2004, while transaction monitoring activity will be the main area of bank AML expenditure over the next triennium. Some banks surveyed also found that computer training of staff in STR and KYC – utilised by two-thirds of respondents – was effective in only 22 per cent of cases.[18] Consequently, the Third Money Laundering Directive and AML will require significant future investments by the EU financial sector, a cost which is likely to rise, as the majority of banks surveyed noted that current AML requirements would need to be improved significantly to combat money laundering effectively (KPMG 2004: 44).

A key achievement of European and international organisations is the coordination of national FIUs, which are statutorily empowered to receive and disseminate information to combat crimes such as money laundering, terrorist financing, and criminal utilisation of *hawala* systems. FATF member countries report that fraud and embezzlement are more common activities than money laundering, and FIUs have much greater access to diverse sources of information than do individual financial institutions. In many instances, the institution itself is the victim, and FIUs can therefore provide greater protection against risk, irrespective of whether the activity is criminal or terrorism-related. The BCCI case, for example, is a well-documented instance of what can occur when there is lax financial supervision and an absence of coordinated financial intelligence, while 9/11 demonstrated that the formal banking system could easily be employed by terrorists if suspicious transaction reporting is insufficiently rigorous. Social stability, financial institutions and national economic systems can be threatened by the transnational drug trade, money laundering, financial fraud, counterfeiting and corruption, and for these reasons it is clear why many European countries view organised crime as a threat to national security. The challenge for the CoE, the EU and the FATF is to ensure adequate supervision of the financial services sector, while also ensuring that financial institutions and markets throughout Europe are not subject to excessive regulation that imposes unreasonable burdens and costs upon the sector.

The EU itself scarcely comes to the table with clean hands. Systemic cronyism and fraud within the Commission, estimated at several billion Euros, was revealed in 1999. This resulted in the resignation of the Santer Commission and the establishment of OLAF, the EU's anti-fraud office, as well as a widening of the powers exercised by the EU Ombudsman's office. Moreover, there remain serious gaps in some EU jurisdictions. For example, France is not among the nine EU countries that have implemented the new European Arrest Warrant, a linchpin in the coordination of JHA, despite the French government's original sponsorship of the initiative in September 2001 (Davison 2004: 73).[19]

Some key issues remain unresolved. The focus of European organisations upon the legitimate banking system reveals a number of limitations. Although this constitutes a significant step, given the use of the formal financial system by criminal and terrorist organisations, it is difficult to combat the *hawala* system or the underground banking system's employment of either cash or in-kind transactions. For example, unless comparatively large sums (in excess of $US10,000) are deposited with the formal banking system, they are unlikely to be the subject of an STR. As a consequence, perhaps the next stage for European and other IGOs is to establish a system for the monitoring of informal transnational financial transfers. Although AML and counter-terrorist financing measures are far from complete, it appears reasonable to assume that terrorist organisations will be obliged to have a decreasing reliance upon formal financial systems (as the 9/11 attackers did), and a heavier dependence upon *hawala* transactions and other informal channels of finance.

NOTES

1. Author's calculations, based upon February 2005 exchange rates to take into account the significant fall in US dollar values since 2001.
2. The Republic of Macedonia has now submitted its accession instruments to GRECO.
3. At the time of writing, some provisions of the Second Money Laundering Directive had not been enacted in France, Greece and Sweden.
4. Promulgated in June 2003.
5. The European Bar Association argues that the proposed Third Directive discriminates against lawyers, as opposed to jewellers, whom the Association argues are more likely to be recipients of dirty money (see Council of the Bars and Law Societies of the European Union 2004).
6. Critics of the Third Money Laundering Directive argue that both legitimate and illegitimate capital is likely to be drawn to the 'unregulated' professions, at the expense of 'regulated' professions, such as lawyers. Such an outcome might also introduce competition amongst unregulated professions in market sectors such as consumer and business financial services.
7. Octopus II's recommendations have also had country-specific application. For example, Octopus II's report on Ukraine concluded that a law establishing the National Bureau of Investigations be drafted, and that amendments should be made to the Code of Criminal Procedure (see further Council of Europe 2000).
8. The FATF is not a permanent international organisation, although the 1998 FATF Ministerial agreed to extend its tenure to 2004. The FATF XV review (May 2004) approved a further mandate of eight years for the FATF (see Financial Action Task Force 2004).
9. China was admitted to observer status at the FATF in January 2005.
10. The FATF's ESR No. 8 notes that non-profit organisations are 'particularly vulnerable' to abuse. For example, the ESRs state that non-profit organisations may be employed as legitimate entities used to raise finances – or for the purpose of escaping asset-freezing measures. The Council on Foreign Relations' 2002 report on terrorist financing notes that terrorist groups have utilised charities for decades as fronts for shifting funds from one jurisdiction to another, of which IRA-organised charities in New York and Boston were merely the most prominent (Council on Foreign Relations 2002: 9–10).
11. *Hawala* is an ancient underground banking system. It is rooted in family businesses, which have often operated as hawaladars for generations. The system is based upon trust and ethnic or familial ties, which allow debts to be carried for extensive periods. Thus, cash does not necessarily need to cross borders. Moreover, in the Middle East and South Asia, the cash economy is much more prevalent than in Europe or the US, so that hawaladars can avoid official scrutiny or regulation. See further Council on Foreign Relations (2002).
12. British Chancellor Gordon Brown noted in July 2005 that £345,000 in funds in 100 bank accounts, allegedly from criminal sources, had been frozen as a result of British regulatory and

police inquiries. By contrast, US regulators and law-enforcement agencies had frozen over $US300 million in bank accounts by July 2005. See British Broadcasting Corporation (2005a).

13. The criminal financing of Al Qaeda cells in Europe included drug trafficking in Frankfurt, and arms, explosives and chemical weapons trafficking in Milan. The Hamburg cell did engage in criminal activities, and Hamburg was also used as a base for wire transfers and ATM fund transfers to the 9/11 hijackers.

14. Problems concerning accuracy of statistical data also arose in the EU during the 1990s, when it ceased collecting data on the value of traded goods at customs checkpoints, and switched to a business reporting system as a means of data-gathering in order to estimate intra-EU trade volumes. The EU argues that this results in quantitative data that more accurately and reliably reflect the value of intra-EU traded goods. However, some critics have argued that this is an exceedingly dubious means of measurement (see Davison 2000).

15. There have been calls for Rosfinmonitoring to be endowed with increased powers, and it may also be transformed, ultimately, into a law-enforcement agency. However, critics of the expansion of Rosfinmonitoring's powers point to its lack of personnel and technical resources. Critics argue that the successful implementation of AML strategies require significant resources, which are available to the Interior Ministry, for example (see *Rossiiskaya Gazeta* 2004).

16. Indonesia undertook major financial sector deregulation programs during 1983 and 1988, and again – under IMF supervision – following the 1997 Asian economic crisis.

17. Amended 1997.

18. This survey covered more than 200 banks based in Western Europe, Africa, North America, the Middle East, Latin America, Russia and the Asia-Pacific.

19. Germany resisted implementation of the European Arrest Warrant until July 2005. However, there are caveats to the application of the Warrant in Germany, as the Constitutional Court has ruled its extradition provisions unconstitutional (British Broadcasting Corporation 2005b).

5. The Corruption–Organised Crime Nexus in Central and Eastern Europe

Leslie Holmes[1]

The collapse of communist power at the end of the 1980s and beginning of the 1990s led many to assume that the formerly communist states of Central and Eastern Europe (hereafter CEE) would, with a little assistance, soon make the transition from a communist planned and state-owned economy with a *de facto* one-party political system to a marketised and largely privatised economy with a democratic political system.[2] A decade and a half later, it had become clear that there was a great deal of naïveté in such assumptions. Although eight of these countries were eventually – in May 2004 – admitted to the European Union (EU), and in this sense could be argued to have been accepted as 'normal' European states, it is important to be aware that the EU even as it existed until May 2004 contained a wide variety of states. In terms of corruption, for instance, it included several of what, according to perception surveys, appeared to be the world's least corrupt states (notably Denmark, Finland and Sweden), and some whose reputation for corruption was among the worst in Europe (Italy, Greece). It was thus far from clear that merely being admitted to the EU would substantially improve the corruption situation in the new member states.

As with the 'old' (that is pre-May 2004) EU countries, perception indices suggested that the corruption situation varied markedly across the CEE states. While the differences were most marked between some of the Central European states (least corrupt) and CIS states (most corrupt), there were substantial differences even among the new EU member states. Thus Estonia and Slovenia consistently emerged in perception indices as far less corrupt than countries such as Latvia, Poland and Slovakia.

Moreover, it appeared that some CEE states had a far more serious problem with organised crime than did others. One such was Russia. While it is impossible to measure either the scale or the economic impact of organised crime with a high level of precision or certainty, it is interesting to note that even *Izvestiya*, which has a reputation for being less sensationalist than most of the Russian media, reported in January 1994 that Russian organised crime (the so-called Mafia) controlled some 70–80% of banking and private business in the country (Goldman 2003: 177). While this may well have been an exaggeration, criminality of this type and on this scale becomes a serious problem for other countries too when it spreads across borders.[3] Smuggling of various kinds is an obvious example of this.

Although the primary focus of this chapter is on corruption, organised crime, and the connections between them in CEE, it must be borne in mind that both can have connections to terrorism, and that the three are sometimes closely entwined. The clearest example of this is in Russia – especially vis-à-vis Chechnya, though there are other examples, as in the Russian Far East (see Holmes 2004). The chapter is subdivided into five parts. The first provides evidence of connections between organised crime and corruption, while the second considers the results of just a few of the numerous opinion and experiential surveys conducted in CEE relating to corruption and organised crime. The third part seeks to explain both phenomena, and the reasons why they so often appear to be linked. The fourth section outlines some of the principal methods used to combat both types of crime, and is followed by a concluding section that summarises and analyses over time changes. The basic argument is that there are many structural reasons for the symbiotic relationship between corruption and organised crime, but that it is possible to break the nexus and reduce the incidence of both criminal phenomena.

EVIDENCE OF COLLUSION BETWEEN CORRUPT OFFICIALS AND ORGANISED CRIME GANGS

While there is an abundance of empirical material on corruption in the CEE, and no shortage of it on organised crime, much of the so-called evidence of collusion is circumstantial – claims by analysts such as Voronin (1997: esp. 57–8) notwithstanding. But some proof does exist. Moreover, Rawlinson (1997: 29) makes a valid point when she argues that 'Organized crime ... needs to interact with the legitimate structures in order to expand its activities.' The issue is important, so that it is worth attempting to maximise our knowledge base, despite the fact that some of the data are clearly soft and questionable, and that it is sometimes necessary to use experience-based inference and even intuition. Here, examples both of proven collusion, and collusion for which the circumstantial evidence is strong, will be cited.

A case of corruption in the Bulgarian police force was reported in mid-1997, when two police officers were arrested for alleged involvement in people smuggling (*SWB/EE*, 3 July 1997). The so-called Vasi Iliev Security 2 group, based in the south-east of Bulgaria, was reported by Bulgarian authorities and crime experts to have collaborated both with local politicians and police officers during the 1990s; some of the latter have been directly involved in the gang's activities (United Nations Office on Drugs and Crime 2002: 111). More recently, a report produced by the Bulgarian Ministry of the Interior in April 2003 referred to connections between politicians and judges on the one hand, and suspicious businesspeople believed to have links with organised crime gangs on the other. It named Minister of Finance Milen Velchev as an example of a senior politician suspected of involvement in a large-scale cigarette smuggling operation; the Minister resigned in August, but retracted this a fortnight later (*Sofia Echo*, 7 August 2003 online; *RFE/RL Newsline*, 8 August 2003; *EBBOY 2004*: 373).[4]

A major Polish scandal in recent years has been the 'Orlengate' corruption case. This has implicated various leading figures, including the then President's wife, Jolanta Kwaśniewska.[5] Of relevance here are the allegations concerning one ramification of this, the so-called fuel octopus scandal; there have been claims in the Polish media that this directly involved the former police chief of Silesia. According to some reports, police (regular and secret) and military officers, as well as senior politicians, have been involved with organised crime gangs – the so-called fuel mafia – in selling hundreds of thousands of tonnes of black market low-grade fuel similar to diesel oil not only to farmers, but also to the Polish military. A member of the Orlen Parliamentary Investigative Committee, Antoni Macierewicz, has claimed that this racket was not masterminded by organised crime gangs, but by parliamentarians from both chambers and members of the Polish secret services (all from Jones 2005).

There is further evidence of collusion between the Polish police and organised crime gangs. One example, which appears not to be well-documented but was related to the author during a June–July 2005 visit to Warsaw, relates to street prostitution. Particular stretches of highway in Poland are known to be pick-up areas for prostitutes; scantily clad women stand at fairly regular intervals along these highways offering sexual services (see Markiewicz 2000). Evidently, there are well-defined boundaries between different gangs' or single pimps' sections of such highways. In the early 2000s, it was allegedly common for such gangs to pay members of local police patrols approximately 100 złoty (c. US$35) per month for each woman on 'their' stretch of the highway. In return, the police officers would normally turn a blind eye to the (typically very obvious) prostitution. The Polish media have occasionally carried details of direct police involvement in gang-organised prostitution. Thus a 28 year–old officer from Katowice was reported to have linked up with a local gang and to have recruited teenage girls for prostitution for them, in return for free use of the gang's prostitutes (*Gazeta Wyborcza*, 24 March 2004).

According to Lindberg and Markovic (2000), Russian street prostitutes typically retain only 20% of the sums they charge; the remaining 80% is evenly divided between organised crime gangs and corrupt police officers. More generally relating to the improper linkages between state officials and criminals, the Russian police uncovered more than 700 cases linking corrupt bureaucrats with organised crime between 1995 and 1997 (Glinkina 1998: 17). A number of legal cases in the United States concerning questionable adoption of Russian orphans have implicated corrupt court and adoption officials in Russia, Romania, Ukraine and other post-communist states, who have allegedly falsified or turned a blind eye to incorrect paperwork regarding adoptions, in return for bribes (*Mosnews*, 18 April 2005, as reported in *Johnson's Russia List*, #9123, 18 April 2005).

The police and judiciary are not the only security or legal officers of the state who sometimes 'climb into bed' with organised crime. Another group that sometimes does – almost literally – is military officers involved in peacekeeping in war-torn parts of the post-communist world. Corrin (2005) has argued forcefully that the militarisation of parts of South-Eastern Europe has been a major factor in the marked increase in the number of women trafficked into places such as Kosova, as the demand for prostitutes from both military personnel and officials from international organisations has risen. This particular situation highlights two points. First, it indicates that the connections between officials and organised crime do not always have to be direct to have an impact on societies; market demand from the former can provide a stimulus and increased profit to the latter. Second, officials who have connections with organised crime are not invariably local; they can emanate from distant lands.

This point noted, the trafficking of persons – mostly women and children – into countries or regions that have recently experienced war is often directly facilitated by corrupt local officials, especially border guards, customs officials and police (Mavris 2002: 2; for details on human trafficking primarily from Russia and Ukraine to the US see Stoecker and Shelley 2005). Occasionally, such behaviour is in part a legacy of improper behaviour that was explicitly encouraged during a war period. Thus the Serbian Prosecutor-General admitted in 1996 that the authorities had actually encouraged various forms of economic crime during the war with Bosnia, as a way of circumventing international sanctions (*OMRI Daily Digest II,* 23 January 1996). While some border officials were complicit during the war in *de facto* permitting the smuggling of weapons, oil and other 'necessities' into Serbia, and drugs through it, the fact that they had become used to turning a blind eye to smuggling, often in return for bribes, makes it easier to understand how and why they continued such practices in peacetime. More recently, two senior judicial officials were arrested in Serbia in autumn 2005 for alleged links with organised crime (*Transitions Online,* 22 September 2005, visited September 2005). Next door, in Montenegro, President Milo Djukanović has been accused in recent years of corruption and collusion with organised crime, including in human trafficking and cigarette smuggling (Association of Young Journalists of Montenegro 2002: 25, 30; *EBBOY 2004*: 460). And the death of Olena Popik, a trafficked woman who had worked as a prostitute in Bosnia and Slovenia and who died of multiple illnesses, led to speculation in the Slovene press that senior officials (including politicians) who had used her services would have contracted various sexual diseases from her (*Slovenia Bulletin,* 27 November 2004). While it is not possible on the basis of available evidence to prove that senior officials did have illicit sex with this woman, it is highly probable that some politicians in CEE – as elsewhere – use prostitutes, and are thus at least indirectly contributing to the welfare and profits of organised crime. Along similar lines, the 'Ivana' case reported in the British media (*BBC News online,* 3 November 2004, visited February 2006) involved a trafficker who alleged that high level police and diplomatic officials in both Eastern and Western Europe were involved in 'one way or another' in various trafficking operations, including by accepting bribes not to blow the whistle on these activities.

The organised crime–corruption nexus is all too often fatal for those affected by it. Following the assassination of Prime Minister Zoran Djindjić in March 2003, the Serbian authorities rounded up thousands of people, including a large number of former government, military, judicial and police officials who allegedly had links with organised crime (*Worldpress* online, 8 April 2003, visited September 2005; *EBBOY 2004*: 459). The investigations into the assassination are said to have demonstrated an extensive connection between organised crime and corruption in Serbia (Stephens 2004).

It is not only war-torn parts of South Eastern Europe that have witnessed cooperation between corrupt officials and organised crime gangs. For instance, there have been numerous proven or alleged cases of such collusion in Albania (see Myrtaj 2003; Magistrali 2004: 74). In November 2002, the Albanian state prosecutor announced an investigation into allegations made by opposition parliamentarian Nikolle Lesi that prime minister Fatos Nano had been involved in arms smuggling to Kosovar Albanians in the late 1990s. The Albanian parliament finally voted in November 2004 not to launch a special inquiry into the matter, but doubts about the case remained (*BBC News* online, 23 November 2004, visited March 2005).

Finally, there is evidence of collusion even in what regularly emerge as the least corrupt post-communist states, and that this can sometimes be a major concern for other states. One Slovenian case was cited above. In addition, Slovenia is seen by some specialists as a European hub for human trafficking that is organised jointly by crime gangs, customs officers and police officers.[6] And an example from Estonia is of a senior military official who was accused in 1995 of having engaged in illegal arms deals with organised crime gangs (*Baltic Independent*, 17 November 1995).

Despite the fact that this chapter focuses on connections only between corruption and organised crime, one of the volume's overall objectives is to consider bilateral and trilateral relations between terrorism, organised crime and corruption. Given this, it is worth pointing out here that a UN analysis of 40 organised crime gangs, seven of them based in post-communist CEE states and operating in the late 1990s, reports that the 'Syzranskaya Grupirovka' in Russia both made use of corrupt officials and was in an 'apparent coalescence with an *armed political group* in Afghanistan' (emphasis added – LTH), from where it secured narcotics that it sold in Russia and Western Europe.[7] Another Russian group – identified only as 'Group 20', operating in the Northern Caucasus – was believed *not* to have made use of corrupt officials, but to have provided support to terrorist groups targeting Russia (United Nations Office on Drugs and Crime 2002: 107–8).

Many more examples of collusion from around the post-communist world could be cited. But the cases cited here, while not addressing the issue of the *scale* of such linkages, do at least prove the existence of a problem.

PUBLIC PERCEPTIONS, ATTITUDES AND BELIEFS

Selected official statistics on corruption and organised crime are published in several post-communist states. Most of these refer to investigations of alleged or suspected cases, prosecutions and convictions.[8] However, there are several reasons why such data are at best only a guideline, and almost certainly only the tip of the iceberg. First, some corrupt acts have no obvious victims to report them; the victim is often 'the state' and/or 'society' in a very abstract sense.[9] Second, even when corrupt and organised crime acts do have clear victims, the latter often have understandable reasons for not reporting the crime; where unwilling citizens are involved (for example in being 'required' to pay a bribe to an official), they are typically afraid to inform the authorities, since they themselves have also broken the law. Third, definitions of both corruption and organised crime are contested, both across countries, and even within countries. Finally, and again for a variety of reasons, state authorities often seek to record and report fewer crimes than they are actually aware of, especially if their record of solving cases is poor.

Given all these problems, analysts have devised alternative methods of assessing the scale and nature of corruption across polities. The most common method is surveying, and as awareness of corruption has grown in CEE, so too has the number of surveys. These can be classified under two broad headings – perception-based and experience-based. As can be inferred from these labels, the former are concerned with people's beliefs, opinions and attitudes about corruption in their society, whereas the latter focus on their actual experiences of it. In both cases, surveys can be further sub-divided in terms of *who* is surveyed; the most common groups are public officials, businesspeople and the general public, although there are also a number of surveys of journalists, country 'experts', politicians, and others.

The most widely-known and commonly cited perception index is that produced annually since 1995 by the Berlin-based international NGO Transparency International (TI), the Corruption Perceptions Index (CPI). It would be impossible in a paper of this scale to analyse the eleven indices that had appeared by the end of 2005 in terms of all 27 CEE countries, so that just a few key points will be highlighted.[10] First, the CPIs must be treated with caution, for various reasons. One is that the number of surveys used varies from year to year, so that it is in most cases better to cite a country's *score* on the 0–10 scale than its ranking. Another is that the methodology varies somewhat over time, so that extreme caution must be exercised in using the data on a time-series basis.[11] Despite these problems, there is sufficient homogeneity in the CPIs to permit cautious comparative and even over time analysis. Thus, Estonia and Slovenia have consistently emerged in recent years as the CEE states least prone to corruption (though still more corrupt than most West European states). At the other end of the spectrum, the most corrupt post-communist states appear to be many of those in Central Asia and the Caucasus; Ukraine also fares badly.

The TI CPI is based primarily on the perceptions of businesspeople, and is thus not necessarily representative of the views of the general public. Whilst there does not appear to be such a comprehensive mass-based survey as the TI CPI, there have been some genuinely comparative, cross-polity surveys. One of the most comprehensive was that produced by the Prague branch of GfK in 2001. This was based on ten states – nine post-communist ones, plus Austria. The survey (GfK 2001: 8) reveals that, averaging across the countries surveyed in terms of the perceived level of corruption in various state offices, the health services were considered the most corrupt, followed by – in descending order of corruptness – 'red tape' (offices and bureaux), courts of law, customs offices, the police, ministries, and the military.

It is very difficult to gauge the extent to which perception-based surveys reflect the *actual* corruption situation in any country, given the problematic nature of official (legal) statistics noted above (the latter issue is one major reason why perception-based surveys have become so popular). But the fact that nobody can be certain of the extent to which they reflect reality should not cause excessive concern, since perceptions are often at least as important in politics as 'reality'. Nevertheless, some analysts have sought to measure corruption using experiential surveys, in which respondents are asked about their own experiences of corruption, rather than their opinions about it. There are two particularly well-known sets of such surveys for CEE – those by a three-person team led by Prof. William Miller at the University of Glasgow, and those produced by the World Bank since the late 1990s.

The 'Glasgow team' – Miller himself, plus Åse Grødeland and Tatyana Koshechkina – surveyed citizens in four CEE states (Bulgaria, Czechia, Hungary and Slovakia) in the 1990s. Among their numerous fascinating findings was that, while the percentage of citizens in 1997–98 who had in the previous 4–5 years been directly solicited for a bribe by public officials was *relatively* low – at 11% in Ukraine, 7% in Bulgaria, 4% in Slovakia and 2% in Czechia – these figures rose dramatically if citizens were asked if they believed that an official, while not directly demanding a bribe, was expecting something. Thus the percentages answering affirmatively on this question shot up to 39% in Bulgaria, 44% in Czechia, 56% in Ukraine, and a staggering 64% in Slovakia (Miller *et al.* 1998: 14–16). Combining the two sets of figures, to produce an aggregate percentage of respondents who were either directly asked for a bribe or else believed that an official had been hinting that s/he would appreciate one, yields totals of 46% of both Bulgarians and Czechs, 67% of Ukrainians and 68% of Slovaks. Such data are disturbing.[12]

The World Bank has conducted a series of experiential surveys (as well as perception-based surveys). Probably the best known is the Business Environment and Enterprise Performance Surveys (BEEPS) that have so far been conducted three times; in 1999, 2002 and 2005. These surveyed enterprise managers in most CEE states, and sought to discover how often they had to pay bribes, and how much, in order to obtain permits, and so on from public officials. The findings are too numerous and complex to summarise here. But it is worth noting that there were some areas of corruption in which the situation appeared to have improved in the three-year period between the first two surveys (see Pradhan *et al.* 2000; Gray *et al.* 2004), and further still in 2005 (*BEEPS III.ppt*, 15 February 2006 at http://www1.worldbank.org, visited March 2006). Thus, while the improvements were usually modest, and even though the situation remained a serious concern regarding many aspects of the relationship between the private sector and the state, the authors of the analysis of the 2002 survey concluded that their results were 'mixed but somewhat encouraging' compared with 1999 (Gray *et al.* 2004: xii, 5, 45). This all said, it should also be noted that most CEE firms surveyed in 2002 believed that there was either a net benefit, or at most no net disadvantage, in paying bribes to state officials. Moreover, this applied not only at the level of administrative corruption (obtaining permits, and so on), but also with regard to political decision-makers (Gray *et al.* 2004: xv, 46–8) – so that 'state capture', or using corrupt methods to influence policies and legislation, appears to remain a serious problem in most CEE states. The 2005 results were in many ways more encouraging. Thus, in comparison with 2002, the frequency of bribes decreased in the new EU post-communist member states and the CIS – though it must be acknowledged that they increased in the South East European (sometimes called Balkan) states (*BEEPS III.ppt*, Slide 9). Moreover, corruption was perceived to be less of a problem for enterprises in *all* regions, while the percentage of revenues spent on bribes had declined in all regions too (*BEEPS III.ppt*, Slides 9 and 10). However, these are aggregate findings. When they are disaggregated into types of state agency and activity, it emerges that some forms of corruption had increased between 2002 and 2005. This was true of the court system and bidding for government contracts, for example (*BEEPS III.ppt*, Slide 12).

Unfortunately, there have been far fewer surveys of attitudes towards, and experiences of, organised crime activity. But some data are available. Two of the most useful sets of sources are the International Crime Victim Surveys (ICVS) and the International Crime Business Survey (ICBS) and its predecessor, the International Commercial Crime Survey (ICCS). The ICVS have been running since 1989; at the time of writing, four had been completed and a fifth was in preparation. The first ICCS was carried out in 1994 (see van Dijk and Terlouw 1996), while the ICBS dates only from 2000;[13] the ICBS is particularly germane here, since it was conducted in the capitals of nine CEE states (Albania, Belarus, Bulgaria, Croatia, Hungary, Lithuania, Romania, Russia and Ukraine).

A number of findings from the 2000 ICBS are of significance to this analysis. First, some 9% of businesses surveyed – which were overwhelmingly relatively small enterprises – had experienced intimidation and/or extortion during 1999; the figure reached a scary 29% in the Belarusian capital. Violent threats, in the form of weapons being used, featured in 9% of these cases. But interestingly, it was the view of an overwhelming majority of respondents that *international* organised crime groups were *not* involved in this intimidation or extortion; rather, it was local (domestic) groups. Similarly, some 8% of these CEE businesses (a staggering one third in Minsk) had been coerced into paying protection money during 1999, of which only 8% believed that international gangs had been involved. In the case of both types of crime, some 70% of respondents did not report the crimes to the police. However, and of direct relevance to this study, this was mostly not out of fear that the police might be colluding with the criminals. Rather, victims lacked confidence in the capacity or willingness of the police to do anything, fear of reprisals from the gangs, and other reasons.[14] Given these data, it might appear that the police in CEE are treated merely as incompetent in one way or another, rather than actually involved in criminal activity themselves. It is therefore important to note that, when asked for their reasons for being dissatisfied with the police, the number one reason cited by businesses in the 2000 ICBS was a belief that the police were corrupt (all from Alvazzi del Frate 2004: esp. 150–52, 156–7).

But it is also important to interrogate the finding that international organised crime is not seen by most CEE businesses as a major player in crime that directly involves those businesses. This is not necessarily surprising. Although there is ample evidence that international organised crime has sought to become more involved in legitimate or semi-legitimate business in recent years, the circumstantial evidence, when linked with the experiential data just cited, suggests that the core business of such conglomerates remains highly profitable *illegal* activities, such as the smuggling and trafficking of drugs, people and arms. Attempting to survey the victims of such activities is even more fraught with difficulties than surveying businesses about illegal and grey area activities. One example of how problematic this can be is provided by research conducted into human trafficking in Poland in the late 1990s. Male

researchers were sent to pick up highway prostitutes, whom they then paid –
but to answer a survey questionnaire, rather than for sex. The researchers were
disappointed by the results, since they discovered little about the women's
experiences using this method. But it should be fairly obvious that such a
method is unlikely to be productive. Many women – who were *de facto* slaves
to crime gangs or individual pimps – would have been at least apprehensive,
probably scared, about answering such sensitive questions to complete
strangers. The latter could be undercover police officers or, often worse,
associates of the pimps testing the women's loyalty.

There have been even fewer surveys of perceptions of and attitudes towards
the *collusion* between corrupt officials and organised crime gangs. One of the
most significant polls on organised crime is that conducted by the UNODC
that was published in the early 2000s. From our perspective, this generally
very useful analysis raises a number of problems. For instance, the study
surveyed primarily state authorities and 'experts' (mainly in universities and
research centres), not citizens (United Nations Office on Drugs and Crime
2002: 12), so that it does not, strictly speaking, tell us about public
perceptions. The extent of this particular problem can be exaggerated,
however; since the respondents based their answers primarily on published
reports, both official and in the media, it is reasonable to infer that there would
be *some* resonance between their perceptions and those of the public.

Another problem is that, of the 16 countries involved in the survey, only
two – Czechia and Russia – were post-communist. However, the survey did
incorporate findings from a similar UNICRI study to expand the database on
CEE states (United Nations Office on Drugs and Crime 2002: 11).
Unfortunately for our purposes, most of the findings in the UN analysis are
presented in aggregate form, and it is not possible to isolate the data on CEE
states to the extent one would wish. But summaries of each of the 40 organised
crime groups analysed are provided in Appendix B of the report, and it is
possible to use those to create a sub-grouping of the seven CEE gangs and
analyse them in isolation. Thus, despite the various problems, it *is* worth
trawling the report; given the general paucity of data on this topic, some of the
findings can and should be cited here.

One of the aggregated findings (that is based on *all* of the groups analysed,
not just those in CEE) in the 2002 report was that 'corruption was essential to
the primary activity of the criminal group' in almost half the cases (18 out of
40), and was occasionally used by a further 12 groups. Thus three-quarters of
all groups used corruption either as a key element or on a more infrequent
basis to pursue their aims. Furthermore, just over one half (21 out of 40) of the

groups were seen to have exerted political influence at either the local, regional or national level (United Nations Office on Drugs and Crime 2002: 25–6). Isolating the seven CEE crime gangs, it emerges that four had clearly interacted with corrupt officials, one had not, and the situation was unclear in the case of the remaining two. Similarly, four of the seven had clearly been able to exert political influence – though in all cases this was only at the local or regional level (United Nations Office on Drugs and Crime 2002: 107–13).

Turning now to consider *citizen* perceptions, a survey conducted in CEE by the author in mid-2000 produced some disturbing results. Similarly worded questionnaires in four post-communist states revealed that 53.7% of Poles, 54.3% of Bulgarians, 60.2% of Hungarians and a staggering 86.7% of Russians believed that there were either close or very close connections between corrupt officials and organised crime gangs.[15] While the accuracy of such perceptions cannot be determined, and there are no time-series data, they do paint a disturbing picture in terms of system legitimacy.

CAUSES

There are so many causes of corruption and organised crime in any society that it would be impossible to explore or even list them all in a chapter of this scale. Rather, the focus will be on three sets of explanations of particular relevance to post-communist states: the communist legacy; aspects of the multiple and simultaneous transition; and the international neo-liberal (or Washington Consensus) climate in which these transitions occurred. There will also be consideration of a fourth factor that is not peculiar to post-communist states, but that has become particularly salient in recent years, namely technological development.

Numerous aspects of the communist legacy help to explain corruption in the post-communist era. Several relate directly to the centrally-planned economy. Given the fairly rigid vertical organization of such economies, initiative and creative responsibility were not generally encouraged. This produced a situation in which many people had few reservations about simply helping themselves to state property, given so few outlets for private entrepreneurial activities, and there was a lowly developed sense of personal responsibility. The shortages of consumer goods – both durable and non-durable – in most communist states resulted in various coping mechanisms amongst citizens. Perhaps the best know example is of the culture of *blat* in Russian society (see Ledeneva 1998; Lovell *et al.*, 2000). This culture of coping in times of adversity, and of mutual assistance between friends, is compatible with the development of a culture of corruption.

The impact of the communist legacy on organised crime is in many ways less direct. Certainly there were organised crime gangs in the USSR, the so-called thieves in law (*vory v zakone*) being the most obvious example (see Gurov and Ryabinin 1991; Razinkin 1995). But from the 1980s (at the latest) on, and accelerating in the 1990s following the collapse of Soviet power, new groups emerged that rejected the approach of the thieves in law. For instance, many of the new gangs refused to abide by self-imposed codes of behaviour that were a feature of the thieves in law (and explains why the latter are so called). The often rather arbitrary approach of the new gangs is compatible with their more frequent use of violence, including against ordinary citizens.[16] In this, there is a resonance between the approaches of the new criminal organisations and most terrorist groups.

Another aspect of the communist legacy was the near breakdown of both legal and security systems. In part as a reaction to the more or less (depending on the country) totalitarian systems, new elites sought to distance themselves from the past in part by substantially reducing the state security services, especially the clandestine ones – the secret police. Not only did this mean that the state was spying less on its citizens, but also that large numbers of former secret police agents were retrenched. These unemployed former security officers often constituted an easy prey for criminal elements, who either used them as bodyguards or else enrolled them into gangs. Such former officers were highly trained in weapons-use and, in the chaos of early post-communism, were all too frequently able to access the weapons they had previously wielded on behalf of the state.

What *might* also be a law-related ramification of the rejection of the past – that is post-communist officials not wanting to appear to be as arbitrary and draconian as their communist predecessors – is the relatively mild sentences given to both corrupt officials and violent criminals. For example, in the period 1995–99, 151 people were found guilty of inducing or facilitating prostitution in Poland, of whom only *one* received a prison sentence of more than five years; 50 were imprisoned for periods of between two and five years, 47 were imprisoned for less than two years; and the others (approximately one third of the total) received even milder punishments (Markiewicz 2000). In many CEE states, a somewhat similar situation exists regarding officials found guilty of corruption. For example, only 18 out of 183 convicted for bribery in Hungary in 1997 were imprisoned; the others received either suspended prison sentences or were fined (Ministry of the Interior 2000: 33). Luneev (1997:

277–8) reports that, of the three main types of corruption case (embezzlement, bribery and abuse of office) registered in Russia during the 1990s, only one in eleven resulted in any form of conviction. Whether or not such mild punishments and low conviction rates do relate to the past,[17] the fact is that amoral or immoral rational individuals will often discover that a simple cost–benefit analysis or risk assessment will encourage them to engage in illegal and improper practices.

The transitions in post-communist states were necessarily more complex and more comprehensive than transitions in other parts of the world, such as Latin America and Southern Europe. Although the latter had to undergo radical political change following the collapse of various kinds of dictatorship, typically there already existed a privatised economy and a bourgeois class even under the old authoritarian systems. Moreover, citizens were mostly able to practise religion without major state interference, which meant that many people had an ethical code that could readily be transferred from the old system to the new. The post-communist states had not only to create new political systems, but also radically different economic systems. Since they had no bourgeoisies to speak of, it was unclear how the privatisation (more than marketisation, which was a simpler change) would occur. Since so many communist states began their transitions at more or less the same time, between 1989 and 1991, and since much of the West was in or close to recession at the time, the possibilities for privatising through foreign investment were severely limited. The problem was compounded by the fact that most new ownership laws – where there were any – were typically ambiguous in the early days of post-communism, which made many potential foreign investors apprehensive about investing. On the other side of the coin, several states – with Hungary being a notable exception – were initially reluctant to encourage much foreign investment anyway. Having just escaped the domination of the USSR, they were unwilling to subordinate themselves to other powerful foreign states. For various reasons, some were particularly anxious not to become dependent on German capital; Czechia exemplifies such an attitude. There was also a need for new ethical codes; while religion provided this for some, many other post-communist citizens were unable to relate to the church.

The near-absence of indigenous bourgeoisies and limited foreign investment are major factors explaining how and why corruption became such a problem in so many CEE countries. Some post-communist leaders were surprisingly frank in acknowledging that they basically did not care about the origins of investment funds, as long as they were forthcoming. A prime example was Václav Klaus in Czechia, who, as prime minister in the mid 1990s, 'brushed aside such objections [that 'dirty money' was funding much of the Czech privatisation process – LTH], saying the origin of funds invested in the country's economic transformation was irrelevant, and that the only important matter was that the process begin quickly and not be delayed by such quibbles' (Kettle 1995: 39).

The fact that new elites were often more interested in benefiting from the confusion of early post-communism than in establishing effective democracy and the rule of law not only helps to explain why corruption increased, but also how and why organised crime could thrive. Many of those formally responsible for the operation of the state were more focused on maximising their own incomes and property than on carrying out their duties, which partly explains the initial weakness of so many post-communist states. In weak states, the law is poorly enforced. In such a situation, it is hardly surprising that organised crime flourished.

Turning to our third category of explanations, whilst most neo-liberals would baulk at the suggestion that their *Weltanschauung* had anything to do with communism, there are in fact some interesting parallels. One is that both neo-liberals and communists advocate – consciously or otherwise – a blurring of the boundary between the state and the economy. One ramification of this is a fuzzy division of labour between institutions, which in turn encourages both a reticence by individuals to accept responsibility, and a lack of appreciation of the meaning or implications of the concept of conflict of interest. Another similarity is the privileging of ends over means, and a consequent lack of respect for due process. All this is conducive to corruption, with its knock-on effects for organised crime.

A significant way in which neo-liberalism can impact upon corruption levels is in its devaluing of loyalty among the state's officers. Neo-liberals typically place a form of economic rationalism ahead of concepts such as social capital or the collective good, and officers of the state who have worked effectively, honestly and loyally for many years can suddenly discover they are being retrenched, as the state offloads functions onto the private sector. Neo-liberalism was spreading from the Anglophone world (especially the USA, UK, Australia and New Zealand) to continental Europe by the time of the anti-communist revolutions of 1989–91, and this impacted upon the general (international) ideological climate into which the post-communist states were born. Given this, the *gap* between the old (communist) system and the new (capitalist) was much larger than would have been the case had the countries exiting communism been transiting to a less radically different system, notably a social democratic arrangement with a well-developed welfare state. According to this argument – the *transition gap thesis* – levels of insecurity and alienation were higher among both officials and ordinary citizens than they would have been under different circumstances. Thus, had the anti-communist revolutions occurred when social democracy in continental Europe was at its zenith, the gap, and feelings of insecurity, in the transition states would have been smaller. *Ceteris paribus*, this may well have resulted in lower levels of corruption than existed in the 1990s.

However, there is a crucial point to bear in mind about the transition gap thesis. This is that well-functioning welfare democracy is only ever a realistic option for wealthy states.[18] Given the sorry state of the economy in *all* communist countries by the end of the 1980s, the social democratic option was simply not viable in early post-communism, even had the international ideological climate been more conducive to it. The *normative* antagonism here towards neo-liberalism does not prevent the recognition of certain harsh realities.

Neo-liberalism can also be seen to have impacted upon organised crime. In addition to rendering some officials more susceptible to approaches from gangsters (that is because of increasing insecurity, decreasing loyalty to the state, and relatively low levels of risk), one of the many ramifications of the Washington Consensus approach to economics and trade is that it encourages more porous borders. Within Europe, the clearest symbol of this has been the creation of the Schengen zone. First formally discussed by five of the original six members of the EC (Italy was not involved at that stage) in 1985, the Schengen Treaty eventually became effective in 1995, and made movement between the member countries much easier.[19] Admittedly, some aspects of the Schengen Treaty are specifically designed to *counter* transnational organised crime, in particular concerning drug-related crime. Thus there is supposed to be greater judicial and police cooperation and harmonisation. And, while movement *within* the Schengen member states has become much easier, entry *into* the Schengen zone has in various ways become more difficult, leading some to refer to 'Fortress Europe', and promoting a growth in people-smuggling. Nevertheless, the apparent continued growth of organised crime suggests that the counter-measures are proving to be less effective than they should be; ongoing tensions between notions of national sovereignty and the liberalisation of markets suggest that this growth could continue (though see below, on the ramifications of the 9/11 events).

Our final factor, technological development, is by no means peculiar to the post-communist world. But it would constitute a serious lacuna in the analysis were there to be no reference to the fact that the development of the internet, mobile telephone systems, bankomats, and other technologies since the early 1990s has opened up new channels and possibilities for transnational crime and corruption (Shelley 1998), just as it has for terrorism (Johnson 2005). For instance, there is considerable evidence that criminals in CEE and the CIS have over the past decade moved heavily into credit card fraud, made easier for them by the large-scale move to online banking and the substantial increase in the use of this form of payment (for details of a Bulgarian case see *Trud*, 24 November 2004).

MEASURES FOR CURBING CORRUPTION AND ORGANISED CRIME

Since both organised crime and corruption can be found in almost all societies, it would be naïve to suggest that they can be eradicated from CEE states. On the other hand, since these phenomena appear to be more salient in many post-communist states than in most West European countries (Italy is a notable exception), it is reasonable to suggest that they could be reduced to more manageable levels. A full exposition of the many ways in which different agencies and practices could play a role in reducing corruption and organised crime would require far more space than is available here, and only a highly selective approach is offered. Methods can be grouped under three broad headings – those used by individual states; those adopted by international organizations; and those available to civil society. Unfortunately, even these three classifications have to be analysed cursorily here; readers interested in a much fuller exposition should refer to other sources (for example L. Holmes 2006: 211–69).

One of the most common methods used by post-communist states has been anti-corruption campaigns. Several of these have been named after the Italian anti-corruption campaign of the early 1990s, 'Clean Hands'. Unfortunately, the evidence indicates that such campaigns are often not only ineffective, but may even be counter-productive. Unless the authorities can demonstrate real and fairly rapid successes with such campaigns, the public quickly becomes disillusioned with them, all too often seeing them as cynical exercises engaged in by elites who want to *appear* to be doing something about a problem which they are not serious about *actually* addressing. If the public believes that the elites are engaging in them essentially as a cover-up for those elites' own misdemeanours (including corruption), anti-corruption campaigns can even have a delegitimising effect.

Another common method is to establish new agencies specifically designed to target corruption and/or organised crime. One example was the establishment in 1991 of the Bulgarian National Service for Combating Organised Crime (NSCOC). Given the earlier reference to the new opportunities for criminals created by technological development, it is worth noting that the NSCOC recently added 'the detection and prevention of cyber crimes' to its list of primary objectives (www.mvr.bg).[20]

In countries in which corruption and involvement with criminal elements appear to be so widespread that it would be difficult to find an incorrupt group to combat these phenomena, it might be necessary to consider extreme measures such as amnesties. Clearly, such an approach is far from optimal, since ordinary citizens can feel that their own honesty – or lack of opportunities! – has counted for little, and that political elites and criminals are getting away with their questionable or clearly illegal profiteering. Hence, this method too can exert a delegitimising influence. But an important point needs to be borne in mind. This is that such systems are *already* experiencing serious problems of legitimation if corruption – particularly high level – and organised crime are salient features. If amnesties are effective, legitimacy will begin to increase. Certainly, a number of CEE states have either proposed or actually introduced amnesties concerning corruption or organised crime; they include Poland (1992), Romania (1997), Albania (1999), Russia (2000), Ukraine (2000) and Kazakhstan (2001).

Another radical approach that can be highly effective – particularly at levels below the political elite – is to use plants and sting operations to detect both corrupt officials and organised crime activities. Unfortunately, it appears that the communist legacy can interfere with such approaches in post-communist states. Thus many legislators and law-enforcement officers have serious reservations about using such techniques because they are reminiscent of the informer and undercover operations of the communist-era secret police agencies. For such post-communist officials, it would be anathema to resort to such measures, which they often perceive to be anti-democratic and at odds with their commitment to civil liberties. It will take time for a more nuanced culture to develop, in which evils are relativised and it is better understood that actual or potential victims should have at least as many rights as actual or suspected criminals.

At a less radical level, and as a longer term measure, it is vital for CEE and CIS states to work hard on developing a rule of law culture. Such a culture was not a feature of the communist era, and cannot be created overnight. But now that many of the laws relating to the multiple and simultaneous revolution have been passed, it is time to refine these, ensure the political independence of the judiciary, depoliticise police forces, and generally improve the level of institutionalisation of post-communist states. Only in this way will corruption become less of a systemic feature, and based more on individual cases. Reducing corruption should lead to a reduction in organised crime, as well as in the connections between both types of malfeasance.

It comes as a surprise to many to learn that, as pointed out in Chapter 1, it is only since the mid-1990s that international organisations have begun to treat corruption as a serious issue, and even more recently that the connections between corruption and organised crime have been explicitly recognised. The reasons for such late awareness were outlined in that earlier chapter, so that the focus here is on ways in which international organisations have identified and attempted to deal with corruption specifically in CEE states.

Most international organisations that have adopted guidelines and measures to combat corruption, including the OECD (see Organisation for Economic Co-operation and Development 1997) and the UN (see United Nations 2004), have done so on an essentially global basis. But there have been a number of programs and approaches tailor-made for the transition states of CEE. At a more general level, the EU produced a document in 1997 – *Agenda 2000* – that spelt out the conditions applicant states would have to meet if they were to be admitted to its ranks. In addition to the general document, the EU produced individual analyses of each applicant state, identifying specific problem areas to be addressed. The analyses were divided into three main sections, one of which was the political sphere. Whereas some variables – such as the treatment of minorities – could be found in several countries' analyses, only one was common to *every* CEE applicant state. That problem was corruption, and each CEE applicant state was required to tackle the problem before it could be admitted to the EU.

Together with the EU (via the PHARE program), the Council of Europe adopted the 'Octopus' program in 1996. This was targeted specifically at the post-communist states, and involved 16 countries. It ran for 18 months, following which the Council made specific recommendations for individual countries. Although the program was officially deemed a success, its work was considered still incomplete, so that a follow-up program – Octopus II – was launched in February 1999, and ran until December 2000. One of its primary objectives was to bring corruption and organised crime down to manageable levels specifically in those countries likely to be admitted to the EU in 2004.

While its successes were patchy (see Economic Crime Division 2002), its very existence testified to the commitment of major European organisations to fight corruption and organised crime in CEE.

Several CEE states have also collaborated closely with the USA's FBI. Offices of the FBI have been established in a number of capital cities (Almaty, Bucharest, Kiev, Moscow, Prague, Sofia, Tallinn, Tbilisi and Warsaw – listed on the FBI website), in many cases because the US has been concerned about the international impact of gangs based or operating in those countries. In other countries, domestic police forces have worked together with the FBI to target particular areas. For example, Latvian police and the FBI collaborated in the investigation into the August 2000 bombing of a popular department store in Riga (*Central Europe Review*, 2/29, 4 September 2000).

Many of the methods designed to combat corruption and organised crime are essentially reactive, and are used when the problem of these crimes has already emerged. But, as Williams and Godson (2002) have argued, another potentially powerful approach to countering them is to predict and anticipate the kinds of situations in which these anti-social activities are likely to arise, and take pre-emptive measures. Such prediction will often be based on previous experience, and constitutes a form of risk-assessment.

While it is in general desirable that as many agencies as possible, including international ones, become involved in the fight against corruption – and, often as a corollary, organised crime – it should be noted that there have been some powerful criticisms of such activity as a form of illegitimate interference and because of its ambiguity. For instance, it can be argued that the EU's conditionality vis-à-vis corruption was not taken as seriously by Brussels as it could have been. Support for such an argument is provided by Poland, which was admitted to the EU in May 2004, despite there being considerable evidence, and a widespread perception, that corruption rates had *increased* in the early 2000s. Conversely, Bulgaria appears to have made real progress since the end of the 1990s in curbing both corruption and organised crime, yet was not admitted to the EU in the 2004 enlargement. A number of writers from CEE itself (for example Cirtautas 2001; Sajó 2002, 2003) have criticised the often hypocritical position of the West on corruption in CEE states; while such arguments sometimes overstate the case, there is undoubtedly some validity to many of them.[21]

Criticisms of the West's methods and interference have sometimes also been directed towards the role played by civil society in fighting CEE corruption and organised crime. A major reason relates to the fact that many aspects of civil society involving self-initiated citizen action in the political sphere have not developed well in most CEE states (see Howard 2003). Partly to compensate for this inauspicious start to post-communist civil society and promote the latter's development, many Western states and organisations have been funding NGOs within CEE states. Several of these NGOs are concerned with fighting corruption and crime. Most do this largely through various forms of consciousness-raising. But critics such as Krastev (2004) argue that this can encourage NGOs in post-communist states to exaggerate the scale of these phenomena, since their funding and future largely depend on there being serious problems for them to tackle. Thus, the role, nature and success rate of these agencies is contested.

Another important component of civil society is the media. Many media, both printed and broadcast, have played a major role in highlighting the problems of corruption and organised crime in CEE states (see for example *Bulgarian Media on Corruption Weekly Review*, online; Kislinskaya 2000). But this role is not invariably positive. All too often, newspapers and other media make allegations without sufficient investigation; if their allegations are in fact groundless, citizens can form an impression that a situation is worse than it really is.

CONCLUSIONS

The connections, both proven and either alleged or inferred, between corruption and organised crime have been a serious problem in CEE since the collapse of communist power. The limited evidence available suggests that rates of both soared in the 1990s, but that they have either plateaued or even begun to decline in several states in the 2000s. Several factors help to explain this development.

First, privatisation processes have been more or less completed in many countries, reducing opportunities for privatisation-related crime. While this applies primarily to the opportunities for corruption, it needs to be remembered that improper privatisation deals have in the past often involved collusion between corrupt officials and 'businesspeople' for whom honesty and integrity are not major concerns.

Second, the economies of many states in the region have rebounded in recent years. As late as 1999, in only three CEE states – Poland, Slovakia and Slovenia – was the GDP anticipated to exceed that of 1989 (that is the last year of economic activity in the communist era – EBRD data, as published in *The Economist*, 24–30 April 1999: 112); by 2000, only five states (Albania,

Hungary, Poland, Slovakia, Slovenia) had surpassed their 1990 real GDP levels (Mitra and Selowsky 2002: 5). But as more countries have joined these ranks in the early 2000s, so what some have seen as the *need* for corruption among lower level state officials has declined. During the 1990s, after all, some state officials were either underpaid or, in extreme cases, not paid at all for months on end, so that obtaining extra income through illicit means was often perceived to be a survival mechanism.

Third, many states have stabilised in comparison with the 1990s. While the still highly volatile situation of political parties even in countries such as Poland means that it remains premature to describe most of these countries as consolidated democracies, several have largely caught up with the legislative lag that typified early post-communism. This means, *inter alia*, that there is less confusion about what are and are not crimes; corruption levels at least – organised crime rates less so – are sometimes related to the degree of ambiguity or visibility of legislation.

Related both to the last point and to the economic improvements is that many states have become stronger, and more consolidated as democracies, than they were in the 1990s. High levels of corruption are correlated *inter alia* with weak and less democratic states (Buscaglia and van Dijk 2003; Holmes 2005), so that strengthening states and consolidating democracy should improve the crime situation. Certainly, the domestic security and judicial agencies in many CEE states are now operating better than they were, and it should not be overlooked that they *are* scoring successes in their fight against crime. A recent example is that the Bulgarian police, working with their Turkish counterparts, were able to intercept a major consignment (267 kg) of amphetamine drugs in August 2005; these were being illegally transported from Bulgaria to Turkey by a drug-smuggling syndicate (*24 Chasa*, 21 August 2005). Bulgaria, Czechia and Slovenia also exemplify CEE states that, according to most of our subjective methods of measurement (for example the TI CPI), have become less corrupt in recent years. And the *perception* that crime is a major threat in society is declining in some CEE states, even where it is not clear that crime rates really are falling to any significant extent (for example in Poland – see Public Opinion Research Center CBOS 2005: 3–4).

Finally, CEE has not escaped the ripple effects of the 9/11 terrorist attacks. Thus, as in many Western states, political elites in several CEE countries have had to reassess their attitudes towards the balance between civil liberties and national security. This has led in some cases to a reconsideration of the 1990s attitudes – referred to above – towards undercover activity by state operatives. While such reassessments have occurred primarily because of concerns about terrorism, changing policies on citizens' privacy – for instance, in terms of telephone tapping or accessing information on bank accounts – have clear and tangible ramifications for the fight against corruption and organised crime. This is yet another way in which the linkages between terrorism, organised crime and corruption manifest themselves.

But much remains to be done. One of the most significant aspects of corruption and organised crime is that a state's inability to make inroads in combating them can be a major source of delegitimation. That such lack of success can be a serious political factor can be inferred from a 2005 Polish survey, which invited respondents to identify the biggest failures of Solidarity since 1989. Corruption was the second most frequently cited factor after unemployment, and was considered a worse problem than, for instance, poverty or healthcare. It can further be noted that 'the dishonesty of politicians' – which almost certainly overlaps with corruption – was seen as the fourth worst failing, and 'crime' (though not specifically organised crime) was ranked seventh (*Rzeczpospolita*, 16 August 2005). Given that transition states are generally less stable than established Western states, and that the rule of law culture – which can buttress a system in hard times – has not yet become deeply entrenched in such countries, official and organised crime greatly hinder the legitimation and hence consolidation process.

NOTES

1. I wish to thank the Australian Research Council (ARC) for the considerable financial assistance they have provided to me to research this topic (Award Nos. A79930728 and DP0558453). Thanks, too, to the Melbourne Research and Innovation Office at the University of Melbourne for a seeding grant in 2004 that enabled me to conduct initial research into the links between corruption and organised crime (with particular reference to people-smuggling) in Europe. Finally, particular thanks to my Polish and Bulgarian Research Assistants, Kasia Lach and Katia Malinova, for their diligence in finding material relevant to this chapter from Polish, Bulgarian and other CEE sources.
2. For the purposes of this chapter, CEE is understood very broadly, to include all the member-states of the Commonwealth of Independent States (CIS). This is geographically questionable, since some of the states are clearly located in Asia; but the practice has been adopted by the International Council for Central and East European Studies (ICCEES), and is followed here.
3. For an argument that crime figures have been artificially inflated in Russia, and suggestions why, see Bäckman (1998). However, Bäckman acknowledges a substantial rise in organised crime activity in Russia in the early-to-mid-1990s, and argues (p. 30) that, '. . . the threat of Russian crime is a European threat'.
4. The official reason for Velchev's resignation was disagreement with much of the rest of the government over economic policy. But Velchev is alleged also to have been concerned over

the claims made about him in connection with the so-called 'Yacht scandal'. Whereas this allegation related to organised crime and smuggling, another concerned more straightforward corruption relating to foreign companies holding Bulgarian bonds – see *Sofia Echo* online, 14 August 2003. It must be emphasised, however, that Velchev's involvement in any improper behaviour has not been proven, and the various rumours may be mere vicious gossip; but they could affect public perceptions and hence regime legitimacy, which is of particular concern in fledgling democracies and countries seeking EU membership.

5. At the time of writing, however, it appeared likely that the President's wife had not in fact done anything improper. Suspicions were sown originally when it was alleged that a charity foundation she headed – Porozumienie bez Barier (Understanding without Barriers) – had received a substantial donation from a businessman who was later called in for police questioning, and then released, in connection with the assassination of Polish national police commissioner Marek Papała. Leading Polish newspaper *Rzeczpospolita* (11 May 2005) published a photo of the first lady with the businessman at a formal function in Washington DC. But her foundation continued to deny the two had ever met. The evidence suggests to this analyst that the photo was of a very brief introduction at a reception, so that the first lady's claims not to have met him were in essence true. Ms Kwaśniewska agreed to be publicly interrogated about the affair; the interview was broadcast live on Polish television – for some six hours! – on 2 July 2005, and the first lady was highly persuasive that she had done nothing wrong.

6. This point was made to the author by two specialists at a conference held in Bologna, November 2004, specifically on people-smuggling and human trafficking. However, most maps of major smuggling and trafficking routes in Europe suggest that other parts of former Yugoslavia are more significant – see for example Center for the Study of Democracy (2002: 49–52); Hajdinjak (2002: 47–56). For an analysis of the differences between people smuggling and human trafficking see Iselin and Adams (2003).

7. Of the seven organised crime groups analysed in the UN study, four were based in Russia, and one each in Bulgaria, Lithuania and Ukraine. For those readers interested in the 'quasi-' post-communist state of China, the report also includes details on three Chinese gangs.

8. For example, the Bulgarian Prosecutor's Office worked on 1138 cases of suspected organised crime in the period January–November 2004, during which time 93 people were imprisoned for organised criminal activity (*Trud*, 24 November 2004). In the period January 2002 to October 2004, a total of 111 employees of the Bulgarian Ministry of the Interior alone were dismissed for corruption (official data from the Ministry, www.mvr.bg 29 October 2004, visited November 2005). According to the Deputy Director of the Warsaw Police Command's Central Bureau of Investigation, Tadeusz Kotuła, some 240 organised crime gangs were operating in Poland as of early 2000, approximately 70 of which were international (*Gazeta Wyborcza*, 15–16 April 2000: 2); the total number appears to have increased to more than 350 by early 2004, though the proportion of international gangs declined (to 62 – *Gazeta Wyborcza*, 9 February 2004: 6). For comparative overall crime statistics on CEE 1985–97 see Holmes 2001: 197.

9. However, it must be acknowledged that there is typically a substantial difference between the number of crimes – of all sorts – committed in any country and the number of convictions.

10. The TI CPIs can be found online; visit http://www.transparency.org/cpi/2005/cpi2005_ infocus.html and follow the links.

11. For far more detailed analyses of the potential hazards involved in using the CPIs see Sik (2002); Kaufmann *et al.* (2003: 32–9); Galtung (2006).

12. Miller *et al.* (2001) have produced a large number of articles based on their research and – probably as the best overview of their work – a book.

13. The 2000 ICBS questionnaire related to experiences in 1999.

14. For recent survey evidence on the reasons why Bulgarians often do not report crimes (of various kinds) to the police see Bezlov and Gounev (2005: 28–33).

15. The surveys were conducted by Vitosha Research in Bulgaria, TÁRKI in Hungary, CBOS in Poland, and VTsIOM in Russia; the number of valid responses (here, this includes the 'don't know' category) was 1870, 1526, 1066, and 1000 respectively.

16. It is not always sufficiently appreciated that much of organised crime's violence is directed against its own people, rather than the public; however, many ordinary citizens are directly affected. For Russian analyses – often sensationalist – of Russian organised crime see for example Gurov (1995); Modestov (1996); Razzakov (1997). A more sober – but less colourful – analysis is Frisby (1998). For a fascinating study of the symbolism and history of tattoos used by Russian criminals see Baldaev and Plutser-Sarno (2003).

17. Another possibility is that countries attempting to move towards a rule of law culture require more persuasive evidence of guilt than more authoritarian systems typically do. It is difficult – perhaps impossible – to disentangle motives. In the situation being considered here, for instance, do lower conviction rates in the post-communist era represent a new commitment to the rule of law, an attempt by post-communist authorities to appear very different from their communist predecessors, or merely indifference? Could it be a mixture of all of these motives? For our purposes, the answer is not important; the relevant point is that interest-maximising individuals perceive that risks are lower than in the past.

18. Though even the wealthy European states have in recent years had to attempt to cut back in an era of globalisation, declining birth rates, ever more sophisticated medical technology and greying populations.

19. Whereas most of the Schengen states are also EU member-states, some of the latter – notably the UK and Ireland – are not signatories to Schengen, while some non-EU countries (Norway, Iceland) are. It is acknowledged that movement across frontiers became easier for citizens anyway with the collapse of communist power (communist states were in general highly restrictive in terms of permitting citizens to travel abroad). Nevertheless, some boundaries have become even more porous as a direct result of the neo-liberal advocacy of maximally free movement of capital and labour, rendering it easier for criminals to move around many parts of Europe.

20. Another of the NSCOC's tasks is to combat 'terrorist activities' – so that it is an example of a CEE agency that explicitly recognises possible linkages between organised crime and terrorism. A related example, which links all three of the phenomena on which this book focuses, can be found in the Defence Strategy of Serbia and Montenegro, adopted in November 2004. That document, having argued that military 'challenges, risks and threats' have been reduced while non-military ones have grown, proceeds to identify the most likely non-military threats to security as 'terrorism, organized crime and corruption'. Although it does not directly link terrorism with the other two forms of criminality, it does explicitly refer to the 'interrelation' between organised crime and corruption (Kovac 2005: 8–9).

21. For a recent comparative analysis of the ambivalent attitudes of many political elites (especially in Australia, Italy, the USA and the USSR) towards combating corruption see Maor (2004).

6. All in the Dutch Construction Family: Cartel Building and Organised Crime

Petrus C. van Duyne and Maarten van Dijck

INTRODUCTION

The oft-repeated adage of open competition, the free market and analogous statements gives the impression that these refer to a kind of 'natural state' of trade and industry. As is the case with most moral adages, nothing is further from the truth. Psychologically, free markets and open competition, a kind of regulated 'commercial war of all against all', are perhaps quite unnatural. For humans, it appears to be more natural to strive to an absolute domination of one's entrepreneurial surroundings. However, few entrepreneurs are either strong or cunning enough to succeed in such an uphill struggle. Hence, the next natural tendency is cooperation intended to carve up the market and allot a part to each player. Indeed, rational entrepreneurs who know they cannot *de facto* monopolise the market through cut-throat competition will prefer to look for arrangements involving a common commercial shelter. Why should they engage in unpleasant commercial fights if they can agree to a mutual sharing of the profits? But such an arrangement implies agreeing on a commercial truce, stopping the fierce fight for prices and market share, and trading in peace. Of course, such an armistice is not intended as a prelude to a general long-term peace encompassing all combatants. Far from it: rather, while it can settle relations between those parties that have sufficient commercial weight and exclude others in the short to medium term, the 'market hostilities' can be resumed at any time. The partners in such a commercial production and price alliance form a cartel.

At present, the word cartel has a negative connotation, since it is associated with secret price manipulation, self-enrichment and unfair exclusion of other market players. In the end, consumers typically pay a higher price for a lower quality of goods and services than they would do under 'fair competition', for which reason cartels have been banned in the EU, while anti-cartel enforcement has been intensified (Evenett *et al.* 2001). Yet despite this negative image, private regulation of markets by means of agreements on prices or production does not *a priori* need to be considered as negative. It may guarantee a 'fair' minimum level of revenue for the entrepreneurs, while at the same time tempering volatile fluctuations in supply and prices. This provides a certain amount of protection, which may be beneficial to industrial sectors. To this end, industrial partners may agree on *vertical* agreements between the chains of production (from raw material to the retail market) or on *horizontal* agreements between enterprises at the same level of production (basic production, semi-manufacture, end product).

Historically, such protective private sector regulations have not always been unwelcome to government authorities, which typically also had an interest in fostering industrial peace. In fact, many industrialised countries stimulated and regulated cartels for decades (Barjot 1993; Quaedvlieg 2001). Accommodation by means of consultation may not have produced the theoretically perfect solution (that is free trade), but at least results that have had broad support from industrial sectors.

Despite such good intentions and the smoothing effect on industrial relations, many industrialised countries, including the US and the EU, have banned private agreements to regulate prices, volumes of products or access to markets. So-called good intentions often proved to be in the interests of neither consumers nor those enterprises that found themselves excluded from these opaque relationships. But since those entrepreneurs who benefit from such relationships see little evil in them, violations of cartel prohibitions are entirely predictable.

It is not easy to find a common denominator for the successful emergence of a cartel (Levenstein and Suslow 2004). Perhaps counter-intuitively, industrial sectors with a high degree of concentration appear to be less prone to cartel forming than sectors with low concentration. Trade or industry associations also appear to be a facilitating factor (Levenstein and Suslow 2004). In addition, a permissive legal environment is highly conducive to the emergence of cartels. This is certainly to be expected in a socio-economic landscape in which 'accommodation by consultation' is historically fostered by both private and public partners.

The Netherlands provide such a landscape in the form of the famous 'polder model', allegedly characterised by extensive consultations. In the Netherlands, modest cartel building was tolerated and sometimes officially encouraged for decades. After 1992, when it became illegal, this tradition did not change but simply went underground, and secret cartels continued to thrive. How serious are these prohibited cartels? How is this illegality organised, and can it be classified as organised crime, given its organised and conspiratorial mode of operating? And if the definition of organised crime also covers illegal cartel formation, why has this transgression remained outside the organised crime literature? This chapter will address these questions, based on evidence from the Dutch Parliamentary investigation of the scandal in the construction industry – the so-called building fraud.

Before this scandal emerged, there was little interest in this phenomenon, which continued virtually unopposed for years. However, a desperately goaded informant, together with a clumsily responding Public Prosecution Office, changed the perception of this situation dramatically: a nationwide cartel of construction firms appeared to be fleecing public funds to the tune of hundreds of millions of euros.

UPHEAVAL IN THE POLDER

The Building Scandal Erupts

In November 2001, the Dutch public was able to watch a most revealing television programme: a previous executive director of one of the largest construction companies, Mr Bos, revealed the so-called 'shadow bookkeeping' of his former employer. The bookkeeping, of which he showed a few pages, contained the secret dealings of his previous firm with many other firms. This shadow bookkeeping related to the mutual price rigging and division of the market of transport infrastructure in which virtually all the major construction firms in the Netherlands participated. It contained various 'IOU' statements: for example, firm A owed €20,000 to firms B and C because these allowed it the lowest subscription to a tender to construct a flyover or a road. The ex-director – Bos himself – had been heavily involved in this wheeling and dealing by his boss's corporation, on whose behalf he frequently corrupted civil servants in order to obtain building contracts. Now he had been sacked and was hawking these ledgers for financial gain.

In the latter undertaking, he was unsuccessful. His own boss, one of the main culprits – whose firm's name appeared frequently in the shadow bookkeeping – considered himself untouchable, and did not allow himself to be pressurised into paying for these ledgers. Subsequently, Mr Bos turned to the authorities, primarily the Competition Authority and the Public Prosecution

Office. He was bitterly disappointed: neither of these agencies showed much interest, let alone that they wanted to pay for this explosive information. In the end, exasperated, he went public, and a 50-minute television program was devoted to what came to be known as 'the building fraud'. The broadcast shocked the public on two major fronts. On the one hand, there was the staggering scale of the cartel scheme, in terms of both financial damage and the broad involvement of virtually the entire road-building branch. On the other hand, the program revealed the unprofessional, clumsy and offhand way in which the authorities appeared to have handled this most valuable information. In fact, despite being fully informed, they preferred to do nothing, and may have succeeded in maintaining their state of torpor had Mr Bos not gone public.

In short, a double scandal had been brought to light: on the one hand, widescale fraud and corruption, with allegedly hundreds of millions of euros' worth of damage and, on the other hand, the obviously incompetent law enforcement authorities, particularly the Public Prosecution Office. Questions were asked in Parliament, and pressure built up for a Parliamentary investigation. A Parliamentary Investigation Committee was duly established in February 2002 to examine the extent and nature of the 'building fraud', which concerned mainly public contracts for transport infrastructure: road, channels and other transport-related construction projects.[1]

The Myth of the 'Polder' Explanation

The Parliamentary Committee investigated the functioning of the construction branch, particularly in the public construction sector, as well as the social and economic backgrounds to the whole affair. The latter aspects are important because many exculpating arguments were supposed to derive from the characteristic Dutch consultative culture – the so-called 'polder model' referred to above.

It is generally assumed that this culture of consultation developed from the Middle Ages, when the Dutch started to wrest their lowlands from the water. In the developing polders,[2] the small communities had to consult with each other because of the common 'enemy': the water. No one in the polder communities, the water bordered districts, could avoid the regular deliberations about dikes and canals. This is claimed to be the basis of later forms of Dutch democratic government. Speculative statements were derived from this 'historic' assumption, such as 'consultation of the construction firms is part of their (Dutch polder) heritage'. In fact, these speculations about the legacy of historical cooperative forms of local government against the water are based on a grave misreading of Dutch history (Price 1994).

The romantic image of a people tenaciously fighting the water by consultation, consent and endless deliberation has little to do with the emergence of the form of government in the time of the Dutch Republic (1588–1795), which was no democracy at all. The elite of the Dutch Republic, the ruling regents, did not deliberate about canals and dikes in democratic polder societies. The Dutch Republic was based on towns represented in the States, the provinces. And in the towns, the framework of actual rule consisted of the interconnected wealthy merchant families. It was a network of regent families, held together by means of family contracts that arranged the sale of profitable jobs (Schutte 1988). The Dutch administrative model was born not out of a common fight against the water in the polder, but out of an elitist high-handed division of the spoils of sinecures among ruling families and factions.

Regarding the tendering processes, the building cartels are therefore neither a typical Dutch 'polder product' nor the outcome of a particular social and cultural determination shared by the players in this market. They are the outcome of a traditional social and economic market ordering, which grates inconveniently against the imposed formal ordering of free competition. Regarding the latter, the authorities have a responsibility concerning enforcement, with equally traditional traits. In the enforcement of economic law, it is not unusual to find a permissive regime with enforcement officers who do not feel they are dealing with 'crime'. Enforcement officers may also feel discouraged from pressing for prosecution because of the lenient sentences they expect to be handed down (Croall 1993). In the history of building fraud, the elements of traditional consultation and slack law enforcement fused. But how should this be interpreted from a penal law perspective? Did the tradition of consultation, which had gone underground, get out of hand, or was there a conspiracy that could be classified as 'organised crime'? What characteristics and labels best characterise the illegal conduct of the principal market players?

'ALL FOR THE COMMON INTEREST', AND STILL ILLEGAL

Traditionally, economic penal law faces the social problem of recognisability (Sutherland 1945; Levi 1980). The protection of the integrity of life, body and possessions against intruders is clear to everybody's image of law enforcement. However, the protection of economic and legal interests, like good faith or equity, remains in most cases abstract and 'bloodless', though the directly harmed victims will think otherwise (Shover *et al.* 1994). Concerning cartel forming, this has its historical background too. The historical guilds are a good example of authorities that regulated the economy in which the principles of equity and trust played an important and at that time very deeply internalised role. In their ideal form, the guilds strove to protect the recognised entrepreneurs (master artisans) by guaranteeing them a 'fair price' for their product by impeding competition. The customers were protected too by the strict control of prices and quality of the merchandise: they also had to trust that they were paying a 'fair price for a fair product'. To the city governments in which the guilds were represented, a strict enforcement of these economic laws was a serious matter. In their judgements, they were not affected by subtleties like 'labelling theory',[3] and they took severe measures in the protection of this economic order. Transgressors of economic regulations were harshly punished: fines, banishment, and forfeiture of all possessions were common, while some even found themselves being cooked in hot oil in the municipal cauldron.

While the need to protect trust in the economic order and in a fair distribution of scarce resources remained important, the unfolding of the young capitalism brought with it a new entrepreneurial dynamic of commerce. On the one hand, the capitalist evasion of the old order induced feelings of injustice, while on the other, it revealed a hesitant attitude on the part of law enforcement agencies regarding economic changes. Commercial interests began to override those of the guilds (Braudel 1982). What was still a 'fair' wage or a 'fair' market price in the era of developing early capitalism? Surveying such questions in a broader time span, it is striking how recognisable the 'old' issues and complaints are. These concerned the big players on the emerging West European capitalist markets, who succeeded in undermining the municipal cartels of the guilds through their international cartels. At that time, this also led to 'parliamentary investigations', as happened in Nürnberg (1522), in which the council committee remarked that, 'While petty robbers and thieves are punished severely, rich companies and their associates, who have done more injury to the common good than all highwaymen and petty thieves together, live in extravagant luxury' (Strieder 1967). This complaint, directed against the copper monopoly of the South German banker family Fugger, could not have been formulated in a more contemporary way. It reads like a Renaissance indictment against white-collar crime, and that without the aid of modern criminology.

The fact that this 500 years old indictment is so recognisable and worded in such a modern way indicates that, with regard to economic regulations, we continue to struggle with its penal law aspects. For example, what kinds of transgressions are to be labelled as 'criminal'? And is it appropriate to use this loaded label 'criminal' when it applies primarily to corporations (Geis and Dimento 1995)? This traditional uncertainty regarding economic delinquency has also played an important role in the emergence and evaluation of illegal cartel building in the construction branch.

Without rehearsing the development of economic penal law, a few words about the protection of the free market against cartel building are appropriate. A cartel is a market-regulating form of horizontal or vertical cooperation. Construction firms (in this scandal, mostly road building companies) can enter into agreements not only on prices and the allocation of projects (horizontal), but also on the delivery of essential raw materials such as sand and asphalt (vertical). As argued above, such agreements are not necessarily 'evil'. For centuries, in fact, the archetype of cartels, the guilds, provided European entrepreneurs and employees a decent, 'fair' income. However, this fixed economic order actually hampered the development of new production management. Countries such as England, in which the closed system of guilds was dismantled early on, took the lead in economic development in the 18th and 19th centuries compared with France or Germany, where the local authorities stuck to their old 'municipal cartels' (Dillard 1967). This did not conform with the capitalistic philosophy of a free market, as represented by the developing liberalism.

However, the so-called free market was an ideal that was never fully achieved, since there were many national interests to be protected, and cartels proved to a valuable mechanism (Quaedvlieg 2001). The free market has many uncertainties, depressions as well as booms, which entrepreneurs seek to reduce by narrowing the free market space. The worst depression was the major crisis in the 1930s following the Great Crash of October 1929 (see Galbraith 1961). Free but 'cut-throat' competition, with falling prices in a time of on-going depression, evoked in 1935 the return of the idea of market regulation in the Netherlands. Cartels to further the improvement of the Dutch economy were introduced. For their own good or for the common interest, companies could even be forced to cooperate with cartel agreements. These cartels were supervised by the authorities; in cases of abuse, they could declare a cartel (agreement) void (Quaedvlieg 2001).[4]

For more than 50 years, the Dutch authorities furthered cartel building. Particularly after the Second World War, trade and industry were organised in 'corporatist' entrepreneurial sectors. On the basis of 'good consultation', preferably informally, the interests of the participants were taken care of. Though informal 'good understanding' prevailed, the Law on Economic Crime contained a number of orders and prohibitions; but penal enforcement of this law hardly ever took place. Rather, the Ministry of Economic Affairs attempted to bring trespassers back on the right track by informal consultation and persuasion. The transfer of economic sinners to the police and Public Prosecutors did not fit into this approach. Those who promised to better their (economic) life could expect lenient treatment. Dutch economic law enforcement was characterized by widescale pampering (van Duyne 1988).

It is important to project the cartel maintenance against this general climate of economic law enforcement. Until the late 1970s, economic crime was hardly a political and social issue. This was not unique to the Netherlands: observations of permissive enforcement in other jurisdictions abound (Levi 1980, 1983). Even serious forms of economic crime, such as (organised) fraud, attracted little attention, even from the police and the Public Prosecution Office (van Duyne 1983; Sackers and Mevis 2000). Only after a few young public prosecutors repeatedly drew media attention to widespread tax and social security fraud (by employers and 'spongers') did fraud (against public funds) get onto the political agenda as a *criminal* law enforcement problem.

Social class characteristics could further explain political recognition of the problem. The phenomenon of illegal subcontracting by professional freebooters of the criminal labour market attracted broad media attention, not least because they withheld millions in social security contributions. But these crime-entrepreneurs were also from a different (lower) social class, and were considered big-time crooks, so that they 'deserved' a full penal law approach (Brants and Brants 1984). Despite this media attention and social labelling, accompanied by firm government statements, an anti-fraud policy concerning social security fraud (by employers as well as by employees) developed only slowly. It took six years to enact the law that made principals liable for the financial misconduct of their subcontractors (van Duyne 1988).[5] For a while, the anti-fraud policy was pursued more vigorously. But after 1985, this heightened law enforcement activity sunk silently down, like an artificially induced wave. The same applies to the intensification of environmental policy. In the 1980s, this was high on the political and law enforcement agenda; but following the prosecution of a few miscreants, the policy returned to the normal restraint. As before, this policy is characterised by giving warnings, toleration, administrative fines and an occasional real prosecution and trial.

But even then, the rhetoric of the criminal law is never stressed in relation to pollution offences (Richardson *et al.* 1983).

Against these backgrounds of officially encouraged cartel building and a general lack of interest in economic crime, the Parliamentary Committee should have had few grounds for demonstrating surprise about violations of the Law of Competition, or irritation about the very moderate penal law enforcement. This moderate enforcement did not change when the new cartel norms were handed down by Brussels in 1992 and were reluctantly accepted. Given the fact that the Dutch authorities were (erroneously) of the opinion that the cartel portfolio was well under control, it is understandable that they did not interpret the new EU norms in terms of criminal law. In addition, most of the criminal law enforcement energy was devoted at that time to 'real' organised crime, or to safety in the public domain. The result was that cartel violations were fully shifted to the field of *administrative* enforcement. This implied prohibitions, but not criminal offences. Expressing this another way, they were 'illegal, but not criminal'. This choice was clarified in the explanatory memorandum on the Law on Competition (Second Chamber, 1995/96, 24707, No. 3: 42), which deserves full quotation:

> In the Cabinet position, the criteria are also discussed to determine which legal norms are suitable for an administrative enforcement. The norms in this bill ... satisfy a number of such criteria, such as the *low normative loading*, the fact that violations do not cause harm to persons or goods, and far-reaching interventions like detention or other drastic measures are not required. [Despite the contra-indication concerning the complexity of the violations] it is acceptable to opt for enforcement by means of administrative fines .... In addition, the Law on Competition [would be] one of the many laws to be maintained by the criminal law organs. In relation to the limited processing capacities on the one hand, and the complexity of competition cases on the other, and the relatively minor disturbance that these infractions create, the Public Prosecution Office is likely to dismiss the case or to settle it out of court. (Italics added)

The wording of the justification of this choice reflects the sense of justice and the related 'sense of urgency' that could be found in broad circles concerning the (disguised) cartel building. It was perceived to be not really bad, and certainly not criminal. It is noteworthy that the memorandum makes no mention at all of the financial harm that cartel violations may inflict on society. Comparing the anti-fraud policy against criminal subcontractors on the 'black' labour market in the first half of the 1980s with this stance some fifteen years later, we observe a remarkable cooling of interest in the financial harm done to public funds. Perhaps the concern about the infringement of the public funds was at that time (partly) artificial and media driven. As soon as the media heat had passed, the level of concern about economic crime returned to its traditional level; a television broadcast was needed to raise it again.

In 1998, while international cartel enforcement received increased attention (Evenett *et al.* 2001), the Dutch decriminalized violation of the cartel prohibition by transferring it to the *administrative* Competition Law, with only administrative sanctions. Meanwhile the building sector community was widely engaged in a kind of collective economic 'shadow behaviour', though it was formally only 'administrative' misconduct. Nevertheless, it led to significant criminal follow-up offences that were required to cover up that misconduct. Could the authorities have foreseen this development?

Looking back again at the first phase of massive fraud in the construction sector by the aforementioned criminal subcontractors, one has to conclude that the competent ministries cannot be characterised as 'learning organisations'. Likewise, the massive violations at that time did not start in a criminal law setting, but with an *administrative* law to prevent the fiscal abuse of temporary workers. Subsequently, employment agents who could not obtain a licence devised a trick whereby they pretended to subcontract a work, while all they were really doing was loaning personnel to construction firms (van Duyne and Houtzager 2005). This constituted document fraud. This resulted in structural advantages for all parties involved: lower building costs, continuity and timely completions because of guaranteed staff, and additional income for the 'black' workers. Concerning cartel violations, the authorities could have identified similar structural circumstances stimulating widespread law breaking, starting again with an administrative law. A rational, 'learning' legislator could have learned from history that any (administrative) intervention in market relations increases not only predictable evasions, but also the likelihood of criminal follow-up activities. The only lesson from history that the minister of justice appears to have learned was that it is better not to entrust the public prosecutors with overly complicated economic cases. Though this proved to be a correct assessment of the general competence of the Public Prosecution Office, the related follow-up criminal acts would sooner or later impose themselves. As far as the Public Prosecution Office was concerned, that 'later' would rather be 'never'. The wish was not fulfilled.

FROM RATIONALISED 'SHADOW BEHAVIOUR' TO CRIMES

As indicated in the previous section, the evasion of the cartel prohibition became widespread. Both cultural and technical circumstances and features contributed to this development. As a cultural element, the Parliamentary Committee referred to the so-called 'freebooter mentality' of the builders, though it rated this element as less important than the corporate rationality and the shared conception of what was proper entrepreneurial conduct. As proper entrepreneurial conduct is largely determined by corporate rationality, there is some circularity in this justification.

Summarising the nature of the entrepreneurial rationality, the following elements are important (Meeuws and Schoorl 2002). The building activities are usually spread over a wide area, are labour intensive, and are sensitive to the nature and supply of material, particularly concerning the transport infrastructure. The production place is literally the building site, which makes the distances between the firm and the site's running costs significant, not only because of the distance between raw materials and components, but also because of the transport of workers. The execution of the construction requires scarce skilled workers, who cannot be dismissed at will when there is a discontinuity in the supply of work and re-hired as soon as new orders have been obtained. Moreover, some of the essential building materials, particularly for road construction, cannot be stored while waiting for new contracts: cement and asphalt will harden if not used in time. Unlike the situation in a goods production firm, builders cannot bridge slackness in trade by forming stock. In short, there are many technical, 'rational' reasons that stimulate law breaking, and since there are so many participants – all with similar 'technical reasons' – the law breaking becomes socially and economically systemic. Socially, it creates a work-related subculture with its own ideas of proper conduct (Coleman 1987).

A first brief consideration of the ways in which this collective deviant 'shadow behaviour' was rationalised evokes many *déjà vu* feelings because of the self-justifying bromides: there are no 'real' victims, or the victim (the government) is to be blamed itself, and everybody does it and (therefore) 'we did not know better'. It would be more satisfactory to admit that the European Commission imposed a norm nobody wanted – neither the Dutch government, nor the entrepreneurial community, and the builders least of all. Evasion did not lead to serious disapproval by the law enforcement agencies. Actually, the Cabinet and Parliament opted for transferring the enforcement to an administrative, non-penal law regime. Hence, everybody could maintain that this behaviour was 'illegal, but not criminal', like the price-rigging in the US electrical equipment industry (Conklin 1977; Geis 1978). This was no more than a shallow sophism: as with the illegal subcontractors, to cover the breaking of the administrative law, the culprits often had to commit other more serious criminal offences like fraud. As this had to be carried out collectively and systematically, the rationalising arguments acquire a really hollow appearance.

The transition from non-criminal violations of the cartel regulations to criminal offences appeared to be a consequential act born out of sheer necessity: the cartel participants did not *intend* to tamper with their books, but were sometimes technically forced to do so if their clearance system produced surpluses. To clarify this, we summarise a case described by the Parliamentary Committee (TK, 28244: 87).

The city of The Hague seeks a tender by private contract for a viaduct. In such a situation, a limited number of contractors is invited, let us say five: *A*, *B*, *C*, *D* and *E*. The contracting authority has made an estimate of the maximum costs involved: €5 million. An information day is announced, at which the contracting authority comments on the specifications tender, following which the five contractors (all present) can ask questions. By noon ten days later, the contractors must have submitted their price estimates, in closed envelopes. What happens after the information day? Building firm *A*, which is eager to secure the contract, contacts the other four invited builders for an informal preliminary consultation on the morning before the offers have to be submitted. During this consultation, *A* urges the other firms to concede the contract to him, in exchange for which he will later concede a future contract of the same magnitude to them (that is 25% of the contract sum to each). If *B*, *C*, *D* and *E* agree, then there is a market division based on a *turnover* list. Although this represents a transgression of the cartel regulations, the impropriety of this kind of tender-cartel is at least open to debate, since there is no inflation of the price.

Unfortunately, firm *A* meets opposition: the other four firms all want the contract too. Instead of departing and independently submitting their price estimates, they decide that each represented firm will write down on a piece of paper the price for which they would carry out the work, and agree that the lowest subscriber will secure the contract. The numbers mentioned on the notes give the following price picture: *A* wants to carry out the work for €4.7 million; *B* for €5 million; *C* for €4.9 million, *D* for €5 million and *E* for €4.8 million. All of them are at or slightly below the allowed maximum building costs. Thereupon they decide to increase the offers by €250,000 each, so that *A* is still under the maximum tender sum. If the city grants him the work, the conspirators can perceive their agreement as not harmful at all, even if the building price is higher than it would have been without this preliminary consultation. But the city is supposed to be ignorant.

The advantage granted to *A* is not an act of charity by his fellow builders. His colleagues want their share from his extra €250,000. According to 'good custom', each participant of the cartel receives an equal share, in this case €250,000 ÷ 5 = €50,000. However, *A* will not pay his partners the money at that time: that would be inefficient, since one of the others would gain an advantage the next time, in the sharing and distribution of which he has to participate too. Paying the debts in 'real time' would entail the risk of a constant flow of money not covered by invoices, or else to be covered by false invoices. Instead of taking this risk, mutual 'rights' or claims are tallied and cleared at the end of the year.[6] Such year-end settlements are not uncommon in cartel relationships, the art being to avoid creating documentary evidence in handling side payments (Marshall *et al.* 2003).

What does this clearing imply in terms of criminal law? This question is important because of potential document fraud. *A* will record his obligations to his partners *B–E*, who will also record their claims on *A*. To indicate that these registrations are not a part of the regular paperwork, they are denoted as 'extra-accountable', a euphemism for the aforementioned 'shadow bookkeeping'. More important is the question of whether this shadow bookkeeping consisted of false documents, such as false invoices. This is not the case: the shadow bookkeeping is a survey of mutual claims arising from the division of the market. If the market (the total of works) appeared at the end of the year to be equally divided, the claims are mutually cancelled, ending up as a zero-sum. In that case, the shadow bookkeeping of that year is only a historical document of the mutual claims. In the regular accounting of the firms, no false invoices would be adopted to veil hidden payments or revenues, since none exist. All the book-keeping entries are in agreement with real contracts.

It goes without saying that the world is more complicated than this simple example would suggest. The shadow bookkeeping of the informant Mr Bos reveals that about 600 colluding building firms participated, in changing compositions, in this preliminary consultation carousel. As this concerned only the province of North-Holland, and taking into account that this carousel was nationwide, it becomes obvious that a very complex and dense system of mutual claims developed, which had to be administrated and cleared in an orderly manner. Needless to say, a huge amount of money was involved, while the participants strove to avoid as much as possible direct payments that would have to have been covered by (false) invoices. To accomplish this complicated clearing task, regional 'settlement funds' were created. These professional accountancy units had to put all the little bits and pieces of the puzzle together such that all the claims and debts were cancelled and the year ended with an ideal zero-sum situation: there were to be no leftover claims.

Despite this professional clearance system, there were frequently unsettled claims at the end of the year. Some participants preferred to shift these to the following year, because such claims would constitute new 'building rights' in following contract rounds. If unsettled claims had to be paid, the forms of payment could range from the delivery *in natura* to settlements with false invoices. Where did the participants cross the dividing line between civil and criminal law? Let us consider various settlement methods:

- a neutral settlement in kind and without (false) invoices – such as the delivery of material to the amount of the claim or of labourers who remain in the service of the debtor firm;
- material is delivered with an invoice, but a discount is given, or the price is increased to the amount of the debt or the claim;
- invoices are made for the delivery of non-existing services or goods, such as the hire of a crane;
- cash payments are made without any invoice. This method is rarely used, as the major players in the building sector have only small cash flows. Large cash payments require withdrawals, which show up in bank accounts.

It is interesting to observe that so many illegal acts could be settled without technically committing fraud. Only the third method implies actual fraud. Delivering sand or asphalt free is not *per se* fraudulent, because there are no papers and no payment, while delivering it at a reduced price with an invoice does not constitute fraud either: parties are free to determine prices, the amount of goods delivered is quoted exactly on the receipts, the bank transfers are duly entered in the books, and the price includes VAT, which is regularly paid. In the perception of the builders, there was no crime involved in these forms of settling debts and claims, with the exception of phony invoices.

It is interesting that the violation of an administrative norm, not protected by criminal law, led to a nationwide system of market division, with shared shadow bookkeeping that in many cases contained no fraud – yet the municipal, provincial and central authorities were fleeced for hundreds of millions of euros.[7]

This brings us to the interaction between the conspirators and the entrepreneurial landscape – the scale of the organised illegality, and the role of condoning third parties, such as the state authorities and accountants.

A MAKE-BELIEVE WORLD OF REAL MONEY

The most disquieting aspect of the building fraud is the participation of broad circles which took part in or knew of this make-believe world of fair competition, free enterprise and good governance. In this fantasy world, the active parties danced their economic *danse masqué* while secretly dividing the dance floor. The central and local authorities, which until 1992 had encouraged preliminary consultations, now naïvely (or knowingly) took the masked cartel dance as representing free and open competition. The accountants also took part in the dance, by issuing their yearly audit certificates to the annual accounts of the cartel firms. There were also passive parties, such as the Dutch Competition Authority, just watching idly because it claimed to be very busy elsewhere. The Public Prosecution Office, having recently blundered in a €10 million subsidy fraud case (by some of the same conspirators), was eager to declare itself not competent because of the decriminalisation of the cartel prohibition. It did not occur to the prosecutors that there were related cover-up frauds or the little used article 328 bis of the Criminal Code (see note 7). And if they were aware of this clause, the low maximum punishment did not stir them to action either.

The metaphor of the *danse masqué* should not disguise the underlying economic reality, which had a very compelling social and economic nature. Entrepreneurs could be banned from the dance floor, or could be compelled to participate or face economic doom. For example, a German road building firm was barred from the Dutch market because the Dutch companies that delivered asphalt denied service.[8] In economic (organised) crime settings, it is not necessary to draw guns to pose an effective (economic) threat.

In the building community, certainly in the market of large infrastructural works, there was no need for more coercion. On the contrary, firms also participated in private tendering procedures and delivered an offer, even if they had no intention at all of fulfilling the tendered contract. They simply took a figure from their neighbour. The reason for this fake subscription was that the firm established a claim for a later round. In addition, such an action notified the tendering authority of a company's interest in similar works.

During the Parliamentary Committee hearings, the question was raised whether and to what extent the sums of money in the shadow bookkeeping were 'real'. After all, if the claims and debts balanced and the outcome was zero, no money changed hands. This implied that there were no 'black funds' hidden somewhere. Another consequence was that the fiscal police of the Inland Revenue Service had no grounds for suspicion, let alone for starting investigations. The whole edifice was 'clean', and the tax money was duly paid.

Nevertheless, behind this edifice the make-believe world of the cartel generated real money, even according to the Parliamentary Committee (final report: 106–110). Firms could construct for higher prices, and the Parliamentary Committee deduced from one of the instances of shadow bookkeeping a plausible estimate of an 8.8% price increase in cases of private tendering. If the prelude to secret consultations was a *danse masqué*, the real outcomes were tangible constructions for too much and hard money.

CARTELS AND 'ORGANISED CRIME'

The connection between organised crime and cartels is obvious to everybody if the place of residence is Cali or Medellin. The connection is less obvious if a construction firm is based in The Hague. The irony is that the so-called cartels of Medellin or Cali were actually no cartels at all (Verbeek 2001; Zaitch 2002), while the illegal building cartels in the Dutch building scandal were real and would have fully deserved classification as examples of 'organised crime', if only the cartel prohibition had been included in the Criminal Code. While the penal climate in the Netherlands during the past 15 years has in some ways become harsher – with much tough talk of taking action, longer sentences and a disgraceful cutback in expenditure concerning rehabilitation of prisoners – and whereas the old idea of decriminalisation was virtually dead, the government decriminalised cartel formation on the grounds of insufficient seriousness and an incompetent Public Prosecution Office (the latter was probably the only correct judgment). Otherwise, all the criteria mentioned in the Dutch clause on organised crime, the UN convention on organised crime, or that of the EU are fulfilled:

- 'there are more than three persons involved': hundreds of firms appear to have taken part in the conspiracy;
- 'activities that have a structural nature': the nationwide systematic price rigging and market division was by its very nature structured and lasted for years;
- 'already has or aims at acquiring criminal assets of more than €500,000': this needs no further clarification;
- 'crimes punishable with a four year prison sentence': cartel forming was decriminalised, which cancels out this criterion but
- follow-up offences like false invoicing are punishable with up to six year prison sentences;
- 'has a specific task distribution': in order to clear claims and debts, regional 'clearance units' were established with specialised staff;
- 'has a positive or negative system of sanctions': woe betide the firm that did not play the game, as it was mercilessly pressed out of the market;
- 'makes use of corruptive contacts': corruption of civil servants in charge of tendering was a common procedure.

Will these firms and their executives slip off the 'organised crime hook'? Probably not, because the Public Prosecution Office has finally recovered (or yielded to public and political pressure) from its aloofness, and has begun to charge managing directors of the major building corporations with 'participation in a criminal organisation'. However, the public prosecutors will face formidable legal obstacles.

The circumstance that cartel formation is literally 'illegal but not criminal' does not make it easy for public prosecutors to prove their case in court: there are only derivative crimes, such as the false invoices and the bribing of a number of civil servants. *Intent* to defraud, even if not planned, can be proved, while those who succeeded in settling their claims and debts without false invoices still took part in an organisation in which the commission of fraud was taken for granted. The builders willingly accepted that, due to their own systems, false invoices had to be used year after year as an 'accountancy patch'. This constitutes an organised criminal system.

The point of *money laundering* may be difficult to prove, because there is no predicate crime, though there are illegal advantages. Moreover, these illegal advantages are not disguised or hidden, but neatly entered into the books – not as illegal advantages, of course, but as licit incomes from civil contracts. If false invoices were used, these were not instruments for hiding crime-money, but served to settle the mutual debts and claims. As mentioned above, there is another predicate offence: criminal deception of the tendering authorities, according to article 328 bis Criminal Code that criminalises the extension or maintenance of one's market share by deceiving the public or any other person.

However, the role of many local authorities in all this appeared to be somewhat dubious. Many civil servants in local building departments had a very detailed knowledge of how the system of preliminary consultations operated. Hence they were knowingly deceived; but they did not care as long as the building sum remained less than the sum of the tender (Dohmen and Verlaan 2003). They let these cases pass, not because they may have been bribed (although some were), but because of a mutual – often tacit – recognition of interests: as long as the builders did not raise prices above the determined budget limits, the competent functionary would not be motivated to meddle in their dealings.

This attitude provided the conspiring builders with ample self-justifications. Even if the sums contracted for would have been lower with fair play, the builders could quote Clinton's excuse for using marijuana: 'I did not inhale'. In their perception, they did everything to satisfy the authorities. They usually remained within the authorities' cost estimates, knowing that the latter were not the goose that laid the golden eggs, but a hand that fed them. They cherished that hand, if necessary with corrupting pleasures of the flesh. While hosting the heads of the building departments in a plush brothel, no one thought of a criminal conspiracy, let alone 'organised crime'. Rather, the builders were concerned to obtain the correct receipt for that evening, in order to enter it in the books as legitimate, deductible 'representation *and procurement* costs'.

ORGANISED CRIME CONCERNS AND CARTELS

From social-psychological and political perspectives, it remains intriguing how the representations of 'organised crime' and 'economic crime' remain mentally so separate while they share so many characteristics. The following case description exemplifies this.

Three offenders from three countries conspired for years illegally to maximise their trading profits. To achieve this aim, they convened regularly at secret places. A Swiss trustee (Treuhand) functioned as caretaker, secretary and host, but had no other dealings with their businesses. He knew the trade figures, which the participants received a day before the meeting, and which were not permitted to be taken home. After each meeting, all documentary evidence was destroyed. No-one was allowed to use the fixed telephone line or fax, so only used their pre-paid mobile phones. In the town where they met, they were forbidden from using credit cards, taking money from cash dispensers, or performing any other transaction that might leave traces. For the same reason, the Treuhand paid the hotel bills in cash, with no names mentioned. The conspirators arrived by different modes of transport, which was another method for avoiding suspicion.

How would these criminal conspirators' *modi operandi* be classified had they been involved in weapons or drug dealing? There is little doubt that the label 'organised crime' would be an obvious choice. However, the persons involved were managers from three major chemical internationals: the Dutch chemical corporation AKZO, the German Peroxide Chemicals and the French Atochem, which between them controlled approximately 85 per cent of the European market in organic peroxides. For some 30 years they formed a cartel, until personal relationships soured and AKZO stepped out of the cartel – and ratted.[9] Though the long duration of this cartel is unusual, its conspiratorial conduct is not exceptional. The offenders in an electrical equipment cartel described the attendance roster as a Christmas card list, and their meetings as 'choir practice' (Geis 1978). In other documented cases, an elaborate division of labour was observed: higher management, nicknamed the 'masters', met secretly to determine the broad outlines, while the executives, the so-called sherpas, met monthly to run the business (Levenstein and Suslow 2004).

Comparing the nature of the behaviour of organised business crime and traditional organised crime in the way Sutherland (1961) did (and as we repeated above), his conclusion appears very compelling: 'white collar crime' *is* organised crime. Despite this oft-quoted phrase, and while nobody appears to have heeded its consequences, this statement is far from clear, as the phrases on both sides of the copula are ill-defined. In the first place, the 'white' versus 'blue' collar distinction has lost much of its distinctive value as far as fraudulent behaviour is concerned. Fraud cuts through all social classes (van Duyne 1988). Second, the concept of organised crime is far from clear. The definitions put forward thus far fail to delineate the intended phenomenon (van Duyne 2003). The fact that the organised crime concept has become a component of the international law enforcement arena has not contributed to clarity either. The definition used by the EU and the UN, which we have used in this chapter, includes features that overlap, while it is also heavily contaminated by the *seriousness* component. Organised crime is, firstly, a form of *serious* crime. The UN convention defines 'serious crime' as those offences that are punishable with a maximum prison term ('deprivation of liberty') of at least four years. Following this definition, we have to conclude that, in the Netherlands, the cartel-forming itself is not an organised crime offence; yet covering this activity up with false invoices does ultimately render this label applicable. The situation is different in the UK, where, since 2002, the authorities have taken strong measures against 'cartelists', and have bestowed additional powers on the Office of Fair Trading (S. Holmes *et al.* 2004). Under the British Enterprise Act, individuals found guilty can be imprisoned for up to five years. This brings cartel violation within the organised crime orbit. It is an intriguing intellectual exercise to contemplate the juridical position of the offenders in an international Dutch–UK cartel. The Dutch offenders may feel at ease for being only in breach of an administrative law within the Netherlands. They are wrong to believe they are safe. Even if these Dutch accomplices cannot be extradited for cartel violations, they can still be apprehended on the basis of the crimes on the list of the European Arrest Warrant. Subsuming the components of the UK cartel violations into the EU organised crime definition may very well yield an unavoidable arrest and extradition request for participating in a criminal organisation.

The Council of Europe 2004 report on organised crime recognises that organised and economic crime share many characteristics, and that the division between the two would seem artificial. We are of the opinion that this more flexible point of view should be taken one step further, with which we depart from the rather fruitless 'what is organised crime?' debate. It is preferable to side with the authors who addressed this issue from the gerund perspective – organis*ing* crime, a concept first suggested by Block (1991), whose argument was much in line with Smith's (1978, 1980) crime-entrepreneur perspective, and was applied in the first Dutch research on organised crime (van Duyne 1991) and further elaborated by Levi (2002). Instead of looking at an elusive 'organised crime' phenomenon, the more interesting question is: how do offenders organise their law breaking? Taking behaviour as the point of departure, we can look at the entrepreneurs exploiting the advantages of their surroundings and their culture, as well as their concrete organisational activities. Whether or not they arrive at a real criminal 'organisation' is a corollary of the requirements of doing crime-business. In contrast to criminal 'underground entrepreneurs' dealing with prohibited merchandise such as drugs, organising business criminals need formal organisations as 'weapons' in the commission of their crimes (Tilman and Pontell 1995).

Forming and successfully maintaining a cartel requires much organisational thinking. Being a secret arrangement, agreements can be evaded: the possibilities for cheating constitute one of the weak points of an operating cartel. Our colluding constructors may have realised the importance of avoiding mutual cheating and, as has been observed with other successful cartels, designed provisions for a 'fair' settling of accounts. They did not start by establishing separate clearing units as organisational tools for settling their claims. But they eventually had to, because the scale of the price-rigging became too large and complex, and disgruntled cartel members may pose a threat to cosy arrangements. Once this establishment occurred, our colluding constructors were sooner or later bound to develop a criminal organisation. What else could they do?

NOTES

1. The reports of the Committee were published in 2003 (TK, 28244)
2. A polder is a piece of low-lying land that has been reclaimed from the sea.
3. Labelling theory refers to the process by which socially and economically dominating groups define what constitutes crime and stigmatise perpetrators as 'criminal'. Labelling can be selective: economic perpetrators are less likely to be labelled 'criminal' if they only commit economic crime (and do not deviate too much from other entrepreneurial norms) – see Lemert (1967).
4. In 1935 the Dutch legislator created the Business Agreement Act (Ondernemerso vereenkomstenwet 1935).
5. 1982: Wet Ketenaansprakelijkheid (Law on Chain Liability). As criminal subcontractors intentionally used to bankrupt their firms, which left the Insurance Board or the Inland Revenue Service empty handed, this law enabled these agencies to ignore the bankruptcy of the subcontractor(s) and address the principal for all unpaid dues lower in the chain of subcontracting (van Duyne and Houtzager 2005).
6. Final report of the Parliamentary Committee Construction Sector TK 28244 2002–2003, Nos. 5–6: 48.
7. Though according to section 328 bis of the Criminal Code, the secret agreements between the different construction companies constitute a crime: deceptive deeds to establish, maintain or increase one's market share, if that damages a third party. As this crime is punishable with a maximum of only one year's imprisonment, it is hardly ever used.
8. There are about 50 asphalt plants in the Netherlands, of which 30 are exploited by cooperatives of road constructors. After the building scandal, the Dutch Competition Authority demanded a reduction of these cooperatives.
9. Because AKZO mentioned the cartel itself, its fine of €240 million was remitted.

7. The State, Business and Corruption in Russia

Yuri Tsyganov[1]

The transition in Russia has seen the rise of traditional forms of economic, social and political coordination. This involves a significant role for specific groupings, which can be called clans. This name is somewhat artificial, since such clans usually have nothing to do with kinship and family ties; rather, they are often based on a common origin (for example the 'Moscow group') and/or professional ties (for example the 'Gazprom group'). In advancing their economic and political interests, such groupings do not use official procedures. The latter are only a cover for a hidden mechanism designed to balance and promote their interests: the groupings simply buy the governmental decisions they are interested in, or else exert pressure on government bodies through the mass media that they control.

The accession to power of Vladimir Putin was accompanied by broad expectations that he would put an end to the system of clans. But what we see today is a new round of the clans' struggle, with a new group brought to the top by Putin that has started to fight the 'old' oligarchs. Paradoxically, the fight against corruption has become a bargaining chip in this struggle. There is nothing new in this. For example, in 1997 the so-called 'writers' case' – when it was alleged that the participation in a book on Russian privatisation by several high ranking officials was in fact a cover-up for paying them bribes – was used as a tool to root the 'young reformers' (Anatoly Chubais and others) out of the government. However, despite much discussion of and symbolic campaigns against corruption, the problem remains essentially unaddressed. Moreover, the struggle between the leading political and economic groups provides fertile soil for it.

BUSINESS THROUGH INFORMAL CONNECTIONS

The clan system received a significant boost in the 1990s, due to the fact that Yeltsin's government lacked a proper legislative basis,[2] and there was mutual mistrust between the central administration and the state bureaucracy. Yeltsin's administration attempted to address important issues by using personal ties, bypassing the government apparatus. This later developed into a vital link between the government and the 'approved' financial groups. A special theory was introduced to explain that the government should support selected individuals in creating financial and industrial groups (FIGs), since these individuals, as heads of FIGs, were expected to become the driving force of market reform. Kryshtanovskaya (2002) has called this pattern a system of 'business by approval' that had its roots in the 'komsomol[3] economy' (the Communist *nomenklatura* started its experiments in exchanging political power for economic resources and property by appointing young Communists to positions where they were allowed to engage in business).

Yeltsin's reforms destroyed the old mechanism of macroeconomic management based on a system of industrial ministries. The rapid privatisation undermined the very basis of this system.[4] At the same time, the view that large FIGs should play the key role in Russia's economy – they were seen as the units that could close the management gap and accumulate serious resources for development – became increasingly popular. The Japanese *zaibatsu* and Korean *chaebol* were often cited as models to emulate. The 'loans for shares' scheme of 1995–96 triggered the process of creating FIGs headed by the most influential banks. By 1998, there were more than 70 such groups, and, as a result, large joint-stock companies became key elements of the national economy in the late 1990s.

One of the most important features of the FIGs is a high level of ownership concentration. Moscow-based economists Peter Boone and Denis Rodionov of UBS Brunswick Warburg, analysing 64 of Russia's largest non-government companies, found that 85 per cent of the capital was controlled by just eight shareholder groups (Rodionov and Boone 2002) (see Table 7.1). According to Alexandr Dynkin, of Moscow's Institute of World Economy and International Relations (IMEMO), the eight groups account for 40 per cent of industrial output, 30 per cent of exports, and 1.6 per cent of the labour force (Sergeev 2003). Observing this concentration of ownership in Russia, some analysts (for example Cottrell 2002) speak of a 'chaebolisation' of the economy – comparing the rise of FIGs to the rise of the chaebol business groups in South Korea.

Table 7.1 Russian integrated business groups

Business Group	Number of Companies in the Group
Lukoil	378
Alfa-Group – Renova	193
YuKOS	312
Basic Element – Sibneft	138
InterRos	201
SurgutNefteGaz	51
AFK 'System'	169
Severstal	136

Source: Strana.Ru, 31 January 2003, http://www.strana.ru/stories/02/02/06/2462/170352.html, visited January 2005.

The informal connections between business groups and the government not only provided the latter with important information and a source of alternative advice, but also created opportunities for the political participation of business tycoons, later known as oligarchs. After the 1996 presidential elections, the oligarchs positioned themselves as groups of political influence, and this influence had little to do with the interests of the majority of society. The influence was supported by strong financial flows over which they had obtained control.

The new business structures headed by oligarchs seriously changed the political landscape. They were not simply making strenuous lobbying efforts, but were starting to participate in politics directly, interfering in decision-making and the administration of political appointments. Under such circumstances, corruption turned out to be the most efficient method of 'privatising the government'. The situation was complicated further by the 'semi-official' nature of political participation. Glinkina (1998: 18) is correct in arguing that the uncertain legality, together with the extensive practice of 'telephone rule', gave politicians, bureaucrats and judges an unusually free hand to apply their own assessments of right and wrong.

FROM YELTSINISM TO PUTINISM

The political struggle of 1997–99 revealed that the political structure of Yeltsinism – with the clan system as a part of it – had started to destroy itself from within. The 1993 Constitution granted extremely broad powers to the President. As a result, he was expected to play the role of referee between all the clans and political groups. However, being created around Boris Yeltsin's personality, the system of 'super-presidentialism' appeared to be equal in its strength to the political weight of the man. For reasons relating both to his poor physical health and to the political situation, Yeltsin failed to play the expected role, and the country found itself in a political deadlock.

Although Yeltsin's positioning of himself as the only barrier against Gennady Zyuganov's accession to the President's office and an eventual Communist restoration did help him to win the 1996 presidential election, 1998 saw Yeltsin's rating fall to the 2 per cent mark. Yeltsin lost popular support, and he had neither sought support from an existing political party nor tried to create a new party to acquire such support. His health problems aggravated the situation. At the end of the day, he could rely only on his administration and the inner circle – the so-called 'Family'. Migranyan (2004) has pointed out that the super-presidential republic created by the 1993 Constitution had by 1996 lost its substance. The President had the authority to dismiss the Cabinet or sack a minister, and even to decide the fate of a governor or an oligarch. However, in reality, the President's authority was limited to downtown Moscow.

In early 1999, Yeltsin's weakness encouraged a struggle for power between four major players: the Family, the Communists, Yevgeny Primakov's group and Yury Luzhkov's 'Fatherland'. Unlike its political rivals, the Family did not have a political structure as well as a candidate to run for the presidential office. At the end of 1998, it seemed to be a loser. But then it put a final stake on Vladimir Putin. Unexpectedly, the Family managed to create a new 'party of power' to provide support for Putin. Changing personalities in the President's office, curbing the clans' political activities, and suppressing 'unapproved' competitors aspiring to the main office, were seen as a way out of the political crisis. Striving for independence from the oligarchs, the Family was also successful in increasing the level of autonomy of the government. Putin, who did not belong to any major political group and had carefully hidden his political preferences, was viewed as a suitable person to become a successor.

Putin came to office being promoted by the mass media as a strong man able to solve a broad range of problems – from eliminating the Chechens' rebellion to bringing the oligarchs under government control. By this time, the political elites and ordinary people had developed a consensus that the country did not want new shocks, even for the sake of reforms. Putin emerged as a symbol of the new stability. He completely hid his political and economic views, so as not to give observers an opportunity to interpret his stance in the interests of the particular social groups they represented. He was backed by the freshly established 'Unity' party (now transformed into 'United Russia'), which also declared no political or economic goals – other than support for the President.

The political elites and clans agreed to a policy of 'equal distancing' from state power. This meant that no business group or political clan would receive preferences on an individual basis. Putin tried to roll back the practice known as 'privatisation of power' and to rebuild the so-called power vertical. The two strategies are similar, in that they consider large corporations to be the only significant political force, and ignore small and medium sized businesses. The major difference between these two practices lies in their methods of interaction. Informal ties of exchanging money for power (official decisions) were substituted by the principle of 'equal distancing', which emphasised the leading role of the government in decision making. The capacity of big business directly to influence official appointments and other governmental decisions was significantly reduced.

Some steps were taken to create a more transparent mechanism of contact between the government and the so-called oligarchs (business tycoons). The latter turned towards the Russian Alliance of Industrialists and Businesspersons, which was initially established as a representative body for the so-called red directors.[5] In 2000–01, nearly all large-scale businesspeople joined the Alliance. It was an attempt to change a pattern: instead of individual bargaining, which was common when Boris Yeltsin was in power, businesspeople had shown their readiness to act in the framework of a body representing the entire business community. This also changed the agenda – the state and businesspeople started to discuss broader issues of economic policy (for example taxation, currency control, joining the WTO). Big business acquired a structure for their participation in determining strategic approaches to the social and economic situation in particular regions and in the country as a whole.

Despite this stabilisation policy, two oligarchs became the targets of instant attacks by law enforcement bodies supported by Putin's administration. Boris Berezovsky demanded special status for himself as an author of 'project Putin'. Vladimir Gusinsky also wanted to gain exclusive benefits from the government, using his NTV company – the only independent national television channel in Russia – as leverage. Moreover, Gusinsky had refused to grant NTV's support to Putin and the 'Unity' party, and was put on the

Kremlin's 'black list'. Both oligarchs acted against the informal agreement struck between Putin and the oligarchs in July 2000, and were punished accordingly. They lost their stakes in two major national television channels, ORT and NTV respectively, and were squeezed out of Russia.[6] This seemed to be in line with the rules of the new game of 'equal distancing'. Nevertheless, it later became obvious that Putin was playing another game, and was gradually appointing former secret service officers to government bodies, and expanding their control over mineral and financial resources.

Looking back to 1999, we can see that the quick recovery of the Family was ensured by a new approach to methods of political financing. The Family made a titanic effort to bring financial flows under its control. On the basis of personal ties and selective appointments of heads of government bodies, the group obtained access to budget and other government financial resources as a source of political financing. Thus, by the end of 1999, the oligarchs had lost their importance as a source of funds that could be allocated to election campaigns. In 1996 the oligarchs had supported Boris Yeltsin through converting budget funds into anonymous monies (for example, in the famous case of 'a box for a Xerox machine'). During the elections of 1999 and 2000, the Family did not need the service of the oligarchs' banks any more. The oligarchs lost their significance after emerging as a pillar in the political structure under Boris Yeltsin. Thus, the earlier mechanism of buying governmental decisions was undermined.

Putin, who had had no personal support basis in the government apparatus, took advantage of these changes. He began to promote his protégés to government positions, gradually increasing the political significance of the newcomers. In 2001, Sergey Ivanov became the Defence Minister, Boris Gryzlov was appointed Interior Minister, Alexandr Rumyantsev became the head of the Ministry of Nuclear Energy, and Mikhail Fradkov was appointed head of the Taxation Police and subsequently Prime Minister. Practically all these people had come from St Petersburg. Alexandr Miller, who also represents the Petersburg group, was elected Chairman of Gazprom, the largest company in Russia. According to a report by the Russian Academy of Sciences' Institute of Sociology, in 2001–03 up to 22% of the top officials (3500 positions were analysed) were newcomers. Former military and secret service officers constituted 70% of the administration in federal districts, and 35% of deputy ministers. Their numbers among governors increased twofold. Big business controlled 16% of the top official positions, 17% of the Federal Council, and 5% of the government. The 'old *nomenklatura*' – those who had worked for the state during Brezhnev's times – accounted for up to 30% of the top bureaucrats in the early Putin era (Kaftan 2003).

The former military and secret service officers have a good understanding of, and broad experience with, the mechanisms of Communist society, and the current ruling group is trying to restore many aspects of the Communist-style system of governance. Putin's slogan of 'strengthening of the power vertical' implies such a restoration. The current president's political structure relies on the so-called administrative resource, coupled with a policy of intimidation; there appear to be attempts to create an atmosphere of Andropov-style 'low level fear', which can be seen in the apparently fabricated spy cases of Sutyagin, Pasko, Moiseev, Danilov, Nikitin, and so on. Valentin Moiseev, a former leading Korea specialist in the Russian Foreign Ministry, argues that the fabrication of spy cases and anti-spy paranoia are aimed at strengthening the position of the secret service and intimidating society (Moiseev 2003).[7]

At the same time, the secret service conducts covert operations against the rare critics of Putin's regime. This can be in the form of a grenade exploding near the door of an apartment owned by the author of an anti-Kremlin book, or a visit by professionally equipped burglars stealing a notebook and a PC hard drive from a journalist critical of Putin's foreign policy. Baker (2004) writes that, in certain circles, fear is creeping back into Russia. As a result, self-censorship has developed. For example, the NTV channel, in contrast to the two governmental television channels, is believed to be exempt from direct Kremlin advice or instructions, but checks (censors) its own broadcasts to avoid any potential difficulties (Mursalieva 2004). Thus, in early June 2004, NTV's management closed a popular program by Leonid Parfenov and dismissed him. Parfenov was 'guilty' of publishing an interview with the widow of Zelimkhan Yandarbiev, a former Chechen leader, killed in Qatar by Russian agents.

There were serious institutional changes that ensured 'strengthening of the power vertical'. This policy of Putin included three major steps that virtually substituted the government structures with unconstitutional bodies. First, the country was divided into seven federal districts headed by the President's representatives. Second, the regional governors were moved from the Federation Council (according to the Constitution, the Upper House of the legislature) to a new consultative body – the State Council. Subsequently, the Federation Council lost its power. Third, the federal bodies were granted the right to interfere in the regions, to dismiss governors and regional legislatures. Furthermore, in September 2004 Putin used the tragedy in Beslan to sneak in his proposal to abandon direct elections of governors. This unconstitutional structure of political management is oriented exclusively towards the President, and is not subject to control by society. Thus, Putin created a new mechanism for the super-presidentialism inherited from Boris Yeltsin.

Petrov (2004) points out that the federal districts coincide with the boundaries of regional deployment of Internal Forces of the Interior Ministry. Five of the seven President's representatives are military generals. Their offices, as well as the offices of federal inspectors, have been filled by former military and secret service officers. The President's representatives are members of the Security Council and regularly report the situation in their districts to the President. In the districts, they created special structures to control all military-like and law enforcement bodies. There is no transparency in the activities of the President's representatives, and there is no clear review of their competence.

Interestingly, the architect of *perestroika*, Alexandr Yakovlev, testifies that the former KGB head and then Communist General Secretary Yury Andropov advocated a system of vertical management based on seven to ten federal districts (Bykov 2004). In this context, it is noteworthy that, in June 2004, the 90th anniversary of Andropov's birth was widely celebrated in Russia, and he was portrayed as a reformer. Clearly, Putin took the old KGB's project from a dusty shelf and is implementing it 20 years after the death of its notorious author.

Significant changes in the political landscape of Russia allow us to speak of a serious transformation of the regime established by Boris Yeltsin and inherited by Vladimir Putin. Boris Nemtsov and Vladimir Kara-Murza argue that there is a new political formation – Putinism. It is a mix of a one-party system, censorship, a manipulated parliament, the absence of independent courts, a high level of power and finance centralisation, uncontrollable secret services and bureaucracy, and the subordinate position of business (Nemtsov and Kara-Murza 2004). Medushevsky (2001) has emphasised the system's dual legitimation (a combination of democracy and autocracy), 'technical' government and the emerging personality cult, and suggests that the regime is moving towards a form of classical Bonapartism.

'MANAGED DEMOCRACY' MEANS RESTORATION

The reliance on the 'administrative resource' increases the role of bureaucracy, undermines positions of previous favourites, and turns bargaining into a hidden process inside the system. The 'administrative resource' is the main driving force for the so-called managed democracy. The term 'managed democracy' in regard to the Russian political system was introduced by the former editor-in-chief of the daily newspaper *Nezavisimaya Gazeta*, Vitaly Tretyakov. Describing the political agenda of President Putin, Tretyakov (2000) argued that the president, without restraining democratic institutions and freezing political freedom, could ignore the Parliament, mass media, and the opposition if this was beneficial for national development. Such a system is supported by the political elite, which has no romantic expectations or illusions about Russia's political system.

Many observers have pointed out that the victory of the managed democracy policy can be seen clearly in the last parliamentary and presidential elections. For example, the main reason for the extraordinary efforts the regional authorities exerted in mobilising the electorate and ensuring a high level of participation in the 2004 presidential election was an informal promise by the Finance Ministry to allocate budget funds according to the level of participation (Butrin 2004). The most undeveloped regions showed the highest achievement; Chechnya, Ingushetia and Chukotka demonstrated the best results in terms of participation and support granted to Putin.

However, this is not a new phenomenon. The presidential and parliamentary elections of 1996 and 1999–2000 revealed a similar pattern. In a sense, the elections of 1999–2000 were even more remarkable: the Kremlin's political manipulations turned a hastily gathered group of people into the 'party of power', and an unknown mid-level official into the president. Yevgeny Yasin, Russia's economic guru, argues that the only alternatives in 1996 to managed democracy were a Communist restoration or a new coup (Yasin 2001: 43). In 1999–2000, the Family used managed democracy to protect itself against Luzhkov's and Primakov's 'Fatherland' that sought to revise Yeltsin's policies. Yasin (2001: 47) insists that the system of managed democracy, with its undercover political struggle, has now reached a dead end. Perhaps such a system was to a certain extent acceptable in 1996–2000, but it is not now beneficial for either society or the government itself. Shevtsova (2004b) argues that the current system is, in fact, a system of self-preservation and status quo, but which provides no basis for development. With this system, running in a circle produces an illusion of real movement.

The essence of Putin's stabilisation is the fact that managed democracy has given new opportunities to bureaucracy. Former Deputy Head of the Central Bank Oleg Viugin calls Putin a leader of the new *nomenklatura* (Yasin 2001: 62–3). According to Viugin, Putin's policy reflects the interests of this stratum. The *nomenklatura* has rearranged its relations with the oligarchs. Viugin is correct that the oligarchs have adopted a misguided approach, believing that power comes with money. But the formula is contrariwise – power leads to money. Those who agreed with the latter formula see their businesses flourishing; those who did not were ousted from business, and in several cases from the country. The policy of 'equal distancing' has significantly undermined the oligarchs' capacity for influencing the decision-making process in government bodies. However, this has not stopped what Yasin (2001: 68) has called the 'privatisation of power'. One group is prevented from further participation in such privatisation, but this only means that a much larger group – the *nomenklatura* – no longer has any competition. Managed democracy appears to be a system allowing an unchallenged position for the *nomenklatura*.

It should be noted that the *nomenklatura* was disorganised and disoriented in the early 1990s, due to both the new policies and the inflow of newcomers with academic backgrounds to government offices. But it never lost its position as a major element of the political system. Albats (2000) argues that Russia's liberal reforms should have gone further than simply introducing the market instead of the planning system and allowing private ownership. It should have included the elimination of absolutism and the bureaucratic state that was a tradition in Russia for many centuries. The last two centuries have seen significant changes in social relations, the structuring of elites, ideology and ownership. However, the bureaucratic nature of the state persists, and the unlimited power is still in the hands of the bureaucracy. On this point, the events of 1991–92 were not a revolution, but rather yet another attempt to modernise the bureaucratic state. The reforms of 1991–92 legalised the *nomenklatura* privatisation of 1985–91, and permitted a change in elites. Citing Sergei Kovalev, the famous human rights activist, Albats (2000) further suggests that Boris Yeltsin deliberately rejected the reform of the government apparatus. According to Kovalev, Yeltsin as a politician and a public manager developed within the Soviet party bureaucratic system. As such, he tended to preserve the basis of the *nomenklatura*'s existence, despite bringing in reformers and creating links to the FIGs. Having extremely good skills in 'backstage management' and in *nomenklatura* intrigues, Yeltsin was afraid that under a new system he could lose control over government bodies.

Olga Kryshtanovskaya points to the fact that during Yeltsin's presidency the 'political longevity' of people in the ruling elite decreased dramatically (Naryshkina 2003). Under Brezhnev, top officials enjoyed about 18 years on average in the elite. Yeltsin, who was quick to dismiss people, cut this period to 1.7 years. This was a dramatic purge of the system. However, it created a large group of disaffected people, who formed the basis of the opposition to the regime; this opposition included younger officials (those who were 30 to 40 years old when the reforms started) who had planned their careers in the *nomenklatura* hierarchy, and who suffered when the old ladder of gradual career movement was abandoned along with the Communist system. The opposition was not necessarily against the new political course: rather, their chief concern was to regain their positions and opportunities. Putin increased the average tenure in the elite to more than 3 years, and 'normalised' the situation (Naryshkina 2003). The *nomenklatura* regained a feeling of stability. At the same time, the Communist practice of creating sinecures for dismissed officials was re-established. This effectively undermined the opposition.

THE PHOENIX OF THE *NOMENKLATURA*

Voslensky (1984: 441) has described the *nomenklatura* as a class of privileged exploiters that acquired wealth from power, not power from wealth. This privileged position was made possible by monopoly – monopoly in ownership and monopoly in power. The last two decades have provided a brilliant opportunity to the members of the *nomenklatura* to cut personal pieces of their own from the pie of the former 'all-people's' economy. Many of them welcomed this opportunity. Abandoning the 'all-people's' – that is state – ownership has allowed a conversion of official privileges into real property rights. Paradoxically, it has also undermined the very foundation of the *nomenklatura*'s existence, since it created some level of competition in economic and political life.

The period of chaos that followed the USSR's collapse was a period that gave people from all walks of life the opportunities to capture pieces of the value that the *nomenklatura* intended to divide among themselves. There were many reasons for this, including a lack of control, propagandistic measures (for example a simulation of equal opportunities), and the necessity to have a group of pioneers who were to examine the new opportunities and show the way (appointees to the role of businesspeople, who were mentioned above). It should also be noted that the changes came so quickly, and the internal transformation of the *nomenklatura* was so significant – it lost the ideological axis that provided legitimation of its privileged position – that it simply lost its grip on the national assets.

Now the *nomenklatura* is restoring its position. Certainly, the restoration includes an attempt to re-establish control over the most important assets in the country. Under such circumstances, the attack against the oligarchs became inevitable. It started when YuKOS, Russia's second largest oil company, found itself under pressure from the authorities. The use of tax exemptions granted earlier was declared to be an illegal activity, as a result of which the company producing 20% of Russia's crude oil output, and the second largest taxpayer in the country, was brought to the brink of liquidation. The Kremlin actually destroyed this lucrative business in order to teach others a lesson.

Big business is to be a part of the new system, but in a subordinate position. Prime Minister Mikhail Fradkov explicitly called on the oligarchs to 'turn themselves' to solving the problems the government faced (Obukhova and Skornyakova 2004). Blant (2004) suggests that now the oligarchs do not need their 'trade union' that was previously oriented to a dialogue with the Kremlin. The Russian Alliance of Industrialists and Businesspeople can be closed, since it has become obvious that there would be no such dialogue in the new conditions. Now the Kremlin prefers to speak through the office of the Prosecutor General, as the case of Mikhail Khodorkovsky and his company YuKOS made absolutely clear. Judging by the lack of serious protests on the part of businesspeople, it is clear that they have submitted to the new pattern of relations between business and power. This is despite the possibility that more of them might follow Mikhail Khodorkovsky in the near future.

Besides the *nomenklatura* and the oligarchs, there are other participants in Russia's politics that cannot be ignored. Avtorkhanov (1991) has described three major political elements of Brezhnev's regime – the party, the police and the army. He suggests that the political balance between these three 'corporations' was a result of recognising the fact that the Communist Party could not rule without the support provided by the police and the army. In the triangle, the army technically was the strongest part; yet it was the least independent in terms of realising its corporate interests. At the same time, it was the corporation most influenced by patriotic slogans. The police and the party were initially two parts of one political mechanism, but later the two corporations clashed in a battle for control of the state.

After Stalin's death, Nikita Khrushchev organised a coup against the police (as a result of which Lavrenty Beria, three ministers of national security, and thousands of secret service officers were killed). He later ousted Marshal Zhukov, then Defence Minister, who had ensured military support for the party leaders in this struggle. Thousands of military and party officers were moved to leading positions in the police apparatus. The party control over the other two pillars of the regime was restored. However, the police gradually regained its influence, and the 1970s saw the above-mentioned balance re-emerge, with its hidden struggle for power.

One more player should be added to Avtorkhanov's analysis – a very important part of the Soviet *nomenklatura*, the state bureaucracy (opposed and at the same time complementary to the party apparatus). Obviously, the specialisation in political and economic management created two relatively separate parts of the Communist hierarchy – the state and party *nomenklatura*. In the late 1980s, the state *nomenklatura* used Gorbachev's *perestroika* to seize the leading position in the power structure. Yeltsin effectively destroyed the party hierarchy, but hardly touched the state *nomenklatura*. There were also hectic attempts to reform the police structures, but these mostly failed.

In the end, three out of the four major political elements of the Communist regime (the police, the armed forces and the state *nomenklatura*) survived and started to adapt themselves to the new conditions. In addition, a newcomer appeared on the scene – a group of businesspeople holding significant assets created by privatisation. They often originated from the party, government or secret service structures, but now had independent interests. Kurginyan (1998) has an interesting argument about oligarchs (whom he calls 'appointees to the role of so-called "oligarchs"'). He argues that the essence of the emergence of the group that called themselves oligarchs was not in their political role or position. Rather, what was really important was the fact that a certain group actually called itself a new class. They openly stated that they did not belong to the *nomenklatura* and did not want to. Demonstrating political ambitions and aspiring to power, the group became an obvious 'antipode' to the *nomenklatura*.

In the rectangle of four competing forces, the police currently seem to be the most successful. Portnikov (2003) has pointed to the struggle between the army and the police (*'chekists'*[8]). Since Communist times, there have been special controlling bodies ensuring the *chekists'* control over the army. Now the main referee that resolved the conflicts between the military and the *chekists* – the party *nomenklatura* – has gone. The *chekists* appear to have gained the upper hand in the struggle. Former KGB officer Sergey Ivanov was appointed Defence Minister. His appointment probably represents additional control over the top brass. At the same time, the role of the General Staff was downgraded, as it lost its functions of operational command. It is also important to note that the FSB (the successor organisation to the KGB) regained control over the border guard troops, which gave the service a significant boost in real military strength.

SILOVIKI[9]: THE AVANT-GARDE OF THE *NOMENKLATURA*

Today there exists an interesting situation in Russia. The army is controlled by the representatives of the secret services. *Chekists* have flooded into many offices and appear to have managed to outclass the *nomenklatura*. However, it is probably correct to speak of a kind of emergency team recruited both to restore the hierarchy of state management that collapsed more than a decade ago, and to fill leading positions of the *nomenklatura* in Russian society. Indeed, Putin and many of those who rose with him had either retired from the service or else had hardly had a chance to reach the top of the KGB, not to speak of their domination in the current Russian government.[10] Moreover, the collapse of the Communist system undermined demand for the services of the political police. The cooperation with the rival corporation (the state *nomenklatura*) has opened up a new career path for the *chekists*. The *nomenklatura* has its benefits too; while the oligarchs showed them the path to personal wealth, the *chekists* could help re-establish the privileged position of the *nomenklatura* and protect its wealth. No wonder then that officials of all ranks and kinds quickly adapted to the new rules of the game, and showed no opposition to the Kremlin's attempts to 'put the screws on'.

In most cases, the former members of the democratic movement that was born out of *perestroika*, and the independent representatives of the intelligentsia who became officials in the late 1980s and early 1990s, have now been ousted from office. As in Communist times, only affiliation with a particular group can secure a place within the ruling elite. Gradually increasing its strength, the 'Petersburg Group' initially found its place at the top exclusively due to its old ties with Vladimir Putin. The newcomers brought their own mates to the government offices, and this turned into a self-sustaining process. The ten years 1993–2002 saw a serious qualitative change in the ruling elite (see Table 7.2). Although the number of people with a tertiary education remains high, the share of those who had an equivalent of a PhD declined 2.5 times. This fact clearly mirrors the exit of intellectuals from the elite, who were substituted by people with a military or similar background. The unchanged proportion of economists and lawyers can be explained by the fact that the elite recognises their utility, while pushing out other 'academics'.

The recruitment of officials following the principle of common origin is an old political tradition in Russia. Leonid Brezhnev brought to the top his comrades from his native region – the so-called Dnepropetrovsk mafia. Mikhail Gorbachev promoted people from his native city of Stavropol. Boris

Yeltsin opened excellent career opportunities for the natives of Sverdlovsk (now Ekaterinburg). Today the doors are open for those coming from St Petersburg, especially for Putin's former colleagues from the KGB.

Table 7.2 Ruling elites under Yeltsin and Putin

		Yeltsin's elite (1993)	Putin's elite (2002)
Average age	Years	51.3	51.5
Women	%	2.9	1.7
Those from rural areas	%	23.1	31.0
Persons with tertiary education	%	99.0	100.0
Research degree holders[a]	%	52.5	20.9
Persons with military education	%	6.7	26.6
Persons with economic or law education	%	24.5	25.7
Persons graduated from prestigious tertiary institutions[b]	%	35.4	23.4
Those from the President's native city[c]	%	13.2	21.3
Representatives of business	%	1.6	11.3
Military	%	11.2	25.1

Notes:
a. PhD equivalent
b. Moscow University, Moscow Institute of International Relations, Moscow Institute of Foreign Relations, Party High School, Academy of National Economy, Academy of Social Sciences (now Academy of Government Service), Finance Academy, Foreign Trade Academy and Diplomatic Academy
c. Yekaterinburg or St Petersburg respectively

Source: Institute of Sociology, Russian Academy of Sciences. *Pro et Contra*, 7 (4), Fall 2002: 162.

However, the *scale* of the 'Petersburg invasion' is really unprecedented. Many joke that nowadays the place of birth or dwelling registration in Petersburg is the main – if not the only – requirement for promotion to a senior position. In fact, this joke contains some truth. Very often, Putin's protégés cannot demonstrate any significant achievements or strong skills and knowledge that would justify their appointments to the leading posts in Russia's political hierarchy. However, these people do have one valuable feature – namely absolute loyalty to the group and its leader. Bulavinov (2003) argues that it was his undoubted loyalty to the leader that opened the doors of the President's office for Vladimir Putin. Now the same 'key' is opening the doors for his former colleagues and fellow Petersburgers.

The years between Putin's first and second elections became a period of significant change in the clan structuring of the ruling group. The Family that recruited Putin to the post of the system's stabiliser (Shevtsova 2004a: 1) managed to recover its political position, which had been undermined after the 1998 crisis. Putin came in as a guarantee that there would be no significant forcible redistribution in the ownership of property. Together with the new guarantees for the *nomenklatura*, this was the basis for Putin's 'consolidation'.

At the same time, during recent years the Family has passed through a series of transformations. Boris Berezovsky, who used to be the major author of political schemes in the group, lost its support. Subsequently, his former protégé Roman Abramovich became the leader in this informal association; but then his influence drastically diminished too. Following the agreement on the merger of oil companies YuKOS and Sibneft, Mikhail Khodorkovsky assumed the leader's role. By approving Khodorkovsky's arrest and ousting both Mikhail Kasyanov (the former prime minister) and Aleksandr Voloshin (former head of the President's Administration), Vladimir Putin has shown that he now feels free of any obligations to the group.

In parallel, several new clan-type groupings emerged. The most important one is the 'Petersburg *chekists*' (that is KGB-FSB people originating from Petersburg). They derived their political (and economic) influence from their support for President Putin. There are three major players promoting the economic interests of this group: two leading figures in the President's Administration, Viktor Ivanov and Igor Sechin, plus Sergey Pugachev, commonly known as the 'orthodox oligarch'. The economic basis of the group is its close connections with MezhPromBank, Rosneft state oil company and Gazprom.

At a certain point, the newcomers, who favour an increase of government interference in the economy, attempted to gain access not only to government resources, but also to those that had already been transferred to new owners during privatisation. Their basic approach is to reinstitute the hierarchical lines of power, which were one of the main features of the Communist system. Instead of several clans or groupings competing for control over the government, one particular group made attempts to monopolise this control and to use it to establish control over economic resources. Businesses are to be integrated into this system.

Although Putin had promised not to revise the results of privatisation, the draft reforms of the fuel and energy sector that were introduced by his administration in 2002 advocated the nationalisation of oil and gas deposits, and the conversion of oil companies into contractors (Subbotin 2002: 58–60). If this program is implemented, the Rosneft company controlled by the government (and 'the Petersburg *chekists*') will deprive other oil companies of their vast resources, and will become the major player in the market. The idea of nationalisation was subsequently abandoned, but the administration became the driving force in expanding centralised control over gas and oil resources. Clearly, YuKOS became their first target.

The main stockholder of YuKOS, Mikhail Khodorkovsky, refused to incorporate his business into the new 'vertical' system. He proclaimed certain political interests and eventually clashed directly with the new grouping expanding its power. It should be noted that, at the same time, some 70% of the capitalisation of Russia's stock market came from oil companies, including some 35% from YuKOS and Sibneft alone. It is not surprising that YuKOS – which, after acquiring Sibneft, became the largest oil company in Russia – found itself under open attack sanctioned by the highest authorities, for both political and economic reasons.

Khodorkovsky's intention to sell 40–50% of YuKOS shares to an American company (Exxon or Chevron) triggered the attack against him and the company. This decision had the potential to weaken the efforts of Putin's administration to enhance Russia's economic ties with, and leverage over, the West, in particular the USA. It was not about the economic exchange *per se*, but rather about who would control it and how. Apparently, it is much easier to control the process when Russia's major oil company is fully Russian owned. Although the government announced in early October 2003 that there were no regulations that could obstruct the deal, three weeks later they arrested Khodorkovsky (Gurova and Privalov 2003).

The possible deal was criticised by pro-Kremlin observers as an enormous threat to the fundamentals of Russia's political system (see for example Svyatenkov 2003). They produced a threatening forecast. The oligarchs, who have obtained former government companies – above all in the oil industry – for bargain prices and/or for privatisation vouchers, are seeking business alliances to sell the assets to foreign partners, so as to obtain 'real money' for what was purchased at knockdown prices. For example, British Petroleum bought 50% of the TNK oil company. The InterRos group was considering the possibility of inviting a foreign investor to participate in the holding. YuKOS was preparing the sale of a significant share to US corporations. The critics argued that, as a result of such transactions, the Russian government could lose much of its control over the oligarchs' activities, since the oligarchs would obtain a certain amount of protection from the West. Under such circumstances, it was maintained, the oligarchs would turn into 'agents of the Western bourgeoisie'. Leaving corporate management to their foreign partners, the oligarchs would turn their focus onto politics. Building political influence on foreign capital, they could turn the country into a Western colony and a banana republic. The fact that the oil industry is of strategic importance further aggravates the situation. To avoid such developments threatening national security, strengthening government control over the gas and oil industries, by means of nationalisation or increasing the level of taxation, was proposed. The oligarchs, initially portrayed as engines of reform, are now considered to be 'demons' conspiring against the nation.

Piontkovsky (2004) has addressed the issue of whether or not Putin's group is opposed to private ownership; his conclusion is that it is not at all. He argues that the conflict between *chekists* and oligarchs is 'a rebellion of dollar millionaires against dollar billionaires'. What makes this rebellion – the current redistribution of assets from Yeltsin's oligarchs to Putin's *chekists* – easy is a low level of legal protection for property rights. Sergey Peregudov cites Ya. Pappe, who argued that in Russia an owner must effectively participate in the tactical and operational management of his assets. Otherwise, he will fail to realise his rights and will be considered not a 'real' owner by all interested parties (Peregudov 2002: 85). This means that an owner cannot expect his property rights to be effectively protected by the law. He has to ensure this protection through participation in management. From this point of view, it is clear that there is no need to undertake some form of nationalisation or other expropriation steps. It is enough to separate the owner and his assets. This is what was effectively achieved through the arrest (and threat of arrest) of major YuKOS stockholders, above all Mikhail Khodorkovsky.

Yulia Latynina discusses the same problem. According to her, private ownership does not exist in Russia. In ownership relations, the law is substituted by personal connections. Private ownership appears to be a system of vassal rights connecting the business owner with a governor, a president's representative, the taxation police chief, the FSB head, and so on (Latynina 2001). Oligarchs are at the top of this chain, and are dependent on the Kremlin. At the regional level, many businesspeople are dependent on friendship with the local governor.

The *chekists*' desire to redistribute the assets acquired by the oligarchs in the process of privatisation coincides with the understandable intention of the *nomenklatura* to restore its position in the economy. Putin's group thus looks like a kind of ice-breaker, leading the charge on the assets redistribution process. The result of this should be a new economic structure, in which the government formally controls major assets, but which in practice benefits certain groups inside the *nomenklatura*. Such a structure resembles the Communist system of industrial ministries, though with elements of a market economy.

MAKING THE MOST OF A PUBLIC 'BAD'[11]

There are no contradictions between the restoration of the *nomenklatura*'s positions and the new round of struggles for wealth redistribution. Naishul (2004) argues that the Communist economy was not a command economy, but an economy of agreements. This system is known as an administrative market. It is a hierarchy based on bargaining, including horizontal bargaining between subjects independent of each other, and vertical bargaining between subjects superior or inferior to each other. Relations between a boss and an employee were also based on bargaining. That is why Brezhnev's epoch can be called a time of bargaining. This system was ready for the exchange ties long before the reforms. The essence of the recent reforms was to introduce money into this system. The current system is basically the same administrative market. The difference is that now, together with power, it recognises the importance of money (Naishul 2004). 'Administrative resources' and 'administrative currency' are the key concepts of this system. The negative consequence of the system is rampant corruption.

Corruption is obviously a public 'bad', that is something of which a normal society prefers to have as little as possible. However, it has now become an important element of the Russian regime. The system of administrative bargaining provides officials with excellent opportunities for profiteering. On the other hand, corruption has turned into an effective method of ensuring loyalty. Corrupt officials, military officers with 'business interests', and businesspeople who acquired their assets through various schemes are subjects who provide a convenient leverage against themselves; the leverage is the compromising information about their involvement in certain wrongdoings. Thus, the ruling group converts this social 'bad' to their own good, consolidating their power and creating the illusion of stabilisation.

According to research by the Indem foundation, 82% of Russian businesspeople pay bribes (Litvinenko and Belimov 2004). In the years 2001 to 2005, the total annual sum that went into the pockets of Russian officials increased from US$33.5 billion to US$316 billion (Indem 2005). Each citizen spends an average of US$100 a year in bribes; each businessperson spends approximately US$244,000 (http://2005. novayagazeta.ru/nomer/ 2005/55n/at06-big.jpg, visited 2 August 2005). The businesspeople agree to pay because they are aware of close informal ties between local officials and local law enforcement bodies. The latter are dependent on the former for receiving housing and other benefits. At present, the members of local legislative bodies are usually strongly influenced by the executive. As a result, local legislatures cannot control their executive counterparts, which, according to the same research by Indem, take 87% of bribes in the country (http://2005. novayagazeta.ru/nomer/2005/55n/at07-big.jpg, visited 2 August 2005). At the same time, local governors, mayors and local governments have bought stakes in local mass media, either directly or through businesses loyal to them. Thus, there is no control from this side either.

The problem of corruption became the last straw that triggered the attack against YuKOS. Meeting Vladimir Putin in February 2003, Mikhail Khodorkovsky blamed the government for turning a blind eye to the problem of corruption. Khodorkovsky addressed the case of the Northern Oil Company. On his retirement, Deputy Finance Minister Andrei Vavilov had bought the company. In March 2001, the company managed to win the tender for a large oil deposit in Nenetsky Autonomous district, offering a bonus of only $US7 million, while other companies (for example, Lukoil and SurgutNefteGaz) had offered $US70–100 million. The better offers were not considered at all (Latynina 2004). The Ministry of Natural Resources subsequently had to annul the license for the deposit, but the company continued the development. Lukoil, YuKOS, SurgutNefteGaz, TNK and Sibneft appealed to the Arbitration Court, pointing to the preferential treatment of Northern Oil during the tender. Seemingly because of the scandals, Vavilov opted to sell the company. With an estimated market value of $US300 million, Northern Oil was sold to Rosneft for $US600 million. Rosneft, which is under state ownership, is known for close ties with Viktor Ivanov and Igor Sechin, both of whom belong to Putin's inner circle.

The striking gap between the estimated market value and the real sum paid drew attention to the deal. Following a request from the Russian Alliance of Industrialists and Businesspeople, Mikhail Khodorkovsky asked Vladimir Putin about his attitude towards the abnormally expensive sale of Northern Oil to Rosneft (Latynina 2004). Putin was apparently extremely angry to be asked who benefited from the deal; it appears that Khodorkovsky openly pointed to the alleged corruption involving people from the President's administration. Putin's response was to go on the attack, claiming that the sources of Khodorkovsky's own enormous wealth were illegal. In June 2003, the Office of the Prosecutor General opened a case against one of YuKOS's employees. In the following month, YuKOS's top manager, Platon Lebedev, was arrested. The arrest of Khodorkovsky followed in October. In July 2004, YuKOS was brought to the brink of liquidation by the Taxation Ministry and the Office of the Prosecutor General, who used legal procedures to achieve unlawful results. Mikhail Khodorkovsky called the YuKOS case 'a demonstration of force indifferent to the law, though observing legal rituals and procedures' that was extremely dangerous to Russia's development prospects (Mikhail Khodorkovsky Press-centre 2004).

It is not surprising that the Office of the Prosecutor General has turned into a tool for suppressing any business group that tries to demonstrate its independence. The office itself has not once responded to questions about corruption in its own ranks. The Commission for Public Control in the 'Anti-Corruption' Union has compiled a list of questions about activities of allegedly corrupt officials (Samotorova 2004).[12] The first question refers to two deputies to the Prosecutor General, Yury Biriukov and Vasily Kholmogorov.[13] The Anti-Corruption Commission of the previous State Duma demanded their dismissal, but failed in this attempt. Both officials were accused of creating obstacles to the anti-corruption investigation into the activities of several federal officials, even though there was serious documented evidence. The Anti-Corruption Commission tried to initiate investigations regarding Transportation Minister Sergey Frank, the head of MinAtom, Yevgeny Adamov, and the former head of the Chechen Republic, Mikhail Babich. The Prosecutor General deputies recognised that the facts stated by the Commission were correct, but refused to open an investigation. The 'Anti-Corruption' Union is attempting to investigate the motives behind this.

Now the Office of the Prosecutor General has its own material interests in participating in the investigations into numerous economic cases. In January 2000, Putin approved the regulations for the Foundation for the Development of the Office of Prosecutor General. The foundation was granted the right to accumulate 10% of all monies that were received from companies and organisations following the Office's initiative. These funds can be used not only for the needs of the Office itself, but also for the private needs of its employees, such as housing, holidays, interest free loans, and so on. All economic entities are obliged to pay 10% when they file lawsuits. The percentage has to be paid irrespective of whether the case reaches the courtroom or not. Similar foundations were established for the Interior Ministry and the secret service. Zamoshkin (2000) has pointed out the inherent threat of corruption in these arrangements.

The situation in the Interior Ministry (militia) is even more dangerous. Yury Levada's Analytical Centre revealed the results of a survey conducted in 12 large cities in May 2004 (Kolesnichenko 2004). Respondents were asked about their attitudes towards the Russian militia (police). Some 64% said that they did not trust the militia, while only 24% trusted them fully, and a further 10% trusted them to some extent. Some 46% were actually afraid of the militia, while no less than 78% believed that the militia in their city was corrupt. More than half (58%) agreed that bribe-taking by police officers had become systemic, while 40% believed that the militia had criminal connections. Approximately 46% claimed that they had been arrested or searched unlawfully during the previous three years, and fully a quarter had been victims of the militia's violence. Some 61% considered recent measures against dirty police officers – the case of the so-called 'werewolves in uniforms' and operation 'clean hands' – to be purely political campaigns that would not improve the situation. Experts from the Analytical Centre have argued that the 'strengthening of the power vertical' has not changed the situation (Kolesnichenko 2004). On the contrary, during the previous three years it had become even worse. In reality, the government does not control and manage its police force effectively.

Corruption has become normal for the Russian Armed Forces, too. Just one example will be cited. Russia's Navy Chief, Vladimir Kuroedov, is very close to Boris Kuzyk, a former Yeltsin advisor and now the owner of the Northern Shipyards company. It is said to have been Kuroedov who helped the company to secure a lucrative Chinese contract for two destroyers of the Sovremenny class, worth US$1 billion. Despite a government decision to award the contract to Baltic Plant, Kuroedov allegedly managed to transfer the contract to his friend. He also allegedly ordered the write-off of one relatively new destroyer from the Northern Fleet. Later, components from this ship were used to build destroyers for the Chinese Navy (Milashina 2004). There is a long list of similar records of 'commercial activities' by Admiral Kuroedov.

But Kuroedov is evidently only one of many. In July 2003 *Komsomol'skaya Pravda* published a list of 120 generals and admirals who were accused of various crimes, including bribery, embezzlement, abuse of office, and so on ('"Nepodsudnye" Generaly' 2003). Although the total loss to the budget due to their activities amounted to 43 billion roubles, none of them was sentenced to jail. The newspaper failed to gain access to dozens of other criminal cases of high-ranking officers. Meanwhile, a large proportion of crimes conducted by them remained hidden. Thus, the newspaper suggested, the real loss was much more serious.

CONCLUSIONS

On the whole, despite much discussion of corruption and dozens of commissions to combat it, Russia's authorities have not really addressed the problem. Firstly, it is extremely widespread, and a real struggle against this social evil would affect the interests of many groups, including the ruling elite. It is, moreover, a convenient tool for ensuring the loyalty of officials at all levels and from all fields. Thirdly, as mentioned above, the President's circle is allegedly not free from corruption. And finally, the current version of *nomenklatura* promotes corruption, making it a feature of the system.

The five years of Putin's presidency have been a period of further attempts to strengthen the power hierarchy on the basis of Yeltsin's model of 'super-presidentialism'. To this end, a series of unconstitutional measures has been undertaken. This was designed to introduce a functioning mechanism to the model that initially existed only on paper, and did not work under Yeltsin.

At the same time, Vladimir Putin proclaimed a policy of 'equal distancing' of big business from the government. The policy turned into a purging of oligarchs from the economy, that is the removal of businessmen who acquired their wealth through close connections with Yeltsin's group. Now those who came with Putin are redistributing the wealth to their benefit. Putin's 'strengthening of the power vertical' provides excellent opportunities for this.

The interests of people that followed Putin to government offices (former KGB/FSB officers and those from St Petersburg) coincided with the broader interests of the *nomenklatura*. As a result, the latter received 'fresh blood' and actively restored its position in society. The system that seemed to collapse in 1991 is re-emerging without its axis of Communist ideology. This ideology has been substituted by the pursuit of wealth.

The Communist system that evolved after two coups – Khrushchev's and then Brezhnev's – was a system of bargaining. It was based on 'administrative' exchange, and money was not important for it. Recent reforms introduced money into it, and money exchange became a norm for the system. Nowadays everything can be bought or sold within the system – from the lives of entire army battalions to ministerial offices. For example, the terrorists who seized the school in Beslan in September 2004 paid bribes to the local police to turn a blind eye to their preparations; this allegedly even extended to escorting them. The suicide bombers who blew up two Russian airplanes in August 2004 also paid bribes in order to get on board. The system is working for itself, ignoring national interests. Rampant corruption promoted by the system is a serious obstacle for national development. However, paradoxically, it also destroys the system from within and prevents the country from falling into real authoritarianism, a propensity to which was obvious during Yeltsin's presidency and which became a state policy under Putin.

NOTES

1. I owe thanks to Dr Catherine Hirst for her help in preparing this chapter.
2. Boris Yeltsin used to his benefit the August 1991 coup that was a conspiracy of the state *nomenklatura* dissatisfied with Gorbachev's rule.
3. Komsomol is an abbreviation for the All-Union Young Communists League.
4. Aslund and Boone (2002) point out that, ' . . . whereas only 10 years ago Russia's industry was fully state-owned, today 90 per cent of it is privatised and 61 per cent of the companies have one controlling shareholder group'.
5. 'Red directors' is a euphemism for directors and managers appointed by the Communist party, who tried to stay loyal to the old system.
6. In May 2004 the European Court of Human Rights ruled that the three-day arrest of Vladimir Gusinsky in 2000 (after which he chose to sell his NTV channel and to leave the country) was unlawful (*Moscow News*, No.18, 2004, http://www.mn.ru/issue.php?2004-17-58).
7. Valentin Moiseev was a Deputy Head of the First Asian Department, Ministry of Foreign Affairs. He was sentenced to four and a half years in prison for transferring a paper, 'Russian Policy on the Korean Peninsula', to a representative of the South Korean National Security Agency. Moiseev and his lawyers insist that the paper was an academic one and contained no confidential information. They have applied to the European Court of Human Rights, claiming that Moiseev was a victim of a violation of The Convention for the Protection of Human Rights and Fundamental Freedoms.
8. Officers of the Russian secret service still often call themselves 'chekists'. The name derives from the acronym of ChK – the Extraordinary Commission for Combating Counterrevolution and Sabotage – that was established in December 1917.
9. This term refers to representatives of the secret service, law enforcement bodies and the military.
10. Vladimir Putin's transformation is a good illustration of this process. A low-ranking KGB officer, Putin was appointed to a position in East Germany. Later he recognised that he had preferred this appointment to a more serious professional career within the USSR, because he wanted to go abroad (working in a foreign country meant a much higher standard of living) (Gevorkyan *et al.* 2000: 50). Since Putin had no special achievements, after several years of service he was transferred to an insignificant position at the local university in Leningrad (St Petersburg). Seeing no prospects in his KGB career, he retired, and was later invited by his former university professor to take the office of deputy-mayor of St Petersburg. His movement

into the *nomenklatura* ranks was finalised when he secured a position in the Kremlin administration. Vladimir Putin then returned to the FSB (KGB) as its director. But this awesome career jump became possible only due to the fact that Putin was an appointee of the 'Family'. Later, in the same manner, he was appointed as Boris Yeltsin's successor.

11. I use the term 'bads' as opposed to 'goods'. 'Goods' are the cases in which more of a commodity/service is preferred to less, while in the case of 'bads', less of them is preferred to more (Pindyck and Rubinfeld 2001: 70). Since services provided by officials can be treated as public goods, phenomena such as corruption will be public bads.

12. The Anti-Corruption Union was created 8 April 2004 by the Indem Foundation, the National Anti-Corruption Committee, and the All-Russian Organisation for Small and Medium Entrepreneurship (OPORA).

13. Yury Biriukov played an active role in the case of YuKOS; Vasily Kolmogorov was in charge of Berezovsky's and Gusinsky's cases.

8. Political Corruption and the Law-Governed Post-Communist State: the Polish Case and Broader Applications

Adam Czarnota

INTRODUCTION

Common sense knowledge tells us that corruption is nearly everywhere. Perhaps a society of angels is without corruption; but at the same time we cannot empirically confirm that such a society really exists. So back to Earth and earthly societies, where there is unquestionably corruption. But this does not mean that the level and functions of corruption are everywhere the same.

The aim of this chapter is to analyse corruption in post-communist countries from the perspective of the dual character of post-communist transformation in the context of a proclaimed democratic law-governed state. The focus is on political corruption at the highest level of the state. I am not going to provide a definition of corruption, but will focus on the place and functions of corruption in the structure of the process of the transformation of society, economy and political structure in the former communist states of Central and Eastern Europe (CEE). It will be argued that corruption in these countries during the process of transformation is not merely something that could easily be described as social pathology – some deviation from normality, something abnormal. Rather, the situation is more complicated than it appears. Corruption has become a structural, that is to say *constitutional*, feature of these societies. Corruption fulfils a role, and has become functional in post-communist societies under transformation.

My hypothesis is that the principle of the democratic law-governed state was introduced too early in the transformation process, and that the rule of law, in the form in which it was introduced in post-communist states, provided a space for corruption. This means that the introduction of rule of law principles prematurely has been functional for corruption. I will suggest that corruption has not a single but a dual character. There is a visible transformation of political, economic and social institutions, on which the attention of dominant parts of the media and social sciences focus, and a hidden dimension of the transformation in which corruption is one of the central elements.

In the final part of the chapter, I will focus on the early proclamation of a law-governed state by the new political class. I will argue that a narrow and formalistic conception of a law-governed state introduced at the time of the transfer of power is functional from the point of view of both visible and hidden dimensions of transformation. In the long run, the social effects of the formalistic law-governed state are destructive for the proper functioning of the new social and economic system being created. I will use examples from Poland, the CEE country with which I am most familiar; but the theoretical conclusions are applicable to all countries of the region. In order to paint the full picture, it will still be necessary to add local elements and peculiarities.

INFORMATION ON SOME POLISH CASES

The visitor to Poland is struck by the enormous mass of daily information about corruption scandals at all level of society. Between 2003 and 2005, the Polish *Sejm* (Diet) – the lower chamber of the Polish parliament – set up three investigating commissions in relation to corruption at the highest level of government. The first of the three commissions was established to investigate the so-called Rywin case. Mr Lew Rywin, a person well known in the Polish cultural and political establishment, owner of a television and movie producing company and co-producer of Roman Polański's movie 'The Pianist', made a terrible error of judgement; and in April 2004, it was revealed that, nearly two years after having committed his act, Rywin had at last been imprisoned. In July 2002, on behalf of the so-called power-holding group, he approached the media house Agora with a request for a payment of more than US$17 million in exchange for favourable provisions for Agora in a new and much debated media law. Adam Michnik, hero of the former KOR dissident movement and editor in chief of the daily newspaper *Gazeta Wyborcza*, the flagship title of Agora, taped the conversation and made the meeting public about six months later (December 2002), when *Gazeta Wyborcza* published the article 'Przychodzi Rywin do Michnika' (Rywin comes to Michnik).

When knowledge of the corrupt offer became public, the *Sejm* set up an investigative commission, and for several months, the entire nation was both mesmerised and entertained by direct telecasts from the commission's hearings. During the hearings, surprised, so-called normal, relatively honest, law-abiding, average citizens learnt about the corruption networks in the Polish Third Republic. As of mid-2005, the heated atmosphere connected with the Rywin case had still not completely dissipated. Rywin was sentenced to imprisonment by the court of first instance, which found him guilty of attempting to corrupt. However, the judges also found that he had acted alone. Both he and the public prosecutor's office appealed the verdict of the first court. The appellate court found him guilty – but also that he had not acted alone, but on behalf of a 'power-holding group'. Meanwhile, a number of the members of the *Sejm's* special investigating commission wrote their reports, which was in itself very interesting. One of the most radical, written by the member of the opposition party Law and Justice, was in the end accepted by the *Sejm*. The report indicated that responsibility lay at that time with the Prime Minister and leader of the post-communist SLD party, Leszek Miller, as well as some others occupying senior offices in the state. Yet nothing happened. The report is sitting somewhere on a shelf, and no action against the suspects has been taken. It is true that Leszek Miller lost office, but long after the scandal broke, and in different circumstances (he resigned in early May 2004, claiming that this was related to the state of the economy).

Some people, and especially a few members of the special commission, made political gains, and the public learnt that corruption exists at the highest level. That only confirmed popular beliefs that corruption is everywhere and that it is impossible to fight against it, since the politicians and other top officials in the so-called democratic law-governed state are immune from any accountability.

But not everything was lost. After the lessons with the first *Sejm* investigating commission and its huge impact on society, a new commission was set up. At the end of 2004, the *Sejm* established another investigating commission in relation to the suspicious arrest and removal of the executive president of the state-owned company ORLEN – the monopolist on the Polish market in the import and refinery of oil. The problem was extremely delicate and important, since it related to the security of the state.

This time, there were more members of the Parliament who wanted to become members of the commission, knowing from the experience with the former commission how huge the political gains could be. The commission soon began work, and nearly every day of investigation revealed new facts about the dense networks of informal connections between high-level members of the political class, the new capitalist class, and the special services. The picture that emerges from the information gathered during these hearings is that both political and economic life are shaped by networks of informal connections and peculiar, non-transparent dealings. The hearings confirm how great is the impact of the members of the former communist secret services and the contemporary secret services on the economic decisions of the state. The commission was still operating at the time of writing, but the materials and information received during the hearings show that there are deeper layers of networks of power, hidden structures and even criminal connections that not only exist, but exert considerable influence on the country. That influence is outside the legally defined institutional life of the Third Polish Republic.

It is disturbing to learn that there were meetings held in the dead of night between the Prime Minister, the President and the richest man in Poland, Jan Kulczyk, regarding the appointment of the chairman of the state-owned company; that the richest man flew to Vienna to meet with a former Soviet spy operating in Poland; that the meeting was organised by so-called Polish businesspeople with criminal records; and that such people were guests at functions organised by the President's Office. At the time of writing, it was impossible to predict the political outcome of the work of the special commission to investigate the so-called ORLEN affair. But as far as the increase of public awareness of the true nature of power is concerned, the commission had already done a great deal. The most unfortunate aspect of all this is that the revelations unveiled by the hearings of the commissions undermined the very tiny amount of legitimacy enjoyed by the new democratic institutions and the rule of law.

Even more recently, in February 2005, the Polish *Sejm* established a third special commission, this time to investigate the process of privatisation of PZU (the biggest insurance company in the country). The audience soon learnt that there was a political battle regarding which party would control the PZU privatisation process; that the small unknown Portuguese company that bought the Polish insurance giant did not have sufficient funds to pay for it; and that the highest officials in the country were interested in the process, and applied pressure to secure the greatest advantage from the PZU privatisation.

There are also some major criminal cases. The most important is the FOZZ case. A special fund for servicing the Polish foreign debt – FOZZ – was set up by the former communist government before the transfer of power in 1989. Surprisingly, millions of dollars allocated to the fund disappeared. Journalists called FOZZ the mother of all corruption affairs. The entire institution was used to transfer money from the state budget to private pockets. The legal process against the people responsible for the FOZZ scandal took nearly 13 years, and the statute of limitation will soon apply to some charges.

There was also information about the arrest of a post-communist SLD (Democratic Left Alliance) MP from Łódź, Mr Andrzej Pęczak, on corruption charges. The Agency for Internal Security taped a conversation Pęczak had with Mr Marek Dochnal – officially a lobbyist – regarding economic favours, in the form of the latest model of Mercedes Benz (with tinted windows, as insisted on by the prime minister) in return for favourable decisions in the privatisation process that would allow him to acquire some state-owned enterprise for nothing.

Only a few examples of the most recent and biggest corruption scandals that have come to light in Poland have been mentioned here. In popular consciousness, there prevails the opinion that all politics is a dirty and corrupt game, politicians are not accountable, and the entire system – including the legal system – works in their interest. There is a widespread popular belief that corruption is everywhere. It is argued here that social scientists should treat that common opinion seriously, and not simply ignore it. Such opinions constitute social facts in themselves. But they also indicate areas which should become objects of serious investigation.

ONE OR TWO POST-COMMUNIST TRANSFORMATIONS?

The Polish sociologist Zdzislaw Krasnodębski recently formulated a thesis about two post-communist transformations. He claimed that actually both types – one open and transparent, the other hidden – had taken place in Poland. The open and transparent one was the transformation of the institutional structures of the communist state into the formal institutions of parliamentary democracy. The second, parallel transformation – the hidden one – was the process of local modification and concretisation of the new institutions of the state and market economy and their rules to work in the interests of the transformed communist elites and co-opted segments of the former oppositional elites (Krasnodębski 2004). Earlier, and in a different but related way that referred specifically to political life, another Polish sociologist, Andrzej Rychard (2002), formulated a thesis concerning two levels or scenes of conducting politics in post-communist Poland.

I accept the thesis that there were and still are two dimensions of social life. The standard criticism of such a broad thesis is that transformation is only a partly controlled process that is also rather spontaneous, and that the spontaneous dimension creates side effects which later figure as the phenomena Krasnodębski classifies as a hidden transformation. Potential critics representing such a position could be partly correct. Post-communist transformation *is* a partly spontaneous process – but only partly. It is enough to control crucial strategic points in order to have an influence on nearly the entire process of transformation. That does not, of course, mean that someone or some centre is able to control *all* elements of transformations. But as argued above, it is enough to have a major influence on the outcome of transformation. Such a position has nothing to do with a 'conspiratorial view of history', but rightly stresses the possibility of constructing social reality after communism. Anybody who studies the matrix of communist societies and states knows that there was a similar dichotomy present in them too: they too had visible and invisible dimensions of life. Invisible factors were more important than visible ones. The entire system was constructed around that double structure. Institutions in the communist era had their façades and their real contents. It is difficult to argue against the notion that such a double structure was likely to survive the transfer of power.

It is accepted here that there were and still are two dimensions of transformation, as articulated by Krasnodębski. The next logical step is to identify that hidden dimension of transformation. From a common sense perspective, all processes and mechanisms that are not open and transparent are hidden. The hidden dimension of transformation has a different meaning. It relates to the creation of a network of groups of vested interests that used the formal, open institutions to promote and pursue those interests. It means that the hidden dimension of transformation is in symbiosis with the open dimension of the transformation – that legally formal and *prima facie* open institutions in time become dependent for their functioning on the hidden elements of transformation. It means further that the two dimensions become functionally dependent on each other in fulfilling their respective functions. In other words, the hidden structure of the transformation became structural or constitutive for the entire process.

The post-transformation period was officially about the creation of new democratic institutions that would be open and transparent in their operation. It was the popular belief and conviction that these institutions would establish a framework for an open public space after communism. The operation of new institutions would be based on transparent rules based on law, and they would work in an impersonal way. Although expectations were very high, they were also based on realism. The main arguments used in discussion within the political class after 1989 were opposed to overly adventurous experimentation and any notion of a 'third way'. The new ruling elites chose to transplant institutions and recipes from developed market liberal democracies in the West. So a market economy, human rights, the rule of law and democracy were on the menu of the day.

But there was a problem. This was that the cooks were not properly trained, and did not know what ingredients should be used in the preparation of the menu. Understanding the basic ideas appeared to be rather simple, and was connected with the beliefs and convictions that, after the initial period of the introduction of institutional change, there would be a healthy system with a strong and open public space for discussion, coupled with strong but limited state institutions capable of implementing and guaranteeing the rule of law, justice and the realisation of the public good by the state's institutions and apparatus. In short, there was an expectation that the state's institutions would operate basically in accordance with the formal rationality described by Max Weber. That blueprint was not implemented. So the question arises: what went wrong? Why, from the perspectives of both popular consciousness and the sophisticated analyses of social scientists – including sociologists, political scientists and academic lawyers dealing with the operation of the legal system – does such a dark picture emerge (see for example Hausner and Marody 2000; Mariański 2002; Mokrzycki *et al.* 2002; Krasnodębski 2003; Jarosz 2004)?

ON THE SINS OF TRANSFORMATIONS – BUT ESPECIALLY ON ITS ORIGINAL SIN

In searching for the answer to the question of the negative image, social scientists look back to the beginning of transformation as the source of future problems and dissatisfaction. However, they differ on when to locate the beginning of the transformation. Some claim that it started in 1989, with the transfer of power from the communists. Others – albeit a minority – claim that it started much earlier, at the beginning of the 1980s, with the imposition of martial law in Poland by General Jaruzelski's government.

Without empirical evidence, that issue cannot be resolved at present. But it is not particularly important from our point of view anyway. What *is* important is that there is a general consensus among social scientists that something went wrong with the transformation process, and that the outcome of this is a problem with the functioning of the institutions of state.

The problem with the transformation is that it was not and is not restricted to politics, but also included the economy and all other areas of social life. Most important from the point of view of effects have been the connections between politics and the economy. The political class chose the wrong model of economic transformation. The same basic model of transformation of property relations was implemented in all former communist countries.

We can answer the question of who was responsible for the adoption and implantation of that model. There are two positions. Some claim that it was Western agents and forces pursuing their interests in the countries that were joining the world market (Wedel 2001; Wincenty 2002). A second position claims that the political class in post-communist countries is responsible, and has been more interested in this version than in another model of changes in the system of property rights (Zybertowicz 1993). The collapse of the Iron Curtain opened up all the countries of the former CMEA (Comecon) to global market forces; but that opening did not predetermine the choice of economic policies. Again it is not the intention here finally to resolve the issue of who was responsible for the adoption of the preferred model. More important is the outcome of the adopted model of economic change. One effect is a hybrid economic system, in which one part of it functions according to the classical model of the free market, while another still operates according to the old communist system of conscious steering of the economy.

The same hybrid system functions at the level of the state. The state is operating on the basis of contradictory principles, and is in effect dysfunctional. Different types of rationalities regulate the functioning of different parts of the state. On the most general level, the state still performs the function of a proprietor, and is involved in both the governance of the economic units and the redistribution of wealth. On the other hand, the state itself created different types of funds and special economic agencies, in order to terminate its own involvement in economic decision-making and processes. Jadwiga Staniszkis – in my opinion, the most interesting commentator on the post-communist transformation – has written of the commercialisation of state economic assets, including the commercialisation of the traditional functions of the state. That commercialisation process does not mean that the state is free from economic responsibilities – far from it. What has changed is that formally commercialised state economic assets became prey for the politically dominant group. In other words, commercialisation is connected with political capitalism – the type of system in which political position translates easily and without any restriction not only into the extraction of economic rent, but also into a dominant economic position.

Contradictions in the economic and political system have an impact on the social fabric, and through society are further reinforced. After more than fifteen years of transformation, it is justifiable to claim that the system of change has not achieved the expected aims. Instead, a system based on different types of rationality is being created. External observers easily see a façade, comprising institutions that look from a distance like typical institutions of a western market liberal democracy. From within, however, and using different cognitive powers, it is possible not so much to see but more to observe in its effects the operation of the hidden dimensions of the transformations.

Different rationalities and hidden dimensions of the entire system translate themselves to the legal system as well. Perhaps it would be more important to note that the legal system itself reflects this dual character of the transformation, and is deeply anchored in systemic contradictions (for examples of the privatisation law in Poland see Kosikowski 2003: 41). Law is playing the function of regulator of the re-transformation processes in the economy and a tool that provides a framework for planning and control of these processes.

A LAW-GOVERNED STATE – BUT BASED ON PARTLY ROTTEN LAW?

Legal scholars usually look overwhelmingly at legal texts; only a small fraction of them, as well as legal sociologists, are interested in the actual *functioning* of the legal system. But even this small cohort is subject to a problem when approaching hidden dimensions of the operation of the law. This is due to the dominant role of legal positivism as a paradigm both for law itself and for thinking about law. What interests lawyers is positively existing legal principles, norms, and rules – not the substance or functioning of law, but only positive law.

After World War II, Professor Gustav Radbruch formulated his famous thesis that legal positivism disarmed German lawyers in the face of Nazism. This severe criticism of legal positivism was made by a former minister of justice and law professor during the Weimar Republic, who for years had himself been a legal positivist in Germany. The dominant type of legal theory during communism was simplistic legal positivism in Marxist packaging.

Marxist philosophy provided a sort of rhetoric, but was not taken seriously by either legal academia or the legal profession. Vulgar legal positivism was functional and instrumental for justifying any new type of regulation. There was no questioning of the 'holders of power'. Unquestioning acceptance of any command of the sovereign was the rule. The entire legal system, as well as legal education, was based on this type of communist version of vulgar legal positivism. There were a few individual lawyers representing a non-conformist approach, but they were outside the system of the institutions of justice. In the process of implementing the lustration law in Poland, we learnt how broad and deep was the penetration of the legal profession by the secret services during the communist era, and how many judges, procurators and advocates were secret collaborators with these services, against the official professional ethics. Such a legal profession cannot guarantee the autonomy of law.

Did something change after the collapse of communism? On the surface it looks as if it did, since one of the first amendments to constitutions was the introduction of the concept of the 'democratic law-governed state'. In addition, there were declarations of a serious approach to and implementation of a bill of rights, especially concerning liberties that were suppressed during the communist era. The belief was that freedom and democracy would flourish when political power – the government – was fully subject to and controlled by the law, as a result of which citizens would be guaranteed the possibility of enjoying their rights. After more than 15 years of the transformation, it is possible to claim that the entire ideology of the post-communist transformation can be reduced to a few keywords, such as democracy, the rule of law, rights – and later one major keyword that, if it did not entirely replace, at least overshadowed the former three: that keyword was the market economy. This combination in practice created a problem. The rule of law means that law plays a special – privileged – role in society, by both providing a framework for actions and acting as a medium for communication. To play such a role, as a foundation of expected rational behaviour, law has to be relatively stable, as well as relatively autonomous from politics and the economy.

But there were structural obstacles to the implementation of the law's autonomy, which were of a different nature from the above-mentioned character of the legal profession. Post-communist transformation requires changes in the institutional framework of the state and society. The economic changes – the process of building the market – are carried out by the political power. Decisions about commercialisation and then privatisation of the state's assets are taken by the government. This may not sound particularly alarming; something rather similar occurs with the process of privatisation in established market economies. But there is one important difference. This is that, in established market economies, even the most radical privatisation decisions are taken and conducted by the government in a market environment. The market and its institutions operate as relatively autonomous domains in relation to politics. In the former communist countries, in contrast, market institutions were created from scratch by political decision. The market is still not an autonomous institution. Law played a crucial role in the creation of the market institutions. Given the character of the transformation itself, there was no scope for the law to operate as an autonomous system. Rather, law has been an expression of the will of the sovereign, with virtually no limitation.

At first glance, this might not seem to be much of a problem. If law in the transformation process was an expression of political will, and the legal profession inherited from the communist system was a rather vulgar form of legal positivism, then the implementation of law adopted by the political power should proceed smoothly. But nothing could be further from the truth. Since the beginning of the transformation, there have been complaints about the operation of the courts, procuracy, public administration and later on local government as well. Some fifteen years after the introduction of the change, the situation is, at least according to public opinion, worse rather than better.

One of the elements that needs to be taken into account is that the main element of the transformation – the one that really caused rapid changes in social institutions and the fabric of society – was economic change, in particular changes in the distribution of property rights. The creation of the market economy promised in Poland's so-called Balcerowicz plan had a profound impact on society. It was not only an economic impact, but also a moral one. Implementation of the plan created opportunities to become rich quickly, to acquire property rights in former state assets. Members of the new political class adopted laws that established criteria for commercialisation and privatisation of state-owned assets. The implementation of these laws was then in the hands of the state administration, dependent on its political masters.

Part of the law created by the legislators (the parliaments) in post-communist countries is so-called bad law. It did not reflect or adhere to the rules of a high standard of legislation. This was only partly due to the huge legislative demand – the need to regulate whole areas of social life under the relentless pressure of time. It is true that the parliaments in all the countries in transition from communism were exceptionally creative and the numbers of new statutes adopted huge. However, in addition to this problem of overload, the other cause of bad law was the concern of parts of the ruling class to realise the particular interests of their political base and/or particular groups. An example is Lew Rywin's offer on behalf of the 'power-holding group' to have the regulations in the statute on media ownership constructed in such a way that the Agora Group would have been granted a dominant position in the market.

Rywin's offer probably represents only a tiny tip of a huge iceberg. The investigation conducted by the special parliamentary commission made public other interesting and not readily comprehensible facts. Among these were that the Prime Minister at the time knew about Rywin's offer, yet did not even inform the Minister of Justice about it. The President of the Republic also knew about it and did nothing either; nor did other less senior people holding public office. All this confirmed that the institutions of the state are not oriented towards, and are not acting for, the realisation of the public good during the difficult process of transformation. Rather, people occupying the highest public offices realise the interests of their political support group. It is more than clientelism (on clientelism see Mączak 1994). Clientelism could work for the public good when there exists in post-communist systems such interconnectedness between groups of specific and vested interests that they hinder the development of the entire system (see the insightful Zybertowicz 2005). András Sajó, the distinguished Hungarian scholar, has written in relation to post-communist East European countries in transformation that, '
... political corruption is not just about corruption of the public/private sphere, or about bribery in governmental offices and parties; it constitutes a series of events dictated by the needs of the political structures. It is political in the sense that it is the political structure itself that enables and requires corrupt practices that become a structural (constitutive) phenomenon of society' (Sajó 2003: 171). This thesis captures very well the peculiarities of corruption in the post-communist countries.

Law and the *dual structure* of that symbiosis are involved in the process of the creation of bad law. The bad law is full of inconsistencies and contradictions. At the same time, it is very complicated, which allows interested parties and groups to interpret it to their advantage. Another characteristic is the delegation of discretionary regulation. The justification given for that delegation to particular ministers is in terms of the needs of transformation, but in practice that discretionary delegation is used for the subordination of the realisation of parties' interests in accordance with the so-called 'booty law'. At the same time, governance by the discretionary powers of particular ministers destabilises the law. So far, and paying lip service to the rule of law, all political parties have treated the existing regulations in a rather loose manner for the realisation of their particular interests.

THE RULE OF LAW AND POST-COMMUNIST TRANSFORMATION

To this point, I have established that the post-communist transformation has a dual character, visible and hidden, and that political corruption is different from the traditional blurred border between public and private domains. As also argued, law is functional in that system of structural corruption. That the law is bad law and in the background, or is an outcome of corruption, are propositions that can easily be supported.

The question remains: what is the relationship between the law-governed democratic state or democratic rule of law concept and the structural corruption in post-communist states? The rule of law is about transparency, accountability and predictability. This last element of predictability is a necessary foundation for rationality. Rationality on the other hand is a necessary precondition for a market capitalist economy, according to Max Weber. It seems to me that the rule of law in post-communist states plays a façade role for masking the structural corruption of the state. After more than a decade and a half of dual transformation, in which the rule of law played the role of a façade, some states have arrived at the point where that dual role has started to reproduce itself. We therefore face a new type of situation in which the system, with a façade and institutions behind it, is reproducing itself.

Shortly after the transfer of power in 1989, the new ruling elites agreed to implement the rule of law in the countries under consideration here. The rule of law was understood in a formal positivistic way, and reduced to the concept of legality and rule according to the legal text. That implementation was signalled by changes in the constitutions, which spelled out that the state was henceforth a 'democratic law-governed state', and then various institutional changes necessary for the implantation of the rule of law. The most important of those changes was the introduction of an independent judiciary. In Poland, the National Council of the Judiciary was established as an independent self-governing body. The main function of that body was to safeguard the independent position of the judiciary. From a material perspective, the salaries of the judges increased, but only marginally. In effect, independence and secure tenure were granted to a professional group that in the communist past had been totally dependent on political power. Former Chief Justice of the Supreme Court of Poland, Professor Strzembosz, believed that the judiciary would purge itself of compromised judges, but without pressure being exerted on the entire profession. This cleansing process did not happen, and compromised judges are still in their positions. One of the social preconditions of the rule of law, namely the independence of the judiciary, was introduced too early in the process of transformation, with serious outcomes for the rule of law. This means that the entire court system in Poland is generally not efficient; but it is especially inefficient as far as corruption matters are concerned. In a number of cases, the statute of limitation already applies and the cases cannot be continued.

Another dimension is corruption among judges themselves. The well-regarded daily Polish newspaper *Rzeczpospolita* made public information about the connections between judges and criminals. Especially widely publicised were the cases of a judge from Toruń – who handed down a favourable verdict in a criminal case in return for economic advantage – and another in Lublin. In both cases, the procedure for removing the judges was exceedingly protracted. At the beginning of 2005, the media made public the scope of corruption within the judiciary in Olsztyn, the capital city of a north-eastern province.

Until the introduction of the 1997 lustration law (amended 1998), the number of judges who were secret collaborators with the communist secret services was unknown. Since 1999, while we still do not know the overall numbers, the names of members of the judiciary who have returned positive lustration declarations have been published in the *Monitor Polski*, the governmental gazette. But since the Polish lustration law penalises only those who lie during the lustration process, these named judges still occupy their positions. Attempts to remove them by disciplinary procedure, on the basis of breaches of the judicial oath, have met with vigorous resistance from the profession.

It is possible to mention many other examples of corrupt behaviour by the legal profession and reflect upon some of the causes of that behaviour. It seems to me that introducing the concept of the 'democratic law-governed state' too soon played a crucial role in the institutionalisation of the dual character of the transformation.

The constitutional provision of the 'democratic law-governed state' was interpreted in a narrow positivistic way as legality. The legal profession interpreted that regulative constitutional principle in that way. This narrow interpretation blocked the flexibility necessary in steering the process of transformation, but also blocked any possibility of interpreting legal norms from the point of view of their merits or a substantive conception of justice, not to mention the crucial issue of transitional justice. Too early and narrow an interpretation of the 'democratic law-governed state' principle allows old networks smoothly to embrace the new reality and in time control that new reality. In other words, the rule of law has been functional to the creation of the dual character of the transformation. It works to provide legitimacy to the new regime, while, at the same time, its narrow interpretation allows abuse of the new institutions and rules by the hidden networks of interests.

The noble principle that was supposed to regulate the operation of the political system was turned into its opposite. The case of the post-communist state in which the function of the rule of law is the opposite of what was expected probably cannot be treated as universally valid, but is nevertheless worthy of study.

9. Countering Corruption: An Australian Perspective

George Gilligan and Diana Bowman[1]

INTRODUCTION – THE PHENOMENON THAT IS CORRUPTION

At the time of writing (March 2005), there is extensive coverage in the media of the report by the UK Government's Commission for Africa. The Commission is strongly supported by UK Prime Minister Tony Blair and his Chancellor of the Exchequer, Gordon Brown, and is being promoted as '… the most serious analysis of Africa's problems for a generation' (World Bank 2005: 1). The Commission for Africa Report argues that 'the issue of good governance and capacity-building is what we believe lies at the core of all Africa's problems' (Commission for Africa 2005: 29). The Report states that widescale corruption adds at least 25 per cent to the costs of government procurement, and reiterates the very sensible truism that countering corruption involves tackling those who offer bribes as well as those who take them (Commission for Africa 2005: 37). The vast majority of people in Africa have suffered greatly from the effects of corruption, but it is important to remember that, although the impact of corruption can be acute in less developed and transitional economies, corruption blights all continents, not just Africa, and can harm all types of societies and organisations (Bowles 1998).

Corruption is an enduring social problem that has featured to some extent in most societies, in most eras. Corruption can cause significant harm to economic, social and political structures at local, regional, national and international levels. Its corrosive effects can distort markets, undermine the rule of law, facilitate the incubation and growth of terrorism, stimulate the growth and impact of organised crime, delegitimise political processes, and generally reduce the standard of living of most people in those societies that it affects. The durability of corruption is testimony to its often low visibility within prevailing sets of power relations, as well as the ensuing difficulties associated with producing policy initiatives that can combine effectively with specific law enforcement responses to counter the prevalence of corruption (Gilligan 1999).

Despite increasing attention in recent years to corruption by, amongst others, governments, pressure groups, academics and non-governmental organisations around the world, there remains a lack of consensus about how corruption should be defined (Jain 1998). This is not surprising, and reflects the complexity of corruption as a phenomenon. For example, Tanzi (1998: 564) notes that 'corruption has been defined in many different ways, each lacking in some aspect'. The process of attempting to define corruption has been going on for a long time. For instance, in the United Kingdom, various statutory instruments have attempted to define what constitutes corrupt behaviour, such as the *Public Bodies Corrupt Practices Act 1889* and the *Prevention of Corruption Act 1906*. Some analysts centre on abuse of public office – for example, Bardhan (1996), who sees public sector corruption as the use of public office for private gain. Many definitions involve some conception of the public interest and an element of private gain for money, power or prestige, but have varying degrees of delineation. Shleifer and Vishny (1993) seek to differentiate between corruption involving theft and corruption without theft. Heidenheimer *et al.* (1989: 8–11) examined the subject of defining corruption and identified three broad types of definition: *public-office-centered*; *public-interest-centered*; and *market-centered*.

Given the multi-faceted nature of corruption and the levels of ambiguity that surround it, some variation in the definition and explanation of corruption is inevitable. However, in general, definitional models of corruption usually include some degree of cooptation or capture of public agencies and officials, and generally cite behaviours such as bribery, misappropriation and nepotism as typifying corruption. Nevertheless, corruption should not be perceived solely as a public sector phenomenon, since it can be a feature of intrinsically private sets of relationships and exchange. Indeed, corruption problems in the private sector can be just as intractable and damaging as those in the public sector. It should be clear then that corruption may be present in both large and small organisational structures, and in both the public and the private sectors. It follows therefore that corporate entities are a significant conduit for much corruption and other forms of associated misconduct. Many individuals and organisations around the world continue to try to define corruption so that it might be possible to identify acts of corruption and measure their effects (Philp 1997; Johnston 2001). Some examples can be seen in Table 9.1.

Table 9.1   Defining the corruption phenomenon

Jurisdiction	Definition
International	'The misuse of public powers, office and authority for private gain through bribery, extortion, influence, peddling, nepotism, fraud, speed money or embezzlement' (United Nations Development Programme 1999: 7)
Europe	'Requesting, offering, giving or accepting, directly or indirectly, a bribe or any other undue advantage or prospect thereof, which distorts the proper performance of any duty or behaviour required of the recipient of the bribe, the undue advantage or the prospect thereof' (Council of Europe 1999)
Africa	'The soliciting, accepting, obtaining, giving, promising or offering of gratification by way of a bribe or other personal temptations of inducement or the misuse or abuse of a public office for private advantage or benefit' (Zambia Anti-Corruption Commission 1996, s.3)
Asia	'Corruption is the asking, receiving or agreeing to receive, giving, promising or offering of any gratification as an inducement or reward to a person to do or not to do any act, with a corrupt intention' (Corruption Prevention Investigation Bureau, Singapore 2001)
Middle East	'Corruption is the behaviour of private individuals or public officials who deviate from set responsibilities and use their position of power in order to serve private ends and secure private gains' (Lebanon Anti-Corruption Initiative Report 1999)
North America	'The misuse of public office for private gain' (United States Agency for International Development 2003)
Academic	'The use of public office for private advantage, the latter term understood not only in a pecuniary sense but also in terms of status and influence' (Palmier 1983: 207)

As shown by Table 9.1, there are many different approaches to defining the phenomenon of corruption, and although the lack of uniformity between regional definitions may make the study of corruption more difficult (Jain 2001), it does seek to highlight how cultural differences may underpin perceptions of corruption. Table 9.2 lists some of the commonalities and differences between various attempts at definition:

Table 9.2 Common threads and tensions in defining corruption

Threads	Tensions
The misuse of discretionary power	Generally a much greater focus on the public sector, and less on the private
Active	Generally economic in motivation with less consideration given to alternative motivations of the actions
Gain/benefit may be for the individual or for others	
Violation, e.g. of trust, position	Must the gain/benefit be pecuniary? Or may the advantage be social/hierarchical?
Positive result for one or more parties, with generally a negative consequence for society	
Socially aggregated phenomenon	Can corruption ever be seen as advantageous – even if only in the short term?

This variance reflects the fact that the shape and scale of corruption varies among and within societies (Johnston 2000: 1). As such, if one is seeking to deconstruct notions of corruption, then it is helpful to consider corruption not as an *inherent type* of behaviour, but instead as a *negotiated classification* of behaviour (Chibnall and Saunders 1977). The advantage of this approach is that it alleviates the difficulties of being locked into assumptions about what constitutes corruption that may have some purchase in one country, culture or industry over time, but which may have limited relevance in another country, culture or industry over time. Stereotypical assumptions regarding corruption that possess limited explanatory power can bog down analysis of what is a cross-cultural – and indeed global – phenomenon. The need for explanations that are sufficiently flexible to be generalised across cultures, industries or countries is clear.

This need is accentuated when one considers how assumptions, classifications and understandings of what constitutes corruption, or who is corrupt, may change substantially over a relatively short period within a single country, or even within a single industry. For example, in the United States during the nineteenth century, individuals such as Thomas Carnegie, Daniel Drew and Leland Stanford moved swiftly from the status of 'Robber Barons' to scions of the establishment

(Abadinsky 1977). A similar process is underway in contemporary Russia and some of the other sovereign states of the former USSR. So when one considers this innate structural flexibility surrounding corruption, any universally accepted template of what corruption actually is must be seen as something of a *definitional holy grail*.

The definitional difficulties are accentuated by the potential that corruption offers for political influence. This is evident in many contemporary regimes around the world, and was very evident in the past as well. One example is in municipal politics in the United States, such as Chicago in the 1920s and 1930s, when norms regarding corruption were manipulated by both politicians and organised crime actors to distort political processes, and amass wealth and influence (Albanese 1996). This manipulation is made possible because, in comparison with many other forms of harmful behaviour, corruption is a low-visibility phenomenon (Grabosky and Larmour 2001: 3). This contributes to very substantial conceptual and methodological problems associated with measuring the incidence of corruption and its costs.

THE COSTS OF CORRUPTION AND INTERNATIONAL RESPONSES TO COUNTER ITS EFFECTS

In terms of furthering research agendas on corruption, there have been a number of initiatives around the world in recent years. These include the work of the United Nations Office for Drug Control and Crime Prevention (now UNODC), which published its Global Programme Against Corruption that featured the Anti-Corruption Tool Kit. The Internet Centre for Corruption Research based at The University of Passau in Germany has sought to act in a clearing-house role regarding research into corruption issues. Similarly, the Organisation for Economic Co-operation and Development (OECD) provides a worldwide resource on corruption and bribery. In recent years, debates about corruption often make reference to the Transparency International (TI) Corruption Perceptions Index (CPI). TI seeks to measure perceptions of corruption around the world, based largely on surveys. For example, the TI CPI 2004 surveyed 146 jurisdictions; Australia scored 8.8 and was ranked ninth in terms of being least affected by corruption. Finland, with a score of 9.7, was considered by TI to be the jurisdiction least affected by corruption, while Bangladesh and Haiti both scored 1.5 and were considered by TI to be the countries most afflicted with corruption among those surveyed (Transparency International 2004b).

The often clandestine nature of corruption, which makes it so difficult to define, likewise impacts on the ability to model and measure the impact of corruption (Jain 2001). Similarly, the inability to define the outer boundaries of corrupt behaviour ensures that even if empirical research into the scale and costs of corruption could be undertaken with greater veracity, the blurred boundaries of illegal and legal behaviour would result in many corrupt activities being unaccounted for (Johnston 2000). What is generally true about corruption is that it is often necessary, in order to facilitate the smooth interaction of the legitimate and illegitimate sectors of the economy. However, the level and intensity of corruption required will fluctuate between different economies, and indeed within the same economy over time. Interestingly, corruption is part of a broader societal behavioural continuum (Moran 1998). This is because similar processes to conventional western understandings of corruption may be employed by powerful nations, corporations and individuals in the course of conventional business in all types of states, whether capitalist, communist, or various types of authoritarian regimes. Specific examples of these processes being part of *normal business* include the arms industry and major infrastructure projects overseas.

It is not uncommon for a whole range of inducements to be offered by major contractors in their efforts to bid successfully for large military hardware defence contracts, or to win the tenders for major projects, such as the construction of airports and energy systems. These enormous pressures of commercial competition can lead to corruption, especially in less developed countries, and increasingly these linkages between conventional business practice and corruption are being acknowledged at the highest levels – for example, by the OECD in its *Convention on Combating Bribery of Officials in International Business Transactions*, 21 November 1997, Article 7; by the Council of Europe in the *Criminal Law Convention on Corruption ETS No.173*, Article 13; and in the US by Senator Carl Levin, who sits as the senior Democrat on the United States Senate Permanent Subcommittee on Investigations, and who has criticised aspects of the growing industry of private banking and its linkages to corrupt political figures in a number of jurisdictions (United States Senate Permanent Subcommittee on Investigations 1999).

Nevertheless, it is not surprising that in an increasingly globalised economy, economic actors will continue to make what appear to them to be economically rational decisions as to *how to do business* in different countries and cultures. Corruption has been in the past, is currently, and will continue to be in the future, a very significant factor in a host of rational business decision-making processes, in a wide range of increasingly inter-linked scenarios. This commercial reality can actually stimulate levels of competitive corruption, as economic actors such as transnational corporations (TNCs) and smaller locally-based firms seek to exploit market opportunities. These economic pressures interact with political factors, thereby creating environments in which corruption can sometimes deliver specific selective benefits to a state, community or individuals. This can be seen, for example, in the role of corruption in the *narco economy* in Colombia in the last 30 years (Lupsha 1991). Accurate data are difficult to gather (for obvious reasons), but it is widely acknowledged that cocaine exports – not necessarily grown or manufactured there, but which are directed by Colombian interests – have been larger, in foreign revenue terms, than the combined totals of all of Colombia's conventional industries. Much of the profit from the *cocaine economy* goes to the larger cartels and their associates, but historically there have also been significant *trickle-down* effects to the general population, as large amounts of drugs-stimulated foreign currency flow back into the Colombian economy (MacDonald 1988).

Corruption can generate benefits in specific contexts - for example, being successful in a tender process or winning a contract. But the influence of corruption is in general a repressive one. Langseth and Michael (1998) made a specific attempt to measure the positive and negative effects of corruption by utilising empirical evidence from Tanzania to demonstrate that the general effect of bribes is to obstruct rather than facilitate economic transactions. They found that, overall, bribes act as grit rather than grease in the engine of the economy. The problem of corruption may not simply be one that is found in business, governments or those holding public office; it is also a very real issue for law enforcement agencies themselves. Most law enforcement agents are not well paid, and the attractions of pecuniary reward from corrupt sources can be overwhelming. Similarly, the business sense for organised crime in bribing law enforcement agents is clear, given the vast profits of much organised crime activity. Unsurprisingly, the problem of poorly resourced and/or corrupt law enforcement agencies varies between countries.

There have been a number of empirical studies undertaken by international organisations and social scientists seeking to quantify the economic impact of corruption. Ongoing research by the Governance Division of the World Bank has estimated that the value of bribes paid *each year* in developing and developed countries is greater than $US1 trillion. This estimate 'does not include embezzlement of public funds or theft of public assets' (World Bank 2004) – suggesting that the true scale of international corruption is far greater than this initial figure. Attempts have also been made to measure corruption at the national and regional levels. Hevesi (2003), citing a Brookings Institute report, has stated that corporate corruption in the US alone costs the national economy $US35 billion per year. In Cambodia, the World Bank (2002) found that low income households are disproportionately affected by corruption. The survey found that poorer households were, on average, required to spend approximately 2.3 per cent of their household income on paying bribes, compared to 0.9 per cent for higher income households. At the regional level, Nakata (1978) noted that studies on government procurement policies in several countries in Asia 'reveal that these governments have paid from 20 to 100 percent more for goods and services than they would have otherwise'. In Africa, Celarier (1996: 49) cites Frank Vogl, a former World Bank executive, who suggested that 'some $US30 billion of ... aid has ended up in Swiss Bank accounts'.

While these figures provide a scale as to the cost of corruption, the actual cost and incidence of corruption at the national, regional or international level is unlikely to be determined with any great accuracy (Hindess 2004). While the veracity of corruption measures is therefore unknown, these empirical studies are worth highlighting, as they bring into the spotlight the losses associated with corruption, while clearly illustrating that corruption is more than simply a public sector phenomenon and more than just a problem for the developing world.

There is a growing literature on corruption that has helped to produce a number of initiatives both theoretical and practical in nature (see for example Rose-Ackerman 1978; Klitgaard 1988; Tanzi 1994; Gorta and Forell 1995; Mauro 1995). Some of the more significant initiatives include typologies of corrupt behaviours; profiles of actual and/or potential offenders; and templates of risk minimisation strategies. A common difficulty confronting these types of initiative is their capacity to be transferred effectively between cultures, countries and industries. Given the diverse range of economic, social, political and cultural considerations that can have an impact, it is not surprising that different countries have varying levels of commitment to fighting corruption.

The United States has been in the vanguard of positive reform efforts. It introduced the Racketeer Influenced and Corrupt Organizations (RICO) provisions as part of the *Organized Crime Act 1970*. The RICO provisions targeted organised crime groups, in particular the mafia, and allowed for enhanced prison terms and fines for participation in corrupt organisations. The United States was the first jurisdiction to outlaw the act of bribery of foreign officials through the *Foreign Corrupt Practices Act 1977* (FCPA), which was passed by Congress without a single dissenting vote. The FCPA imposes substantive compliance and reporting requirements upon US corporations regarding their business arrangements. Breaches of the FCPA can result in criminal penalties (including prison terms of up to five years), fines for individuals of up to US$250,000, and fines for firms of up to US$2,000,000. The United States followed up the FCPA with the *International Anti-Bribery and Fair Competition Act 1998* and the *International Anti-Corruption and Good Governance Act 2000.* Table 9.3 lists examples of other national responses to corruption.

Table 9.3   Key national anti-corruption responses

Country	Program
Brunei	Anti-Corruption Bureau Established 1982 in order to uphold the integrity of the Public Service by means of eradicating and abolishing corruption, and to bring those involved in corruption to justice
Bulgaria	Coalition 2000 Founded in May 1997, Coalition 2000 'is an initiative of a number of Bulgarian non-governmental organizations aimed at combating corruption through a process of cooperation among governmental institutions, NGOs and individuals drafting an Anti-Corruption Action Plan for Bulgaria, implementing an Anti-Corruption Awareness Campaign and a Corruption Monitoring System' (Coalition 2000 1998: 2)
Georgia	Transnational Crime and Corruption Centre Established in 1999, this NGO is focused on actively promoting transparency in government, broadening rights of NGOs and drafting anti-corruption laws
Hong Kong	The Independent Commission Against Crime Established in 1974 to investigate corruption within the public and private sectors. Achieves these goals through investigation, education and prevention
Singapore	Corrupt Practices Investigation Bureau Founded in 1952 for the purpose of preventing corruption in both the public and private sectors. Achieves these goals through investigation and prevention

Organised institutional responses to corruption have been around for many decades, as can be seen by the establishment of the Corrupt Practices Investigation Bureau in Singapore as early as 1952. This table is only a snapshot of the many oversight bodies and anti-corruption agencies of various models that now exist throughout South and North America, Africa, Australasia, Europe and the Middle East. Table 9.4 lists some of the major multilateral anti-corruption instruments, and Table 9.5 some of the multilateral responses to corruption, which in recent years have been key drivers in the continuing emergence of anti-corruption agencies in so many jurisdictions, reflecting a greater emphasis on international cooperative efforts against corruption.

Table 9.4   Multilateral anti-corruption instruments

Body	Instruments
Council of Europe	Criminal Law Convention on Corruption (CETS No.173),[2] which entered into force on 1 July 2002
	Group of States Against Corruption (GRECO), which monitors the observance of the Guiding Principles for the Fight Against Corruption (1997)
Organisation for Economic Co-operation & Development	OECD Convention on Combating Bribery of Foreign Public Officials in International Business Transactions (1999)
Organisation of American States	OAS Inter-American Convention Against Corruption (1996)
United Nations	United Nations Convention Against Transnational Organized Crime (2000)
	United Nations Convention Against Corruption (2003)

The implementation of anti-corruption programs by key international and transnational organisations including the United Nations, the World Bank and the OECD is a visible commitment to the fight against corruption. Importantly, this commitment highlights the truly multi-jurisdictional nature of corruption, with corrupt transactions having the ability to permeate beyond national boundaries. Such initiatives are crucial in countering corruption, and have spawned specific national responses, illustrating the reflexive relationship between national and international efforts. For example, Australia adopted the main features of the OECD Convention in the *Criminal Code Amendment (Bribery of Foreign Public Officials) Act 1999*. These multi-lateral initiatives can help national and regional governments not only in establishing regulatory and specific law enforcement initiatives against corruption, but also in fostering beliefs and practices in the business and broader community that will not tolerate the corrosive existence of corruption. The latter objectives are less tangible than establishing a new law or task force, but ultimately are just as important (Huberts 1998). There processes can manifest themselves in many positive developments, such as:

- regulatory requirements for greater transparency in commercial practices;
- sensible risk management strategies in both public and private organisations;
- substantive checks and balances in local and national political structures, in particular, mandatory codes for ethical practice; and
- corruption awareness education programmes within government, commerce and the general community.

Table 9.5   Multilateral responses to corruption

International Organisations	Programs and Agencies
OECD	Anti-Corruption Division
The World Bank	Anti-Corruption Knowledge Resource Centre, in conjunction with a range of Public Sector governance programs.
Transparency International	TI, through its International Secretariat and more than 85 independent national chapters around the world, focuses on strengthening national integrity systems.
United Nations	Crime and Justice Information Program, Centre for International Crime Prevention.
International Monetary Fund	Reports on the Observance of Standards and Codes (ROSCs)
World Bank and International Financial Corporation (IFC)	Foreign Investment Advisory Centre

The impact of anti-corruption initiatives can vary tremendously across and even within jurisdictions, but some do have very substantial effects. For example, the National Counter Corruption Commission in Thailand has been rated in opinion polls in that country to be '... Thailand's most trusted government body' (*Economist* 2002: 25). The focus in the following section is on the Australian context, and how differential responses to corruption have emerged within a jurisdiction that is federal, and sees anti-corruption efforts being the responsibility of a number of different governments at both the state and federal levels.

THE AUSTRALIAN SITUATION

As stated earlier, Australia has performed consistently well in terms of international comparative studies on perceptions of corruption such as the TI CPI, being ranked ninth least affected country in the world in 2004, eighth in 2003, eleventh in both 2002 and 2001, and thirteenth in 2000 (Transparency International 2004b, 2003, 2002, 2001, 2000). Obviously one would prefer one's country to be ranked eighth rather than one hundred and eighth, but it would be naïve to suggest that Australia remains largely corruption free. The reality is that corruption does exist in Australia, and that in certain contexts it may be widespread and systemic in nature. Notable royal commissions and commissions of inquiry – such as the Fitzgerald Inquiry (1989); the WA Inc. Royal Commission (1992); the Wood Royal Commission (1997); the Kennedy Royal Commission (2003); and the HIH Royal Commission (2003) – illustrate clearly that instances of serious corruption do occur. Similarly, corruption scandals and their aftermath receive extensive coverage from the electronic and print media, and are often front page news.

While the majority of counter corruption responses in Australia have been initiated and implemented in the public sector, there is an increasing focus on countering corruption in the private sector as well. For example, the Corporations Law Economic Reform Program (CLERP) 'is a comprehensive initiative to improve Australia's business and company regulation' (Department of Treasury 1998: iii). The program has sought to promote transparency and accountability within the private sector, with the most recent reforms under CLERP 9 extending to corporate disclosure requirements (Department of Treasury 2004). There have been numerous other initiatives launched by individual private sector organisations and professional associations, but the focus for this chapter will be on the various Australian public sector institutional arrangements implemented to counter corruption and promote integrity and good governance arrangements. Prominent in these arrangements has been the Office of the Auditor-General, which traditionally has been charged with the functions of ensuring financial probity, public sector accountability and performance, and which has become an increasingly important component of Australia's anti-corruption effort (Coghill 2004). The history of this independent institutional agency is a long one, with Auditor-Generals and Audit Offices having an institutional presence as far back as 1826. By the end of the nineteenth century, Tasmania, Victoria and Western Australia had established independent Audit agencies, accountable to their respective parliaments. In 1901, the Commonwealth followed this lead, as did

Queensland in 1908 and South Australia in 1939. By the conclusion of the twentieth century, each state and the Commonwealth had introduced a number of additional institutional actors within the public sector. As illustrated by Table 9.6, chief among these was the introduction of the Commonwealth and state Ombudsman schemes, as well as a number of sector-specific institutional responses.

Table 9.6 Key institutional responses to corruption in Australia

Jurisdiction	Oversight Body	Established	Accountable to...
Commonwealth	Commonwealth Ombudsman	1976	Commonwealth Parliament
Australian Capital Territory	ACT Ombudsman	1901	Parliament
New South Wales	NSW Ombudsman	1974	Parliament
Northern Territory	NT Ombudsman	1978	Parliament
Queensland	QLD Ombudsman	1974	Parliament
South Australia.	SA Ombudsman	1972	Parliament
	South Australian Police Complaints Authority	1995	Parliament
Tasmania	Tasmanian Ombudsman	1978	Parliament
Victoria	Victorian Ombudsman/OPI	1973	Parliament
	Ethical Standards Department (Police)	1996	Chief Commissioner/ Ombudsman
Western Australia	Parliamentary Commissioners for Administrative Investigations (PCAI)	1971	Parliament

	Investigative Powers		
	Investigation of Complaints/ Allegations	Own motion powers to investigate?	Compel witnesses to give evidence
Commonwealth	Yes	Yes	Yes
Australian Capital Territory	Yes	Yes	Yes
New South Wales	Yes	Yes	Yes
Northern Territory	Yes	No	Yes
Queensland	Yes	Yes	Yes
South Australia.	Yes	Yes	Yes
Tasmania	Yes	Yes	Yes
Victoria	Yes	Yes	Yes
Western Australia	Yes	Yes	Yes

	Power to conduct hearings in public or private	Telecomm-unication interception powers	Powers to enter and search
Commonwealth	Private	No	Yes
Australian Capital Territory	Private	No	Yes
New South Wales	Private	Yes	Yes
Northern Territory	Private	No	Yes
Queensland	Private	No	Yes
South Australia	Private	No	Yes
Tasmania	Private	No	Yes
Victoria	Private	No	Yes
Western Australia	Private	No	Yes

Sources: Ombudsman Act (Commonwealth of Australia) 1976; Ombudsman Act (Australian Capital Territory) 1989; Ombudsman Act (New South Wales) 1974; Ombudsman Act (Northern Territory) 1977; Ombudsman Act (Queensland) 2001; Ombudsman Act (South Australia) 2001; Royal Commission Act (South Australia) 1917; Police (Complaints and Disciplinary Proceedings) Act (South Australia) 1985; Ombudsman Act (Tasmania) 1978; Ombudsman Act (Victoria) 1973; Police Regulation Act (Victoria) 1958; Parliamentary Commissioner Act (Western Australia) 1971; Royal Commission Act (Western Australia) 1968.

The role of the Ombudsman at both the state and Commonwealth levels traditionally has been to investigate complaints against public sector employees. To undertake this accountability function, the Australian Ombudsmen have been vested with a range of investigative powers, as shown by Table 9.6. Recent legislative changes in a number of states, including Queensland, South Australia and Victoria, have resulted in a broadening of many of these investigative powers. The Queensland Ombudsman (2003) however asserts that these new powers are 'appropriate investigative powers . .

[that] clarify the type of information we may seek and the protection and privileges people have'. Arguably, the compulsion powers available to the Commonwealth Ombudsman and all state Ombudsmen have provided these organisations with the authority 'needed to investigate organised crime and corruption' (Lewis 2004). In such jurisdictions, the Ombudsmen have the compulsive power to make witnesses testify, with witnesses who refuse to answer questions, or obstruct an investigation, subject to contempt or other serious offences. Overall then it would appear that each jurisdiction has adopted and implemented a number of institutional responses to corruption. However, the practical impact of each of these agencies to act as key anti-corruption agencies within Australia is dependent upon the interaction of their various legal and regulatory regimes, underpinned by the powers instilled

within the various agencies, available resources and other prevailing external influences.

Table 9.7 The evolution of specific anti-corruption responses in Australia

Jurisdiction	Anti-Corruption Agency	Estab-lished	Legislation	Agency accountable to
New South Wales	Independent Commission Against Corruption (ICAC)	1989	Independent Commission Against Corruption Act (NSW) 1988	Parliamentary Joint Committee
	Police Integrity Commission	1996	Police Integrity Commission Act (NSW) 1996	Parliamentary Joint Committee
Queensland	Criminal Justice Commission (CJC)	1989 – 2001	Criminal Justice Act (QLD) 1989	Parliamentary Committee
	Crime and Misconduct Commission (CMC)	2001	Crime and Misconduct Act (QLD) 2001	Parliamentary Committee
Western Australia	Official Corruption Commission (OCC)	1989 – 1996	Official Corruption Commission Act (WA) 1988	Parliamentary Committee
	Anti-Corruption Commission (ACC)	1996 - 2004	Anti-Corruption Commission Act (WA) 1996	Parliamentary Committee Joint
	Corruption and Crime Commission (CCC)	2004	Corruption and Crime Commission Act 2003	Parliamentary Committee
Victoria	Office of Police Integrity (OPI)	2004	Major Crime Legislation (Office of Police Integrity) Act 2004	Parliament

In considering the more specific public sector institutional responses to corruption, such as the establishment of anti-corruption commissions and independent crime commissions in Australia, it is important to acknowledge the role that royal commissions and other public inquiries have played, because often they have been the stimulus for the establishment of specific anti-corruption bodies. Perhaps the most notable in this regard have been the Commission of Inquiry into Possible Illegal Activities and Associated Police Misconduct (1989), the Royal Commission into Commercial Activities of Government and Other Matters (1992), the Royal Commission into the New South Wales Police Service (1997), and the Royal Commission into Police Corruption (2003). It has been a feature of Australia's political and social history since European settlement of Australia that many royal commissions and other such inquiries have not only played an influential role in official discourse, but have also resulted in significant policy and related institutional change (Gilligan 2002). Table 9.7 provides an overview of the key anti-corruption agencies that have existed within the Australian context since the late 1980s, and traces the succession that has occurred in Queensland and Western Australia. Specific institutional responses to corruption in New South Wales, Queensland and Western Australia have been in existence since 1989. In both Queensland and Western Australia, these original anti-corruption bodies have been replaced by restructured agencies, with Western Australia recently implementing its third such body in less than 20 years. Related royal commissions and other formal inquiries have provided much of the momentum for these initiatives and any subsequent overhauls.

Interestingly, of the four states listed in Table 9.7, Victoria has been the last to implement an independent anti-corruption agency, the Office of Police Integrity (OPI). The impetus for the recently established OPI is entwined with what has been described as 'the state's worst outbreak of police corruption in living memory' (Munro *et al.* 2004: 1). Instances of police corruption linked to Melbourne's underworld and a recent spate of gangland killings have prompted leading commentators such as Lewis (2004) to demand an independent inquiry into what they perceive as systemic corruption within the state's policing body. The Victorian Government has resisted calls for a royal commission of inquiry into corruption in Victoria (Gilchrist and Murphy 2004), and some analysts view the OPI as a specific strategy to avoid such a public inquiry and the establishment of any subsequent permanent anti-corruption body (Moor 2005b). Unlike the New South Wales-based Independent Commission Against Corruption (ICAC) and Police Integrity Commission (PIC), the Queensland-based Crime and Misconduct Commission

(CMC), and the Corruption and Crime Commission (CCC) in Western Australia – which are all independent entities – the OPI has been established within the Victorian Ombudsman's office, with the Victorian Ombudsman also acting as the director of the OPI. Table 9.8 provides an overview of the key investigative powers not only of the OPI, but also of other key anti-corruption agencies across the four largest states in Australia.

Table 9.8   Investigative powers of current anti-corruption agencies

Investigative Powers	New South Wales		Queens-land	Vic-toria	Western Australia
	ICAC	PIC	CMC	OPI	CCC
Investigation of complaints/allegations	Yes	Yes	Yes	Yes	Yes
Own motion to initiate investigation	Yes	Yes	Yes	Yes	Yes
Compel witnesses to give evidence	Yes	Yes	Yes	Yes	Yes
Arrest warrant to ensure attendance by witnesses (subject to conditions)	Yes	Yes	Yes	Yes	Yes
Power to conduct hearings in public and/or private	Yes	Yes	Yes	Yes	Yes
Telephone interception powers (receiver or intercept TI products)	No	Yes	Yes	Yes	Yes
Powers to enter and search property	Yes	Yes	Yes	Yes	Yes
Power to seize property	Yes	Yes	Yes	Yes	Yes

Sources: Independent Commission Against Corruption Act (NSW) 1988; Police Integrity Commission Act (NSW) 1996; Crime and Misconduct Act (QLD) 2001; Corruption and Crime Commission Act 2003; Major Crime Legislation (Office of Police Integrity) (Vic) Act 2004.

Table 9.8 illustrates that all five agencies have extensive investigative powers – powers that experience around the world demonstrates are fundamental for any agency that seeks to counter corruption in any meaningful fashion, because they enable watchdog agencies to be proactive and initiate their own investigations, rather than simply be reactive to external forces. But available powers are only part of the picture. Other factors – including how an agency conducts its investigations, operational outputs, resources, and legislative framework – are critical in determining institutional capacity. Table 9.9 provides an outline of these factors for specialist anti-corruption agencies in Australia.

Table 9.9   Resourcing and outputs of current anti-corruption agencies

Resource Allocation and Output (2003–04) financial year	New South Wales		Queens-land	Victoria	Western Australia
	ICAC	PIC	CMC	OPI	CCC
Operating budget	$A16.8 million	$A16.0 million	$A31.0 million	$A16.0 million[3]	$A6.1 million
Approximate staff numbers	101	107	276	80[4]	100
Number of (new) complaints received	901	833	3964	N/A	208[5]
Number of new investigations	34[6]	56[7]	105[8]	N/A	7[9]

Sources: Bottom and Medew (2004); Corruption and Crime Commission (2004); Crime and Misconduct Commission (2004); Independent Commission Against Corruption (2004); Moor (2005a); Police Integrity Commission (2004).

Table 9.9 suggests that the financial resourcing of anti-corruption initiatives has been relatively low and, in the view of some commentators, arguably symbolic at best (Brown and Head 2004). For example, in a state such as New South Wales with a population of approximately 6.7 million (Australian Bureau of Statistics 2004), and a police force of 17,000 sworn and unsworn members (New South Wales Police 2004), it is not hard to make the case that their specialised bodies, the ICAC and the PIC, do not have sufficient resources to investigate adequately all complaints brought to their attention. This pattern of under-resourcing is repeated in the cases of the CMC, the CCC and OPI, and has prompted some commentators to criticise governments – of all political persuasions – in Australia as lacking '... the political will to seriously tackle police accountability and corruption issues in [these] states' (Lewis 2004). So when attempting to evaluate the efforts of Australian anti-corruption agencies, it is important to take note of the prevailing political and economic realities within which they must function. The establishment of the CCC in January 2004 and the OPI in November 2004 has resulted, understandably, in them focusing on internal capacity building. For the remaining three agencies – the ICAC, the PIC and the CMC – even where output data are available, there is a lack of consistency between the state institutions in the corporate reporting of investigative activities and operational results. In the pursuit of operational information, one must resort to trawling through annual reports of these agencies to find what should be easily accessible information. Even when such information is gleaned from the reports, the issue remains that they are different in character, so that one might be trying to compare apples with oranges. The diversity of institutional arrangements, resourcing and outputs of anti-corruption agencies in Australia ensures that comparing their institutional capacity and effectiveness is extremely difficult. However, Table 9.10 lists some of the features that seem to recur across Australia's various anti-corruption bodies, and the contexts in which these bodies must operate.

Table 9.10 Recurring characteristics of anti-corruption bodies in Australia

• Ambiguity in terms of mandate	• Monitoring function responsibility
• Appearance of political independence	• Multifaceted
• Broad investigative powers	• No single model
• Compulsion powers	• Potential deterrence
• Defined by the interactions between politics, economics, social and environmental conditions	• Public sector emphasis
	• Range of control mechanisms
	• Symbolic in reality?
	• Transparency
• Focus on good governance	• Underpinned by access to a strongly independent judicial system
• Goals driven by both external and internal factors	
• Limited evaluation processes	

CONCLUSIONS

The discussion above indicates that the current capacity to evaluate anti-corruption efforts in Australia appears very limited. This is not unexpected, since there is no strong evidence available from overseas to suggest that any jurisdiction has yet developed a robust framework for measuring the efficiency of counter-corruption activity. This is unsurprising, given the multifaceted nature of corruption. Nevertheless, it remains a cause for concern, because, as stated at the beginning of this chapter, it seems that corruption and its negative impacts have been for a very long time, and continue to be, an endemic feature of most forms of social organisation. Corruption has even been described by Gibbon (a leading scholar of the Roman Empire) as '... the most infallible symptom of democratic liberty' (cited in T. Williams 1998: 45). However, despite one scholar's perhaps more rosy – or should that be cynical? – view of corruption, it is undeniable that the overall effects of corruption are in general damaging and can be devastating, whether for a single community, a country, or even an entire continent, as in the case of Africa in recent decades. Consequently, there is a premium on trying to evaluate how worthwhile specific initiatives against corruption actually are. This is a massive challenge and raises a number of difficult issues.

First, how should different jurisdictions and different agency models be compared, especially given the lack of independent, systematic evaluations of oversight bodies and specific anti-corruption bodies, which in turn highlights the need for increased evaluation processes within these areas. The description above of the powers, resources and outputs of the various Australian anti-corruption agencies indicates how problematic it can be to make comparisons in one national setting; these difficulties are of course magnified when trying to evaluate across different jurisdictions and cultures regarding the effectiveness or otherwise of anti-corruption initiatives.

Consequently, our second conclusion is that if meaningful evaluation were ever to be achieved, it would appear that there is a requirement for greater consistency between agencies and jurisdictions in reporting methodologies, especially within the areas of outputs and performance. But how to achieve this is a major challenge. Should there be some statutory requirement, or could it be achieved through a voluntary code? The reality is that currently the primary form of evaluation undertaken by specific anti-corruption agencies is *self*-evaluation, and in most cases the very lack of independence within this process has the potential to limit transparency, credibility and objectivity. Should independent evaluation of bodies and agencies be the preferred methodology for any form of performance evaluation, and, if so, how can such independence be achieved under real political and commercial conditions? Also, one should not be too presumptuous on the supposed superiority of independent evaluation, especially given that some commentators such as Brereton (2000) argue that the weight of the available evidence is that external oversight bodies have not achieved consistently better investigation outcomes than their counterparts that are subject to internal evaluation. Uncertainty remains about what are the best methods of evaluation; but what is almost certain is that it is not possible to measure accurately the impact of anti-corruption strategies when there are very limited substantive evaluative data available, as is the case in Australia.

Third, on this issue of data quality, *ex post facto* statistical analysis of data for evaluation purposes appears to be inadequate, due to limitations presented by baseline measurements and trend lines. Other forms of impact evaluation may be superior, such as longitudinal studies, but these have substantial resource and time implications. Similarly, any statistical analysis that proposes to incorporate numerous co-variates must firstly justify them as legitimate for evaluating anti-corruption bodies or practices, and then specify how variables can be operationalised in practice to evaluate integrity systems.

Fourth is the thorny issue of deterrence. Can one reasonably identify and measure the deterrent capability of anti-corruption initiatives and agencies? In doing so, one must consider the host of both primary and secondary factors that may promote deterrence. The challenge, as always in these contexts, is to operationalise these deterrence factors into quantifiable terms in relation to measurable corrupt activity. This is an area that requires a great deal more empirically-oriented research before any substantive conclusions can be drawn.

Fifth, and tying in with this theme of potential deterrence variables, is the question of the effect broader structural and more specific influences have in militating against corruption. For example, what is the influence of the strength of any statutory whistleblower provisions? How influential are the media? What is the involvement of the private sector? What are the effects of scandal? What structures of competitive capitalism help to counteract corruption? What impact does the historical development of a particular industry or sector have on types and levels of corruption? And how significant are cultural and other normative influences?

Finally, what are appropriate pathways for policy reform in countering corruption? Taking a national focus for a moment, does the admittedly limited analysis of the Australian context earlier suggest a need in Australia for a

National Anti-Corruption Commission? An analogy might be drawn with the regulation of corporations, which historically in Australia was under the aegis of the states through their Corporate Affairs Commissions. However, the accumulating costs to business of multiple state-based regulatory systems, the need to keep Australian business competitive, and the broad effects of internationalisation influenced the states to transfer voluntarily their responsibilities in this area to the federal government, so that corporate regulation came under a national system with the *Australian Securities and Investments Act 1989* that established the Australian Securities and Investments Commission (ASIC). A similar process may happen in the future regarding efforts to counter corruption. But a national anti-corruption agency is unlikely at this point in time, given the political reality of Australia as a federal jurisdiction in which crime is primarily a responsibility for state governments and their policing agencies. Nevertheless, there is a case for more coordination regarding the structures and processes of Australia's various anti-corruption agencies. Not only would this help in the micro objective of developing more meaningful performance indicators for the activities of these agencies, but the process of coordination is likely to inject more transparency, as well as greater community and media involvement, into both the discourse and the fight against corruption. This case cannot be proven empirically, but we suspect that these latter components are probably the most significant variables in countering corruption. They represent potentials that should be exploited in any efforts to counter the negative impacts of corruption, terrorism and organised crime on contemporary local, national, regional and global societies.

NOTES

1. The authors would like to thank the Institute for the Study of Global Movements, Monash University, which provided a grant to support this research project.
2. Although the Criminal Law Convention on Corruption opened for signature in Strasbourg on 27 January 1999, the treaty's entry into force was conditional upon its ratification by 14 Member States of the Council of Europe. This occurred on 1 July 2002.
3. Operating Budget for the entire Ombudsman's Office.
4. Project staffing level.
5. For a six month period only.
6. Excluding preliminary investigations.
7. Full and preliminary investigations open during the year, with 29 concluded.
8. Misconduct investigations.
9. For a six month period only.

10. Poodle or Bulldog? Tony Blair and the 'War on Terror'

Peter Shearman

INTRODUCTION

This chapter argues that British Prime Minister Tony Blair has been a leading player in reconceptualising international politics during the past decade. In key policy documents and important speeches, Blair has made explicit his view that threats to global security now arise from non-traditional sources. In particular, Blair identifies a dangerous nexus between terrorism, corrupt and non-democratic regimes, failing states, organised crime, and the proliferation of weapons of mass destruction. Since 9/11, the template of the Cold War has been replaced by the 'global war on terror'. This nomenclature has become shorthand for a wider war: principally against terrorism, but also against corruption and organised crime, and the networks and linkages that bind them together. Tony Blair has played perhaps the most important role of any contemporary political leader in establishing new thinking and new approaches to counter post-Cold War security challenges. Yet this assertion contradicts the many arguments that Blair's foreign and security policies have been devised in Washington, with the US acting out an old-fashioned role in forging a new empire.

The main focus of the chapter will be the role played by Tony Blair in the 'war on terror'. Opinions on both sides of the political spectrum, including at the highest levels of his own government, hold that Blair, in going to war against Iraq, was following a long-standing British tradition and acting out a role as America's supplicant poodle. It has been suggested that in going to war in Iraq '... Britain under Blair is so clearly the leading apologist for US foreign policy, that the relationship seriously resembles that between the former Soviet Union and its satellite republics of Belorussia and Ukraine' (M. Curtis 2003: 112). Curtis goes on to say that Britain has become a '... US client state, while its military has became an effective US proxy force'(Curtis 2003: 112). This conception of the UK as an American poodle has long been the mantra of the more radical left in British politics; but under Blair it has become more widely accepted. In his last column before he died, the influential journalist Hugo Young argued that Blair had taken Britain to war in Iraq due to his loyalty to Washington, and that the UK had '… ceased to be a sovereign nation' (Young 2003). Ross McKibbin claims that Blair's '… vocabulary is determined by American usage', and that he went to war due to his '… deep attachment to the political, social and economic culture of the United States' (McKibbin 2003: 8). Blair has been accused of lying to the public, and of deliberately misleading his own government in order to commit the UK to America's war in Iraq (Wheatcroft 2004).

In short, the widely-held assumption is that Blair, who came to power committed to implementing a radical domestic reform agenda, has simply followed the dictates of Washington in the conduct of his foreign policy. I will demonstrate that this argument does not stand up to scrutiny. One might reasonably claim that some of Blair's most significant policies relating to the war on terror, and especially the war on Iraq, have been misconceived, wrong-headed, dangerous, and ultimately serving to undermine rather than protect British long-term interests. But it should be recognised that they have been the independent policies of the British Prime Minister, pursued often in the face of strong domestic opposition, including within the Parliamentary Labour Party and even the Cabinet. It is nevertheless the case that it would not have been possible when he came to power to have anticipated that Blair would become a leading advocate of the war against Iraq in 2003, for he had previously shown himself to be both uninterested in international affairs and risk-averse in policy making. In taking Britain to war in Iraq, Blair put his own position as Prime Minster at very real and serious risk. He did not do this out of loyalty to Washington.

When he brought New Labour to power in 1997, Tony Blair was perhaps the least prepared British Prime Minister in the field of foreign affairs in half a century. Blair was relatively young, had become politically active only after graduating from university, and had never experienced ministerial office of any kind. The last Labour Prime Minister, James Callaghan, had, in contrast, previously held all the principal offices of state, having served as Home Secretary, Foreign Secretary and Chancellor, before taking over as head of government. Blair himself recognised that his experience of government was limited, and that his knowledge of the past was shallow, once admitting to Roy Jenkins that he wished he had read history, instead of law, while at Oxford

(Naughtie 2004: 142). As one writer remarked of the new Prime Minister, this '... was not a politician closely associated with the political geography of the world, nor was he an eager student of diplomacy' (P. Stephens 2004: 149). Insofar as Blair had any inclinations in foreign policy in 1997, it was to ensure that the UK played a leading and positive role in Europe, rather than acting as the reluctant European as under previous British governments. Indeed, the Labour Party Manifesto in 1997 (entitled 'Britain in Europe') made barely a mention of the United States. Blair, fluent in French, knew Europe well. One of the first moves of the new government was to sign Britain up to the social chapters of the Maastricht Treaty, which the previous Major government had rejected. Blair worked closely with the German Chancellor to produce a paper on the 'Third Way'; and he worked with the French President, through the St Malo initiative, on developing European defence cooperation. Blair also expressed his support for Britain adopting the European currency. He was the most committed European to head a British government since Edward Heath. In contrast, on coming to power he knew very little of the United States (although he had been influenced by the domestic reforms undertaken by Bill Clinton in the fields of welfare and social policy).

A one-time (reluctant) member of the Campaign for Nuclear Disarmament, Blair married a successful barrister who had become a socialist at the age of sixteen. Becoming a close friend and political soulmate of President Bill Clinton, it would have been very difficult to predict Blair's subsequent partnership with George W. Bush in the war on Iraq. In the context of British politics, Blair was unusual in not having been reared in strong political traditions. He came from a privileged social background, having been educated at Fettes (The Scottish 'Eton') before going on to Oxford and then to London's Inns of Court, and eventually Westminster. However, Blair pushed beyond the old boundaries of 'left' and 'right', taking his fundamental values from his Christian faith. Blair saw himself as leader of the wider nation; he lacked tribal loyalty to his party, and was not wedded to any political dogma. As one close acquaintance of Blair put it, he is '... the only prime minister I can recall who both believes in God and loves his family' (P. Stephens 2004: 26). Blair at one stage seriously considered a vocation in the Church, but instead '... politics became a vehicle for his moral commitment' (Rentoul 2002: 44). At a time when many other young students were actively engaged in politics, Blair, in the mid-1970s, chose confirmation in the Church of England. Faith came before politics, and would always inform both his thinking and his policies.

LEARNING THROUGH DOING

It was events in Europe that first led Blair to take a keen interest in foreign policy and international security. Blair was forced through changing international circumstances to turn his attention to foreign affairs. He was required to learn quickly on the job. The source of Blair's new ideas on security matters was the conflicts in the former Yugoslavia. Due in part to his opposition to humanitarian intervention in Bosnia, Jack Cunningham was replaced by Robin Cook as Shadow Foreign Secretary before the election in 1997, for Blair wanted someone in that portfolio who shared his views on this issue. Blair became convinced that the world had changed fundamentally, and that, as he would put it '… we are all internationalists now' (Blair 1999a). The Party Manifesto in 1997 boldly asserted that the goal of New Labour was to '… make the protection and promotion of human rights a central part of our foreign policy'. Recognising the forces of globalisation in the fields of economics and trade, Blair pushed for new thinking too in the realm of security, which was also becoming global, and should therefore in his view no longer be the limited preserve of the sovereign nation state. Globalisation needed a 'security component'. Blair perceived the wars in the former Yugoslavia in global terms, with a linkage between bad regimes, organised crime and ethnic conflict, and the dangers these held for undermining wider international stability. More fundamentally for his own thinking on these issues was what he considered to be the evil of the Milošević regime in Serbia.

For Blair, countering the threats from terrorism, rogue states and the proliferation of weapons of mass destruction became the moral imperative of the new era. Blair articulated views setting out his thesis on international affairs before Bush had even contested his first presidential election, and long before 9/11. During the US election campaign in 2000, the Bush team made it clear that foreign policy priorities would be based on traditional notions of the national interest. The ABC (anything but Clinton) of the Bush foreign policy program was to ensure American national interests were maintained through policies of containment and deterrence, and only when *vital* US interests were threatened would force be considered. The incoming US administration's foreign policy and strategic thinking were based upon the Cold War doctrines of containment and deterrence, with Condoleezza Rice, who became Bush's National Security Advisor in his first term, influential in setting out the parameters. Rice was schooled in the old traditions, having produced a doctorate on the Soviet military, and having served in the previous Bush administration as a Soviet specialist. She believed that states like North Korea could still be contained and deterred, and that the US should not waste its resources on international 'social work' (Rice 2000). It is illogical and ahistorical to ascribe pressures to conform to US policies as the driver of Blair's foreign policy; for it is the Bush foreign policy that has altered to fit more closely with that of Blair's, rather than the other way around. This is not to suggest that Blair had a direct influence on thinking in Washington, but rather that he had already concluded himself – before Bush took office – that these non-traditional threats were paramount. He had learned this from direct experience in dealing with contemporary security challenges. It would take the strategic shock of 9/11 to fully alert the Bush administration to these different types of challenges.

It simply does not make sense to argue, as so many do, that Blair has been blindly following the lead of the US in the war on terror. There are always going to be contradictions and complexities involved in trying to conduct an ethical foreign policy when faced with stark choices that risk the lives of others, including one's own citizens. Blair recognises that it is neither possible nor desirable to intervene for humanitarian purposes in all cases of abuse by dictators. However, the atrocities in Kosovo marked a turning point for Blair. In an April 1999 speech to the Economic Club in Chicago, the Prime Minister sought to develop a framework for determining when military intervention in another state's affairs could be justified. He made the case for intervention not only when innocents were subject to genocide, but also when 'turning a blind eye' could impact negatively on one's own long-term security. Blair stated that we 'cannot turn our backs on conflicts and the violations of human rights within other countries if we want to be secure' (Blair 1999a), and called for new ways of organising international institutions, positing that the principle of non-intervention should be qualified. Dictators, he argued, should no longer be allowed to get away with inflicting ethnic cleansing or genocide on their own population under the cover of sovereignty, stating that '… acts of genocide cannot be a purely internal matter'. Blair went on to specify five conditions under which it would be appropriate to intervene for humanitarian purposes, even if this would violate traditional principles of state sovereignty. Thus it was necessary:

1. to be certain of the cause;
2. to have exhausted all other alternatives;
3. to then be prudent and proportionate in the use of military force;
4. to be prepared for the long term;
5. to ensure that national interests are involved.

By this time, Blair had already become a major international figure in redefining both the thinking and practice of international relations to account for the new non-traditional security threats. More than two years *before* 9/11, he had developed what was essentially a grand strategic doctrine of prevention – one based upon ethical foundations, which had nothing to do with the thinking then dominant in Washington. Whereas George W. Bush, before becoming President, denied the very existence of an international community, this idea was central to Blair's thinking. During the 2000 US presidential election campaign, Rice set out the essence of what American foreign policy would look like under a Bush administration. She stated that it would '... proceed from the firm ground of the national interest, not from the interests of an illusory international community' (Rice 2000: 62). In contrast, Blair has always expressed a moral purpose for defending the values that should be cherished: not the narrow values of a specific form of 'western democracy', but the universal values relating to fundamental human rights, especially those guaranteeing security against physical harm. Blair would state to the Labour Party Conference that '[O]ur values aren't western values. They're human values...Around these values we build our global partnership' (Blair 2002). Blair articulated the idealistic assumption that the spreading of these values would make the whole world safer. Blair's speech in Chicago, rather grandly entitled the 'Doctrine of the International Community', offered a non-traditional and broad conception of security, one that did not simply focus on states and the balance of power. Blair has stated on a number of occasions that we must move beyond what he described as the sterile, outmoded thinking that sees states operating in a hostile anarchic environment within shifting balances of power. Former British conservative Prime Minister Margaret Thatcher has taken issue with Blair's conception of the international community, arguing that it is a '... prescription for strategic muddle, military overstretch and ultimately, in the wake of inevitable failure, for an American retreat from global responsibility' (Thatcher 2003: 35). Like George W. Bush (at least before 9/11), Thatcher (writing here after 9/11) is wary of any doctrine of humanitarian intervention or the use of military power except when it is absolutely necessary to defend against real and imminent threats. She warns against the '... trap of imagining the West can remake societies' (Thatcher 2003: 37). Blair's views are based upon more idealistic, normative and moral foundations.

It is worth recalling here that in the late 1990s, Blair played an important role in forcing Milošević from power. Whereas Clinton, in countering Serbian atrocities in Kosovo, was only prepared to allow aerial bombardment at safe altitudes, Blair was willing to countenance a land offensive that would have put NATO troops directly in harm's way. Clinton was opposed to the use of ground forces, and he was clearly and openly irritated by Blair's push for their deployment against Milošević in Kosovo. At a 1999 meeting in Washington celebrating NATO's 50th anniversary, standing on the White House steps, Blair dispensed with protocol and told Clinton that NATO's credibility would be undermined if it were not prepared to 'put boots on the ground' in Kosovo. Even the Prime Minister's own advisers were shocked by '... the directness of his approach', and one present at the ceremony stated that you '... don't usually start like that with a US president' (P. Stephens 2004: 227). Outraged by the atrocities committed by Milošević earlier in Bosnia, Blair was adamant that he should not get away with this again in Kosovo. Blair made his case on American television (*Larry King Live*); and he sent a clear message to Milošević: 'You will be made to withdraw from Kosovo. There will be an international military force that will go in to secure the land for the people to whom it belongs. Our determination is absolute' (Blair 1999c). As one biographer of the British Prime Minister put it, 'Blair's forceful seizure of NATO was startling', for the '... sudden ferocity of his moral vision' (Hennessy 2000: 507). Strobe Talbott, Clinton's Deputy Secretary of State, acidly stated in private that "Winston" Blair was ready to fight to the last American' (Rentoul 2002: 527). And Clinton was concerned that Blair was making a coalition with General Wesley Clarke, the American Commander of NATO troops (Halberstam 2002: 462).

Later, Blair would also come to irritate the neoconservatives in the Bush Administration, as he tried to persuade the US president to seek UN approval for the war against Iraq. Blair might have been on friendly terms with both Clinton and Bush, but one should not view this friendship as a one-way street or free from tensions. Blair was already advocating military strikes against Saddam if he did not comply with UN resolutions while Clinton was still in office. Standing next to Clinton in February 1998, in relation to the question of weapons of mass destruction (WMD) in Iraq, Blair stated that if the UN inspectors were prevented from doing their work '... then we have to make sure, by military means of which we are capable, that, in so far as possible, that capacity ceases' (P. Stephens 2004: 177). Blair also announced at this time deployment of more British fighter aircraft to the Gulf. The subsequent air strikes on Iraq in 1998 were not approved by the UN, were opposed by France, and lacked strict legal legitimation; yet Blair was not apologetic, arguing then that Saddam's defiance of earlier UN resolutions gave legal grounds for the strikes. Already in 1997, during his first year in office, Blair was offering British participation in military action against Iraq (Stephens 2004: 171). In the cases of both Iraq in 1998 and Kosovo in 1999, Blair was acting out of principle, and not kow-towing to Washington. Clinton is assumed by many to have instigated the bombing against Iraq in December 1998 to draw attention away from the Lewinski scandal, and impeachment proceedings then underway in Congress. For Blair, it was the issuing of the Butler Report, detailing Saddam's continuing obstruction of the UN inspectors, that was the key.

In his address to the US Congress, Blair stated that the battle against these new threats could not be fought and defeated solely by military means – by traditional armies in coalitions of states – in conventional ways. In the end, he argued, it was not military power that would defeat contemporary threats to security: '... our ultimate weapon is not our guns, but our beliefs' (Blair 2003b: 249). Three years earlier, in an article in a British newspaper, Blair wrote, in relation to conflict in Kosovo, that this '... is now a battle between good and evil ... It is a battle between civilization and barbarity, democracy against dictatorship' (Blair 1999b).

When New Labour first took power in 1997, the mission statement of the Foreign and Commonwealth Office had as a central objective to '... spread the values of human rights, civil liberties, and democracy' (Foreign and Commonwealth Office 1997), and Cook, the new Foreign Secretary, talked constantly about conducting an 'ethical foreign policy' (Cook 1997). Clare Short was appointed to the newly created post of Minister for International Development, with Cabinet rank, whose job description was to 'eradicate poverty' in the Third World, cutting the figure in half by 2015. Blair immediately set in motion a strategic defence review in which moral considerations should be paramount, with a policy objective of making the UK a 'force for good in the world'.

It should also be noted that the idea that Britain has performed the role of puppet to the American master does not stand up historically. In truth there have always been rifts in the alliance. In 1956, the US put pressure on the UK and France (along with Israel) to withdraw from their campaign in Suez against Nasser. In the 1960s, Harold Wilson successfully resisted US pressure to send troops to South East Asia in support of America's war in Vietnam. Later still, Edward Heath refused to permit the US to use its bases in the UK for sorties during the 1973 war in the Middle East. Ten years later, Margaret Thatcher was incensed when the US invaded Grenada, a commonwealth country, without conferring with the British government. And Blair, despite joining forces with the US in Iraq, has had differences – some of them profound – with the Bush administration over the Kyoto Treaty, the International Criminal Court, trade issues, and the Israeli–Palestinian conflict. Dean Acheson once noted that the relationship between the US and the UK was 'unique', due to a common history and a common language: 'But unique did not mean affectionate. We had fought England as often as we had fought by her side as an ally' (Acheson 1987: 387).

9/11 AND THE WAR ON IRAQ

Blair's war against evil preceded the terrorist attacks of 9/11 in the United States, but the attacks served to reinforce the ideas he had previously been grappling with. Those people close to Blair who disagreed with his position on Iraq did not question his sincerity, his moral stance, or his strategic goals. What many *did* question was the logic of his views and the lack of consistency in applying them. One could point to his support for bombing the Taliban or Saddam's forces while simultaneously supplying arms and support to the brutal regime in Uzbekistan. It should be noted here, however, that Blair has often been frustrated in the face of constrictions in applying his doctrine more widely, in one case telling Clare Short in a private conversation that '… if it were down to me, I'd do Zimbabwe as well' (Kampfner 2004: 76). In his third term as Prime Minister, Blair clearly has to take stock of the problems posed by the invasion and occupation of Iraq. But it should be recognised that in conducting British foreign policy he was acting more as the British bulldog than as a tame poodle of the United States.

The issue of whether we consider Blair's policies to have been right or wrong is irrelevant when it comes to assessing what motivated them. Blair was motivated by moral imperatives moderated by realism. He has tried to take a logical moral stance on international issues where dictators ride roughshod over their own populations under the cover of state sovereignty, or where poverty and underdevelopment create conditions for breeding conflict and terrorism. But he has sought to be realistic in accepting the risks of specific situations that might make it difficult or impossible to intervene. He has also been sensitive to the relativities of power between states in international politics, considering it dangerous to leave the US on its own with the burdens of ensuring international security. In his view, it is better to be on the inside, with some influence over the more militant tendencies of the world's hegemonic power, than an outside critic with no opportunities to help moderate US policy. In a private letter to a 'trusted friend' in March 2002, Blair wrote '[M]y objectives must be to pull the Americans towards a strategy that is sensible in Iraq [and] ... to broaden the strategy so that it is about the wider world, including the Middle East peace process, Africa, staying and seeing it through in Afghanistan' (Seldon 2004: 572). Since 9/11 and the ensuing war on terrorism, the Europeans – 'old' as well as 'new', to use Donald Rumsfeld's misguided labels – have sought the same general objectives in international politics. A comparison of the EU's Security Strategy (European Security Strategy 2003) with the US National Security Strategy (National Security Strategy 2002) demonstrates quite clearly that both sides of the Atlantic share similar perceptions of threat (from rogue or failing states, global terrorism and the uncontrolled proliferation of WMD). Disagreements arise primarily about the *means* to achieve what are essentially common objectives. Blair's conception of the 'international community' is not something shared with the neo-conservatives in Washington. Blair has consistently linked the war on terror, including the war on Iraq, to a wider peace settlement in the Middle East. He has also steadfastly supported multilateral measures to help alleviate poverty and AIDS in Africa, leading an international campaign against global poverty. The Blair government from the outset has also been a strong advocate of environmental measures to mitigate the effects of global climate change, something that contrasts markedly with the thinking and policies pursued in these areas under George W. Bush in the United States.

In the post-9/11 world, Europe no longer dominates in US strategic thinking as it did in the Cold War. Indeed, for the first time in a century, Europe is not at the centre of strategic thinking in Washington. The US is the world's sole superpower, so that it is impossible for Europeans *not* to place the US at the forefront of their strategic thinking. Europe and the US might agree on what threatens international stability; but there are keen differences over how best to counteract such threats. Blair considers it necessary to remain close allies with the US not only because it is the single most powerful state, but also because he believes that the UK and the US share the same basic values. And these are values shared not just between these two Anglophone countries, but also with the rest of the democratic world, especially the rest of Europe. Blair was clearly frustrated when the French and Germans opposed attacking Iraq – not because he disagreed with some of the concerns they were expressing, but because in his view they were acting in old ways, being insufficiently aware of the potential dangers if rogue states are allowed to flout UN laws, develop WMD, and possibly provide a haven for terrorists and criminal networks. Blair was annoyed at the tendency of President Chirac to continue using the outdated discourse of the balance of power. In a private session to Labour MPs before the March 2003 vote in the House of Commons, Blair warned that the French strategy of creating '… rival poles of power' was dangerous: '… that's not diplomacy, that's lunacy', he told them (Ramesh 2003: 50). The French were simply offering outdated methods for dealing with these new and radically different security threats.

The implications of a nexus between global terrorism, organised crime and corruption are clear. The most dangerous scenario is one in which organised criminal networks and corrupt regimes collude to sell weapons of mass destruction to terrorists. Terrorists, organised crime cartels and corrupt regimes all employ the arbitrary use of violence. They also utilise methods of intimidation against individuals, other groups and states; violate international norms, rules and institutions; and target non-combatants. In this, they all represent a threat to international security and global governance. These non-traditional threats cannot be fought by states acting independently. It is not possible to balance such power. Rogue states cannot be contained. It is not possible to negotiate with terrorists whose objective is to destroy the very fabric of democratic society; such groups, in particular those who engage in suicide attacks, cannot be deterred through conventional means. Blair considered that a radically new approach was required to deal with these non-traditional threats.

In his speech designed to persuade the House of Commons to vote for an invasion of Iraq, Blair said that the question most often asked was not why Iraq mattered, but why it mattered so much? He provided this answer: 'Because the outcome of this issue will determine more than the fate of the Iraqi regime and more than the future of the Iraqi people … It will determine the way Britain and the world confront the central security threat of the 21st century … It will determine the pattern of international politics for the next generation' (Blair 2003a). Blair saw Iraq as a threat because of the potential for Saddam to develop weapons of mass destruction that could then fall into the hands of terrorists, either directly from the regime, through corrupt rogue elements, or through organised criminal networks. Blair's '… fundamental commitment to the idea of disarming Saddam was so strong, so intimately bound up in the emotions he felt and the conclusions he reached on 9/11, that it wasn't going to wither away' (Naughtie 2004: 202).

At the end of the day, Blair put his principles on the line in calling for war against Iraq. He risked losing his position, and was prepared for this if the vote in parliament went against him. Blair was opposed by the British people (over one million marched in London against going to war), and opinion polls indicated that less than a third of the population supported war. The trade unions and – more quietly but just as assuredly – the military establishment were also opposed to war. The bulk of his own party outside parliament opposed the Prime Minister, and fully one third of Labour MPs voted against the resolution put to parliament in March 2003. The majority of the UN was opposed to the invasion, as were the other more powerful European partners, Germany and France. Clare Short said that Blair was acting recklessly, and Robin Cook notes in his diaries that there was 'near mutiny in Cabinet when military action was first mentioned against Iraq' (Cook 2003).

INDIVIDUAL AGENCY: HOW IMPORTANT WAS BLAIR?

Assessing the extent to which individuals make a difference in politics is a controversial and difficult matter. Intuitively, one assumes that to some extent individuals *must* have an impact. But how can we evaluate the extent to which this is true in any specific case? One specialist on this issue has suggested that there are three conditions that must be met before we can conclude that an individual has made an impact on history (Greenstein 1987). First, the actions of the person in question must be ones we could not reasonably have expected from other similarly situated individuals. This requires an exercise in counterfactuals: if someone other than Blair had been Prime Minister, would the policies have been different? Here there is a general consensus that if any of the other potential leaders of the Labour Party had been in office in 2003, then Britain would not have gone to war in Iraq. One of Blair's Cabinet colleagues has stated that '[H]ad anyone else been leader we would not have fought alongside Bush' (P. Stephens 2004: 298). Another senior British minister maintains that '[I]f Colin Powell had been US President and Jack Straw Prime Minister you can be pretty sure that there would not have been a war' (Stephens 2004: 319). Gordon Brown was, and is still at the time of writing, the most likely alternative to Blair as leader of the Labour Party. If Brown had been Prime Minister in 2003, it is quite clear, and widely accepted, that he would not have taken Britain to war against Iraq.

A second consideration in assessing the role of individuals is to establish that their own individual actions made a difference to the actual policies adopted. There can be little argument that British policies pursued in the war on terror, and especially in waging war against Iraq, reflected the preferences of Blair, and that he had to utilise his noted powers of persuasion to convince others to accept them. Blair was pushing for joining with Bush against Iraq at a time when negative opinion of the US in the UK was at an all-time high and the majority of the British public strongly opposed going to war. Even waverers in the Cabinet, such as Clare Short, were eventually persuaded to vote for war. Following her subsequent resignation, Short accused Blair of ruling by 'diktat', with the Cabinet no longer a collective decision-making body, but rather a rubber stamp for '... policy initiatives that came from on high' (Riddell 2003: 284). Another Labour MP was critical of Blair's 'messianic sense of mission', while a third stated that he '... thinks he can walk on water' (Kearney 2003: 84). Cabinet government and the doctrine of collective responsibility have given way under Blair's leadership to a form of presidential rule. Meetings of the Cabinet under Blair have become infrequent, short, and more of a rubber stamp for policies already made by the Prime Minister, who takes advice not from professional civil servants, but from unelected and unaccountable political advisers. The role of the Cabinet is to offer a periodical '... series of self-congratulatory remarks' (Hennessy 2000: 507). Kosovo was the making of his leadership and, as Hennessy (2000: 507) has described it, this has been 'hugely impressive' and 'awesome'. Blair is uneasy about sharing power with others, and has created an office of the Prime Minister 'that was of unprecedented authority and reach, more powerful even than that presided over by Margaret Thatcher at her peak' (P. Stephens 2004: 121). Blair's 'autocratic' style of leadership, according to an insider, entrenched 'an oppressive sense of conformity ... few dared question or criticise him' (Seldon 2004: 600). His advisers '... told Blair what he wanted to hear... and Blair was too ready to listen to the people whose advice chimed with his own instincts' (Seldon 2004: 600). Lord Butler, in an unprecedented savage attack on an incumbent Prime Minister from a former Cabinet Secretary, criticised Blair for bypassing the professional public service and the traditional checks and balances of Whitehall (Butler 2004). In the field of foreign policy, neither of Blair's foreign ministers, Cook or Straw, has been part of his inner circle. As one observer noted when Blair came to power '... the Foreign Secretary ... arrived in Whitehall a passenger rather than a pilot' (Rentoul 2002: 420).

Blair's persuasive capabilities extended beyond Westminster to Washington. Cheney was frustrated by the influence Blair held over Bush in taking the Iraq issue to the UN, complaining in private that 'We are there for Blair. There's no other reason, no justification. We're told we have to do it' (Naughtie 2004: 147). Blair spoke almost daily with Bush during the lead-up to war, and he was '... not afraid to talk frankly to the president', pushing

Bush to undertake '... new policies of engagement for all parts of the world, starting with the Middle East' (Stothard 2003: 207). Most officials in the Foreign and Commonwealth Office did not merely have reservations about taking Britain to war in Iraq – they considered it would be a fateful mistake. Gordon Brown's clear lack of obvious support was possibly due to philosophical objections, but in the end he conceded that Iraq was 'transparently Blair's show' (P. Stephens 2004: 580).

A third consideration in assessing the role of Blair relates to the impact of his policies. Having ascertained that he followed policies that could not have been expected from any other possible leader, and that he was instrumental in getting these policies accepted and implemented, it is necessary to assess the extent to which the policies themselves were really important in the conduct of international relations during the period in question. Here it is a self-evident and non-controversial fact that the policies pursued by the British government leading up to the invasion of Iraq had profound effects. Blair's policies led to the most serious rift for decades between the UK and France, and they helped ultimately to undermine rather than reinforce, the role and legitimacy of the UN, to say nothing of the impact they had on the people of Iraq. Clearly, Blair made a difference; and the difference was significant.

One can reasonably conclude that Blair as an individual has been an extremely important figure in the war on terror, and that he has acted out of his own personal convictions. Indeed, although 9/11 clearly had a profound impact on his thinking and the dangers represented by Saddam, Blair had already begun to seriously rethink the nature of international security and to develop a radical approach to deal with new threats. Blair's support for war on Iraq was not out of any loyalty to Bush (although he does consider it desirable to stay on side with the US in an age of unipolarity), but because he held very strong personal views about what needed to be done. Karl Marx (1937) made the point that 'men make their own history' (although not as they please, and in the objective circumstances they face at the time); and E.H. Carr, associated with the Realist school of International Relations, stated '... that human affairs can be directed and modified by human action and human thought is a postulate so fundamental that its rejection seems scarcely compatible with existence as a human being' (Carr 1939). Blair recognised that new security challenges required new thinking and new policies, but he also recognised the objective reality of US power and unipolarity, and the need to work within the confines of this basic, objective material fact. Having said this, it should be stressed that Blair's conception of the international community is certainly not rooted in the idea of US hegemony or a new American empire, but rather in multilateralism, humanitarianism, international institutions and treaties. This can be contrasted with the neo-conservatives in the US, whose conception is rooted in unilateralism, American national interests, and the use of the military to serve the interests of maintaining and enhancing US power and influence in the world.

CONCLUSION

All of this does not portray someone who is acting in accordance with another's wishes, or someone manipulated by others. Blair's own ideas informed his foreign policy. He lacked neither principle nor determination. When Blair had an objective, he stuck to it rigidly and with conviction, following logically his own moral compass. Evidence of his sincerity and seriousness of purpose is the fact that he would not compromise his convictions even when faced with opposition from within his own circle of New Labour colleagues. Roy Jenkins' view of Blair was that 'far from lacking conviction [he] has almost too much, particularly when dealing with the world beyond Britain. He is a little too Manichean for my perhaps now jaded taste, seeing matters in stark terms of good and evil, black and white' (Naughtie 2004: 142). Whether or not one supports Blair's policies, it should be acknowledged that he acted more as a persuader in the showdown with Iraq over the last several years than as the secondary enforcer of US will. Blair's actions in siding with the US over Iraq were based upon strategic calculations, designed to both moderate US unilateralist tendencies and encourage the Bush administration to pursue a wider multilateral engagement in the Middle East. In an interview in October 2001, Blair did not rule out war against Iraq, but did indicate that his support would be dependent upon a US commitment to engage with Israel and Palestine regarding a peace settlement in the Middle East (Kearney 2003). Blair has been consistent in pressing Bush to behave proactively for a settlement of the Arab–Israeli conflict.

Blair has also continued to stress his conviction that poverty poses a threat to global security, evidenced in an article he wrote at the beginning of 2005 setting out an agenda for alleviating poverty in Africa (Blair 2005). Blair argues that poverty in Africa is directly linked to wider security interests, for it triggers mass migration, anarchy, and creates an environment conducive to crime, fanaticism and terrorism. It is in their national interests, therefore, for the strong developed nations to act collectively to deal with the problems posed by global poverty. It is interesting to note here that, since resigning from the US State Department, Colin Powell has expressed views very similar to those of Blair. Powell maintains that the '... United States cannot win the war on terrorism unless we confront the social and political roots of poverty' (Powell 2005). Blair did not send British troops to Iraq out of loyalty to Bush. Although he came to power knowing little of foreign affairs and with no experience of warfare, Blair took Britain to war *five* times in six years. None of these wars can be viewed as being linked to traditional notions of the national interest. He used military force first during his initial year in government, against Iraq, to ensure compliance with UN resolutions. Next, in 1999, he went to war against Milošević in support of the Kosovar Albanians. Then Britain intervened to restore order in Sierra Leone in 2000. By the time Bush came to power, quickly followed by the events of 9/11, Blair was already experienced in waging war, and he had already spent a great deal of time thinking both strategically and tactically about how to respond to what he perceived to be new non-traditional threats in an age of globalisation. Bush did not push Blair into war. Blair went to war alongside the Americans, first in Afghanistan and then in Iraq, due to his own assessments of what was necessary, in his view, for the greater good of humanity.

Yet taking the war on terror to Iraq might actually result, finally, in a self-fulfilling prophecy. Following the US–UK invasion of Iraq, that country quickly became a new magnet and recruitment ground for terrorists; criminal networks emerged, engaged in arms smuggling and money laundering; and the clear lesson for 'rogue states' was that the only deterrence against attack is to acquire nuclear weapons. And instead of democracy developing in Iraq, despite the holding of elections, civil war is as likely, or at least another form of corrupt regime. Perhaps for Blair the main lesson of taking the war to Iraq is that he should have stuck more rigidly to the five conditions for engaging in military intervention that he outlined in his 'doctrine of the international community'. The first condition was not met, for the case against Iraq was not clear. This was evident to many at the time, including UN Inspector Hans Blix and many intelligence agencies. In relation to the second condition, other possibilities had not been fully exhausted, for inspections were not given the time needed to prove whether or not Saddam was concealing weapons of mass destruction. Blix would later ask how it could be that there was 100 percent certainty about the existence of weapons of mass destruction but 'zero percent knowledge about their location' (Blix 2004). The third condition relates to the prudent use of military force, the question of proportionality and avoidance of civilian deaths. This question is always difficult; and although 'precision bombing' and other measures were ostensibly employed to reduce the number of innocent victims, there have been substantial numbers of deaths among innocent non-combatants. The fourth condition is to be willing to stay for the long haul. Yet, just two years after the invasion, the mission had apparently changed, and there was an urgency to establish an Iraqi government able to control the security situation, thereby enabling the invading forces to leave. The final and most important condition (the realistic element in Blair's thinking) is that the national interest must also be involved before contemplating military force. It was never evident exactly in what way Saddam posed a threat to British national interests. Blair was advised against an attack on Iraq by a number of specialists on international relations, Iraq, and the wider Middle East, for the consequences could be extremely damaging to British interests. This advice was given privately, as well as publicly in the letters pages of the British press. Blair ignored this advice. Owen Harries has referred to Blair as the 'British Gorbachev', '... in that he believes that statesmanship consists of taking flying leaps into the future without any clear idea of where one will land' (Harries 2004: 124). Blair's place in history will largely be determined by the long-term consequences of his taking Britain to war in Iraq. One thing is certain, however: he was not acting out a proxy role for the US, but was very much his own man.

11. The 'War on Terror' and the Resuscitation of State Power as an Anti-Corruption Strategy

Mark DaCosta Alleyne

Because the link between terrorism, organised crime and corruption is not immediately obvious, and because the stakes in the financial dimension of the 'war on terror' are much higher for some states than for others, the worldwide campaign to starve terror networks of funding has been as much a discursive project as it has been one of law enforcement. This chapter makes the argument that the States System has used the pretext of being the only mechanism to protect civil society from non-state actor violence in order to justify the comprehensive reassertion of state power in the transnational financial system. In the field of international relations this means that previous contentions that the power of the state had been seriously compromised now need to be reassessed. The case of the reform of the international financial system following 9/11 illustrates quite well how the state deploys its power to define a problem and fashion a response in the interest of maintaining, and even enhancing, its own power.

I will first review the theoretical context in international relations for this analysis. This will be accompanied by an historical review of relevant developments in the international political economy prior to 9/11. A critical analysis of the United States' government's response to the terror attacks will follow. I will show that the response taken by the state was not the only option possible. Finally, I will demonstrate what this has meant for the theorisation of state power in the field of international relations.

THEORETICAL CONTEXT

Following the attacks of 11 September 2001, the United States led the worldwide crusade to link the then liberalising international financial system with the problem of the spread of terrorism. The timing could not have been more opportune for the state. Beginning with the concerns in the late 1960s and early 1970s about the rise of transnational corporations through to neo-liberal theories of interdependence and international regimes in the 1980s, a substantial body of literature had been established with the central theme of showing how state power, especially in the realm of finance and economic production, had diminished (Sampson 1973; Keohane and Nye 1977; Krasner 1983; Goodman 1987). This tendency continued apace in the 1990s with the rise of the neo-liberal transnational economy,[1] the end of the Cold War, and the consequent enhanced role of international organisations in world politics, especially the emergence of the United Nations as global peacekeeper. Although the state continued to enjoy a privileged status, it had to deal with contending forces in international relations. These included social movements 'from below', such as those that took credit for toppling some of the governments of the Communist Bloc and that led a peasant rebellion in Chiapas, Mexico. There was also the challenge from the technological revolution in transport and telecommunication, which made it possible for new nodes of affiliation to be created regardless of geographic distance. No longer was the imagining of nationhood – to paraphrase Anderson (1991) – the only form of imagining there could be. There was now a transnational environmental movement, self-organising by indigenous peoples outside the relatively narrow confines of states, and various diasporic unions of peoples along fault lines of ethnicity and religion, to name but a few. In 1996, Arjun Appadurai argued that this scenario produced 'theory of a break', because there was a sudden and drastic break with the past caused by a revolution in mass media and mass migration that occurred within the time span of just two decades. For Appadurai, we had arrived at a 'post-national' juncture in world history that had three meanings:

> The first is temporal and historical and suggests that we are in the process of moving to a global order in which the nation-state has become obsolete and other formations for allegiance and identity have taken its place. The second is the idea that what are emerging are strong alternative forms for the organization of global traffic in resources, images, and ideas – forms that either contest the nation-state actively or constitute peaceful alternatives for large-scale political loyalties. The third implication is the possibility that, while nations might continue to exist, the steady

erosion of the capabilities of the nation-state to monopolize loyalty will encourage the spread of national forms that are largely divorced from territorial states. These are relevant senses of the term *postnational*, but none of them implies that the nation-state in its classical territorial form is as yet out of business. It is certainly in crisis, and part of the crisis is an increasingly violent relationship between the nation-state and its postnational Others. (Appadurai 1996: 168–9)

This way of theorising the world order was a new discourse on 'globalisation'. One problem with grand neo-realist theories of world order was that they were still preoccupied with the state, which was assumed to be a rational actor still, behaving in its own interest. Now features of the international scene, which were previously obscured by the preoccupation with the power politics of the state, were given as much currency in the evolution of international politics as the traditional aspects of 'high politics' (for example strategy, diplomacy, disarmament, and so on). Globalisation was the 'intensification of global consciousness', and this consciousness had agency (Waters 1995). Similarly, new grand theory that was less blinkered by the perceived need to attend to the institutional aspects of the nation-state, and that looked more at culture and civilisation configurations, could yield new insights into the origins and nature of conflict (Huntington 1993, 1996; Barber 1995).

The coming of globalisation theory to international relations coincided with the arrival of the field's 'Third Debate'. The first two debates were realism versus idealism, and the methodological binary of behaviouralism versus qualitative means of research. This new debate was between the rational choice orthodoxy of the field and those willing to look for means of theorising international relations in places not previously considered, such as the realms of critical theory and postmodernism. By carefully interrogating the 'givens' of international politics and declaring all of them to be social constructions, this constructivist turn opens up the opportunity to question the basic credibility of all centres of power in the global order as somehow being primordial, essentialist and natural. These include the state, the modern state system, racial identity, nationalism, and the very principles of the post-World War II international order, especially the doctrine of universality. Additionally, instead of trying to produce grand theories that purport to explain how international politics works, this paradigm is more content to give 'compelling interpretations and explanations of discrete aspects of world politics, going no further than to offer heavily qualified "contingent generalisations"' (Burchill *et al.* 2001). Communicative practices are very important to this way of viewing the international scene because they are critical to how human beings discursively *construct* their social worlds (Campbell 1998). It is my contention here that such a constructivist approach to the US-led response to the terror challenge provides us with a more sophisticated way of understanding why the so-called 'war on terror' has had such a profound impact on the international financial system.

THE LIBERALISING SYSTEM PRE-9/11

Although the G-7 created the Financial Action Task Force on Money Laundering (FATF) almost 13 years prior to 9/11, it was not until after 11 September 2001 that it was given a specific mandate to suppress the links between money laundering and terrorism, and that this change was accompanied by a number of other initiatives that curbed considerably the liberty of financial institutions internationally. During the previous 20 years, there was a movement to liberalise the transnational flow of money and commerce. This was due to a major policy shift in the leading states of the international economy, 'structural adjustment' initiatives by the Bretton Woods institutions, and an overhaul of the rules of participation at international organisations that diminished the privileges enjoyed by states.

One of the earliest factors in the establishment of the transnational neo-liberal economy was the coincidence of ideologically very similar administrations being elected in three of the world's most powerful economies at the turn of the 1980s. Margaret Thatcher in the United Kingdom, Ronald Reagan in the United States, and Helmut Kohl in West Germany were all fiscal conservatives who reduced government spending on social programs, minimised the state's regulation of business, and promoted the view that an unhindered economic marketplace would be more efficient and generate more wealth than one that was tightly controlled. The policies of the George W. Bush administration with regards to global money flows and terrorism cannot be properly understood unless seen with the Reagan philosophy of deregulation as the backdrop. This is because, with the benefit of hindsight, the Reagan policies brought mixed rewards, at best, and might have facilitated the terrorist exploitation of the liberal financial system they created, at worst. The first most prominent example of this policy failure was the 1980s Savings and Loan crisis in the United States, where a number of these financial institutions failed, due to fraud and mismanagement that was facilitated in the deregulated environment (Strunk and Case 1988; Ely and Vanderhoff 1991; L. White 1992). Twenty years later, the Enron collapse took a high toll on investors when the corporation and its auditor, Arthur Andersen, exploited the government's lack of rigid auditing standards (Staff to the Senate Committee on Governmental Affairs 2002; Culp and Niskanen 2003; Fox 2003).

The second factor in the liberalisation of the world economy prior to 9/11 was the debt crisis that dated back to the early 1980s. It was a situation in which several countries either had great difficulty repaying, or defaulted completely, on their debts to transnational banks. These banks had made large loans to several countries over many years on the premise that states could not go bankrupt. However, that assumption was proven wrong when many countries in the global south could not meet their financial obligations. The consequence of this situation was that the IMF, an institution that was the lender of last resort for countries, gained new power and influence. When states in financial trouble appealed to the IMF for help, that body imposed what became known as 'structural adjustment' programs in those countries as conditions for receiving IMF loans. Structural adjustment policies meant a diminished role for the state in several areas of national economies, especially ownership of public utilities and other social services, such as transportation. The IMF also advocated the end of government subsidies and promoted an increased role for markets in socio-economic decision-making.

The third factor accounting for what has become known as the rise of neo-liberalism was in the realm of international organisation. Although the 1994 decision to create the World Trade Organisation (which was formally established in 1995) has been one of the most controversial events in the international political economy, an equally significant event was occurring *inside* key international institutions at about the same time. This was the move to grant transnational corporations membership in international intergovernmental organisations. In the issue-area of telecommunications in particular, this represented formal acknowledgment of what had been obvious from the earliest days of the technology. Although across the globe the state had maintained ownership of national telecommunication networks for national security and fiscal reasons, many international communication companies – such as Cable & Wireless and AT&T – had far more technical expertise and power within the International Telecommunication Union (ITU) than most states. In 1992, the ITU overhauled its administrative structure entirely and divided its structure into three sectors: Standardisation, Radiocommunication, and Development. It ended the monopoly government officials had enjoyed in formulating ITU policy by allowing private firms to be full members of each sector. The move was the culmination of a gradual trend of increasing involvement by non-governmental entities in the ITU policy-making process. In 1989, the ITU allowed scientific and industrial organisations to be members of its consultative committees; and in April 1992, the ITU created a World Telecom Advisory Council, comprising 18 representatives of the telecommunication industry and chaired by the Chairman and Chief Executive Officer of Siemens AG. The full membership of firms in the ITU was announced in late 1992. By April 1997, over 300 firms were members of one, two, or all three of the ITU's sectors. Telecommunication was critical to the establishment of the post-industrial economies on which neo-liberalism was built, because the growth of the service sector – a key characteristic of post-industrialism – was essentially the increased use of new telecommunication technologies (such as telematics and facsimile) to manipulate symbols in the provision of services, such as banking, insurance and brokerage (Bell 1999).

What happened at the ITU was the best example of a trend occurring in several other sectors of the international political economy. In many issue-areas it was becoming clear that non-governmental transnational economic enterprises wielded more power than states, even though states still exercised regulatory power. Some examples include drug corporations in the field of health (a scenario that inspired much controversy over who should control the provision of AIDS vaccines and under what terms); transnational package delivery firms that took away business from government-run postal authorities; and food processing firms in the area of agriculture, with the power to determine the character of research into (and even patenting of) new breeds of plants.

Although the WTO has been singled out as the archetypal neo-liberal intergovernmental organisation, its creation to spread the gospel of free trade was just one aspect of these more profound changes taking place before 9/11 as part of the expanding international neo-liberal economy. The preference for neo-liberal policies produced a number of initiatives and institutions that were quickly changing the fundamental character of the world political economy. These included IMF–World Bank 'structural adjustment' arrangements that obligated indebted countries to implement neo-liberal programs, even despite public protests; free-trade zones, the best-known being NAFTA (1992) and the EU (formally established 1993, in line with the 1992 Maastricht Treaty); and the privatisation of the Internet (1995).

9/11: SHOCK AND AFTERMATH

The key problem faced by the George W. Bush administration after the 2001 attacks on the United States was not how to find, try, and punish those responsible, but how to prevent additional attacks. A number of resources had to be mobilised in order to minimise the risk. These included a general public that appreciated the nature of the threat; public willingness to accept the compromises the new preventative laws required; and the recruitment of allies around the world to see the problem in the same way as the United States government. So the 'war on terror' was first a discursive project before anything else.

Intellectual elites in the United States have made a considerable investment in promoting 'the mythology of American individual freedom', based on values of self-government, liberty and equality (Calabrese and Burke 1992). These myths, which are used in national identity construction, are important to understand because ' ... [i]f citizens make a strong psychological identification with the nation and internalize national symbols, political leaders are better able to mobilize public sentiment toward a political goal in times of crisis by using communication strategies that emphasize positive themes of national identity' (Hutcheson *et al.* 2004: 29).

In addition to the problem of the highly contested nature of national identity politics that is always present, the George W. Bush administration was confronted with the additional problem of the peculiar nature of the crisis. Two fundamental components of war – the enemy and the enemy's war aims – were very unclear.

Al-Qaeda – the named perpetrator of the 9/11 attacks – is not a state but an ominous network of terrorists that, according to the administration, could be anywhere. So, apart from attempting to put a face on the enemy – that is Osama Bin Laden, the Taliban and Saddam Hussein – the administration's propaganda had to establish what al-Qaeda was supposed to represent. By associating al-Qaeda with the Taliban government of Afghanistan and the Baath regime of Iraq, it was easier to make the case for war, because these regimes were said to be anathema to the most cherished principles of American democracy. They dealt in terrorism, sexism, torture, denial of civil liberties and *weapons of mass destruction*. It is therefore very significant that the two military operations launched by the administration against these two states carried the word *freedom* in their titles: 'Operation Enduring Freedom' (Afghanistan) and 'Operation Iraqi Freedom'.

The administration prepared the population within the United States to accept the sacrifices that were necessary to conduct the war – especially curbs on civil liberties and deaths in military operations – by resorting to the trope of hyper-nationalism. A new Department of *Homeland* Security was established. The set of laws that compromised American freedoms was called the *PATRIOT* Act.[2] All along the way, the administration sustained the notion that the country was under terrorist threat, encouraging people within the United States to identify suspicious individuals and activities and report them to law enforcement agencies. On 26 September 2001, White House Press Secretary Ari Fleischer, in response to a report that a comedian had suggested on TV that the suicide attackers were courageous, famously said that such incidents were ' … reminders to all Americans that they need to watch what they say, watch what they do' (Office of the White House Press Secretary 2001). The Department of Homeland Security established a colour-coded 'Homeland Security Advisory System' that featured various levels of 'Threat Advisory': the higher the threat, the more alert law enforcement agencies would be in imposing public inconveniences, especially more security checks at airports. A key feature of the 'war on terrorism' narrative became the ebbs and flows of these advisories that were said to be based on government intelligence about communication among the terrorists.

The alleged suicide bombers left no statement about why they did what they did and what specific changes they meant to see. Although al-Qaeda was said to be a non-state actor, even previous campaigns of violence by non-state entities included these bodies' statements of purpose. And such entities have always had 'political wings' to complement the work of their 'armed wings'. So, in the absence of an entity that would participate in the international political discourse on behalf of the enemy, the George W. Bush administration was free to set the discursive parameters. The administration read the attacks as a declaration of war on the nation-state that is the United States. In the months and years after 9/11, it reinforced that theme by emphasising that 'the terrorists' sought the elimination of the United States. There was a *de facto* call to all Americans to defend the state (the *Homeland*), and so the symbolism of the state became critical to the discursive sustenance of this discourse. Citizens were asked to reflect on what it meant to be part of the nation-state that is the United States; there were prominent displays of the flag; commemorative events featured the playing of the national anthem; and there were appeals to 'support' the US military, the armed wing of the nation-state. Cause marketing campaigns by the Ad Council – the public service arm of the advertising industry that was actually founded during World War II to conduct this kind of integrative propaganda within the United States – stressed 'American' unity across racial lines, and were part of the wider project that included this trope. The Defense Department started a propaganda campaign, called 'Operation Tribute to Freedom' (Defense Department 2004), to bolster support for the troops. Eager to display their patriotism, a number of personalities and organisations volunteered participation. For example, the National Football League (NFL) dedicated the official start of its 2003–04 season to the 'men and women of the U.S. armed forces', as part of the campaign. The NFL sponsored a free concert on the National Mall in Washington DC, at which members of the military were asked to attend in uniform (Defense Logistics Agency 2003).

JUSTIFYING THE SURVEILLANCE STATE

Contrary to popular media discourse following the passage of the United States PATRIOT Act, the biggest changes on the American scene were not in the area of general civil liberties, such as personal privacy when using public transport or the racial profiling of 'Arabs', but in the realm of markets. The neo-liberal financial system that the United States had itself put in place in the preceding 20 years was suddenly found to be a liability in the 'war on terror', and the discursive project that had to be employed overseas to justify the actions being taken had to be quite different from the propaganda campaign used on the United States public. The President acknowledged as much when he noted at the PATRIOT Act signing ceremony, a month and a half following the attacks, that the war was a 'two-front war – one overseas, and a front here at home' (Bush 2001). Abroad, instead of nationalist appeals, George W. Bush's discursive project was based on appeals that stressed the role of the state as protector. It was very important to provide a seemingly compelling justification for the clampdown on freedom in the global financial system, a move very much at odds with the neo-liberal ethos of the preceding years.

The provisions of the PATRIOT Act (Patriot Act 2001) covering the financial services industry were contained in Title III. They were:

- the criminalisation of bulk cash smuggling and imposing a requirement that underground financial networks be registered;
- updating anti-counterfeiting laws for the digital age;
- restricting the provision of financial services to foreign 'shell' banks by US banks and securities broker-dealers;

- creating a formal system in which the government and businesses collaborate to identify, track and stop terrorists' financial activities;
- imposing the requirement that financial organisations report suspicious activity promptly to law enforcement agencies;
- adding broker-dealers to the list of financial enterprises that must report suspicious activity; and
- imposing the obligation on financial institutions to have formal programs for the identity verification of clients, and the related obligation on clients to provide truthful information to these institutions when opening accounts (Byrne and Kelsey 2004).

It is highly significant that the last four of the seven provisions gave the state increased surveillance powers over the sector. In the month that it took the United States Congress to draft the act, the conclusion was reached that what the state needed to do to *prevent* more terror attacks was to acquire more power to spy on suspected terrorists, collect information on their activities (especially their financial transactions), and to take preemptive action against them before they could strike – panoptic power (Gandy 1993). Banks, brokers, libraries and other social institutions were drafted into this government-run surveillance network on the premise that everyone – not just the government or military – was under threat, so that it would be in the general public good to cooperate.

As was evident in the debate over whether the Iraqi government did or did not have weapons of mass destruction in 2003, much of the power and prestige the state has in international relations is due to the aura of its surveillance capabilities. States by themselves, or as part of a military–industrial complex, claim a technological advantage in the ability to determine the identity and location of threat. The civilian population is asked to trust the credibility of the state when the latter claims it has the information. However, this is a Catch 22 scenario, because there is often no way of verifying that what the state asserts is really true. The state justifies secrecy about its sources and methods of intelligence collection by claiming risk 'to national security' and the need to protect the means by which more intelligence can be collected in the future. When no weapons of mass destruction were found in Iraq, the world discovered once again that grave consequences can result when the military–industrial intelligence complex is wrong. For this state of affairs to remain in place unchallenged, there must be public trust in the state as protector and guardian of the general good.

The Bush administration understood that this psychological mindset towards the state needed to be cultivated and maintained. The international discursive project was not only about Americans trusting and allying themselves with the surveillance apparatus of the American government, but also about foreign publics and their governments doing so as well. So the trope of the state as protector with the power to pre-empt terrorist attacks was a critical part of the discursive strategy. At the same PATRIOT Act signing ceremony, President Bush stressed the value of the new law in allowing 'surveillance of all communications used by terrorists, including e-mails, the Internet, and cell phones'. He emphasised that the law aimed at catching terrorists 'before they strike', and he explained that the 'legislation is essential not only to pursuing and punishing terrorists, but also preventing more atrocities in the hands of evil ones' (Bush 2001).

Almost three years later, when the PATRIOT Act needed to be renewed, Bush justified the continuation of the law by stressing again this notion of the state as protector. He said that making sure that 'our nation is as secure as it can possibly be' was a 'solemn duty' (Bush 2004a). And he continued to emphasise the theme of pre-emption by saying that the ' ... best way to secure America is to bring them to justice before they hurt us again' and that the '... priority of the federal government is now the prevention of another attack'. The following day, in another media event staged with United States law enforcement officials to promote the PATRIOT Act, he asserted that '... your job now is to prevent attack' (Bush 2004b).

President Bush's Attorney General, John Ashcroft, was also employing these themes three years into the 'war on terror'. In attempting to establish the state's profile as protector, Ashcroft noted that some provisions of the PATRIOT Act had made it easier for American law enforcement agencies to crack down on pedophiles who used the Internet to distribute pornography. According to Ashcroft, 'America's families and communities have been safer, and their freedom is enhanced because of the president's resolve and leadership' (Ashcroft 2004).

In the four years following 9/11, other countries had also suffered major terror attacks – for example Bali, Indonesia (October 2002); Mombasa, Kenya (November 2002); Istanbul, Turkey (November 2003); Madrid, Spain (March 2004); London, UK (July 2005); Bali, Indonesia again (October 2005) – which provided the Bush administration and foreign governments with more evidence of the need to guard against the ominous threat. A combination of this recognised threat and the inability of almost all other states to extricate themselves from anti-terrorist obligations of US law due to the powerful reach of US-based firms accounted for why, very soon after 9/11, a number of international measures were in place that collectively enhanced state power considerably. Just a few days after President Bush signed the PATRIOT Act into law, the Financial Action Task Force (FATF), which became fully operational in 1990 following its founding by the G-7 in 1989, expanded its brief from a narrow focus on curbing money laundering to combating terrorist financing. As also pointed out by Rémy Davison in Chapter 4 of the present volume, the FATF's eight 'Special Recommendations on Terrorist Financing' committed members to:

- take immediate steps to ratify and implement the relevant United Nations instruments against terrorism;
- criminalise the financing of terrorism, terrorist acts and terrorist organisations;
- freeze and confiscate terrorist assets;
- report suspicious transactions linked to terrorism;
- provide the widest possible range of assistance to other countries' law enforcement and regulatory authorities for terrorist financing investigations;
- impose anti-money laundering requirements on alternative remittance systems;
- strengthen customer identification measures in international and domestic wire transfers; and
- ensure that entities, in particular non-profit organisations, cannot be misused to finance terrorism (See http://www.fatfgafi.org/dataoecd /55/16/34266142 .pdf).

In other words, the FATF Special Recommendations mirrored the main provisions of the PATRIOT Act as they related to the financial sector. Within two years, they had been accepted by the IMF and the World Bank as the standard for combating the financing of terrorism (Holder 2003). Furthermore, the FATF was able to have reluctant states come on board by threatening sanctions (Anonymous 2003).

Another source of pressure on states to crack down on terrorist financing was the United Nations. Although the UN had already created a body of international law against terrorism between 1963 and 1999, it was not until a few days after the 2001 attacks on the United States that the UN Security Council adopted a resolution that obliged UN member states to become parties to the 12 international anti-terrorist conventions and protocols. Security

Council Resolution 1373 of 28 September 2001 stipulated that UN members should:

- criminalise the financing of terrorism;
- freeze without delay any funds related to persons who commit acts of terrorism;
- deny all forms of financial support for terrorist groups;
- suppress the safe haven, sustenance or support of terrorists;
- share information with other governments in the investigation, detection, arrest, extradition and prosecution of those involved in such acts;
- criminalise active and passive assistance for terrorism in domestic laws and bring violators of these laws to justice; and
- become party as soon as possible to the relevant international conventions and protocols relating to terrorism.[3] (Counter-Terrorism Executive Directorate 2005).

The UN also put bureaucratic measures in place to make sure that the Resolutions provisions would be effective. The new Counter-Terrorism Committee was comprised of all 15 members of the Security Council and had as its brief the promotion and monitoring of implementation of the Resolution. A Counter-Terrorism Executive Directorate, CTED, was created to facilitate technical assistance to states without the resources to implement the Resolution's provisions.

It is noteworthy that only one of the 12 international anti-terrorist instruments passed before 2001 was devoted to terrorist financing. The 1999 International Convention for the Suppression of the Financing of Terrorism required states to take steps to prevent and counteract the financing of terrorists, whether direct or indirect, through groups claiming to have charitable, social or cultural goals or which also engage in illicit activities such as drug trafficking or gun running, and to hold those who finance terrorism criminally, civilly or administratively liable for such acts. It also provided for the identification, freezing and seizure of funds allocated for terrorist activities, as well as for the sharing of the forfeited funds with other states on a case-by-case basis. It eliminated bank secrecy as a justification for refusal to cooperate (Counter-Terrorism Executive Directorate 2005).

While terrorism, organised crime and corruption had not been linked by authorities in the early 1960s when international law-making against terrorism began, they certainly were in the period immediately following 9/11. And the momentum to use restrictions on financial institutions as a preventative measure in the 'war on terror' continued through to 2005, when UN Secretary-General Kofi Annan set out recommendations for suppressing terrorism and organised crime and corruption in the same section of his proposals for UN reform. The document stipulated that Heads of State and Government should:

(e)   Resolve to implement the comprehensive United Nations counterterrorism strategy presented by the Secretary-General to dissuade people from resorting to terrorism or supporting it; deny terrorists access to funds and materials; deter States from sponsoring terrorism; develop State capacity to defeat terrorism; and defend human rights;

(f)   Resolve to accede to all 12 international conventions against terrorism; and instruct their representatives to:
(i) Conclude a convention on nuclear terrorism as a matter of urgency;
(ii) Conclude a comprehensive convention on terrorism before the end of the sixtieth session of the General Assembly;

(g)   Commit themselves to acceding, as soon as possible, to all relevant international conventions on organized crime and corruption, and take all necessary steps to implement them effectively, including by incorporating the provisions of those conventions into national legislation and strengthening criminal justice systems ... (Annan 2005)

STATE MOTIVATIONS FOR JOINING THE ANTI-TERRORIST WAR

The UN participated in the 'war on terror' on the terms of the state because states are the only members of the international society given the privilege of full UN membership. So, despite the many years of claims that state power was declining, when there was a shock to the international system such as 9/11, all other participants in international society were expected to fall into line behind the state. The UN played the role of facilitator of this process.

However, it is important to note that there is no monolithic 'state' position on the 'war on terror'. Even before 9/11, transnational discourse on national security, nuclear weapons and biological warfare had included the discursive construct of 'rogue states' – those states that did not play by the rules of 'international society'. Indeed, the two major wars that resulted from the 2001 attacks – in Afghanistan and Iraq – were both launched by the United States against supposed rogue states. From the start, it was assumed that not all states would undertake a common interest with the United States against the threat to the state posed by the non-state threat of terror networks.

However, in the case of the attempts to suppress terrorist financing in particular, non-compliance by other states is not always due to collusion with terrorists. This is why President Bush's assertion that those states that did not readily join the 'war on terror' were automatically allied with terrorists was deeply flawed logically. The following hypothetical case, in which terrorism, organised crime and corruption are all involved, serves to illustrate this point.

A group in Country A is planning to commit a series of violent acts against civilians in Country B to achieve specific ends, but it needs to transfer money to its cell of collaborators in Country B, who will do the job. One member of the cell establishes a computer software business for the sole purpose of laundering money received for the cell from the collaborators in Country A. To ensure that a new anti-terrorist law – which requires banks to report suspicious accounts to the government of Country B – does not cause problems, the cell arranges bribes for the key officials running the regulatory government department and the money laundering division of Country B's police force. The bribes are accepted, the officials responsible look the other way, the money is successfully laundered, the terror act is committed, and even international investigators are hard pressed to solve the crime and secure arrests – because the bribed officials do not even know that the financing of terrorism was the ultimate goal of the money laundering activity.

Under the scenario described above, the bulk of incentives to make the links between terrorism, organised crime and corruption are firmly on the side of Country B. It is at risk from both terrorist attack and government corruption in the service of terrorism. Country A must be given incentives to regard the problem as seriously as Country B. Many offshore financial havens that are small countries with few enemies, such as Caribbean islands, are potential Country As, especially in light of the fact that they have no military cultures with histories of fighting territorial wars and fending off external attack. This is why the Caribbean was an early front in the financial dimensions of the 'war on terror' (Lambert 2001; Allen 2003; Drayton 2003). The list of incentives that could be used to make Country A compliant include: (1) forms of retaliation from Country B for 'hosting' terrorists, such as military action, severed diplomatic relations or economic sanctions; (2) demonstration and persuasion that it too is vulnerable to terrorism and corruption; and (3) international isolation. However, the problem can be exacerbated for Country B the more Country A shares the claims of the non-state terror actor. The more it shares such 'war aims', the less likely it would be to cooperate in transnational initiatives to put the terrorists out of business, such as intelligence cooperation, surveillance of its financial system and violent action to eliminate the terrorists on its home soil.

CONCLUSION

One way of reading the attacks of 11 September 2001 is as a challenge by non-state actors to the States System. The States System had two main options as a response: (a) consider the claims of the non-state actors by incorporating them more formally into the international order; and (b) taking measures to strengthen the power of the state, as a strategy to neutralise the non-state opposition. The latter action was taken. In adopting this posture, the United States in particular was of the view that suppressing the financing of terrorists should be the priority if more terror attacks were to be prevented.

In the ensuing propaganda war, the non-state actors were at a distinct disadvantage. Although states also engage in violent attacks against civilians, they label terrorists as uncivilised and barbaric for employing such a strategy. The mere discussion of the Geneva Conventions (international law that covers states) in relation to controversies involving the treatment of prisoners held by states gives the impression that states adhere to a higher standard of conduct in international conflict that involves obedience to set rules. Governments can claim legitimacy through democratic elections, but non-state actors cannot. In courting public opinion, states claim they are protecting the civic good and dismiss non-state belligerents as 'radical' fringes bent on destroying civil society. States have the power to continue the exclusion of non-state actors from membership in international organisations. This power imbalance leads non-state actors to employ drastic measures to elicit their objectives, such as videotaping the beheading of civilians. Such acts can strengthen the propaganda hands of states, because they reinforce the theme in state propaganda that a war against terrorism is a struggle against irrational violence.

NOTES

1. Neo-liberalism, as a system of thought, questions the assumption that the state should have a central role in the allocation of scarce public resources and the regulation of utilities such as telecommunications, electricity and gas. It argues that much of welfare state policies are wasteful and inefficient. It believes that free markets are better at allocating resources than government policies. Government policies, it is argued, should encourage expansion and

investment by private firms, and these will in turn generate jobs and income that would then be recycled into the economy. Restrictions on international trade and investment should be reduced or eliminated. Some specific neo-liberal policies include: tax cuts (especially on private companies); reduction or elimination of government spending on many social welfare programs; reduction or elimination of government bureaucracies, especially those regulating utilities and mass communication; government divestment from enterprises that were previously thought to be best owned and run by the state; and the creation of 'free trade' zones.

2. PATRIOT is the acronym for the full title of the legislation: 'Uniting and Strengthening America by Providing Appropriate Tools Required to Intercept and Obstruct Terrorism.'

3. The 12 conventions and protocols were the: Convention on Offences and Certain Other Acts Committed on Board Aircraft ('Tokyo Convention', 1963 – safety of aviation); Convention for the Suppression of Unlawful Seizure of Aircraft ('Hague Convention', 1970 – aircraft hijackings); Convention for the Suppression of Unlawful Acts Against the Safety of Civil Aviation ('Montreal Convention', 1971 – acts of aviation sabotage); Convention on the Prevention and Punishment of Crimes Against Internationally Protected Persons (1973 – outlaws attacks on senior government officials and diplomats); International Convention Against the Taking of Hostages ('Hostages Convention', 1979); Convention on the Physical Protection of Nuclear Material ('Nuclear Materials Convention', 1980 – combats unlawful taking and use of nuclear material); Protocol for the Suppression of Unlawful Acts of Violence at Airports Serving International Civil Aviation, supplementary to the Convention for the Suppression of Unlawful Acts against the Safety of Civil Aviation (1988 - extends and supplements the Montreal Convention of Air Safety); Convention for the Suppression of Unlawful Acts Against the Safety of Maritime Navigation (1988 – applies to terrorist activities on ships); Protocol for the Suppression of Unlawful Acts Against the Safety of Fixed Platforms Located on the Continental Shelf (1988 – applies to terrorist activities on fixed offshore platforms); Convention on the Marking of Plastic Explosives for the Purpose of Detection (1991 – provides for chemical marking to facilitate detection of plastic explosives); International Convention for the Suppression of Terrorist Bombing (1997); and International Convention for the Suppression of the Financing of Terrorism (1999).

12. Some Concluding Observations: A Quadrumvirate in Future?

Leslie Holmes

This collection of essays has highlighted and analysed a variety of aspects of terrorism, organised crime and corruption in different countries and regions of the world, transnationally, and conceptually. Perhaps it raises more questions than it answers. But, as has been shown, the issue of linkages between these three phenomena is relatively new, both as a major field of research and as an official concern, and is very much a live dialogue. This is not to deny that a few analysts considered some of the connections long before the 1990s. Nevertheless, and as argued throughout this book, there has been a recent marked increase in awareness and emphasis.

The collection demonstrates that although the three phenomena can be and often are discrete, there *are* linkages, overlaps and resonances of various kinds between them. It is also clear that the hard evidence on such connections is at present thin. This should not be surprising, given the nature of these three forms of criminality. Corruption, for instance, often appears to be essentially victimless. Even when there *are* clear victims, all too often such people do not report the crime to the authorities, in many cases out of fear that they themselves will be punished for having paid bribes.[1] A similar situation – the fear factor – often pertains to both organised crime and terrorism. Users of illicit drugs are breaking the law, and usually have little incentive to report dealers to the police. Trafficked persons rarely turn to the authorities either, often because they fear that they will be punished for being an illegal immigrant and/or for being involved in an illegal activity (most commonly, certain types of prostitution);[2] given that their claims may not result in any prosecution or conviction of their captors, and that the latter might become even more violent against their 'slaves' if they discover they have been reported, the absence of hard evidence 'from the horse's mouth' is understandable.[3] If citizens know or suspect that their neighbours or workmates are involved in a terrorist organisation, they will often opt not to report this to the authorities, out of fear of possible retribution (as well as for other reasons, of course, such as support for the terrorists' cause).

If those affected by these crimes often have good cause for not reporting them, so do their perpetrators, and not only for the most obvious reason of not wanting to self-incriminate. Another factor explaining the limited hard evidence available on these crimes is the high level of secrecy – a code of silence, typified by the Italian concept of *omertà* ('conspiracy of silence') – that operates within many criminal gangs and terrorist groups.[4] Such a code sometimes also operates within groups of corrupt state officials, such as corrupt police officers in drug and vice squads. There has been a slight improvement in the situation in some countries recently, with an increased number of former mafia members (*pentiti* – repentants) collaborating with the state authorities in Italy, for instance, following 2001 changes to the law (Grupo Abele 2005).[5] Nevertheless, it will be a long time – if ever – before this type of confessional and 'grassing' evidence becomes a major source of information across the spectrum of groups and activities considered in this book. In many countries, for instance, there is either no witness protection program – Russia only passed a law to introduce such a program in July 2004 – or else the program is flawed and/or underfunded. Without such protection programs, there is normally too little incentive for witnesses to report to and cooperate with the authorities, which in turn helps to explain why official statistics are so often of limited value.[6] Then there is the problem, highlighted by Granovetter (2005: 15), that corrupt officials who want to cease their improper activities can find this difficult, because so-called 'corruption entrepreneurs' have collected materials on them that can be used for blackmail. Often, this material will be of more and/or worse misdeeds than the corrupt officials may have considered admitting to the authorities in return for denouncing others and a light sentence.[7] A final factor relating to secrecy, and hence to the shortage of hard data, is that many state authorities are prepared to provide academic researchers with information on terrorism, organised crime, and even corruption, but are highly sensitive about supplying details of *collusion* between their own officers and either criminal gangs or terrorists.

Yet even the circumstantial and limited hard evidence available is sufficient to prove that there is a problem. While the scale of this can be and is disputed, its existence cannot; given the serious negative effects of all three types of anti-social behaviour, it would be irresponsible to understate their impact. For example, there is no shortage of evidence that the use of illicit drugs is highly correlated with crime rates. A 1998 US Congressional hearing was informed that, 'Regarding the well-established link between drug use and crime, the latest Drug Use Forecasting Report from the Department of Justice indicated that over 60 percent of adult male arrestees tested positive for use of at least one drug at the time of arrest' (Congressional Hearings 1998). Rates of drug use are also closely correlated with HIV/AIDS rates, another serious social problem. While the precise scale of this cannot be determined, there is no question that large numbers of women and children are being trafficked and treated as sex slaves in several, probably most, Western countries.[8] Both men and women are also being trafficked for use as ultra-cheap labour in many countries. All this occurs largely because of the role of organised crime in drug and human trafficking, and in part because of the gangs' linkages with corrupt officials, who either turn a blind eye or else collaborate in more active ways.[9]

Those who argue that there are few if any meaningful links between organised crime and terrorism need to provide compelling arguments not only against the admittedly limited hard evidence, but also against common sense inferences that terrorism requires funding and is unlikely to be able to acquire much of this through legal channels. This has become even more the case since the early 2000s, as an increasing number of states and organisations have moved to freeze the assets of groups assumed to be terrorist or linked to terrorists, and have launched a major propaganda war against terrorism.[10] It appears that private sponsorship of terrorism is also in decline, because of the tighter monitoring of the transfer of large-scale funds, and because many former sponsors are becoming less willing to finance the random atrocities committed by terrorist groups.[11]Given all this, there is new pressure on terrorists to obtain funding from alternative sources, which will often involve them either becoming directly involved in organised crime themselves, or linking up with organised crime gangs.[12]

THREE GENERAL OBSERVATIONS

Despite the diverse approaches and foci of the contributors in this book, three closely related points emerge clearly and warrant emphasis in these concluding remarks. First, there is no agreed definition of any of the three concepts. On one level, this is to be expected and even welcomed, in that it testifies to the diversity of the phenomena they cover and the openness of intellectual debate. But on another level, serious *practical* difficulties arise because of this. If neither domestic nor international agencies charged with combating these phenomena can agree on definitions, then there cannot be agreement on exactly what they are seeking to reduce, which in turn means that they will find it more difficult to cooperate with others in the fight against them. All too often, such confusion plays into the hands of criminals, who can exploit legal loopholes and ambiguities, and continue their activities while authorities bicker.

Following on from this, the second point is that measuring these phenomena is highly problematic. While this is partly because of definitional differences, there are at least two further reasons. The first relates to the (in-)visibility and reporting problems mentioned above. Where statistics are available – on the number of reported cases, investigations, prosecutions and convictions for a particular type of crime, for instance, or the amount of drugs seized or illegal migrants intercepted each year – they can only be seen as the tip of the iceberg. This problem is less acute in the case of terrorist acts, the results and victims of which are usually highly visible, than for corruption or organised crime. But even in the case of terrorism, some aspects are often well hidden. One of the most obvious dimensions is precisely its relationship – the networks and linkages – to organised crime and corruption.

A second reason for the measurement problem, especially for comparative research, is that different jurisdictions have different methodologies and cultures for interpreting, classifying and reporting crime. Moreover, the methodologies often change over time. Partly because of this, even *general* crime statistics in most countries are at best unreliable, at worst simply misleading.[13] There is no reason to assume that those on corruption, organised crime, or even terrorist acts are an exception.[14] This is not necessarily a criticism of the agencies that produce such statistics, although some jurisdictions do deserve to be censured for deliberate manipulation of their data. Rather, it is to highlight the difficulties involved in classifying, investigating and accurately registering – and hence measuring – crime levels. Given this, the call from Bovenkerk and Abou Chakra in Chapter 2 for far more case studies is well justified. While this would not actually solve the measurement problem, it would provide more solid evidence on which to base general assessments.

The third comparative observation is that one of the most important ramifications of the problems of definition and measurement is that our *perceptions* of the significance of all three types of crime might be highly distorted, although this cannot ultimately be proven one way or the other. For example, the statistics on any one of them can be either downplayed or exaggerated for political purposes. This has led some to argue that the struggle against one or more of them is primarily a political artifice – the need to construct an enemy or 'other' in the post-Cold War era – rather than a more principled fight against anti-social phenomena.[15] This is going too far; there really are problems of organised crime, corruption and terrorism in today's world. On the other hand, it is accepted here that states and international organisations sometimes label various forms of criminality, and weight the importance they attach to these, in politically loaded and arguably even class-based ways. In order to unpack this issue properly, it is necessary to focus now on a factor that has been considered at various points in this book (notably in the chapter by van Duyne and van Dijck), but that will now be explored more fully and incorporated into the general analytical framework. There is a 'joker in the pack' – another type of crime – that has also become far more visible in recent years, but that still receives less opprobrium than it deserves. Moreover, it is all too rarely linked in the minds of the authorities, the media and the public with the 'sexier' (that is more sensational) crimes on which we have focused. This is corporate and white-collar crime, including that by and within transnational corporations, banks, accounting firms and law firms.

A FOURTH PLAYER

It is true that the Western media have in recent years highlighted the misdemeanours of a small but growing number of corporations and firms accused or found guilty of fraud, deception or other forms of economic crime or impropriety (for example ABB, Adelphia, Arthur Andersen, Elf, Enron, Halliburton, HIH Insurance, Parmalat, Shell, WorldCom – for details on these and further cases see the websites of *Corporate Crime Reporter* and the New York-based Global Policy Forum, while an excellent scholarly analysis of recent corporate scandals in the US is O'Brien 2003). Nor can it be denied that the significance of corporate crime *is* now being better recognised by some states and international organisations. For instance, the USA significantly increased the accountability of company executives under the 2002 Sarbanes-Oxley Act, since when the sentences handed down to senior executives found guilty of improper behaviour have in some cases appeared harsh. Two senior executives of Adelphia Communications – a father and son – were found guilty of various types of white-collar crime in July 2004, and were sentenced almost a year later to 15 and 20 years' imprisonment respectively, while two senior officials of WorldCom were convicted in March 2005, and sentenced to 25 year prison sentences in July 2005. Some German states, such as Hessen, have in recent years blacklisted firms that have paid bribes to state officials or engaged in other forms of corporate crime.

Many international organisations also now explicitly recognise the possibility of links between corporate and organised crime. Thus, with the introduction of its Convention on Combating Bribery of Foreign Public Officials in the late 1990s (adopted 1997, effective 1999), the OECD made it clear to the business world that corporations and firms that had in the past used bribery to secure contracts or obtain other unfair advantage from foreign state authorities would now be treated as breaking the law if they continued to do so. As part of their commitment to this new Convention, states such as Australia, France and Germany that had in the past – surprisingly – allowed tax breaks to companies paying bribes in other countries now amended their laws to end this practice. Another example of such awareness is that the Council of Europe – which has been a trailblazer among international organisations in recognising links between corruption and organised crime – now includes sections on *corporate* crime in its annual *organised* crime report (for example Council of Europe 2005: especially 71–2).

Nevertheless, it is still not sufficiently recognised that the networks and linkages that we have begun to identify here should really incorporate a fourth player. Moreover, despite a growing awareness, there is still a long way to go in terms of treating corporate crime as seriously as it should be. In some cases, there is even reason to question whether the new situation represents any improvement on the old. This can be illustrated by reference to several of the cases and developments just cited.

Thus the WorldCom executives appealed their sentences, and were allowed to remain free pending the outcome of these appeals, while a December 2005 report used detailed evidence from 34 case studies to argue that an increasing number of corporations in the 2000s were concluding deals with US prosecutors whereby prosecution of the corporation was either deferred or avoided altogether (Corporate Crime Reporter 2005).[16] According to the editor of the newsletter that produced the report, Russell Mokhiber, 'It used to be that major corporations caught committing serious crimes would be brought to justice – convicted of a crime and sentenced. No longer' (*Corporate Crime Reporter* online, 28 December 2005, visited May 2006).[17] The Hessen ban on contracts for companies found to have been offering bribes lasted only six months (Hawley 2000), which is very different from the five year bans that Singapore has sometimes imposed, and could be seen as tokenistic. And while most Western firms can no longer secure tax allowances for bribes they have paid overseas, this does not necessarily mean that they have stopped offering bribes to foreign officials. Some are making greater use than before of local 'facilitators', thus continuing to engage in bribery, but with more of an arm's length approach.

It could be argued that the new awareness of the significance of corporate crime, and of its linkages with other types of criminality, can be seen in the shift by agencies such as Transparency International to include corporate crime under corruption. Some of the contributors to this volume (for example Gilligan and Bowman) also accept a broader definition of corruption that sees improper B2B activity as a type of corruption. There is no right and wrong on this; the choice of a broader or narrower approach is ultimately a subjective matter. But it is argued here that it is confusing to use the term corruption for certain activities that involve *only* private sector actors and agencies, and that there is one very good reason for using the narrower approach to corruption and then to identify overlap and resonances with other phenomena. That reason relates to public perceptions of what can be called the umpire role of the state.

One of the primary functions of the modern democratic state should be to act as an arbiter – a referee or umpire – between conflicting interests in society. The state, unlike the market, enjoys a monopoly on defining the ultimate 'rules of the game', and claims the sole right – albeit sometimes within parameters determined by supra- or international organisations of which it is a member – to pass, implement, interpret and enforce laws. A simple way to highlight the unique position of the state is by comparing it with that of private companies. Unlike the latter, few states that are underperforming go bankrupt and cease to exist. More significantly, if I believe that a company is overcharging me, or selling me shoddy goods, I can usually purchase the products of another company; the market allows me choice. But for all intents and purposes, there is no such choice vis-à-vis the state.[18] I cannot opt to pay my taxes to some other entity, or at all, if I believe that the state is in some way short-changing me. But in return for this uniquely privileged monopoly position, many citizens still expect the state to set an example, whereas they understand that private firms exist primarily to make a profit. Thus the nature of the state is, or *should* be, fundamentally different from that of corporations in the market. For this reason, crime purely within the private sector is better classified as either corporate or white-collar crime, depending on its nature.

The former arises, for example, when the management in one firm colludes with management in other firms to fix prices, or secretly agrees on a territorial division of a market. It could also occur if that management opts to use improper methods in its business-dealings with the state, such as offering bribes to secure contracts or expedite licensing procedures. The latter situation means that the firm has been *involved* in corruption. But it is the state officials accepting the bribes who are corrupt; the firm has simply contributed to a corrupt practice. In both scenarios, the action of the firm's management might appear to be entirely for the good of the company, not personal benefit – akin to the actions of politicians who improperly secure financing for their parties but who claim not to benefit *personally* in a direct sense.[19] On the other hand, in the context of the discussion here, it is appropriate to use the term white-collar crime to refer to cases in which individual members of a firm engage in improper or illegal activity – relating to the company, but without its approval, encouragement or even knowledge – for personal benefit.

So far, the discussion of corporate crime has focused on the ways in which it can overlap with corruption. But some have highlighted its similarities with organised crime.[20] Thus, as pointed out by van Duyne and van Dijck in Chapter 6, the 'grandfather' of scholarly analysis of corporate and white-collar crime, Edwin Sutherland, long ago recognised and emphasised that the two types of crime (which he tended to merge) could be seen as forms of organised crime. He first made this argument at a conference in 1939, published an article on the topic in the following year (Sutherland 1940), and within a decade had published his seminal book on the subject (Sutherland 1949).[21] While Sutherland's *overall* argument is persuasive, it should by now be clear that the preference here is to opt for only one term for each form of crime, and to examine overlaps empirically rather than stir up already muddy waters through definitional blurring. For precisely this reason, and despite some sympathy for their position, we also reject the call from Edwards and Gill (2002) to take Sutherland's argument one step further and question the very distinctions usually drawn between licit and illicit behaviour.

To summarise this part of the argument, the above discussion relates very much to the labelling issue in criminology referred to in Chapter 6. As van Duyne and van Dijck point out, with reference to a Nürnberg report from almost five centuries ago, the issue is hardly a new one. But it continues to be contentious. It is maintained here that, rather than conflate several phenomena and add to the confusion by using the same term for related but ultimately distinct concepts, it is preferable to use discrete terms for different phenomena, and *then* to analyse the overlaps, networks and connections between these. In other words, the argument here is in favour of maintaining a clear distinction between *concepts*, while at the same time acknowledging that *practices* often straddle these. Such an approach enjoys the major advantage of being able to identify and to separate related but ultimately distinct concepts and phenomena *at the same time* as it permits acknowledgement and analysis of blurring between them in the real world.

Explicitly including corporate and white-collar crime in our analysis of linkages would, *inter alia*, help to overcome one of the major definitional and demarcational problems identified by Ruggiero (1996), Edwards and Gill (2002), Paoli (2002) and others, and mentioned briefly in Chapter 1 – namely, that the boundaries between transnational organised crime and international corporate crime are often blurred in the real world. By highlighting and interrogating what can in practice be a hazy boundary between these two phenomena, the equally questionable practice of drawing an overly sharp distinction between street or underworld crime on the one hand, and upperworld crime on the other, can be identified and challenged.

There might initially appear to be a contradiction here, given our criticism of the practice of merging concepts. In fact, the position adopted here is perfectly consistent. It is fully recognised that there exist many similarities and overlaps between different forms of criminality; but it is maintained that it is misleading to employ the same term for different types of crime, even if they appear to be related. The very fact that we argue in favour of analysing empirical overlap permits criticism both of labelling that exaggerates differences between various types of crime and of the adoption of a 'moral hierarchy' that can inappropriately treat particular types of crime as less serious and more acceptable than others. Corporate upperworld crime sometimes affects more people, and over a longer period, than many cases of street or underworld crime. For instance, a team of burglars may break into my home and steal my electronic goods; assuming these items are insured, I can soon replace them. But if I have invested most of my life savings – intended for my retirement in five years' time – in the shares of a company that is declared bankrupt because of the criminal behaviour of some of its executives, or if I lose my job with that corporation for the same reason, then the repercussions can be far worse than those of the burglary.[22] Although it is sometimes argued that the burglary is worse because of psychological repercussions – it can induce a sense of insecurity relating to the invasion of my personal space – it is a moot point whether or not this is usually worse than the long-term insecurity I can experience through losing much of my future income.

TWO CASES INVOLVING THE FOURTH PLAYER

The discussion can now focus on actual examples of corporate crime and its relationship with other forms of criminality. Two recent cases of alleged corporate crime – one involving a US corporation, the other an Australian one – demonstrate the need to include this form of venality in future analyses of networks and linkages.

In 2002, following allegations it had been making since at least July 2000 (*BBC News* online, 6 November 2000), the EU opened a lawsuit, and issued a 149-page accusation, against the US-based tobacco corporation R.J. Reynolds. The EU claimed that the company was involved in illegal dealings, including money laundering, with organised crime gangs in Europe, Russia and Latin America (Weinstein and Levin 2002). In January 2003, the European Communities' Court of First Instance found that R.J. Reynolds had indeed been engaging in criminal activities. R.J. Reynolds lodged an appeal against this judgement with the European Communities' Court of Justice in March 2003. But a US court ruled in January 2004 that foreign courts were not mandated to try US companies in this way. Before analysing the significance of all this, it can be noted that the EU charges were not the only ones made against R.J. Reynolds by Europeans; earlier in 2002, for instance, it was announced that US officials were investigating European allegations that the company had broken UN sanctions against Iraq (Levin and Rempel 2002).

The Reynolds case raises a number of important issues. First, the EU initially filed a lawsuit in a civil rather than a criminal court, on the grounds that it was seeking financial compensation rather than punishment (*BBC News* online, 6 November 2000).[23] Such a soft approach must be changed if progress in combating what is here being called the quadrumvirate of crime is to be overcome. Would the EU have sought only compensation, rather than serious punishment, if an organised crime gang had broken into EU headquarters in Brussels and stolen €10 million, or had produced millions of counterfeit Euros? By treating upperworld crime as less serious and more abstract than underworld crime, perceptions of both become distorted. It is high time for more authorities and analysts to move beyond propaganda and class-based analysis of 'their' (the 'others') crimes and 'our' crimes; crime is crime, whether committed by poorly-educated street people or by highly-educated and well-paid state officials and corporate executives, and there should be no privileging of the latter over the former.

Second, the US justice system had acted in a not dissimilar – parochial – way in the past. Thus, US courts had ruled on allegations made formally by the

Canadian government in 1999 that R. J. Reynolds and its affiliates had been smuggling cigarettes into Canada.[24] This case went from a local US court (which cleared Reynolds) to an appellate court, and eventually to the US Supreme Court – which in late 2002 declared that it would not reconsider the appellate court's dismissal of the Canadian appeal. A spokesperson for R. J. Reynolds claimed that this action (or non-action!) by the Supreme Court was another example of the USA showing other countries' governments that they could not attempt to use the American legal system to enforce their own laws. It was hailed as a victory against attempts by foreigners to enforce their tax laws if allegedly broken by American companies (all from *BBC News* online, 5 November 2002; visited February 2006).[25]

The approach of the US legal system sends the unfortunate message that it is unwilling to consider the alleged wrongdoings of American companies overseas. And yet, as has been demonstrated in earlier chapters, these courts are supposed to have been implementing the Foreign Corrupt Practices Act since 1977, and are prepared to consider both international underworld crime and the alleged corruption of foreign officials.[26] Indeed, US authorities – specifically the CIA – have sent operatives to Europe and elsewhere to investigate, transfer and interrogate alleged terrorists when it suits them, under so-called rendition processes (*Washington Post*, 13 March 2005). This double standard – being parochial in some situations, while disregarding sovereignty in others – is fundamentally at odds with almost any notion of the rule of law, and hence with a basic premiss of democracy.[27] Moreover, the US courts' parochialism plays into the hands of transnational crime of whatever sort. The problem is compounded by the USA's refusal to recognise the legitimacy of the International Criminal Court, and to grant only conditional recognition to the International Court of Justice;[28] while, under their terms of reference, neither of these courts is likely to try the types of crimes being considered here, the fact that the USA is basically unwilling fully to recognise various international courts sends a most unfortunate message, and again indirectly assists transnational crime.[29] Similarly, the fact that the countries of Europe still do not have fully harmonised laws, definitions, or extradition rules concerning the types of criminality analysed here is advantageous to transnational crime of various kinds.[30]

Before concluding this analysis of some of the broader issues raised by the Reynolds case, it is important to note that tobacco companies have themselves sometimes alleged that organised crime has moved into cigarette smuggling in a major way that undermines legitimate cigarette trade. If respectable corporations claim that it is necessary to break the law in order to compete with organised crime, it is obvious that there is yet another reason for advocating full-length academic studies of the bilateral, trilateral and occasionally even quadrilateral linkages between the individual components of the quadrumvirate.

The second example is of a major scandal, widely seen as an offshoot of the UN's so-called oil-for-food case, that erupted in Australia in late 2005. As with one of the allegations about R.J. Reynolds, it involves claims of a corporation breaking UN sanctions against Iraq. AWB (formerly the Australian Wheat Board) was accused of having paid substantial bribes (more than US$200 million) over a number of years to Saddam Hussein's regime, and of having contravened UN sanctions. At the time of writing, this case was still under examination by the Cole Commission of Inquiry.[31] But whatever the ultimate findings on this particular case, it raises important theoretical issues.

First, can such actions – assuming they are proven – be described as corrupt? The answer is that they can be and often are so described in everyday and media parlance, but that they do not necessarily constitute corruption in a more technical sense. It has been argued here that corruption must involve state officials; since AWB is not, strictly speaking, a state agency, neither it nor its employees can be corrupt under this approach.[32] Yet this was alleged to be a case of a private corporation paying – albeit at arm's length – what were in essence bribes to state agencies in Iraq. It might therefore appear that the Iraqi agencies were corrupt. But at the time of writing, it was not clear that either Australian employees of AWB or Iraqi officials had engaged in their allegedly improper behaviour for reasons of *private* (personal) gain. Whatever the eventual outcome of this particular case, let us assume that in a similar, hypothetical case, there was no evidence of personal or private gain by employees or officials on either side. The improper activities should not then be described as regular corruption – though they could be described as a combination of bribery and corporate crime. This demonstrates once again why it is important to include other forms of crime when analysing so-called corruption. It is precisely the *networks* and *linkages* between corruption and related crimes that highlight the rottenness of so much economic and political behaviour in the contemporary world. Many more studies of these connections and overlaps are needed.

It has been argued that corporate and white-collar crime should be conceptually distinguished from corruption. It is self-evident that they are also distinct from terrorism, though the possibility of linkages and overlap in the future should not be dismissed; in fact, there were allegations in the late 1990s that the French corporation Elf had been involved in improper arms brokering, which has been seen by some as an example of this (Curtis and Karacan 2002: 17). But since it has also been argued that corporate crime sometimes has links with organised crime but is conceptually distinct from it, it is appropriate to consider some of the differences. First, there is the issue of transparency. Whether or not such documents are always as honest and complete as they should be, most corporations, banks, and so on do provide regular, public reports on their activities; crime gangs do not. Related to this, corporations and firms usually advertise their goods, services and job vacancies openly, whereas crime gangs are typically more circumspect. Third, most corporations allow anyone who wants and is permitted by law to do so to buy shares in them, through being listed on stock exchanges; it would be a very unusual crime gang that sought to do this – in addition to which, most stock exchanges have rules that forbid the listing of such forms of economic activity anyway. Fourth, licit businesses pay taxes; they often seek to minimise these, but through legal means.[33] Finally, licit businesses do not typically employ violence in the way that illicit businesses often do. This is not to deny that corporations sometimes use threatening behaviour – for instance, against their own workers who challenge them, or against local citizens opposed to a project the business wants to develop. But the nature and scale of violence is, ultimately and overwhelmingly, very different from that so often employed by organised crime gangs.[34]

The argument made here in favour of more research into the connections between the quadrumvirate of corruption, organised crime, terrorism and corporate crime does not overlook the fact that some trailblazing analysts and political figures recognised possible linkages – at least bilateral ones – well before the 1990s. Sutherland's contribution has already been noted. Block and Chambliss (1981) published research findings on the nature of the relationship between corrupt politicians, corporate executives, trade union officials and organised crime at the beginning of the 1980s. As Sidoti (1991: 105–6) points out, Joseph LaPalombara (1987: 180) had observed in the 1980s that a number of Italian intellectuals believed that much of the terrorism in their country was connected with multinational corporations and various domestic and foreign state-run intelligence services, including the CIA. But such links were mostly assumed, and there was little empirical evidence. Nor were such claims very common in scholarly analyses. Not until the 1990s did the situation begin to change to any meaningful extent, and there is no question that awareness of linkages has increased significantly in recent years. But all too often, even the new awareness of linkages tends to concentrate on bilateral ties, rather than possible trilateral or quadrilateral ones.

ON LINKAGES AND NETWORKS

Now that the range of possible linkages and networks to be considered has been broadened to include the corporate sector, what conclusions can be drawn about their nature? What kinds of linkages exist? In addition to the most obvious form, (that is direct cooperation and collusion), analysis of which mainly requires far more empirical research in the form of case studies, it has been demonstrated that linkages can sometimes be *indirect*. One example of this cited in Chapter 5 was of foreign military and other officers in former Yugoslavia, who have been contributing to the coffers of organised crime gangs by using prostitutes.

The nature of collusion between the state and organised crime is complex and diverse. Ruggiero (1996) is one of several analysts who maintain that there is active complicity by some governments in permitting organised crime to thrive. Thus states will sometimes seek to contain the problem of organised crime by turning a blind eye to some of its activities, in return for a tacit agreement that the gangs will stay away from other areas. For example, Fabre (2003: 89) claims that Yakuza organisations have not been involved in a major way in heroin production or distribution, in return for which the Japanese authorities have been less strict about policing other areas of drug-dealing and illegal activity. Much of the time, such an approach by the state does not involve corruption as such. Rather, it often testifies to the state's limited capacity, as it targets some areas of criminality (presumably, those it perceives to represent the most serious threats to the public or to itself or to both) while largely ignoring others.

The relationship of the state to terrorism is also typically complex, and sometimes highly questionable. From what was known of the AWB scandal at the time of writing, the Australian state might have played some indirect (and unintended) role in funding Iraqi terrorism. *If* it is concluded by the Cole Inquiry that the Australian government had advised AWB that its extra payments to Iraq were acceptable, and that it was breaking UN sanctions against the Saddam regime, and *if* it transpires or appears highly probable that some of that money was later used by Iraqis to purchase weapons and munitions which they then deployed against other Iraqis and foreign troops after Saddam's fall, then it becomes clear why it would be appropriate to refer to the state's indirect role – in this case via alleged corporate crime – in funding terrorists.[35]

Turning away from the state towards other forms of linkage, another less than obvious one is *transmutation* (or metamorphosis), that is the conversion of one kind of criminality into another. A frequently cited example of this is of the Chinese Triads. These started life as a violent political movement to counter the Qing dynasty; but they eventually mutated into straightforward organised crime groups, oriented to profit-making rather than political activism. Much more recently, many former members of the military in several South-East European states became involved in the dealing and/or smuggling of arms and other products following the end of conflicts in which they had been involved. This type of transmutation, which can also be found among former terrorists such as some former IRA members, is sometimes called the 'fighters turned felons' syndrome (Curtis and Karacan 2002: 4, 23).

Now that a start has been made at knitting corporate crime into the patchwork quilt, yet another form of transmutation can be identified. This is that of the so-called robber barons of early capitalism into respected corporate leaders. Although it is too early to argue that any of the Russian oligarchs – assuming some survive the clash with the *chekists* analysed by Yuri Tsyganov in Chapter 7 – will become respected pillars of the community in a similar way to the early robber barons in the USA, signs of a somewhat similar mutation beginning to occur can already be identified in other transition societies. The so-called wrestlers in Bulgaria constitute a good example. These people were widely perceived to be engaged in running illegal protection rackets in the early-to-mid-1990s, but were then, at about the time of the introduction of the 1997 Bulgarian Insurance Act, forced by the government to move into more lawful security or insurance businesses (see Stanchev 2001). My own frequent visits to Bulgaria lead me to conclude that many Bulgarians do see the 'wrestlers' as having become more respectable and businesslike, and unquestionably less violent, since that change.

In some cases, one type of criminal group can engage in other forms of crime, as distinct from linking up with other groups in those different branches of crime. In addition to the *sequential* or transmutational forms already noted – the 'fighters turned felons' syndrome – groups may engage in two or more forms *simultaneously*. Typically, this is a temporary phase, though there is no logical reason why it needs to be. A putative example of this sometimes cited is the so-called 'mafia terrorism' of the 1980s (Grupo Abele 2005: 67–77). However, caution needs to be exercised when identifying such overlaps (here, of organised crime and terrorism). In the case of the mafia, it was usually clear why they had targeted a given individual or group. Moreover, the mafia's objective was mostly to dissuade state authorities from investigating its illegal profit-making activities, rather than to challenge the political system as a whole. Thus, although the activities could by some criteria be called 'political' (that is because the mafia was challenging the state's right and capacity to interfere in its illegal activities), they were not comparable with the broader and more overtly political objectives of groups such as the Red Brigades or ETA. Given the approach to terrorism adopted in Chapter 1, most of the mafia actions in the 1980s described by others as terrorism would not be classified as such here. Rather, they were examples of violence by organised crime gangs, directed at officers of the state, for the purpose of protecting the gangs' criminal interests. Conversely, the alleged involvement of the IRA in the December 2004 bank robbery referred to in Chapter 1 *might* constitute the type of simultaneous activity being identified here, unless the IRA continues to adhere fully to its recent renunciation of terrorism.[36]

GOVERNANCE AND POLICY ASPECTS

Devising tactics and strategies for dealing with any one of the three types of criminality analysed in this book is a complex process, and merely listing the various methods available in 'toolkits' would require more space than is available here.[37] To do this for all three – four, if corporate crime is included – and include an overview of methods for identifying and breaking linkages would be unrealistic and require a separate volume. The objectives in this section are far more modest: to relate the conceptual blurring that has occurred in recent years to the neo-liberal approach to governance, and to foster even broader recognition of the possible connections between the four types of crime when devising policies for overcoming them individually.

The plea for much more empirical research into linkages and networks, based on more case studies, is related to the need for more evidence to support a more general argument made here against neo-liberalism, economic globalisation, and so-called rational choice approaches to human behaviour.[38] The blurring of boundaries, the privileging of ends (outcomes) over means (due process), and the insecurity associated with neo-liberal approaches to economics, politics and society help to explain not only much of the temptation to engage in the various types of anti-social behaviour described in this book, but also the networks and linkages between them. For as long as states and international organisations continue to promote the ideology of neo-liberal – or Washington Consensus, or Lisbon Strategy – economics, their struggles against corruption, organised crime, terrorism and corporate crime are doomed to be at best only partly successful.[39] All too often, Western states and international organisations claim that poverty is the principal reason for

corruption and organised crime. There can be no question that this often *is* a
major factor. But, as argued in Chapter 1, focusing only on poverty can blind
us to the fact that many middle-class and relatively affluent people also engage
in economic crime (various forms of corruption, as well as corporate and
white-collar crime) and terrorism, and that poverty is often only a contributory
factor to these crimes, rather than the actual trigger. There needs to be far
broader acknowledgement of the fundamental contradiction between the
widespread commitment to gung-ho economics and the irresponsible state on
the one hand, and the commitment to fighting serious crime on the other. Until
there is such recognition, policies designed to counter these problems will be
based on a superficial understanding of them, and are therefore bound to be
limited in their effectiveness. Moreover, until states and international
organisations set a better example, the scale of these four often interrelated
types of criminal behaviour is unlikely to be reduced to manageable levels, and
could increase.[40]

However, an important caveat to the above needs to be made. It has just
been argued that there must be much deeper analysis of the underlying causes
of the various crimes considered here, and of the resonances and linkages
between them; the ramifications of neo-liberalism have been identified as a
major one. Yet it is often maintained that one of the main reasons corporations
sometimes engage in corporate crime, including bribery of state officials, is
because states over-regulate, leading firms to seek ways to circumvent
excessive bureaucracy. This argument is frequently used to explain higher
rates of corruption and corporate crime in economically developing states, in
which officials often have considerably more discretionary powers than do
their peers in economically developed states. If this is true, it might appear to
undermine our argument about the negative effects of neo-liberalism; after all,
the latter, as an ideology, advocates minimal state involvement in the
economy, and hence deregulation. But, as with any ideology, there is often a
considerable gap between the ideal and the practice. The progressive
introduction of neo-liberalism into Europe and Australasia, for instance, has
not been onto a *tabula rasa*; whether in Western Europe, CEE, Australia or
New Zealand, there was a tradition – and hence a widespread popular
expectation – that the state would continue to accept at least indirect
responsibility for many aspects of everyday life. Since the state typically
sought to offload these responsibilities, but could not change popular culture
overnight, it introduced an increasing number of compliance regulations, so as
to appear to be continuing to assume responsibility. By introducing ever more
such regulations – on health and safety in the workplace, or on the purity of

water supplies, or on the punctuality and reliability of privately-run public transport, or on the impact of university researchers – it could appear to be continuing to accept responsibilities the public apparently expected of it. And it believed it could do so for a fraction of the cost it used to bear when it was genuinely responsible for the provision of such services and supervision.

All the above has significant public policy and governance implications. By acknowledging underlying ideological factors, and by more fully recognising the connections and similarities between corporate and organised crime, for instance, or between corruption and corporate crime – while not conflating them – states and international organisations would be better placed for dealing with each. As demonstrated in this volume, various agencies *have* now begun to accept that there often exist connections as well as similarities – shared characteristics – between these various types of anomic behaviour. Nevertheless, there is still some way to go in raising awareness of links, especially trilateral or quadrilateral ones.

A policy-related implication of the resistance to conceptual blurring advocated above is that it can help policy-makers avoid the temptation to assume that there are general approaches that can be applied in most situations. If the phenomena are treated discretely – even while linkages and overlaps are recognised – and as complex even within themselves, it becomes more obvious that and why no 'one size fits all' approach will be effective in attempting to manage them. Individual states' cultures and structures, plus their level of integration into the international community, their leaders' political will and the state's capacity – these and other variables all have to be factored in. Caution therefore needs to be used in considering global approaches to reducing these crimes. Often, the better policies are the tailored ones, such as the Octopus programs for combating corruption and organised crime specifically in CEE that were introduced from 1996 (see Chapters 4 and 5). While it cannot be denied that this process of nuancing and differentiation *has* now begun, this is a relatively recent development. Moreover, there is always a danger of backsliding.

Despite the cautionary note of the preceding paragraph, which urges the adoption of tailored polices, there are three general approaches that are crucial in the fight by most states and international organisations against all four forms of criminality considered here. One is ultimately a long-term one: education. Only by educating people about the significant dangers of corruption, organised crime, corporate crime and even terrorism is there likely to be a more long-term solution to growth in these activities.[41] Although this general approach is likely to take years to become really effective, short-term components can be introduced immediately, and can have an almost instant effect. For example, a number of European anti-trafficking NGOs have in recent years run intensive courses for police officers, designed to raise the latters' awareness of the fact that trafficked persons are victims rather than criminals, and should be treated quite differently from the ways in which crime gangs and corrupt officials involved in their trafficking are handled. Inasmuch as the NGOs are typically paid by the state to run these courses, this is further evidence of many states' rising consciousness in this area. But such practices are still relatively new in many countries, and are not as widespread as they need to be.

A second general approach focuses on the need to reinstate clear distinctions between the state and the market, and to treat officers of the state in a different way from, for example, private-sector employees. This point has already been elaborated in the discussion of the state's umpire role. It involves a reduction in the salience of the neo-liberal approaches of so many governments.

Third, there is the all-important issue of political will. Unless political leaders are genuinely committed to combating these crimes, the struggle against them will be at best partly successful. Ambiguity plays into the hands of criminals. This said, will alone is a necessary but not a sufficient condition. There must also be institutional capacity to implement political will. The weakness of so many CEE transition states during the 1990s and into the early 21st century is directly related to much of the apparent growth in Europe and beyond of both domestic and transnational serious crime. It can only be hoped that the current consolidation of an increasing number of these states – a process almost certainly assisted by the admission of many of them to the EU – will have a positive knock-on effect in terms of the fight against crime.

WHO IS TO BLAME?

Further increasing awareness among states and international organisations of the various linkages considered here is not enough; ordinary citizens also need to have their consciousness raised. Similarly, simply blaming and criticising states or international organisations for doing too little to combat any or all of the types of anti-social behaviour analysed in this book is simplistic and unfair. A game needs an umpire – but it also needs players. Society and individuals must *also* shoulder some of the responsibility for the current situation. For a start, legislatures are elected in democracies; to a limited extent, voters therefore have some say over the type of economic policy states pursue.[42] But there are even more direct, effective, everyday ways in which individuals can contribute to a reduction in crime. Every time someone – a politician, a corporate executive, a soldier, or the person on the street – purchases illicit drugs or under-the-counter cigarettes or pirated DVDs or the services of a prostitute, there is a strong possibility that they are feeding organised crime and/or corruption, and in some cases also corporate crime or even terrorist organisations. With reference to the first of these (that is the purchase of illicit drugs), the UNODC announced in June 2005 that, according to its calculations, some 5% of the world's population – approximately 200 million people aged 15–64 – had taken illegal drugs in the previous twelve months (*EBBOY* 2006: 208). Hence, at least 200 million people had a direct role to play in reducing the illicit drug supply and the criminal activity that accompanied it. If the growth of organised crime, corruption, terrorism and corporate crime is to be contained, let alone reversed, ordinary citizens will have to be involved, and can be in many of their simple everyday activities. Contrary to the usual wisdom on this, they do not even have to aggregate into civil society groupings to be effective; *individuals* each have their role to play. They can do this in the way they shop – what they buy, and deciding whether or not prices are suspiciously *too* low. And they can do it by showing greater respect for others. Being treated as 'other', which so often implies being treated as inferior, is by definition alienating; such treatment can encourage anti-social behaviour and a desire to seek membership of more welcoming groups, be they terrorist cells or organised crime gangs. It would be grossly naïve to assume that simply treating others with greater respect will have a sudden and major impact on the complex phenomena we have analysed here. But it would be a start, and it is within the capacity of each one of us.

NOTES

1. The fact that many states describe the offering of a bribe as 'active bribery' and the acceptance of one as 'passive bribery' only adds to the perception that citizens are sometimes treated by authorities as more blameworthy than corrupt state officials.
2. An exception to this general rule is Italy, which leads Europe in considering trafficked persons as victims who should be treated sympathetically; it has done so under Article 18 of Legislative Decree No. 286 (Immigration Law) since 1998 (OSCE Office for Democratic Institutions and Human Rights 2001?: 84–5; Orfano 2002). Belgium also has some of the most progressive legislation in this area.
3. These are not the only reasons for non-reporting, of course. Another of direct relevance to our analysis is the fear that the authorities to whom one turns might themselves be corrupt, and

colluding with the gangsters being reported. There is also the very real concern, especially in weak and impoverished states, that the authorities have too little power and too few resources to do anything – or are simply incompetent. And many trafficked persons become psychologically and emotionally dependent on their captors/traffickers, in a version of the so-called Stockholm syndrome.

4. A popular novel based on the concept of *omertà* is Puzo (2000).

5. This is not to overlook the groundbreaking research undertaken in the early 1990s by Diego Gambetta (1993), who cites the trial confessions of eight Mafiosi. But the Italian situation for researchers has now significantly improved. Even before these trials of Mafiosi, the emergence of 'supergrasses' in the UK in the early 1970s constituted another exception to the generalisation being made here about codes of silence (Levi 1998: 339). Nevertheless, there has been positive change recently in Europe. This said, some idea of the continuing problematic nature of this type of research is conveyed by the author's own experience in investigating corruption and organised crime in China. During a 2005 visit to the PRC, a police official raised the possibility of conducting interviews on my behalf among prisoners convicted of either corruption or organised crime activity. This was a tempting suggestion, since it appeared likely to yield a unique data-base. Unfortunately, China is said to use torture against prisoners to extract information – so that a member of my University ethics team (understandably) advised me not even to apply for ethics clearance for this type of survey.

6. Even where there are such programs and they are well-funded, some potential witnesses will decide that the costs of testifying in court – perhaps endangering one's family, or else resulting in the perceived need to move permanently to another town, reduce one's ties to family and friends, or even undergo plastic surgery – are simply too high.

7. A possible solution to this particular problem is for states to declare amnesties for corrupt officials and members of organised crime gangs or terrorist organisations. But most states are reluctant to do this, for the understandable reason that it might then look to the citizenry as if the state is either condoning improper wealth accumulation and/or has been too weak or incompetent in the past to control corruption, organised crime and terrorism. This issue of amnesties is a difficult one. In many ways, it is states whose elites believe they enjoy either very high or very low levels of legitimacy, or who are highly coercive, that are most likely to feel able to introduce them. In the first case, the assumption will be that the problem (for example corruption) is not so widespread or deeply engrained that revealing more of it through an amnesty will undermine the system. An elite that believes it enjoys a low level of legitimacy anyway may decide that it has little to lose, but perhaps a lot to gain, if the amnesty appears to make significant inroads into a problem that the elite knows is a concern to large numbers of citizens. The coercive elite does not feel particularly threatened anyway (which may be a seriously misguided perception!), but may prefer to exercise power more through legitimacy than through coercion, so that a policy that appears likely in the medium term to enhance its legitimacy will be adopted.

8. A 2006 report estimated that some 60,000 women from Poland and Ukraine were being forced to work in the British sex industry alone, and that human traffickers were using 300 flights per week (*Gazeta Wyborcza*, 27 April 2006). Unfortunately, and in line with the argument here about the difficulties involved in securing hard data, the number of prosecutions and convictions relating to trafficking of women is low in most countries. In the period 1995–2003, for example, Polish authorities conducted 304 initial proceedings for this crime, eventually resulting in 181 convictions, and 62 prison sentences of between two and five years. A total of 1511 female victims were identified in these cases (Ministerstwo Sprawiedliwości 2006: 4).

9. As will be clear by now, researching such linkages is fraught with difficulties, and all we can hope to do is gradually to create more complete case studies on the basis of snippets of information and circumstantial evidence. For instance, one former prostitute in Germany informed members of a German anti-trafficking NGO that she had been transported through Poland in a van. Just before the van reached the crossing into Germany, the driver parked it for several hours, and awaited the next shift of Polish customs officers. It does not require an over-fertile or conspiratorial imagination to assume that this was because there was at least one officer who was cooperating with the traffickers, who were waiting for him or her to come on duty. But proving this is extremely difficult.

10. As Alleyne points out in Chapter 11, UN pressure to criminalise terrorist financing essentially post-dates the 9/11 attacks.

11. Some terrorist organisations have in the past successfully engaged in fundraising, particularly among diaspora groups; the IRA, raising funds from Irish Americans, is an oft-cited example.

12. Some terrorist organisations have themselves reduced or renounced violence in recent years, the IRA and ETA being prime examples. It remains to be seen whether or not these commitments to non-violent methods continue to be respected. See too below, on the 'fighters turned felons' syndrome.

13. It should be noted in this context that Interpol ceased posting comparative international crime statistics on the web in late 2004, largely on the grounds that too many states appeared to be providing questionable data.

14. The reader is reminded of the reference in Chapter 1 to changes made in 2005 and 2006 by US authorities in their assessment of the number and nature of terrorist acts worldwide.

15. For examples of both sides of this argument, with particular reference to organised crime, see Edwards and Gill (2002: 207).

16. It will be instructive to see the eventual outcome of the case involving one of the two very senior Enron executives convicted in May 2006 (the other died in July 2006) for fraud and conspiracy; sentencing was scheduled for October 2006, following which there could be an appeal. It is because of the kinds of delay, referred to both here and in the text, in actually enforcing prison sentences that the words 'appeared harsh' are used.

17. Trade-offs for prosecutors vary. They include the go-ahead from the corporation to prosecute individual executives; acceptance by firms of changes to the corporate structure, designed to improve monitoring mechanisms; and a promise from the corporation to create new jobs.

18. The term 'for all intents and purposes' is used here as a way of acknowledging that citizens can sometimes appeal to courts above their state. But such situations are relatively rare, and are too marginal to undermine our basic argument.

19. The word 'direct' has been consciously included here. In the case of the company executives who engage in shady practices 'for the sake of' their company, the fact that improperly acquired business is likely to increase profit margins means that those executives are likely to benefit personally in the longer term, through bonus schemes, salary increases, promotions, and so on. Similarly, politicians involved in improper fund-raising for their political party could well benefit personally, for example in securing a salaried parliamentary seat at the next election.

20. There is no question that there have been some excellent scholarly analyses of the linkages between organised crime and corporations. But many of these (for example Block 1991; Abadinsky 2000) focus more on the ways in which organised crime has become enmeshed in the licit economy in countries such as the US, rather than on the ways in which corporations themselves sometimes operate in ways that resemble organised crime activity.

21. The original 1949 book based on Sutherland's research omitted many names and case-study details because of concerns about possible libel charges. But an uncensored version was eventually published (Sutherland 1983). A more recent analysis of the relations between organised crime and corporate crime that has already established itself as a classic is Ruggiero (1996).

22. The collapse of Enron resulted in the loss of more than 5000 jobs, and in excess of US$2.1 billion in retirement savings. It remains to be seen how much of the latter is eventually retrieved and returned to those affected.

23. The reader is reminded from Chapter 6 that van Duyne and van Dijck point to the soft treatment often accorded to Dutch companies by the Dutch state; corporate crime in the Netherlands has frequently been treated as illegal but not criminal. Fortunately, the Dutch authorities appear to be tightening up now in this area, while the UK introduced what was intended to be much tougher anti-cartel legislation in 2002, under its Enterprise Act. Regarding the issue of the most appropriate type of law to apply, Sutherland was decades ago calling for many forms of corporate crime to be treated as criminal rather than civil misdemeanours.

24. Ironically, the cigarettes in question had apparently been manufactured in Canada, then taken to the USA, then smuggled back in to avoid recently raised Canadian taxes on cigarettes.

25. The victory may in some ways be seen as pyrrhic, however – at least for some of the Reynolds' workforce. In September 2003, R. J. Reynolds announced widescale layoffs.

26. A prime recent example is of former Ukrainian prime minister Pavlo Lazarenko, who went on trial in San Francisco in March 2004 for alleged corruption in Ukraine in the mid-1990s (*RFE/RL OCTW*, 4/12, 2004). He was found guilty by an American jury of using his public position in Ukraine improperly to enrich himself, but then lodged an appeal against his conviction. The final outcome of this case was still unclear at the time of writing.

27. The Council of Europe claimed in 2006 that no fewer than 14 European states had colluded with the CIA in the policy of rendition (*BBC News* online, 7 June 2006, visited June 2006). This is another symbol of the general move by Western democracies away from the rule of law towards security as a more important objective.

28. The International Criminal Court is new, having commenced work only in March 2003; its primary focus is on war crimes and genocide. The US, under President Clinton, initially signed a treaty recognising this Court. But the US did not formally ratify the treaty at that time, and President George W. Bush nullified his predecessor's signature in 2001. The International Court of Justice is much older, and the USA fully recognised it until 1986. But in that year, the Court ruled in favour of a plaintiff against the US, since when the US has reserved the right to decide which rulings it will recognise.

29. Two international courts the US does fully recognise are the Hague-based Permanent Court of Arbitration (established 1899, also known as the Hague Tribunal) and the Paris-based International Court of Arbitration (established 1923) attached to the International Chamber of Commerce.

30. Levi (1998: 341–3) has made the point that 'turf wars' between local and central police authorities in the UK help to explain fundamentally different assessments between forces on the nature and scale of organised crime, which in turn means differences over preferred means for dealing with it. If such 'internecine quarrels' (Levi 1998: 343) exist even within one country, it should be obvious how much more complicated it is to achieve consensus across several jurisdictions, some of them federal. Despite this, some progress has been made in recent years, as the creation of Europol (operational from October 1998) indicates. Europol's primary brief is to coordinate efforts against terrorism and various forms of organised crime.

31. One sign of how serious this case was perceived to be was that the Cole Inquiry required the Australian prime minister, deputy prime minister and foreign minister to testify before it. However, the Commission's terms of reference precluded the possibility that these very senior ministers could be charged with any misdemeanour. Moreover, President Bush made it clear during a visit by Prime Minister Howard to the USA in May 2006 that he was satisfied with the way in which the Australian government was handling the case. Yet again, this sends an unfortunate message. However, in an interesting twist of direct relevance to our argument, US and Canadian wheat farmers announced in June 2006 that they would be attempting to use laws originally designed to deal with organised crime (the 1970 Racketeer Influenced and Corrupt Organizations Act, better known as the RICO Act) to claim damages from AWB (*The Australian*, 30 June 2006: 1–2).

32. The Australian Wheat Board was state-owned until the late-1990s. But it was privatised as AWB Ltd. in 1999 (and listed on the stock exchange in 2001) – which, according to the UN's Volcker Report, was the first year AWB made questionable payments to the Iraqi government, via a Jordanian front organisation. Although it is technically a private company, AWB had until 2006 a state-guaranteed monopoly on foreign sales of wheat – an interesting concept, especially given the Howard government's professed commitment to free trade and economic competition.

33. Kerry Packer, head of Australian Consolidated Press and Australia's wealthiest man at the time of his death in December 2005, used to make it clear that he sought to minimise his taxes. In 1991, the Australian Tax Office began an attempt to challenge the fact that Packer had not paid any personal income taxes in recent times. Eventually, they sought to charge him a notional Aus\$30.55 (less than US\$25) for the years 1990–92; but Packer refused on principle to pay even this. After a seven-year legal process, in 1998 an Australian court found the billionaire not liable for any income tax for the years 1990–92. In the same year, the Australian Tax Office failed in its bid to secure an additional Aus\$260 million in back taxes from Consolidated Press (Australian Broadcasting Corporation, *The World Today Archive*, 7 September 1999, online at http://www.abc.net.au/worldtoday /stories/s49926.htm, visited March 2006), and it was revealed that Consolidated Press had paid no company tax on the more than Aus\$600 million profit it had made over the previous two years (*The Age*, 23 November 1998: 1–2; *Canberra Times*, 24 November 1998: A2). The Australian government under John Howard's leadership organised a publicly-funded state memorial service – usually reserved for leading political figures – for Packer in February 2006, which surely indicated endorsement of the late billionaire's approach to wealth accumulation and taxes.

34. It is sometimes argued that a sixth distinguishing feature is the nature of the products in which corporations and crime gangs deal. But this is a murky area. On the one hand, the actual products might be the same – for instance, cars or weapons. Admittedly, a distinction can often be drawn here between stolen or fake goods and legitimate ones. On the other hand, social labelling sometimes classifies essentially similar products in a rather arbitrary way as either legal or illegal. Thus alcohol, cigarettes and cannabis are all addictive drugs – yet selling the first two is legal in most societies, while selling the third is not. Hence manufacturers of and dealers in alcohol and cigarettes may more or less openly advertise their products, whereas cannabis manufacturers may not. The fact that many states have in recent years tightened the legislation on alcohol and tobacco advertising, and sometimes liberalised the laws on cannabis, only strengthens the argument about blurred boundaries and often arbitrary social labelling.

35. The wording here has had to be circumspect and tentative because of the ongoing nature of the Cole Inquiry at the time of writing. An unambiguous case of a state improperly supporting terrorism was by the USA in the so-called Iran-Contra affair of the 1980s.

36. The IRA declared a formal ceasefire in August 2004, and was declared to have destroyed its entire arsenal in September 2005.

37. A number of states' and international organisations' documents on methods for combating the three types of crime, plus scholarly analyses of such techniques, have been referred to in earlier chapters. Additional starting sources include R. Williams and Doig (2000) (on corruption), P. Williams and Godson (2002) (on organised crime), and Yim (2004) (on terrorism).

38. For a debate on whether or not globalisation is still a meaningful concept, see Rosenberg (2005), and the various contributors challenging Rosenberg in *International Politics*, 42 (3), 2005: 352–99. Our own perspective is very clear; as with the concept of a nation, it is not objective characteristics but perception that identifies globalisation. If large numbers of people around the world believe that it exists, and are prepared to act politically on that belief, then it exists. The classic critique of rational choice theory remains Green and Shapiro (1994).

39. The Lisbon Strategy or Agenda was adopted by the EU's European Council in March 2000. It is very similar to other neo-liberal packages, though with arguably more overt emphasis on the 'knowledge economy' than most.

40. The reference to states setting an example relates to the corruption scandals in numerous countries mentioned at various points in this book. Examples of corruption scandals in international organisations include the so-called oil-for-food scandal in the UN, and, within the EU, the Santer Commission and Eurostat scandals of 1999 and 2003 respectively. As for states and organisations often being ambiguous in their attitudes towards crime, it is worth recalling Charles Tilly's fascinating and provocative essay comparing the emergence of modern European states with organised crime, in which he describes European state-making as 'quintessential protection rackets with the advantage of legitimacy' (Tilly 1985: passim, but here at 169).

41. The violence-related dangers of both organised crime and terrorism are obvious to most people. But other dangers are less so, including the attraction of both kinds of activity to those who might be tempted to engage in them. Their romantic connotations to some must be acknowledged and addressed, if recruitment into organised crime gang and terrorist ranks is to be checked. In his song 'Both Sides of the Story' (1993), British singer Phil Collins refers to the ghetto kid who carries a gun as the only way he knows of gaining 'respect' from others. If Francis Fukuyama (1992: esp. 143–208), basing his argument on Plato, Hegel, Havel and others, is correct in maintaining that *thymos* – the need to be recognised and respected by others – is a basic human need, this psycho-social dimension of the dangerous attractions of many forms of criminality warrants more attention.

42. Demonstrations against the neo-liberal 'First Job Contract' in France in early 2006 constituted an example of another way in which citizens can influence a state's economic policy. Following weeks of protest, the government withdrew its proposed new legislation – at least for the time being.

Bibliography

Abadinsky, H. (1977), *Organized Crime* (Chicago: Nelson Hall)

Abadinsky, H. (1990), *Organized Crime* (Chicago: Nelson-Hall)

Abadinsky, H. (2000), *Organized Crime* (6th ed.) (Belmont CA: Wadsworth)

Acheson, D. (1987) (re-issued edition), *Present at the Creation: My Years in the State Department* (New York: Norton)

AFP (2004), 'Film-Maker Killed in Muslim Backlash', *The Australian*, 3 November: 10

Age, The (2004), 'There is No Right to Vilify Others', *The Age*, 20 December: 10

Ahmed, A.S. (2003), *Islam Under Siege: Living Dangerously in a Post-Honor World* (Cambridge: Polity Press)

Ahmed, T. (2004), 'Alienation that Foments Terror', *The Australian*, 16 February: 7

Akbarzadeh, S. (2004), 'Muslims Must Condemn Evil', *The Age*, 17 September: 13

Akbarzadeh, S. and Yasmeen, S. (eds.) (2005), *Islam and the West: Reflections From Australia* (Sydney: University of New South Wales Press)

Albanese, J. (1997), *Organized Crime in America* (Cincinnati: Anderson)

Albats, Ye. (2000), 'Byurokratiya: Borba za vyzhivaniye', *Nezavisimaya Gazeta*, 10 December, http://scenario.ng.ru/expertize/2000-12-10/1_ burokrat.html, visited 31 January 2005

Allen, W. (2003), 'The War Against Terrorism Financing', *Journal of Money Laundering Control*, 6 (4): 306–10

Almond, G., Appleby, R.S. and Sivan, E. (2003), *Strong Religion: The Rise of Fundamentalisms Around the World* (Chicago: University of Chicago Press)

Alvazzi del Frate, A. (2004), 'The International Crime Business Survey: Findings from Nine Central-Eastern European Cities', *European Journal on Criminal Policy and Research*, 10 (2–3): 137–61

Aly, W. (2004a), 'Muslims Have to Help Overcome Prejudice', *The Age*, 22 June: 11

Aly, W. (2004b), 'Muslims are Condemning Terrorism. But is Anyone Listening?', *The Age*, 21 September: 13

Aly, W. (2004c), 'Free Speech, No. It was About the Vilification of Muslims', *The Age*, 30 December: 13

Anderson, B. (1991), *Imagined Communities: Reflections on the Origin and Spread of Nationalism* (London: Verso)

Anderson, M. and Feuell, W. (1999), 'Ukraine: Cornered as the Curtain Closes', *Transitions*, 6 (3): 31–2

Andreopoulos, G. (1991), 'Studying American Grand Strategy: Facets in an "exceptionist" tradition', *Diplomacy and Statecraft*, 2 (2): 211–35

Ang, I. and Stretton, J. (1998), 'Multicultural Imagined Communities: Cultural Difference and National Identity in the USA and Australia', in D. Bennett (ed.), *Multicultural States: Rethinking Difference and Identity* (London: Routledge): 135–62

Annan, K. (2005), *In Larger Freedom: Towards Development, Security and Human Rights for All: Report of the Secretary-General* (New York: United Nations)

Anonymous (2003), 'International Legal Developments', *Journal of Money Laundering Control*, 6 (3): 201–16

Antara (Jakarta) (2003), 'FATF Threatens to Impose Stronger Measure on Indonesia', 9 June: 1

AP (2004), 'Dutch Muslims in Fury Over Rape Film', *The Australian*, 1 September: 10

Appadurai, A. (1996), *Modernity at Large: Cultural Dimensions of Globalization* (Minneapolis: University of Minnesota Press)

Appadurai, A. and Stengou, K. (2000), 'Sustainable Pluralism and the Future of Belief', in *Cultural Diversity, Conflict and Pluralism: UNESCO World Culture Report 2000* (Paris: UNESCO): 111–23

Ashcroft, J. (2004), 'The Patriot Act: Wise Beyond Its Years', *The Wall Street Journal*, 26 October: A24

Asia–Europe Meeting (2002), 'Cooperation Programme on Fighting International Terrorism', ASEM IV – Fourth Asia–Europe Meeting Summit, Copenhagen, September 22–24

Aslund, A. and Boone, P. (2002), 'Russia's surprise economic success', *Financial Times* (US ed.), 9 October. http://www.ceip.org/files/publications/2002-10-09-aslund-ftnew.asp, visited 24 January 2005

Association of Young Journalists of Montenegro (2002), *Monitoring of the Media 16 May–8 June* (Podgorica: Association of Young Journalists of Montenegro)

Australian Bureau of Statistics (2004), 'Population for States and Territories', www.abs.gov.au/Ausstats/abs@.nsf/1020492cfcd63696ca2568a1002477b5/8ca5022b2135f162ca256cd0007bee22!OpenDocument, visited 26 February 2005

Avtorkhanov, A. (1991), *Technologia Vlasti* (Moscow), http://www.lib.ru/POLITOLOG/AWTORHANOW/tehnologiq.txt, visited 18 May 2004

Bäckman, J. (1998), *The Inflation of Crime in Russia* (Helsinki: National Research Institute of Legal Policy)

Baker, P. (2004), 'Russians' fears of Kremlin reemerge', *The Washington Post*, 7 March, http://www.washingtonpost.com/wp-dyn/articles/A36805-2004Mar6 .html, visited 6 June 2004

Baldaev, S. and Plutser-Sarno, A. (2003), *Russian Criminal Tattoo Encyclopaedia* (Göttingen: Steidl/Fuel)

Baldauf, S. (2002), 'The War on Terror's Money: India's Six Month Investigation Offers Lessons on Fighting Underground Banking', *Christian Science Monitor*, 22 July

Barbalet, J.M. (1988), *Citizenship* (Milton Keynes: Open University Press)

Barber, B.R. (1995), *Jihad vs. McWorld* (New York: Times Books)

Bardhan, P. (1996), *The Economics of Corruption in Less Developed Countries: A Review of the Issues* (Paris: OECD)

Barjot, D. (1993), *International Cartels Revisited. Vues nouvelles sur les cartels internationaux 1880–1980* (Caen: Editions du Lys)

Barton, G. (2005) 'Compassion Breaches Islam's Divide', *The Australian*, 7 January: 11

Beare, M. (ed.)(2003), *Critical Reflections on Transnational Organized Crime, Money Laundering, and Corruption* (Toronto: University of Toronto Press)

Behan, T. (1996), *The Camorra* (London: Routledge)

Bell, D. (1999), *The Coming of Post-Industrial Society: A Venture in Social Forecasting* (New York: Basic Books)

Bezlov, T. and Gounev, P. (2005), *Crime Trends in Bulgaria: Police Statistics and Victimization Surveys* (Sofia: Center for the Study of Democracy)

Bichon, F. (2004), 'Dutch Far-Right Hits Muslims', *The Age*, 10 November: 15

Blair, T. (1999a), 'Doctrine of the International Community', speech to Chicago Economic Club, 4 April, www.primeminister.gov.uk, visited February 2005

Blair, T. (1999b) in *The Sun* (UK), 5 April

Blair, T. (1999c), 'Speech to the European Bank for Reconstruction and Development', London, 19 April

Blair, T. (2002), 'Speech to the Labour Party Conference', 1 October
Blair, T. (2003a), 'Speech to the House of Commons', 18 March
Blair, T. (2003b), 'Speech to the US Congress', 18 July, in P. Richards (ed.), *Tony Blair in His Own Words* (London: Politico, 2004): 247–57.
Blair, T. (2005), 'A Year of Huge Challenges', *The Economist*, 1 January: 44–6
Blankenburg, E. (2002), 'From Political Clientelism to Outright Corruption: The Rise of the Scandal Industry', in Kotkin and Sajó 2002: 149–85
Blant, M. (2004), 'Nayedut Na Vsekh', *Ezhenedelnyi Zhurnal*, 25 May, http://supernew.ej.ru/121/tema/02/index.html, visited 4 February 2005
Blix, H. (2004), *Disarming Iraq* (New York: Pantheon Books)
Block, A. (ed.) (1991), *The Business of Crime: A Documentary Study of Organized Crime in the American Economy* (Boulder, CO: Westview)
Block, A. and Chambliss, W. (1981), *Organizing Crime* (New York: Elsevier)
BNA Banking Report (2004), 'EC Seeks Revisions after FATF Report Targets Terrorist Financing, Recordkeeping', *BNA Banking Report*, 83 (1): 35
Bottom, B. and Medew, J. (2004), 'The Unfair Fight: Why Corruption's Unchecked', *The Sunday Age* (Melbourne), 23 May: 8
Bouma, G., Daw, J. and Munawar, R. (2001), 'Muslims Managing Religious Diversity', in Saeed and Akbarzadeh 2001: 53–77
Bouma, G. (2004), 'Why Costello is Wrong on Vilification Laws', *The Age*, 1 June: 13
Bovenkerk, F. (2000), '"Wanted: Mafia Boss" – Essay on the Personology of Organized Crime', *Crime, Law and Social Change*, 33 (3): 225–42
Bovenkerk, F. and Yesilgöz, Y. (2004), 'Organized Crime in Turkey and the State', in C. Fijnaut and L. Paoli (eds), *Organized Crime in Europe: Concepts, Patterns and Control Policies in the European Union and Beyond* (The Hague: Springer): 585–602
Bowles, R. (1998), 'Minimising Corruption in Tax Affairs', in C. Sandford (ed.), *Further Key Issues in Tax Reform* (Bath: Fiscal Publications): 65–86
Boyes, R. (2004), 'Push to Ban Hate Sermons in Arabic', *The Australian*, 18 November: 9
Brants, C. and Brants, K. (1984), 'Fraudebewustzijn in Nederland: over de sociale constructie van witteboordencriminaliteit', in *Witteboorden-criminaliteit* (Nijmegen: Ars Aequi)
Brasted, H.V. (2001), 'Contested Representations in Historical Perspective: Images of Islam in the Australian Press 1950–2000' in Saeed and Akbarzadeh 2001: 206–27

Braudel, F. (1982), *Civilisation and Capitalism 15th–18th Century: The Wheels of Commerce* (London: Collins)

Bremner, C. (2004), 'Backlash Against Tolerance', *The Australian*, 6 December: 14

Brereton, D. (2000), 'Evaluating the Performance of External Oversight Bodies', in A. Goldsmith and C. Lewis (eds), *Civilian Oversight of Policing: Governance, Democracy and Human Rights* (Portland: Hart): 105–24

British Broadcasting Corporation (2001), 'EU Combats Terror Funding', broadcast 16 October

British Broadcasting Corporation (2005a), 'Britain Freezes Criminal Funds', broadcast 20 July

British Broadcasting Corporation (2005b), 'European Arrest Warrant Faces Obstacles in Germany', broadcast 24 July

Brown, A.J. and Head, B. (2004), 'Ombudsman, Corruption Commission or Police Integrity Authority? Choice for Institutional Capacity in Australia's Integrity Systems', paper presented to the Australasian Political Studies Association Conference, University of Adelaide, 29 September–1 October

Brown, D. (1998), 'The Relationship Between the Current Enlargement to Central and Eastern Europe and the European Union's "Area of Freedom, Security and Justice": An Uneven Impact', paper presented to the International Studies Association Conference, Vienna, 16–19 September

Bruguière, J.-L. (2003), 'Terrorism after the War in Iraq' (Washington DC: Brookings Institution, Center for the United States and France), May, http://www.brookings.edu/fp/cusf/analysis/bruguiere.pdf, visited 29 May 2003

Brunei Anti-Corruption Bureau (2004), 'Background', www.anti-corruption.gov.bn/, visited 12 October 2003

Bulavinov, I. (2003), 'Koloda Rossiiskoi Federatsii', *Kommersant-Vlast*, 17 November: 45, http://www.kommersant.ru/k-vlast/get_page.asp?page_id=20034536-11.htm, visited 7 February 2005

Bull, M. and Newell, J. (eds) (2003), *Corruption in Contemporary Politics* (Basingstoke: Palgrave)

Burchill, S., Devetak, R., Linklater, A., Paterson, M., Reus-Smit, C. and True, J. (2001), *Theories of International Relations* (Basingstoke: Palgrave)

Burnham, B. (2003), 'Measuring Transnational Organised Crime: An empirical study of existing data sets on TOC with particular reference to intergovernmental organisations', in Edwards and Gill 2003: 65–77

Buscaglia, E. and van Dijk, J. (2003), 'Controlling Organized Crime and Corruption in the Public Sector', Forum on Crime and Society, 3 (1–2): 3–34

Bush, G. (2001), 'President Signs Anti-Terrorism Bill', Washington, DC: White House Speech, 26 October, http://www.whitehouse.gov/news/releases/ 2001/10/20011026-5.html, visited October 2005

Bush, G. (2004a), 'President Bush Calls for Renewing the USA Patriot Act', Hershey Penn Speech, 19 April http://www.whitehouse.gov/news/releases/ 2004/04/20040419-4.html, visited October 2005

Bush, G. (2004b), 'President Bush: Information Sharing, Patriot Act Vital to Homeland Security', Buffalo NY Speech, 20 April http://www. whitehouse.gov/news/releases/2004/04/20040420-2.html, visited October 2005

Butler, A. (2005), 'Muzzling Haters Doesn't Mean that Hate Has Vanished', The Age, 4 January: 11

Butler, Lord R. (2004), 'Interview', The Spectator, 11 December: 12–13

Butrin, D. (2004), 'Dolzhnik Svoey Pobedy', Gazeta.Ru., 17 March, http://www.gazeta.ru/comments/2004/03/a_96023.shtml, visited 17 March 2004

Buzan, B. and Little, R. (2000), International Systems in World History: Remaking the Study of International Relations (New York: Oxford University Press)

Buzan, B., Waever, O. and de Wilde, J. (1998), Security: A New Framework for Analysis (Boulder, CO: Lynne Rienner)

Bykov, D. (2004), 'Alexandr Yakovlev: Rynka dlya svobody nedostatochno', Ogoniok, June: 23, http://www.ogoniok.com/win/200423/23-12-14.html, visited 27 January 2005

Byrne, J. and Kelsey, M. (2004), 'USA Patriot Act: Three Years Later: What a Long Strange Trip It's Been (Part 1)', ABA Bank Compliance, 25 (9): 6-13

Cahill, D. and Leahy, M. (2004), Constructing a Local Multifaith Network (Canberra: Department of Immigration and Multicultural Affairs and Australian Multicultural Foundation)

Cahill, D., Bouma, G., Dellal, H. and Leahy, M. (2004), Religion, Cultural Diversity and Safeguarding Australia (Canberra: Department of Immigration and Multicultural Affairs and Australian Multicultural Foundation)

Calabrese, A. and Burke, B. (1992), 'American Identities: Nationalism, the Media, and the Public Sphere', Journal of Communication Inquiry, 16 (2): 52–73

Campbell, D. (1998), *Writing Security: United States Foreign Policy and the Politics of Identity* (Minneapolis: University of Minnesota Press)

Canadian Governmental Ethics Law Project (2003), *Government Ethics Law in Canada*, www3.telus.net/GovtEthicsLaw/Introduction.html, 1 November

Carr, E.H. (1939), *The Twenty Years' Crisis 1919–1939* (London: Macmillan)

Cassella, S.D. (2003), 'Reverse Money Laundering', *Journal of Money Laundering Control*, 7 (1): 92–4

Celarier, M. (1996), 'The Search for the Smoking Gun', *Euromoney*, 329: 49–52

Center for the Study of Democracy (2002), *Corruption, Trafficking and Institutional Reform: Prevention of Trans-Border Crime in Bulgaria (2001–2002)* (Sofia: Center for the Study of Democracy)

Chibnall, S. and Saunders, P. (1977), 'Worlds Apart: Notes on the Social Reality of Corruption', *British Journal of Sociology*, 28 (2): 138–54

Chu Yiu Kong (2002), 'Global Triads: Myth or Reality?' in M. Berdal and M. Serrano (eds), *Transnational Organized Crime and International Security: Business as Usual?* (Boulder, CO: Lynne Rienner): 183–93

Chulov, M. (2003), 'Terror Suspect a "Sleeper Agent"', *The Australian*, 28 October: 1–2

Chulov, M. (2004a), 'Terror in Our Midst', *The Australian*, 23 March

Chulov, M. (2004b), 'Police Too Slow to Act on Tip-Off by Source', *Weekend Australian*, 29–30 May: 10

Chulov, M. and Greenlees, D. (2002), 'Bali Suspects Come into Focus', *The Australian*, 29 October: 1

Cirtautas, A. (2001), 'Corruption and the New Ethical Infrastructure of Capitalism', *East European Constitutional Review*, 10 (2–3): 79–84

Coalition 2000 (1998), *Clean Future* (Sofia: Coalition 2000), http://www.nobribes.org/documents/en/Durban/BulgActPlan.pdf, visited October 2005

Coghill, K. (2004), 'Auditing the Independence of the Auditor-General', Occasional Paper to the *Political Science Program*, Research School of Social Sciences, The Australian National University, Canberra, 11 February

Coleman, J.W. (1987), 'Toward an Integrated Theory of White-Collar Crime', *American Journal of Sociology*, 93 (2): 406–39

Commission for Africa (2005), *Report of the Commission for Africa* (London: Office of the Prime Minister)

Commission of Inquiry into Possible Illegal Activities and Associated Police Misconduct (Fitzgerald, G.E., Chair) (1989), *Report of a Commission of Inquiry Pursuant to Orders in Council* (Brisbane: Government Printer)

Commission of the European Union (2004), *Proposal for Directives of the European Parliament and of the Council* (Brussels: Office for Official Publications, 14 July)

Compliance Reporter (2003), 'EC Interpretation Softens FATF Wire Transfer Recommendation', *Compliance Reporter*, 19 May: 1

Congressional Hearings (1998), 'The Subcommittee on Coast Guard and Maritime Transportation Hearing, June 10 1998: Drug Interdiction and Other Matters Relating to the National Drug Control Policy', http://www.fas.org/irp/congress/1998_hr/06-10-98memo.htm, visited February 2006

Conklin, J.E. (1977), *Illegal but not Criminal: Business Crime in America* (Englewood Cliffs: Prentice Hall)

Connolly, B. (1996), *The Rotten Heart of Europe: the Dirty War for Europe's Money* (London: Faber and Faber)

Cook, R. (1997), 'Speech on Ethical Foreign Policy', *The Guardian*, 12 May

Cook, R. (2003), *The Point of Departure* (London: Simon & Schuster)

Corporate Crime Reporter (2005), *Crime Without Conviction: The Rise of Deferred and Non Prosecution Agreements* (Washington, DC: Corporate Crime Reporter), http://www.corporatecrimereporter.com/deferredreport htm, visited May 2006

Corrin, C. (2005), 'Transitional Road for Traffic: Analysing Trafficking in Women From and Through Central and Eastern Europe', *Europe–Asia Studies*, 57 (4): 543–60

Corruption and Crime Commission (Western Australia) (2004), *Annual Report 2003–04* (Perth: Corruption and Crime Commission)

Corruption Prevention Investigation Bureau, Singapore (2001), 'Frequently Asked Questions – What is Corruption?', www.cpib.gov.sg/faq.htm#2, visited 12 September 2003

Costello, P. (2004), 'The Moral Decay of Australia', *The Age*, 1 June: 13

Cottrell, R. (2002), 'Russia's Rising Tycoons', *Financial Times* (UK ed.), 6 August, http://www.cdi.org/russia/johnson/6388.cfm, visited 24 January 2005

Council of Europe (1959), *European Convention on Mutual Assistance in Criminal Matters*, ETS No. 30

Council of Europe (1977), *European Convention on the Suppression of Terrorism*, ETS No. 90

Council of Europe (1990), *Convention on Laundering, Search, Seizure and Confiscation of the Proceeds from Crime*, ETS No. 141

Council of Europe (1995), *Agreement on Illicit Traffic by Sea, implementing Article 17 of the United Nations Convention against Illicit Traffic in Narcotic Drugs and Psychotropic Substances*, ETS No. 156

Council of Europe (1997), *Second Summit, Final Declaration and Action Plan*, 10–11 October, http://www.coe.int/t/e/human_rights/equality/01._overview /3_coe_summits/09_Summit_Str.asp, visited October 2006

Council of Europe (1998), *Committee of Ministers Resolution (98) 7 Authorizing the Partial and Enlarged Agreement Establishing the 'Group of States against Corruption'* – GRECO,http://www.coe.int/t/dg1/ greco/documents/1999/GRECO(1999)1_EN.pdf, visited October 2006

Council of Europe (1999), *Criminal Law Convention on Corruption*, Strasbourg, 4 November, http://conventions.coe.int/Treaty/EN/ Treaties/Html/174.htm, visited 17 March 2005

Council of Europe (2000), 'Octopus II Program: Country report – Ukraine', Strasbourg, 20 December, http://www.coe.int/T/E/Legal_affairs/Legal_co-operation/Combating_economic_crime/Programme_OCTOPUS/1999-2000/ Octopus(2000)57%20CR%20Ukraine.asp, visited 4 February 2005

Council of Europe (2005), *Organised Crime Situation Report 2005: Focus on the threat of economic crime (provisional)* (Strasbourg: Council of Europe)

Council of the Bars and Law Societies of the European Union (2004), 'CCBE Proposed Amendments to the European Commission Proposal for a Third EU Directive on Money Laundering', http://www.ccbe.org/doc/En/ccbe_ amendments_to_3mld_en.pdf, visited 8 December 2004

Council of the European Union (1991), Council Directive 308/1991

Council on Foreign Relations (2002), *Report of an Independent Task Force on Terrorist Financing* (New York: Council on Foreign Relations)

Counter-Terrorism Executive Directorate (2005), *International Action Against Terrorism: Summary of Legal Instruments* (New York: United Nations Department of Public Information)

Crawford, B. (2003), 'Firebrand Church Faces Hate Case', *The Australian*, 2 October: 4

Crime and Misconduct Commission (2004), *Annual Report 2003–2004* (Brisbane: Crime and Misconduct Commission), http://www. cmc.qld.gov.au/library/CMCWEBSITE/CMCAnnualReport2004.pdf, visited 4 March 2005

Croall, H. (1993), 'Business Offenders in the Criminal Justice System', *Crime, Law and Social Change*, 20 (4): 359–72

Cronin, I. (2002), *Confronting Fear: A History of Terrorism* (New York: Thunder's Mouth Press)

Culp, C. and Niskanen, W. (eds) (2003), *Corporate Aftershock: The Public Policy Lessons from the Collapse of Enron and Other Major Corporations* (Hoboken, NJ: Wiley)

Curtis, G. (ed.) (2003a), *Nations Hospitable to Organized Crime and Terrorism* (Washington, DC: Library of Congress)

Curtis, G. (2003b), 'Former Soviet Union and Eastern Europe', in Curtis 2003a: 32–88

Curtis, G. and Karacan, T. (2002), *The Nexus Among Terrorists, Narcotics Traffickers, Weapons Proliferators, and Organized Crime Networks in Western Europe* (Washington, DC: Library of Congress)

Curtis, M. (2003), *Web of Deceit: Britain's Real Role in the World* (London: Vintage)

Daly, M. (2004), 'Court Told of Canberra Bombing Plot', *The Age*, 18 May: 3

Davison, R. (1998a), 'An Ever Closer Union? Rethinking European Peripheries' in P. Murray and L. Holmes (eds), *Europe: Rethinking the Boundaries* (Aldershot: Ashgate): 63–92.

Davison, R. (1998b), 'Euromoney: From Divergence to Convergence in EU International Monetary Relations?', *Australasian Journal of European Integration*, 1 (1): 79–130

Davison, R. (2000), *Re-evaluating EU Integration: An Economic Assessment of the Impact of the Single European Market*, Working Paper No. 2, Contemporary Europe Research Centre, University of Melbourne

Davison, R. (2002), 'Intervention or Regulation? Competition Policy in Australia and the European Union', *Law in Context: Competition Policy with Legal Form*, special issue, 20 (1): 69–100

Davison, R. (2004), 'French Security after September 11: Franco-American Discord', in P. Shearman and M. Sussex (eds), *European Security After 9/11* (Aldershot: Ashgate): 62–93

Debkafile (2002), 'Terrorists Threaten Europe from Balkan Safe Haven', 11 December, http://www.debka.com/article.php?size=big&aid=220, visited 12 December 2002

Defense Department (2004), *Operation Tribute to Freedom*, www.defenselink.mil/specials/tribute, visited October 2004

Defense Logistics Agency (2003), *Time is Running Out to Register for NFL Kickoff Live Concert*, Defense Logistics Agency; PR News Wire

Della Porta, D. and Mény, Y. (eds) (1997), *Democracy and Corruption in Europe* (London: Pinter)

Deloitte and Touche Financial Services (2004), *A Month in Money Laundering*, December

Deloitte and Touche Financial Services (2005), *A Month in Money Laundering*, January

Department of Commerce (2003), *The Anti-Corruption Review*, http://ita.doc.gov/td/ocg/master.html, visited 8 October 2003

Department of Treasury (1998), *Corporate Law Economic Reform Program – Policy Reforms* (Canberra: Department of Treasury)

Department of Treasury (2004), *Corporate Disclosure – Strengthening the Financial Reporting Framework* (Canberra: Department of Treasury)

Dewhirst, B. (2004), 'Anti-Money Laundering Legislation – Past and Future', Special edition of *Credit Management* on *Financial Crime*: 26–7

Di Fiore, G. (2005), *La Camorra e Le Sue Storie: La criminalità organizzata a Napoli dalle origini alle ultime 'guerre'* (Turin: UTET)

Dijk, J. van and Terlouw, G. (1996), 'An International Perspective of the Business Community as Victims of Fraud and Crime', *Security Journal*, 7 (3): 157–67

Dillard, D. (1967), *Economic Development of the North Atlantic Community: Historical Introduction to Modern Economics* (Englewood Cliffs, NJ: Prentice Hall)

Ding X. L. (2001), 'The Quasi-criminalization of a Business Sector in China', *Crime, Law and Social Change*, 35 (3): 177–201

Dishman, C. (2001), 'Terrorism, Crime and Transformation', *Studies in Conflict and Terrorism*, 24 (1): 43–58

Dohmen, J. and Verlaan, J. (2003), *Kreukbaar Nederland, van bouwput tot beerput* (Amsterdam/Rotterdam: Prometheus)

Dosch, J. (2004), 'Europe and the Asia-Pacific', in M. Connors, R. Davison and J. Dosch, *The New Global Politics of the Asia-Pacific* (London: Routledge): 104–18

Drayton, F.-R. (2003), 'Anti-Money Laundering Legislation in St. Vincent and the Grenadines', *Journal of Money Laundering Control*, 7 (2): 170–4

Duyne, P.C. van (1983), 'Tien jaar fraudebeleid', *Justitiële Verkenningen*, 3: 50–59

Duyne, P.C. van (1988), 'Aard en aanpak van bedrijfsmatige misdaad', *Justitiële Verkenningen*, 1: 7–52

Duyne, P.C. van (1991), 'Crime-Enterprises and the Legitimate Industry', in C. Fijnaut and J. Jacobs (eds), *Organized Crime and its Containment: A Transatlantic Initiative* (Deventer: Kluwer Law and Taxation Publishers)

Duyne, P.C. van (2003), 'Medieval Thinking and Organized Crime Economy', in E. Viano, J. Magallanes and L. Bridel (eds), *Transnational Organized*

Crime: Myth, Power and Profit (Durham, NC: Carolina Academic Press): 23–44

Duyne, P.C. van and Houtzager, M. (2005), 'Criminal Subcontracting in the Netherlands: The Dutch "koppelbaas" as crime-entrepreneur' in P.C. van Duyne and K. von Lampe (eds), *The Organised Crime Economy* (Nijmegen: Wolf legal publisher): 163–88

ECB – see European Central Bank

Economic Crime Division (2002), 'The Prevention of Corruption in Central and Eastern Europe', Activity Report based on Regional Seminar held in Bratislava, 19–21 November 2001 (Strasbourg: Council of Europe – Directorate General 1, Legal Affairs)

Economist (2001), 'The Financial Front Line: Hitting terrorists' cash', 27 October: 108

Economist (2002), 'Beware of the Watchdog', 17 August: 25

Editors of *US Catholic Magazine* (2002), 'The Muslim Vanguard: An Interview with Farid Esack', in M. Wolfe and the Producers of Beliefnet (eds), *Taking Back Islam: American Muslims Reclaim Their Faith* (New York: Rodale): 15–24

Edwards, A. and Gill, P. (2002), 'Crime as Enterprise? The case of "transnational organised crime"', *Crime, Law and Social Change*, 37 (3): 203–23

Edwards, A. and Gill, P. (eds) (2003), *Transnational Organised Crime: Perspectives in Global Security* (London: Routledge)

Egan, C, Kerin, J. and Robinson, N. (2004), 'Another Terrorist Warning Ignored', *The Australian*, 31 May: 1

Ehrenfeld, R. (1990), *Narco-Terrorism* (New York: Basic Books)

Eltahaway, M. (2005), 'Where is the Jihad Against the Tsunamis?', *Muslim Wake Up!*, 3 January,http://www.muslimwakeupcom/main/archives/2005 /01/002558print.php, visited 6 January 2005

Ely, B. and Vanderhoff, V. (1991), *Lessons Learned from the S & L Debacle: The Price of Failed Public Policy* (Lewisville, TX: Institute for Policy Innovation)

Esack, F. (2002), *Qur'an, Liberation, Pluralism* (Oxford: Oneworld Publications)

Esposito, J. L. (2002), *What Everyone Needs to Know About Islam* (Oxford: Oxford University Press)

European Central Bank (2005), *Opinion of the European Central Bank of 4 February 2005 at the request of the Council of the European Union on a proposal for a directive of the European Parliament and of the Council on the prevention of the use of the financial system for the purpose of money laundering, including terrorist financing,* COM(2004, 448 final, CON/2005/2, 2005/C 40/06, 4 February, http://www.ecb.int/ecb/legal /pdf/c_04020050217 en00090013.pdf, visited 5 February 2005

European Report (1999), 'EU Enlargement: Campaign against Corruption and Organized Crime in CEECs', *European Report*, 6 February: 1

European Security Strategy (2003), *A Secure Europe in a Better World* (Brussels: EN), http://ue.eu.int/uedocs/cmsUpload/78367.pdf, visited July 2005

Evenett, S., Levenstein, M. and Suslow, V. (2001), 'International Cartel Enforcement: Lessons from the 1990s', *World Economy*, 24 (9): 1221–45

Fabre, G. (2003), *Criminal Prosperity: Drug Trafficking, Money Laundering and Financial Crisis After the Cold War* (London: RoutledgeCurzon)

Federal Bureau of Investigation (2003), 'Financing of Terrorist and Terrorist Acts and Related Money Laundering', Washington, DC: Department of Justice, 27 March

Financial Action Task Force (1998), 'FATF Report Highlights Money-Laundering Trends', press release, 12 February, http://www .fincen.gov/typonet.html, visited 2 March 2003

Financial Action Task Force (2001), 'Special Recommendations on Terrorist Financing', http://www1.oecd.org/fatf/SRecsTF_en.htm#V.International, visited 15 April 2002

Financial Action Task Force (2003), *Annual Review of Non-Cooperative Countries or Territories* (Paris: FATF)

Financial Action Task Force (2004), *Annual Report 2003–2004* (Paris: FATF)

Finckenauer, J. and Voronin, Yu. (2001), *The Threat of Russian Organized Crime* (Washington, DC: US Department of Justice)

Firestone, T.A. (1993), 'Mafia Memoirs: What they tell us about Organized Crime', *Journal of Contemporary Criminal Law*, 9 (3): 197–220

Forbes, M. (2002), 'Terror Agents Swoop on Homes', *The Age*, 31 October: 2

Forbes, M. and P. Fray (2003), 'Police Confirm Importance of Brigitte', *The Age*, 30 October: 4

Foreign and Commonwealth Office (1997) *Mission Statement,* www.fco.gov.uk/Files/kfile/part1foreword.o.pdf, visited March 2006

Fox, L. (2003), *Enron: The Rise and Fall* (Hoboken, NJ: Wiley)

Freemantle, B. (1995), *The Octopus* (London: Orion)

Frisby, T. (1998), 'The Rise of Organised Crime in Russia: Its Roots and Social Significance', *Europe–Asia Studies*, 50 (1): 27–49

Fukuyama, F. (1992), *The End of History and the Last Man* (New York: Avon Books)

Gabrieli, F. (n.d.), 'Asabiyya'. http://www.muslimphilosophy.com/ei/asbiyah. htm, visited 23 September 2003

Galbraith, J.K. (1961), *The Great Crash 1929* (Harmondsworth: Penguin)

Gal-Or, N. (ed.) (1991), *Tolerating Terrorism in the West: An International Survey* (London: Routledge)

Galtung, F. (2006), 'Measuring the Immeasurable: Boundaries and Functions of (Macro) Corruption Indices', in Sampford *et al.* 2006: 101–30

Gambetta, D. (1993), *The Sicilian Mafia: The Business of Private Protection* (Cambridge, MA: Harvard University Press)

Gandy, O. (1993), *The Panoptic Sort: A Political Economy of Personal Information* (Boulder, CO: Westview)

Gavrilin, Yu. and Smirnov, L. (2003), *Sovremennyi Terrorizm: Sushchnost', Tipologiya, Problemy Protivodeistviya* (Moscow: Knizhnyi Mir)

Geis, G. (1978), 'White Collar Crime: The Heavy Electrical Equipment Antitrust Cases of 1961' in M.D. Ermann and R. Lundman (eds), *Corporate and Governmental Deviance* (Oxford: Oxford University Press)

Geis, G. and Dimento, J. (1995), 'Should We Prosecute Corporations and/or Individuals?', in F. Pearce and L. Snider (eds), *Corporate Crime: Contemporary Debates* (Toronto: University of Toronto Press): 72–86

Gevorkyan, N., Timakova, N. and Kolesnikov, A. (2000), *Ot Pervogo Litsa* (Moscow: Vagrius)

GfK (2001), *Corruption Climate – Central and Eastern Europe: Results of an International Research Project on Corruption in 11 Central and Eastern European Countries* (Prague: GfK Praha)

Giddens, A. (1991), *Modernity and Self-Identity: Self and Society in the Late Modern Age* (Cambridge: Polity Press)

Gilchrist, M. and Murphy, P. (2004), 'Anti-corruption on the Cheap', *The Age*, Melbourne, 1 May: 19

Gilligan, G. (1999), 'Organised Crime and Corrupting the Political System', *Journal of Financial Crime*, 7 (2): 147–54

Gilligan G. (2002), 'Royal Commissions of Inquiry', *The Australian and New Zealand Journal of Criminology*, 35 (3): 289–307

Glinkina, S. (1998), 'The Ominous Landscape of Russian Corruption', *Transitions*, 5 (3): 16–23

Godoy, J. (2004a), 'Finance: Dirty Money Cleaned Here', *Global Information Network*, 2 March: 1

Godoy, J. (2004b), 'Toothless Fight Against Money Laundering', *Global Information Network*, 10 November: 1

Godson, R. and Olson, W. (1993), *International Organized Crime: Emerging Threat to US Security* (Washington, DC: National Strategy Information Center)

Goldman, M. (2003), *The Piratization of Russia: Russian Reform Goes Awry* (London: Routledge)

Goodman, L.W. (1987), *Small Nations, Giant Firms* (New York: Holmes & Meier)

Gorta, A. and Forell, S. (1995), 'Layers of Decision: Linking Social Definitions of Corruption and Willingness to Take Action', *Crime, Law and Social Change*, 23 (4): 315–43

Grabosky, P. and Larmour, P. (2001), *Public Sector Corruption and its Control* (Canberra: AIC)

Granovetter, M. (2005), 'The Social Construction of Corruption', http://www.stanford.edu/dept/soc/people/faculty/granovetter/documents, visited March 2006

Gray, C., Hellman, J. and Ryterman, R. (2004), *Anticorruption in Transition 2: Corruption in Enterprise–State Interactions in Europe and Central Asia 1999–2002* (Washington, DC: The World Bank)

Green, D. and Shapiro, I. (1994), *Pathologies of Rational Choice: A Critique of Applications in Political Science* (New Haven: Yale University Press)

Greenstein, F. (1987), *Personality and Politics: Problems of Evidence, Inference, and Conceptualization* (2nd ed) (Princeton: Princeton University Press)

Grupo Abele (G. Montanaro and F. Silvestri) (2005), *Dalla Mafia allo Stato – I Pentiti: analisie e storie* (Turin: EGA)

Gunning, J. (2003), 'Making Sense of al-Qaeda in Europe', paper presented to 'Muslims in Europe Post 9/11: Understanding and Responding to the Islamic World', St Antony's-Princeton Conference, Oxford, 25–6 April, http://www.sant.ox.ac.uk/princeton/pap-intro-6.shtm, visited 20 October 2003

Gurov, A. (1995), *Krasnaya Mafiya* (Moscow: Samotsvet MIKO 'Kommercheskii Vestnik')

Gurov, A. with Ryabinin, V. (1991), *Ispoved' 'Vora v Zakone'* (Moscow: Rosagropromizdat')

Gurova, T. and Privalov, A. (2003), 'My Teryaem Ego!', *Ekspert*, 41 (396), 3 November, http://www.expert.ru/expert/current/data/ukos-pl.shtml, visited 5 November 2003

Hajdinjak, M. (2002), *Smuggling in Southeast Europe: The Yugoslav Wars and the Development of Regional Criminal Networks in the Balkans* (Sofia: Center for the Study of Democracy)

Halberstam, D. (2002), *War in a Time of Peace: Bush, Clinton and the Generals* (London: Bloomsbury)

Hall, R. (1986), *Disorganized Crime* (St. Lucia: University of Queensland Press)

Hamm, M.S. (2002), *In Bad Company: Inside America's Terrorist Underground* (Boston: Northeastern University Press)

Harries, O. (2004), *Benign or Imperial?* (Sydney: ABC Books)

Harris, T. (2003), 'ASIO Raids Link Man to Terror Boss', *The Australian*, 31 October: 3

Hathout, M. (2003), 'A Valuable Contribution', *South Asia Tribune*, 24–30 August, http://www.satribune.com/archives/aug24_30_03/opinion-book. htm, visited 23 September 2003

Hausner, J. and Marody, M. (eds) (2000), *Jakość rządzenia: Polska bliżej Unii Europejskiej?* (Krakow: Fundacja im. Fridricha Eberta, Malopolska Szkola Administracji Publicznej Akademii Ekonomicznej w Krakowie)

Hawley, S. (2000), 'Exporting Corruption: Privatisation, Multinationals and Bribery', *The Corner House*, Briefing No. 19, online at http://www.thecornerhouse.org.uk/briefing/19bribes.html, visited January 2003

Heidenheimer, A., Johnston, M. and Le Vine, V. (1989), 'Terms, Concepts and Definitions: An Introduction', in A. Heidenheimer, M. Johnston and V. Le Vine (eds), *Political Corruption: A Handbook* (New Brunswick: Transaction Publishers): 3–14

Henderson, G. (2002), 'Islam is No Threat to Australia', *The Age*, 10 September: 11

Henly, J. (2004), 'Paris Urges Training of Moderate Imams', *The Age*, 24 April: 22

Hennessy, P. (2000), *The Prime Minister: The Office and its Holders Since 1945* (London: Penguin)

Hess, H. (2003), 'Like Zealots and Romans: Terrorism and Empire in the 21st Century', *Crime, Law and Social Change*, 39 (4): 339–57

Hevesi, A. (2003), 'News From the Office of the New York State Comptroller: Corporate Corruption Costs New York State's Economy $2.9 Billion, Cut Tax Revenues by $1 Billion and Decreased Pension Fund Value by $9 Billion', Press Release, 20 August,www.osc.state.ny.us/press/release /aug03/082003 .htm, visited 11 October 2003

Hewitt, C. (2002), *Understanding Terrorism in America: From the Klan to Al Qaeda* (London: Routledge)

Higgins, M. (2004a), 'Summary of Reasons for Decision', Victorian Civil and Administrative Tribunal Human Rights Division Anti-Discrimination List, VCAT Reference No. A392/2002, 17 December

Higgins, M. (2004b), 'Reasons for Decision', Victorian Civil and Administrative Tribunal Human Rights Division Anti-Discrimination List, VCAT Reference No. A392/2002

Hindess, B. (2004), *Corruption and Democracy in Australia*, Report No. 3 (Canberra: The Australian National University)

Hizb ut-Tahrir (n.d.), *The Aim of the Hizb ut-Tahrir*, http://www.hizb-ut-tahrir.org/english/english.html, visited 24 February 2005

Hizb ut-Tahrir (1999), *The Methodology of Hizb ut-Tahrir For Change* (London: Al-Khilafah Publications)

Hobbs, D. (1998), 'Going Down the Glocal: The Local Context of Organised Crime', *Howard Journal of Criminal Justice*, 37 (4): 407–22

Hoffman, B. (1998), *Inside Terrorism* (New York: Columbia University Press)

Holder, W. (2003), 'The International Monetary Fund's Involvement in Combating Money Laundering and the Financing of Terrorism', *Journal of Money Laundering Control*, 6 (4): 383–7

Holmes, L. (2001), 'Crime, Corruption and Politics: International and Transnational Factors', in J. Zielonka and A. Pravda (eds), *Democratic Consolidation in Eastern Europe: International and Transnational Factors*, Vol. 2 (Oxford: Oxford University Press): 192–230

Holmes, L. (2004), 'The Impact of Corruption and Organised Crime on North-East Asia', in I.-J. Youn (ed), *The Regional Dynamics of Northeast Asia and Russia's Globalization in the 21st Century* (Seoul: RPGRR): 1–25

Holmes, L. (2005), 'Russian Corruption and State Weakness in Comparative Post-Communist Perspective', in A. Pravda (ed.), *Leading Russia: Putin in Perspective* (Oxford: Oxford University Press): 75–101

Holmes, L. (2006), *Rotten States?: Corruption, Post-Communism and Neoliberalism* (Durham, NC: Duke University Press)

Holmes, S., Turnbull, S. and Farmer, E. (2004), 'Cartels in the UK – OFT Heavily Armed and Ready for Action', *Global Competition Review*, http://www.globalcompetitionreview.com/ear/49_uk_cartels.cfm, visited March 2005

Howard, M. (2003), *The Weakness of Civil Society in Post-Communist Europe* (Cambridge: Cambridge University Press)

Huberts, L. (1998), 'What can be Done Against Public Corruption and Fraud: Expert Views on Strategies to Protect Public Integrity', *Crime Law & Social Change*, 29 (2–3): 209–24

Human Rights and Equal Opportunity Commission (2004), *Ismae-Listen: National Consultations on Eliminating Prejudice Against Arab and Australian Muslims* (Canberra: Human Rights and Equal Opportunity Commission)

Humphrey, M. (2005), 'Australian Islam, The New Global Terrorism and the Limits of Citizenship', in Akbarzadeh and Yasmeen 2005: 132–48

Huntington, S. (1993), 'The Clash of Civilizations?', *Foreign Affairs*, 72 (3): 22–49

Huntington, S. (1996), *The Clash of Civilizations and the Remaking of World Order* (New York: Simon & Schuster)

Hutcheson, J., Domke, D., Billeaudeaux, A. and Garland, P. (2004), 'U.S. National Identity, Political Elites, and a Patriotic Press Following September 11', *Political Communication*, 21 (1): 27–50

Ignatieff, M. (2002), in a Lecture on Human Rights and Terror, 13 June, Amsterdam

Indem (2005), 'Summa Vzyatok v 2.6 Raza Prevyshaet Budget Rossii', *Novaya Gazeta*, 1 August, http://2005.novayagazeta.ru/nomer/2005/55n /n55n-s18. shtml, visited 2 August 2005

Independent Commission Against Corruption (NSW) (2004), *Annual Report 2003–04* (Sydney: ICAC)

Info-Prod Research (Middle East) (2004), 'FATF Awards Saudi Arabia with Clean Bill of Health', 4 April: 1

International Crime Control Strategy (1988) (Washington, DC: US Government), online, visited February 2005

International Monetary Fund (IMF) (2001), 'Financial System Abuse, Financial Crime and Money Laundering', Background Paper, 12 February (Washington, DC: IMF)

Iselin, B. and Adams, M. (2003), *Distinguishing between Human Trafficking and People Smuggling* (Bangkok: UN Office on Drugs and Crime, Regional Centre for East Asia and the Pacific)

Jain, A. (1998), *Economics of Corruption* (Norwell, MA: Kluwer)

Jain, A. (2001), 'Corruption: A Review', *Journal of Economic Surveys*, 15 (1): 71–120

Jarosz, M. (2004), *Władza, przywileje, korupcja* (Warsaw: PWN)

Johnson, J. (2003), 'Repairing Legitimacy after Blacklisting by the Financial Action Task Force', *Journal of Money Laundering Control*, 7 (1): 38–49

Johnson, J. and Lim, Y.C.D. (2002), 'Money Laundering: Has the Financial Action Task Force Made a Difference?', *Journal of Financial Crime*, 10 (1): 7–22

Johnson, T. (2005), 'Cyber Terrorism', in T. Johnson (ed.), *Forensic Computer Crime Investigation* (Boca Raton: CRC)

Johnston, M. (2000), 'The New Corruption Rankings: Implications for Analysis and Reform', paper presented to the Research Committee 24, International Political Science Association World Congress, 2 August, Quebec City, Canada

Johnston, M. (2001), 'The Definitions Debate: Old Conflicts in New Guises', in A. Jain (ed), *The Political Economy of Corruption* (London: Routledge): 11-31

Johnstone, P. and Brown, G. (2004), 'International Controls of Corruption: Recent Responses from the USA and the UK', *Journal of Financial Crime*. 11 (3): 217–48

Jones, E. (2005), 'More than a Circus', *Poland Monthly*, 40 (June): 18–20

Kaftan, L. (2003), 'Kotorye tut yeltsinskie? Slaz!', *Komsomolskaya Pravda*, 6 August, http://www.kp.ru/daily/23086/5402, visited 25 January 2005

Kampfner, J. (2004), *Blair's Wars* (London: Free Press)

Karklins, R. (2005), *The System Made Me Do It: Corruption in Post-Communist Societies* (Armonk, NY: M.E. Sharpe)

Karnelas, P. and Chulov, M. (2002), 'Officers Raid Home of Suspected JI Member', *The Australian*, 30 October: 1, 8

Kaufmann, D., Kraay, A. and Mastruzzi, M. (2003), *Governance Matters III: Governance Indicators for 1996–2002 (Draft)*, World Bank website, visited August 2004

Kearney, M. (2003), 'Blair's Gamble', in S. Beck and M. Downing (eds), *The Battle for Iraq: BBC News Correspondents on the War against Saddam* (London: BBC Books): 79–91

Keohane, R.O. (1982), 'The Demand for International Regimes', *International Organization*, 36 (2): 325–55

Keohane, R.O. and J.S. Nye (1977), *Power and Interdependence: World Politics in Transition* (Boston: Little Brown)

Keohane, R.O. and Nye, J.S. (2001), 'Introduction', in J.S. Nye and J.D. Donohue (eds), *Governance in a Globalizing World* (Washington, DC: Brookings Press): 1–41

Kerin, J., Emerson, S. and Kaszubska, G. (2002) 'Al-Qa'ida Link to Games Bomb Plot', *The Australian*, 30 October: 6

Kettle, S. (1995), 'Of Money and Morality', *Transition,* 1 (3): 36–9

Khan, M and Esposito, J.L. (2005) 'Western Muslims Must Get Tough on Extremism in Our Community', *Muslim Wake Up!*, 18 February, http://www.muslimwakeup.com/main/archives/2005/02/002658print.php, visited 21 February 2005

Khosrokhavar, F. (2003), 'Terrorist Networks in Europe', paper presented to 'Muslims in Europe Post 9/11: Understanding and Responding to the Islamic World', St Antony's-Princeton Conference, Oxford, 25–26 April. http://www.sant.ox.ac.uk/princeton/pap-khosro.htm, visited 20 October 2003

Kimball, C. (2002), *When Religion Becomes Evil* (San Francisco: HarperSanFrancisco)

Kislinskaya, L. (2000), 'Tsentral'naya Pressa Rossii ob Organizovannoi Prestupnosti I Korruptsii (Oktyabr' – Dekabr' 2000 g.)' in Kodan and Brovkin 2000: 87–97

Klitgaard, R. (1988), *Controlling Corruption* (Berkeley: University of California Press)

Kodan, S. and Brovkin, V. (eds) (2000), *Organizovannaya Prestupnost' i Korruptsiya, Vypusk 4* (Ekaterinburg: Tsentr po izucheniyu transnatsional'noi prestupnosti i korruptsii pri Amerikanskom universitete, IITS 'Zertsalo-Ural')

Kolesnichenko, A. (2004), 'Ispytano na Sebe', *Novye Izvestia*, 21 May, http://www.newizv.ru/news/?id_news=6732&date=2004-05-21, visited 24 June 2004

Kosikowski, C. (2003), 'Prawne aspekty prywatyzacji w Polsce w latach 1990-2002' in: M. Jarosz (ed.), *Pułapki prywatyzacji* (Warsaw: Instytut Studiów Politycznych PAN): 27–47

Kotkin, S. and Sajó, A. (eds) (2002), *Political Corruption in Transition: A Skeptic's Handbook* (Budapest: Central European Press)

Kovac, M. (2005), *Defence Strategy of the State Union of Serbia and Montenegro* (Belgrade: Ministry of Defence of Serbia and Montenegro)

KPMG (2004), *Global Anti–Money Laundering Survey 2004: How Banks Are Facing Up to the Challenge*, http://www.kpmginsiders.com/pdf/AML %20A4%20white%20paper%20_web.pdf, visited 8 December 2004

Kramer, M. (2005), 'Guerilla Warfare, Counterinsurgency and Terrorism in the North Caucasus: The Military Dimension of the Russian–Chechen Conflict', *Europe–Asia Studies*, 57 (2): 209–90

Krasner, S.D. (1983), *International Regimes* (Ithaca: Cornell University Press)

Krasnodębski, Z. (2003), *Demokracja peryferii* (Gdansk: Słowo/Obraz/Terytoria)

Krasnodębski, Z. (2004), 'Postkomunizm – życie po życiu', *Rzeczpospolita*, 8 May

Krastev. I. (2004), *Shifting Obsessions: Three Essays on the Politics of Anticorruption* (Budapest: Central University Press)

Kryshtanovskaya, O. (2002). 'Biznes-elita i oligarchi: Itogi desyatiletiya', *Mir Rossii*, 4, http://www.socio.ru/wr/4-02/Kr.doc, visited 24 January 2005

Kurginyan, S. (1998), 'Chem Ne Yavlayetsya Naznacheniye Primakova', *Pravda*, 25 September, http://kurg.rtcomm.ru/publ.shtml?cmd=art& theme =10&auth=10&id=1190, visited 4 February 2005

Lacey, A. (2001), 'Networks of Protest, Communities of Resistance: Autonomous Activism in Contemporary Britain', Clayton, unpublished PhD Dissertation, Centre for European Studies, Monash University

Lambert, A. (2001), 'The Caribbean Anti-Money Laundering Programme', *Journal of Money Laundering Control*, 5 (2): 158–61

Langseth, P. and Michael, B. (1998), 'Are Bribe Payments in Tanzania "Grease" or "Grit"?', *Crime, Law & Social Change*, 29 (2–3): 197–208

LaPalombara, J. (1987), *Democracy, Italian Style* (New Haven, CT: Yale University Press)

Lapidus, I. M. (2002), *A History of Islamic Societies* (2nd ed) (Cambridge: Cambridge University Press)

Laqueur, W. (1999), *The New Terrorism. Fanaticism and the Arms of Mass Destruction* (London: Phoenix Press)

Laqueur, W. (2003), *No End to War: Terrorism in the Twenty-First Century* (London: Continuum)

Latynina, Yu. (2001), 'Zakhvat', *Novaya Gazeta*, 26 March, http://2001.novayagazeta.ru/nomer/2001/21n/n21n-s12.shtml, visited 7 February 2005

Latynina, Yu. (2004), 'Kod Dostupa', *Echo Moskvy*, 8 May, http://echo.msk.ru/programs/code/25612/, visited 7 February 2005

Law Societies, The (2005), 'Sensible Implementation of Third Directive is Key', *Brussels Agenda*, February, http://www.lawsociety.org.uk/secure/file/ 134819/d:/teamsite-deployed/documents/templatedata/Newsletter/Brussels %20Agenda/Documents/brusselsagendafeb05.pdf, visited 5 February 2005

Lebanon Anti-Corruption Initiative Report (1999), cited in United Nations Office of Drugs and Crime (2004), *The Global Programme against Corruption*, www.unodc.org/unodc/en/corruption.html#UN, visited 4 March 2004

Ledeneva, A. (1998), *Russia's Economy of Favours: Blat, Networking and Informal Exchange* (Cambridge: Cambridge University Press)

Lemert, E. (1967), *Human Deviance, Social Problems and Social Control* (New York: Prentice Hall)

Lentini, P. (2003), 'Terrorism and Its (Re) Sources', *Australian and New Zealand Journal of Criminology*, 36 (3): 368–78

Lentini, P. (2004), 'Are Australian Institutions Failing Muslims?', *Muslim Wake Up!*, 3 June, http://www.muslimwakeup.com/mainarchive/2004 /06/000846 print.php, visited 4 June 2004

Levenstein, M. and Suslow, V. (2004), *What Determines Cartel Success?*, January, http://www-unix.oit.umass.edu/~maggiel/JEL-1-04.pdf, visited March 2005

Levi, M. (1980), 'The Sentencing of Long-Firm Frauds', in L. Leigh (ed), *Economic Crime in Europe* (London: Macmillan): 57–77

Levi, M. (1983), 'Blaming the Jury: Frauds on Trial', *Journal of Law and Society*, 10 (2): 257–69

Levi, M. (1998), 'Perspectives on "Organised Crime": An Overview', *The Howard Journal*, 37 (4): 335–45

Levi, M. (2002), 'The Organisation of Serious Crime', in M. Maguire, R. Morgan and R. Reiner (eds), *The Oxford Handbook of Criminology* (Oxford: Oxford University Press)

Levin, M. and Rempel, W. (2002), *Los Angeles Times*, 8 May

Levitt, S. and Dubner, S. (2005), *Freakonomics: A Rogue Economist Explores the Hidden Side of Everything* (New York: HarperCollins)

Lewis, C. (2004), 'Why Our Police Force Must Face a Probe', *The Age*, Melbourne, 6 April: 11

Lifton, R.J. (2000), *Destroying the World to Save It: Aum Shinrikyō and the New Global Terrorism* (New York: Owl Books)

Lindberg, R. and Markovic, V. (2000), 'Organized Crime Outlook in the New Russia', *Search International*, online, visited June 2005

Litvinenko, Yu. and Belimov, V. (2004), 'Peresadyat Ili Peresidyat?', *Ekspert-Ural*, 19, 24 May, http://www.expert.ru/ural/current/ upolk.shtml, visited 29 May 2004

Looney, R. E. (2002), 'Following the Terrorist Informal Money Trail: The *Hawala* Financial Mechanism', *Strategic Insights*, 1 November, http://www.ccc.nps.navy.mil/rsepResources/si/nov02/southAsia.asp, visited 19 October 2003

Lovell, S., Ledeneva, A. and Rogachevskii, A. (eds) (2000), *Bribery and Blat in Russia: Negotiating Reciprocity from the Middle Ages to the 1990s* (Basingstoke: Macmillan)

Luneev, V. (1997), *Prestupnost' XX Veka: Mirovie, regional'nye i rossiiskie tendentsii* (Moscow: Norma)

Lupsha, P. (1991), 'Drug Lords and Narco-Corruption', *Crime, Law and Social Change*, 16 (1): 41–9

Lyman, M.D. and Potter, G. (1997), *Organized Crime* (New York: Prentice Hall)

M2 Presswire (2004), 'World Bank, IMF and Financing', Enhance Efforts at Combating Money Laundering, Terrorist Financing', 5 April: 1

Maas, P. (1997), *Underboss: Sammy the Bull Gravano's Story of Life in the Mafia* (New York: HarperCollins)

MacDonald, S. (1988), *Dancing on a Volcano: The Latin American Drugs Trade* (New York: Praeger)

Mączak, A. (1994), *Klientela. Nieformalny system władzy w Polsce i w Europie XVI-XVIII w.* (Warsaw: Semper)

Magistrali, G. (ed) (2004), *Storie di Vita* (Fusignano: Grafiche Morandi)

Makarenko, T. (2001), 'Transnational Crime and its Evolving Links to Terrorism and Instability', *Jane's Intelligence Review*, November: 22–24

Makarenko, T. (2003), '"The Ties that Bind": Uncovering the Relationship between Organized Crime and Terrorism', in H.G. van de Bunt *et al.* (eds), *Global Organized Crime. Trends and Developments* (The Hague: Kluwer Law International): 159–73

Mansouri, F. (2005), 'Citizenship, Identity and Belonging in Contemporary Australia', in Akbarzadeh and Yasmeen 2005: 149–64

Maor, M. (2004), 'Feeling the Heat? Anticorruption Mechanisms in Comparative Perspective', *Governance*, 17 (1): 1–28

Margalit, A. (2003) 'The Suicide Bombers?', *New York Review of Books*, 50 (1),16 January: 36–9

Mariański, J. (ed) (2002), *Kondycja moralna społeczeństwa polskiego* (Krakow, WAM)

Markiewicz, W. (2000), 'Kobiety przydrożne', *Polityka*, 37 (9 September): 25–7

Markus, A. (2001), *Race: John Howard and the Remaking of Australia* (Crows Nest NSW: Allen & Unwin)

Marshall, R., Marx, L. and Raiff, M. (2003), *Cartel Price Announcements: the Vitamin Industry*, http://faculty.fuqua.duke.edu/~marx/bio/papers/priceann.pdf, visited February 2005

Marx, K. (1937), *The Eighteenth Brumaire of Louis Bonaparte* (Moscow: Progress Publishers)

Masciandaro, D. (1995), 'Money Laundering, Banks and Regulators: An Economic Analysis', *IGIER Working Paper*, No. 73, Bocomni University

Masciandaro, D. (1999), 'Money Laundering: The Economics of Regulation', *European Journal of Law and Economics*, 7 (3): 225–40

Masciandaro, D. and Filotto, U. (2001), 'Money Laundering Regulation and Bank Compliance: What do your Customers Know? Economics and the Italian Experience', *Journal of Money Laundering Control*, 5 (2): 133–45

Mason, C. (2002), 'From Protest to Retribution: The Guerrilla Politics of Pro-Life Violence', in K. Worcester, S.A. Bermanzohn and M. Ungar (eds), *Violence and Politics: Globalization's Paradox* (London: Routledge): 127–45

Massari, M. (1998), *La Sacra Corona Unita: Potere e Segreto* (Rome: Laterza)

Mauro, P. (1995), 'Corruption and Growth', *Quarterly Journal of Economics*, 110 (3): 681–712

Mavris, L. (2002), 'Human Smugglers and Social Networks: Transit Migration through the States of Former Yugoslavia', *New Issues in Refugee Research – Working Paper No. 72* (Geneva: United Nations High Commission for Refugees)

McCoy, J. and Heckel, H. (2001), 'The Emergence of a Global Anti-Corruption Norm', *International Politics*, 38 (1): 65–90

McDermott, J. (2005), 'Cocaine Ring in Ecuador "Sent Profits to Hezbollah"', *Daily Telegraph* (London), 23 June: 12

McKibbin, R. (2003), 'Why Did He Risk It?', *London Review of Books*, 25 (7)

Medushevsky, A. (2001), 'Bonapartistskaya model vlasti dlya Rossii', *Vestnik Evropy*: 1, http://magazines.russ.ru/vestnik/2001/1/medush-pr.html, visited 28 January 2005

Meeuws, J. and Schoorl, J. (2002), *Zand erover. De wereld van de bouwfraude* (Amsterdam: Meulenhof/De Volkskrant)

Mennell, S. (1995), 'The Formation of We-Images: A Process Theory', in Craig Calhoun (ed), *Social Theory and the Politics of Identity* (Oxford: Basil Blackwell): 175–97

Michelson, M. (2004), 'Dutch Filmmaker Cremated as Mosque Attacks Widen', *The Age*, 11 November: 11

Migranyan, A. (2004,), 'What is Putinism?', *Russia in Global Affairs*: 2, April/June, http://eng.globalaffairs.ru/numbers/7/521.html, visited 16 September 2004

Mikhail Khodorkovsky Press-centre (2004), *Process*, 17 July, http://www.khodorkovsky.ru/process/290.html, visited 7 February 2005

Milashina, Ye. (2004), 'Podchinyus Tol'ko Prikazu Presidenta', *Novaya Gazeta*, 24 May, http://2004.novayagazeta.ru/nomer/2004/35n/n35n-s06.shtml, visited 7 February 2005

Miller, W., Grødeland, Å. and Koshechkina, T. (1998), 'Are the People Victims or Accomplices?', *Discussion Papers of the Local Government and Public Service Reform Initiative*, No. 6 (Budapest: Open Society Institute)

Miller, W., Grødeland, Å. and Koshechkina, T. (2001), *A Culture of Corruption: Coping with Government in Post-Communist Europe* (Budapest: Central European Press)

Ministerstwo Sprawiedliwości (2006), *Krajowy Program Zwalczania i Zapobiegania Handlowi Ludźmi Na Lata 2005–2006* (Warsaw: Ministerstwo Sprawiedliwości)

Ministry of the Interior [Hungary] (2000), 'Assessment of Corruption and Elaboration of a National Strategy in Hungary', in United Nations Office for Drug Control and Crime Prevention and United Nations Interregional Crime and Justice Research Institute, 'Joint Project against Corruption in the Republic of Hungary: Preliminary Assessment and Feedback on the Corruption Pilot Study', *Global Programme Against Corruption Working Paper* (Austria: United Nations): 27–41

Miró, R. (2003), *Organized Crime and Terrorist Activity in Mexico, 1999-2002* (Washington, DC: Library of Congress)

Mitra, P. and Selowsky, M. (with others) (2002), *Transition – The First Ten Years: Analysis and Lessons for Eastern Europe and the Former Soviet Union* (Washington, DC: World Bank)

Modestov, N. (1996), *Moskva Banditskaya: Dokumental'naya khronika kriminal'nogo bespredela 80-90-x godov* (Moscow: Tsentrpoligraf)

Moghadam, A. (2003), 'Palestinian Suicide Terrorism in the Second Intifada', *Studies in Conflict and Terrorism*, 26 (1): 65–92

Moiseev, V. (2003), 'Kak ya byl yuzhnokoreiskim shpionom', *Versia*, 44, http://old.versiasovsek.ru/2003/44/weeklyread/5751.html#5751, visited 25 January 2005

Mokrzycki, E., Rychard, A. and Zybertowicz, A. (eds) (2002), *Utracona dynamika? O niedojrzałości polskiej demokracji* (Warsaw: IFiS PAN)

Moor, K. (2005a), 'Walking a Thin Blue Line', *Herald Sun*, 11 March: 29

Moor, K. (2005b), 'Watchdog Tracks Down Bent Cops', *Herald Sun*, 11 March: 10

Moore, M. (2002), 'Indonesia Condemns Home Raids', *The Age*, 1 November: 8

Moran, J. (1998), 'Corruption and NIC Development: A Case Study of South Korea', *Crime Law & Social Change*, 29 (2–3): 161–77

Morris, S. (2002), 'Following the Money Trail: Where Corruption Meets Terrorism', *TI Q*, September 2002: 1, 10

Munro, I., Berry, J. and Moynihan, S. (2004), 'Judge Urges Attack on Corruption', *The Age*, Melbourne, 21 May: 1

Murakami, H. (2001), *Underground: The Tokyo Gas Attack and the Japanese Psyche* (London: Harvill Press)

Mursalieva, G. (2004). 'I eto vse novosti k etomu chasu…', *Novaya Gazeta*, 26 April, http://2004.novayagazeta.ru/nomer/2004/29n/n29n-s18.shtml, visited 27 January 2005

Muslims in Europe Post 9/11 (2003), 'Discussion', 'Muslims in Europe Post 9/11: Understanding and Responding to the Islamic World', St Antony's-Princeton Conference, Oxford, 25–6 April http://www.sant.ox.ac.uk/princeton/discussion-1.shtm, visited 20 October 2003

Myrtaj, F. (2003), 'Albania: Temporary and Permanent Organized Crime', *Aim Dossiers* (France), http://www.aimpress.ch/dyn/dos/archive/data/2003/30725-dose-01-07.htm, visited April 2005

Naím, M. (1995), 'The Corruption Eruption', *Brown Journal of World Affairs*, 2 (2): 245–61

Naishul, V. (2004). 'Otkuda Sut Poshli Reformatory', *Polit.Ru.*, 28 June, http://www.polit.ru/research/lectures/2004/04/21/vaucher.html, visited 7 February 2005

Nakata, T. (1978), 'Corruption in the Thai Bureaucracy: Who Gets What, How and Why in Its Public Expenditure', *Thai Journal of Public Administration*, 18 (January): 102–8, cited in 'The Costs of Corruption', ABD.org. www.adb.org/Documents/Policies/Anticorruption/anticorrupt.400.asp?p=policies, visited 14 October 2003

Napoleoni, L. (2003), *Modern Jihad. Tracing the Dollars Behind the Terror Networks* (London: Pluto Press)

Naryshkina, A. (2003), 'Olga Kryshtanovskaya: Iz elity tol'ko vygonyayut', *Izvestia*, 5 April, http://main.izvestia.ru/community/04-04-03/article 32220, visited 31 January 2005

Nason, D. (2002), 'Raids Divide Papers', *Weekend Australian*, 2–3 November: 10

National Security Strategy of the US (2002), www.whitehouse.gov/usc/nss, visited July 2005

Naughtie, J. (2004), *The Accidental American: Tony Blair and the Presidency* (London: Pan)

Naylor, R. (1997), 'Mafias, Myths and Markets: On the Theory and Practice of Enterprise Crime', *Transnational Organized Crime*, 3 (3): 1–45

Naylor, R. (2002), *Wages of Crime: Black Markets, Illegal Finance, and the Underworld Economy* (Ithaca, NY: Cornell University Press)

Nemtsov, B. and Kara-Murza, V. (2004), 'Ob ugroze putinisma', *Nezavisimaya Gazeta,* 22 January, http://www.ng.ru/politics/2004-01-22/3_letter.html, visited 22 January 2004

"Nepodsudnye" Generaly' (2003), *Komsomol'skaya Pravda*, 8, 9, 10, 12, and 15 July, http://www.kp.ru/daily/23071/4970/, visited 7 February 2005

New South Wales Police (2004), *Profile of the NSW Police*, www.police.nsw.gov.au/about_us, visited 3 March 2005

Nomokonov, V. (2000), 'Transnational Organised Crime in the Russian Far East', paper presented at the 2nd Organised Crime Regional Initiative, Seoul, 6–8 April

Nordstrom, C. (2004), *Shadows of War: Violence, Power, and International Profiteering in the Twenty-First Century* (Berkeley and Los Angeles: University of California Press)

O'Brien, J. (2003), *Wall Street on Trial: A Corrupted State?* (Chichester: Wiley)

Obukhova, Ye. and Skornyakova, A. (2004), 'Vlast' i Biznes ne Ponyali Drug Druga', *Nezavisimaya Gazeta,* 12 April, http://www.ng.ru/economics/2004-04-12/4_fradkov.html, visited 4 February 2005

Office of the White House Press Secretary (2001), *White House Daily Press Briefing September 26* (Washington, DC: Office of the White House Press Secretary)

O'Hara, N. (2004), 'FATF Sets its Sights on Informal Channels', *US Banker*, 114 (8): 17

Ohmae, K. (1990), *The Borderless World: Power and Strategy in the Interlinked Economy* (New York: HarperBusiness)

Ohmae, K. (2005), *The Next Global Stage: The Challenges and Opportunities in Our Borderless World* (Upper Saddle River, NJ: Wharton School Publishing)

Ombudsman South Australia (2003), 'What's New', http://www.ombudsman.sa.gov.au/, visited 15 March 2005

Orfano, I. (ed) (2002), *Article 18: Protection of Victims of Trafficking and Fight Against Crime (Italy and the European Scenarios)* (Martinsicuro: On the Road)

Organisation for Economic Co-operation and Development (1997), *OECD Convention on Combating Bribery of Foreign Public Officials in International Business Transactions*, OECD website, visited July 2005

Organisation for Economic Co-operation and Development (2001), *Behind the Corporate Veil: Using Corporate Entities for Illicit Purposes*, Paris: OECD.

OSCE Office for Democratic Institutions and Human Rights (ed) (2001), *Europa gegen Menschenhandel – Conference Report* (Berlin: Auswärtiges Amt)

Pakulski, J. (1997), 'Cultural Citizenship', *Citizenship Studies*, 1 (1): 73–85

Palmier, L. (1983), 'Bureaucratic Corruption and its Remedies', in M. Clarke (ed.), *Corruption: Causes, Consequences and Control* (London: Frances Pinter): 207–19

Paoli, L. (2000), *Fratelli di Mafia: Cosa Nostra e 'Ndrangheta* (Bologna: Il Mulino)

Paoli, L. (2002), 'The Paradoxes of Organized Crime', *Crime, Law and Social Change*, 37 (1): 51–97

Paoli, L. (2003), *Mafia Brotherhoods: Organized Crime, Italian Style* (Oxford: Oxford University Press)

Patriot Act (2001), *Uniting and Strengthening America by Providing Appropriate Tools Required to Intercept and Obstruct Terrorism (USA Patriot Act) Act of 2001*

Peregudov, S. (2002), 'Korporativanyi Kapital i Instituty Vlasti', *Polis*, 5

Petrov, N. (2004), 'Puzzle federalnoy reformy: 4 goda spustya', *The Moscow Times*, 17 February, http://www.themoscowtimes.com/stories/2004/02/17/006.html, visited 27 January 2005

Philp, M. (1997), 'Defining Political Corruption', *Political Studies*, 45 (3): 435–62

Pieth, M. and Aiolfi, G. (2003), 'The Private Sector becomes Active: The Wolfsberg Process', *Journal of Financial Crime*, 10 (4): 359–65

Pillar, P.R. (2001), *Terrorism and U.S. Foreign Policy* (Washington, DC: Brookings Institution Press)

Pindyck, R. and Rubinfeld, D. (2001), *Microeconomics* (Upper Saddle River, NJ: Prentice Hall): 70

Piontkovsky, A. (2004), 'Vsepobezhdayushchee Ucheniye ChuChe', *Novaya Gazeta*, 22 April, http://2004.novayagazeta.ru/nomer/2004/28n/n28n-s09.shtml, visited 7 February 2005

Police Integrity Commission (2004), *Annual Report 2003–2004* (Sydney: PIC), http://www.pic.nsw.gov.au/PDF_files/2003-2004.pdf, visited 15 March 2005

Portnikov, V. (2003), 'Sluzhili Dva Tovarishcha', *Politcom.ru.*, 15 July, http://www.politcom.ru/2003/zloba2666.php, visited 4 February 2005

Powell, C. (2005), 'No Country Left Behind', *Foreign Policy*, 146 (January–February): 28–35

Powell, S. and Chulov, M. (2002), 'ASIO Raids Target JI Sleeper Cell', *The Australian*, 31 October: 1

Pradhan, S., Anderson, J., Hellman, J., Jones, G., Moore, B., Muller, H., Ryterman, R. and Sutch, H. (2000), *Anticorruption in Transition: A Contribution to the Policy Debate* (Washington, DC: World Bank)

Price, J. (1994), *Holland and the Dutch Republic in the Seventeenth Century* (Oxford: Clarendon Press)

Public Opinion Research Center CBOS (2005), *Polish Public Opinion*, April

Puzo, M. (2000), *Omerta* (New York: Random House)

Quaedvlieg, H.J.M. (2001), *Ondernemende autoriteiten?*, PhD thesis, Rotterdam, Erasmus University

Queensland Ombudsman (2003), 'Legislation', http://www.ombudsman.qld .gov.au/responsibilities/legislation.asp, visited 17 March 2005

Queensland Police Service (2004), *Brief History 2003–2004*, www.police.qld.gov.au/pr/about/history/2003_2004.shtml, visited 3 March 2005

Ramesh, R. (ed.)(2003), *The War We Could Not Stop: The Real Story of the Battle for Iraq* (London: Faber and Faber)

Rapid (1995), '"Post-BCCI" Directive on Reinforcing Prudential Supervision of Financial Services Sector Definitively Adopted', 20 June

Rauschning, H. (1940), *The Voices of Destruction* (New York: Europa Verlag)

Rawlinson, P. (1997), 'Russian Organized Crime: A Brief History', in P. Williams 1997: 28–52

Rayner, M. (2005), 'Why Not Just Let the Truth Speak for Itself?', *The Age*, 6 January: 11

Razinkin, V. (1995), *"Vory v Zakone" i Prestupnye Klany* (Moscow: Kriminologicheskaya Assotsiyatsiya)

Razzakov, F. (1997), *Bandity Vremen Kapitalizma: Khronika Rossiiskoi Prestupnosti 1992–1995* (Moscow: EKSMO)

Reeve, S. (1999), *The New Jackals: Ramzi Yousef, Osama Bin Laden and the Future of Terrorism* (Boston: Northeastern University Press)

Reinikka, R., Svensson, J. and Kurey, B. (2002), 'Public Expenditure Tracking Surveys', online at World Bank website, visited July 2003

Rentoul, J. (2002), *Tony Blair: Prime Minister* (London: Time Warner)

Reuter, P. (1983), *Disorganized Crime: The Economics of the Invisible Hand* (Cambridge, MA: MIT Press)

RIA News Agency [Moscow] (2004), 'International Cooperation Needed Against Terror Funding, Putin tells Conference', 5 October: 1

Rice, C. (2000), 'Promoting the National Interest', *Foreign Affairs*, 79 (1): 45–62

Richardson, G., Ogus, A. and Burrows, P. (1983), *Policing Pollution: A Study of Regulations and Enforcement* (Oxford: Clarendon Press)

Riddell, P. (2003), *Hug Them Close: Blair, Clinton, Bush and the 'Special Relationship'* (London: Politico's Publishing)

Rodionov, D. and Boone, P. (2002), 'Reformed rent-seekers promoting reform?', *Moscow Times*, 23 August,http://www.themoscowtimes. com/stories/2002/08/23/006.html, visited 24 January 2005

Roncesvalles, C. (2004), 'Dirty Money Law Needs More Teeth, Says Report', *BusinessWorld*, 5 March: 1

Rose-Ackerman, S. (1978), *Corruption: A Study in Political Economy* (New York: Academic Press)

Rosenberg, J. (2005), 'Globalization Theory: A Post-Mortem', *International Politics*, 42 (1): 2–74

Rossiiskaya Gazeta (2004), 'Russia Moots New Tactics to Fight Money Laundering', *Rossiiskaya Gazeta*, 12 December: 1, http://www .gateway2russia.com/st/art_259986.php, visited March 2006

Royal Commission into Commercial Activities of Government and Other Matters (WA Inc. Report) (1992), *Final Report* (Perth: Government Printer)

Royal Commission into HIH Insurance Group (Owen, N., Chairman) (2003), *Final Report* (Canberra: Government Printer)

Royal Commission into the New South Wales Police Service (Wood, J., Chairman) (1997), *Final Report* (Sydney: Government Printer)

Royal Commission into Police Corruption (Kennedy, G., Chairman) (2003), *Final Report* (Perth: Government Printer)

Ruggiero, V. (1996), *Organized and Corporate Crime in Europe: Offers That Can't Be Refused* (Aldershot: Dartmouth)

Ruggiero, V. (2000), *Crime and Markets: Essays in Anti-Criminology* (Oxford: Oxford University Press)

Rychard, A. (2002), 'Polityka i społeczeństwo w Polsce: ewolucja porządku instytucjonalnego', in Mokrzycki *et al.* (2002): 147–71

Sackers, H.J.P. and Mevis, P.A.M, (2000), *Fraudedelicten* (Gouda Quint: Deventer)

Saeed, A. (2003), *Islam in Australia* (Crows Nest NSW: Allen & Unwin)

Saeed, A. (2004), *Muslims in Australia: Their Beliefs, Practices and Institutions* (Canberra: Department of Immigration and Multicultural Affairs and Australian Multicultural Foundation)

Saeed, A. and Akbarzadeh, S. (eds) (2001), *Muslim Communities in Australia* (Sydney: University of New South Wales Press)

Sagramoso, D. (2001), *The Proliferation of Illegal Small Arms and Light Weapons in and around the European Union: Instability, Organised Crime and Terrorist Groups* (London: Centre for Defence Studies)

Sajó, A. (2002), 'Introduction – Clientelism and Extortion: Corruption in Transition', in Kotkin and Sajó 2002: 1–21

Sajó, A. (2003), 'From Corruption to Extortion: Conceptualization of Post-Communist Corruption', *Crime, Law and Social Change*, 40 (2–3): 171–94

Salierno, D. (2003), 'FATF Revisits Money Laundering', *The Internal Auditor*, August, 60 (4): 16

Samotorova, A. (2004), 'OSA Zhalit Chinovnikov', *Novye Izvestia*, 26 May, http://www.newizv.ru/news/?id_news=6836&date=2004-05-26, visited 7 February 2005

Sampford, C., Shacklock, A., Connors, C. and Galtung, F. (eds) (2006), *Measuring Corruption* (Aldershot: Ashgate)

Sampson, A. (1973), *The Sovereign State of ITT* (New York: Stein and Day)

Sanders, I. (2004), 'Joining Forces to Counter Terrorism', *Monash News*, December, http://www.monash.edu.an/news/newsline/story.php?story_id =247, visited 16 February 2005

Sandholtz, W. and Gray, M. (2003), 'International Integration and National Corruption', *International Organization*, 57 (4): 761–800

Schelling, T. (1984), *Choice and Consequence* (Cambridge, MA: Harvard University Press)

Schmid, A.P. (1983), *Political Terrorism: A Research Guide to Concepts, Theories, Data Bases and Literature* (Amsterdam and New Brunswick: North-Holland Publishing and Transaction Books)

Schmid, A.P. (1993), 'The Response Problem as a Definition Problem', in A.P. Schmid and R.D. Crelinsten (eds), *Western Responses to Terrorism* (London: Frank Cass): 7–13

Schmid, A.P. (1996), 'The Links Between Transnational Organized Crime and Terrorist Crimes', *Transnational Organized Crime*, 2 (4): 40–82

Schmid, A.P. (2002), 'Links Between Terrorist and Organized Crime Networks: Emerging Patterns and Trends', ISPAC Lecture for the International Conference on Trafficking: Networks and Logistics of Transnational Crime and Terrorism, Courmayeur, Italy

Schutte, G. (1988), 'De Republiek der Verenigde Nederlanden, 1702–1780', in I. Schöffer, H. van der Wee and J.A. Bornewasser (eds), *De Lage landen, 1500–1780* (Amsterdam: Uitgeversmaatschappij Agon)

Schweitzer, G.E. (with C. Dorsch) (1998), *Super-Terrorism: Assassins, Mobsters and Weapons of Mass Destruction* (New York: Plenum)

Seldon, A. (2004), *Blair* (London: Free Press)

Sergeev, M. (2003), 'Dominiruyushchiye nad gosudarstvom biznes gruppy tormozyat modernizatsiyu strany', *Strana.Ru.*, 31 January, http://www.strana.ru/stories/02/02/06/2462/170352.html, visited 24 January 2005

Shelley, L. (1998), 'Crime and Corruption in the Digital Age', *Journal of International Affairs*, 51 (2): 605–20

Shevtsova, L. (2004a), 'President Putin Oformlyaet Sobstvennyi Politicheskiy Rezhim: Chto iz Etogo Sleduet', *Briefing*, 1, January (Moscow: Carnegie Centre)

Shevtsova, L. (2004b), 'Straight Forward into the Past', *Russia in Global Affairs*, 2 (April/June), http://eng.globalaffairs.ru/numbers/7/520.html, visited 20 August 2004

Shleifer, A. and Vishny, R. (1993), 'Corruption', *Quarterly Journal of Economics*, 108 (3): 599–617

Shover, N., Fox, G. L. and Mills, M. (1994), 'Long-term Consequences of Victimization by White-Collar Crime', *Justice Quarterly*, 11 (1): 75–98

Sidoti, F. (1991), 'Terrorism Supporters in the West: the Italian Case', in Gal-Or 1991: 105–42

Sík, E. (2002), 'The Bad, the Worse and the Worst: Guesstimating the Level of Corruption', in Kotkin and Sajó 2002: 91–113

Silke, A. (2003), 'Becoming a Terrorist', in A. Silke (ed), *Terrorists, Victims and Society: Psychological Perspectives on Terrorism and its Consequences* (Chichester: Wiley): 29–54

Skaperdas, S. (2001), 'The Political Economy of Organized Crime: Providing Protection when the State does not', *Economics of Governance*, 2 (3): 173–202

Skelton, R. (2002a), 'Terror "Frontman" Expelled', *The Age*, 29 October: 1–2

Skelton, R (2002b), 'Canberra Defends Deportation of Terror Suspect', *The Age*, 30 October: 4

Smith, D.W. Jnr. (1978), 'Organised Crime and Entrepreneurship', *International Journal of Criminology and Delinquency*, 6: 161–77

Smith, D.W. Jnr. (1980), 'Paragons, Pariahs and Pirates: A Spectrum-Based Theory of Enterprise', *Crime and Delinquency*, 26 (4): 358–86

Speer, L. J. (2004), 'Egypt, Ukraine Escape FATF Blacklist; Countries Discuss Information Exchange', *BNA Banking Report,* 82 (9): 390

Spickard, J.V. (2001), 'Tribes and Cities: Towards an Islamic Sociology of Religion', *Social Compass,* 48 (1): 103–16

Sprinzak, E. (1991), 'The Process of Delegitimization: Towards a Linkage Theory of Political Terrorism', *Terrorism and Political Violence,* 3 (1): 50–68

Sprinzak, E. (1995), 'Right-Wing Terror in a Comparative Perspective: The Case of Split Delegitimization', in T. Bjorgo (ed.), *Terror from the Extreme Right* (London: Frank Cass): 17–43

Sprinzak, E. (1998), 'The Psychopolitical Formation of Extreme Left Terrorism in a Democracy: The Case of the Weathermen', in W. Reich (ed.), *Origins of Terrorism* (Washington, DC: Woodrow Wilson Center Press): 65–85

Staff to the Senate Committee on Governmental Affairs (2002), *Financial Oversight of Enron: the SEC and Private-Sector Watchdogs* (Washington, DC: US Senate Committee on Governmental Affairs): 97–127

Stanchev, K. (2001), 'The Path of Bulgarian Economic Reform', *East European Constitutional Review,* 10 (4): 56–61

Stephens, K. (2004), 'The Current Situation in Serbia: Testimony before the Sub-Committee on Europe, House International Relations Committee', 18 March (Washington, DC: US Department of State), online at http://www.state.gov/p/eur/rls/rm/30561.htm, visited July 2005

Stephens, P. (2004), *Tony Blair: The Price of Leadership* (London: Politicos)

Sterling, C. (1994), *Thieves' World: The Threat of the New Global Network of Organized Crime* (New York: Simon and Schuster)

Stewart, C., Taylor, P., Hickman, B. and Kerin, J. (2004), 'ASIO "Ignores" Terror Call', *Weekend Australian,* 29–30 May: 1, 10

Stoecker, S. and Shelley, L. (eds) (2005), *Human Traffic and Transnational Crime: Eurasian and American Perspectives* (Lanham, MD: Rowman and Littlefield)

Stothard, P. (2003), *30 Days: A Month at the Heart of Blair's War* (London: HarperCollins)

Strange, S. (1982), '*Cave! Hic dragones*: a critique of regime analysis', *International Organization,* 36 (2): 479–96

Strieder, J. (1967), 'Jacob Fugger, the rich merchant and banker of Augsburg', in Dillard 1967

Strunk, N. and Case, F. (1988), *Where Deregulation went Wrong: A Look at the Causes behind Savings and Loan Failures in the 1980s* (Chicago, IL: United States League of Savings Institutions)

Subbotin, M. (2002), 'Zakon "O Nedrakh" – Peizazh Pered Bitvoi', *Oil of Russia*, 12

Sutherland, E. (1940), 'The White Collar Criminal', *American Sociological Review*, 5: 1–12

Sutherland, E. (1945), 'Is "White Collar Crime" Crime?', *American Sociological Review*, 10 (1): 132–9

Sutherland, E. (1949), *White Collar Crime* (New York: Dryden)

Sutherland, E. (1961), *White Collar Crime* (New York: Holt, Rinehart and Winston)

Sutherland, E. (1983), *White Collar Crime: The Uncut Version* (New Haven: Yale University Press)

Svyatenkov, P. (2003), 'Kogda Oligarchy Ushli …', *Russkii Zhurnal*, 27 August, http://www.russ.ru/politics/agenda/20030827-svjat.html, visited 7 February 2005

Szasz, P.C. (1997), 'General Law-Making Processes', in C. Joyner (ed.), *The United Nations and International Law* (Cambridge: Cambridge University Press): 27–64

Tanzi, V. (1994), 'Corruption, Governmental Activities and Markets', *IMF Working Paper*, 94/99

Tanzi, V. (1998), 'Corruption Around the World: Causes, Consequences, Scope and Cures', *IMF Staff Papers*, 45 (4): 559–94

Thatcher, M. (2003), *Statecraft: Strategies for a Changing World* (London: HarperCollins)

Tilman, R. and Pontell, H. (1995), 'Organizations and Fraud in the Savings and Loan Industry', *Social Forces*, 73 (4): 1439–63

Tilly, C. (1985), 'War Making and State Making as Organized Crime', in P. Evans, D. Ruschemeyer and T. Skocpol (eds), *Bringing the State Back In* (Cambridge: Cambridge University Press): 169–91

Times, The, AFP (2004) 'Muslim Radical Held in Film-Maker's Killing', *The Australian*, 5 November: 10

Tishkov, V. (2004), *Chechnya: Life in a War-Torn Society* (Berkeley and Los Angeles CA: University of California Press)

Transnational Crime and Corruption Centre, Georgia (2003), *About Us*, www.traccc.cdn.ge/about/index.html, visited 1 November 2003

Transparency International (1996), *Sharpening the Responses Against Global Corruption* (Berlin: Transparency International)

Transparency International (2000), *Annual Report 2000* (Berlin: TI), http://www.transparency.org/about_ti/annual_rep/ar_2001/annual_report20 01.pdf, visited March 2005

Transparency International (2001), *Annual Report 2001* (Berlin: TI), http://www.transparency.org/about_ti/annual_rep/ar_2001/annual_report20 01.pdf, visited March 2005

Transparency International (2002), *Annual Report 2002* (Berlin: TI), http://www.transparency.org/about_ti/annual_rep/ar_2002/tiar2002.pdf, visited March 2005

Transparency International (2003), *Annual Report 2003* (Berlin: TI), http://www.transparency.org/about_ti/annual_rep/ar_2003/annual_report_2 003.pdf, visited March 2005

Transparency International (2004a), 'Corruption and Money Laundering in the UK: "One Problem, Two Standards". Report on the Regulation of Trust and Company Service Providers', *Policy Research Paper* 003, October

Transparency International (2004b), *Corruption Perceptions Index 2004* (Berlin: TI), www.transparency.org/cpi/2004/dnld/media_pack_en.pdf, visited March 2005

Tretyakov, V. (2000), 'Rossia: Posledniy pryzhok v budushchee', *Nezavisimaya Gazeta*, 24 February, http://www.ng.ru/ideas/2000-02-24/8_lastjump.html, visited 30 January 2005

United Nations (2004), *United Nations Convention against Corruption* (New York: United Nations)

United Nations Development Programme (1999), *Fighting Corruption to Improve Governance* (New York: United Nations Management and Governance Division)

United Nations Development Programme (2000), *Common Country Assessment: Republic of Moldova* (New York: United Nations)

United Nations Office for Drug Control and Crime Prevention (2000), *Anti-Corruption Toolkit* (Vienna: United Nations Office for Drug Control and Crime Prevention), http://www.odccp.org/odccp/corruption_toolkit.html, visited December 2001

United Nations Office on Drugs and Crime (2002), *Results of a Pilot Survey of Forty Selected Organized Criminal Groups in Sixteen Countries* (Vienna: UNODC)

United States Agency for International Development (2003), *Fighting Corruption*, www.usaid.gov/our_work/democracy_and_governance/ technical_areas/anti-corruption/, visited 15 September 2003

United States Senate Permanent Subcommittee on Investigations (1999), *Private Banking and Money Laundering: A Case Study of Opportunities and Vulnerabilities* (Washington, DC: U.S. Congress)

Urrutia, M. (2004), 'The Effect of Crime on Macroeconomic Adjustment', *Journal of Financial Crime*, 12 (1): 53–5

Varese, F. (2001), *The Russian Mafia: Private Protection in a New Market Economy* (Oxford: Oxford University Press)

Verbeek, N. (2001), *De baronnen van de cocaine* (Amstelveen: De Zaak Haes)

Victoria Police (2004), *About Victoria Police,* www.police.vic.gov.au/index.cfm?menuid=1, visited 3 March 2005

Volkov, V. (2002), *Violent Entrepreneurs : The Use of Force in the Making of Russian Capitalism* (New York: Cornell University Press)

Voronin, Yu. (1997), 'The Emerging Criminal State: Economic and Political Aspects of Organized Crime in Russia' in P. Williams 1997: 53–62

Voslensky, M. (1984), *Nomenklatura* (Bodley Head: London)

Wallace, J. (2004), 'Free Speech is the Best Protection Against Extremism', *The Age*, 28 December: 11

Waters, M. (1995), *Globalization* (London: Routledge)

Webster, W. (ed) (1997), *Russian Organized Crime: Global Organized Crime Project* (Washington, DC: Center for Strategic and International Studies)

Wedel, J. (2001), *Collision and Collusion: The Strange Case of Western Aid to Eastern Europe* (New York: Palgrave)

Weinberg, L. and Davis, P. (1989), *Introduction to Political Terrorism* (New York: McGraw-Hill)

Weinstein, H. and Levin, M. (2002), 'EU: R.J. Reynolds tied to mob', *Los Angeles Times*, 31 October

West Australian (2002), 'Muslims Condemn "Heavy-Handed" Raids', *The Age*, 1 November: 1, 8

Wheatcroft, G. (2004), 'The Tragedy of Tony Blair', *The Atlantic*, 293 (5): 56–71

White, J.R. (2004), *Defending the Homeland: Domestic Intelligence, Law Enforcement and Security* (South Melbourne: Thomson/Wadsworth)

White, L.J. (1992), *The S&L Debacle: Public Policy Lessons for Bank and Thrift Regulation* (New York: Oxford University Press)

Wilkinson, P. (1974), *Political Terrorism* (New York: Wiley)

Wilkinson, P. (2001), *Terrorism Versus Democracy: The Liberal State Response* (London: Cass)

Williams, P. (1994), 'Transnational Criminal Organisations and International Security', *Survival*, 36 (1): 96–113

Williams, P. (ed.) (1997), *Russian Organized Crime: The New Threat?* (London: Cass)

Williams, P. and Godson, R. (2002), 'Anticipating Organized and Transnational Crime', *Crime, Law and Social Change*, 37 (4): 311–55

Williams, P. and Savona, E. U. (eds) (1995), 'The United Nations and Transnational Organized Crime', *Transnational Organized Crime*, 1 (1): 1–22

Williams, R. and Doig, A. (eds) (2000), *Controlling Corruption* (Cheltenham, UK and Northampton, MA, USA: Edward Elgar)

Williams, R., Moran, J. and Flanary, R. (eds) (2000), *Corruption in the Developed World* (Cheltenham, UK and Northampton, MA, USA: Edward Elgar)

Williams, T. (1998), 'Formulating a New Offence of Bribery – Catching the Chimera', *Journal of Financial Crime*, 6 (1): 45–9

Williamson, J. (2003), 'Appendix: Our Agenda and the Washington Consensus', in P.-P. Kuczynski and J. Williamson (eds), *After the Washington Consensus: Restarting Growth and Reform in Latin America* (Washington, DC: Institute for International Economics): 323–31

Wincenty, D. (2002): 'Transformacja, prywatyzacja i czołowi aktorzy', *Studia Polityczne*, 13: 353–69

Woodiwiss, M. (2003), 'Transnational Organised Crime: The Global Reach of an American Concept' in Edwards and Gill 2003: 13–27

World Bank (2002), *Anticorruption: Corruption, Poverty and Inequality*, www1.worldbank.org/publicsector/anticorrupt/corpov.htm, visited 18 October 2003

World Bank (2004), 'The Costs of Corruption', *News & Broadcast*, 8 April, http://web.worldbank.org/WBSITE/EXTERNAL/NEWS/0,,contentMDK:2 0190187~menuPK:34457~pagePK:34370~piPK:34424~theSitePK:4607,00. html, visited 4 March 2005

World Bank (2005), 'Blair Targets Corruption in Africa Plan; Commission Also Recommends Doubling Aid', *World Bank Press Review*, 7 March 2005

Wright, R. (2003), 'Putting the Crooks out of Business: The Financial War on Organised Crime and Terror', *Journal of Financial Crime*, 10 (4): 366–9

Wright-Neville, D. (2004), 'Dangerous Dynamics: Activists, Militants and Terrorists in Southeast Asia', *The Pacific Review*, 17 (1): 27–46

Yasin, Ye. (2001), *Novaya Epokha, Starye Trevogi* (Moscow)

Yim, R. (2004), *Combating Terrorism: Evaluation of Selected Characteristics in National Strategies Related to Terrorism* (Washington, DC: United States General Accounting Office)

Young, H. (2003), 'Under Blair, Britain has Ceased to be a Sovereign State', *The Guardian*, 16 September

Zaitch, D. (2002), *Traquedos: Colombian Drug Entrepreneurs in the Netherlands* (The Hague: Kluwer Law International)

Zambia Anti-Corruption Commission (1996), *Anti-Corruption Commission Act No. 42* (Lusaka)

Zamoshkin, S. (2000), 'Prosto Fond Prokurorskogo Reketa', *Moscow News*, 19 September, http://www.compromat.ru/main/ustinov/fond.htm, visited 7 February 2005

Zwartz, B. (2003), 'Q. C. tells of Anti-Muslim Hate Seminar', *The Age*, 23 October: 8

Zwartz, B. (2004), 'Historic Win for Muslims in Religious Hatred Case', *The Age*, 18 December: 3

Zybertowicz, A. (1993), *W uścisku tajnych służb: upadek komunizmu i układ postnomenklaturowy* (Komorów: Antyk)

Zybertowicz, A. (2005), 'Anty Rozwojowe Grupy Interesow. Zarys analizy' in W. Wesołowski and J. Włodarek (eds), *Kręgi integracji i rodzaje tożsamości: Polska, Europa, Świat* (Warsaw: Scholar): 299–324

Index

Despite its loose thread the chapters are successful, as a collective, in navigating a vast topic. Transitioning from the social anthropological study of Australia's Muslim communities to an in depth discussion on EU AML legislation ensures that the book covers a multitude of areas that ultimately allow conclusions to be drawn. Without this diversity the analyses wouldn't be as rich or meaningful. and the reader would leave without a clear appreciation of the networks & linkages of terrorism, OC & corruption.